UNITED STATES MARINE CORPS EMBLEMS

1804 to World War I

FREDERICK L. BRIUER, PH.D.

Schiffer Publishing Ltd
4880 Lower Valley Road • Atglen, PA 19310

Library of Congress Control Number: 2016934806

Cover Design by Matthew Goodman
Designed by Justin Watkinson
Type set in Indispose/Minion Pro/Trade Gothic LT Std

ISBN: 978-0-7643-5068-9
Printed in China

Published by Schiffer Publishing, Ltd.
4880 Lower Valley Road
Atglen, PA 19310
Phone: (610) 593-1777; Fax: (610) 593-2002
E-mail: Info@schifferbooks.com

For our complete selection of fine books on this and related subjects, please visit our website at www.schifferbooks.com.
You may also write for a free catalog.

This book may be purchased from the publisher.
Please try your bookstore first.

We are always looking for people to write books on new and related subjects. If you have an idea for a book, please contact us at proposals@schifferbooks.com.

Schiffer Publishing's titles are available at special discounts for bulk purchases for sales promotions or premiums. Special editions, including personalized covers, corporate imprints, and excerpts, can be created in large quantities for special needs. For more information, contact the publisher.

This effort is dedicated to all those
Marines who honorably served
and proudly wore all the
emblems of their Corps.

CONTENTS

FOREWORD

Since the establishment of the United States Marine Corps in 1798, a series of emblems were prescribed for wear up to 1868, when the famous eagle globe and anchor emblem was approved. The design of this emblem went through many modifications until 1955, when a standardized emblem was approved for enlisted personnel, and in 1960, when a standardized emblem was approved for officers, with no further modifications permitted.

Although many articles have been written about the Marine Corps emblem, including a monograph published in 1971, a detailed study had yet to be undertaken. This void has now been filled by a two-volume, detailed evaluative treatment by Dr. Frederick L. Briuer, a retired US Army Corps of Engineers research archaeologist and former Marine. Volume I traces the development of the Marine Corps emblem from 1804 through WWI. The second volume, in preparation, will cover the development of the emblem from 1919 to the present.

Dr. Briuer's outstanding work covers various aspects of the Marine Corps emblem, such as a description thereof, when it was worn, when it was manufactured, when it was discontinued or replaced along with numerous color photographs to scale for aid in identification. A special effort is made to provide objective criteria for distinguishing authentic Marine Corps emblems from a disturbing and growing number of reproductions and fakes. The work should be of interest to general readers of military history and especially dealers and collectors of Marine Corps emblems.

The author is to be commended for a job well done.

John A. Driscoll
Col., USMCR (Ret.)

ACKNOWLEDGMENTS

This book was made possible by an extensive and truly collaborative effort of many contributors. There were so many people who contributed to the effort that it is not possible to name everyone. Inadvertently, some will be left out. Between the verbal text of acknowledgments, special mention of the major influences for the research, citations and endnotes, photo credits, figure credits, material credits, and an alphabetical listing of contributors by name, in the index, it is hoped that those left out will be few.

A major contributor was the late Maj. Ed Wages, USMC (Ret.). Many pleasant hours were spent in Ed's "Red Room" examining and discussing his extraordinary collection of USMC emblems. Both Ed's collection and his knowledge of the subject were extraordinary. Every time I came to the "Red Room," I learned something new and saw something that had previously been overlooked. Ed like many others in these acknowledgments, was passionate about his phenomenal collection.

Jack McCord, Master Sergeant, USMC (Ret.), was another extraordinary collaborator. His contribution to this work was both highly significant and greatly appreciated. He generously allowed me to photograph and describe, in the time available, a selection of his wonderful collection. Jack also shared with me hard to find research material, which over the years, he had diligently accumulated. Jack McCord also spent considerable time on the phone discussing issues of mutual interest. His enthusiasm for emblems was both extraordinary and infectious.

George Mennegaux, a former WWII Marine, and renowned emblem collector, was well known and respected in the emblem collecting community. When I first contacted him, George was very gracious about assisting. Several visits to the Mennegaux home allowed me to selectively photograph and describe George's wonderful collection. To learn, from his extensive knowledge about emblems, was an extraordinary and never-to-be-forgotten experience. What I saw and had time to photograph and describe was only a fraction of what George had acquired. His extensive photograph collection, wherever it is today, would be of extreme value to future researchers.

I extend special thanks to Col. John A. Driscoll, for reviewing, commenting on the text, and for writing the foreword. John provided over the years much appreciated support and recommendations. Several visits to the Driscoll home were a source of great pleasure and provided many new ideas based on John's fine collection, past research, and writing. Some of John's photographs, graciously given to me, are the only record that we now have of important emblems that have, unfortunately, turned up missing from their original repositories.

It was fortunate for me to know and work with respected collectors and especially knowledgeable persons like Joseph Lowry, a WWII marine, Maj. Rick Spooner, USMC (Ret.), and Col. Frank Heins, USMC (Ret.). All three gentlemen shared fascinating information about the subject and provided source material from their extensive collections. Rick Spooner related to me wonderful stories passed down to him from WWI Marines. Frank Heins, generously gave me copies of some of his original and invaluable emblem research. To Michael Kelly, Col. USMC (Ret.), I am indebted for also loaning, for inclusion in this inventory, select emblems from his fine collection.

A special note of thanks goes to author and consummate researcher Alec Tulkoff, who not only sent copies of many superb photographs but generously shared his thorough research results from the National Archives. A wealth of information, based primarily, but not exclusively, on surviving USMC Quartermaster records, came from Tulkoff's thorough research and his publications. Paul Stine, former US Marine and Lt. Col. Michael Manifor, USMC, assisted me by carefully describing and photographing emblems from their own collections. Besides their excellent photos, Stine and Manifor, carefully described, using my standard format, select emblems from their collections. Without this kind of cooperation, from so many individuals, it would never have been possible to achieve the scope of this book. Stine and Manifor have, for a long time, been in regular contact, sharing mutually interesting information.

Other respected researchers and authors of militaria books and articles made significant contributions. Dr. Albert Scipio, a retired college professor and John Stacey, another former US Marine, hospitably opened their homes and access to their wonderful collections, thereby allowing me to selectively describe and photograph. Dr. Scipio's two-volume work classifying collar discs, kindly given to me, was very heavily relied upon. John Stacey, on several occasions, provided crucial information, based on his many years of thorough research and publication. Stacey's efforts included using his research contacts with the Marine Corps and the US Navy to answer specific and difficult queries. Both of these gentlemen have been very generous in their contributions.

Of the many contributors, one who especially stands out, is Ray Darida. The debt to him is immense. Like the others who welcomed me into their homes, Ray not only gave open access to his collections, but was also an exceptional source of information. I know of no one as knowledgeable as Ray when it comes to nineteenth century military insignia and especially, early insignia die striking technology. The many hours spent with Ray, discussing the subject and carefully taking written notes and tape recordings, was a unique educational experience. Ray also generously gave me examples of all his die struck emblems. These have been included in this inventory.

I am grateful to Jim Phillips of Phillips Publications, who contributed to the number and diversity of emblems in the inventory. Jim Phillips simply mailed some of his most expensive emblems. For this trust, I am particularly grateful. Over the years of preparation for this book, Jim has been another major source of encouragement and support.

The following individuals also offered their hospitality and gave me access to their emblem collections: Bob Gill, Maj., USMCR (Ret.), author and collector Mark Kasal, respected collector, author, and WWII Marine veteran Emile Steffanacii, former Marines Richard King, and Korean War USMC veteran Robert Doss. Grateful acknowledgment is extended Richard Forte, David Callaway, Gregory Walseth, Jack Brown, and Joseph Musso; all contributed collectively and added greater breadth and diversity to this emblem inventory.

When dealing with museum curators and collection managers, I found all to be extremely helpful and eager to assist. Thanks go to Kenneth Smith Christmas, who while still with the Marine History Center, Quantico, Virginia, was an early and avid supporter. Later, Ken provided crucial information that he had independently researched, especially on the problem of recognizing authentic emblems from fakes and reproductions. Later, Neil Abelsma replaced Ken Smith Christmas and also did a remarkable job of supporting me. Neil even came to work on his days off, so that he could better focus on assisting me, without being constantly distracted by his normal, heavy work load. Neil's successor at Quantico, Owen Conner, has also been in regular contact, sending photos and conscientiously answering research questions. Jennifer Castro is also a part of the Quantico team and has generously supported this research. Acknowledgment and grateful thanks are due Ellen Guillemette, archivist Command Museum, Marine Corps Recruit Depot, San Diego. Ellen patiently helped me find and copy important photos and by her remarkable organization of the collections, especially thousands of photographs, was able to efficiently pull all my requests. This efficiency served to shorten the amount of time for research at the Command Museum. Jonathan Casey, archivist for the WWI National Museum in Kansas City, Missouri, is also to be thanked for his enthusiastic and conscientious assistance.

It was extremely fortuitous to have contacted Father Nicholas Schiron, S.J., who kindly sent his photographs and firsthand remembrances of the fascinating story of the Jesuit High School New Orleans, Marine Corps emblem link. I am also indebted to Joe Weingarten for graciously reading a draft on investment castings and fakes. Joe is the most knowledgeable person the writer is aware of on the subject of modern investment casting. He saved me the embarrassment of writing some erroneous and mistaken interpretations about investment casting.

Special thanks are extended to Bruce Bazelon who, through both written and telephone communication, provided valuable information on insignia manufacturers based on his thorough research and publications on military goods manufacturers and dealers. Michael Miller, with the Marine Corps University Library at Quantico, promptly provided copies of images as well as many documents and citations in support of my research. The sound advice on indexing and manuscript organization by the well-known researcher and author William Emerson is most appreciated. Another researcher and well known author, David Sullivan, has been consistently attentive in promptly helping me grapple with various queries over a period of several years.

Susan Lintlemann, librarian at the United States Military Academy, West Point, and Alice Lubrecht, Director, State Library of Pennsylvania, were both most pleasant and prompt in providing digital copies of images and documents requested from their libraries. The same appreciation is extended to Marie Kaljot, USMC photograph collection, Washington Navy Yard, and Peter Harrington, archivist with the military collection, Anne S.K. Brown Library, who along with Vicki Stuart Hill, of the USMC National Museum, provided support with copies of requested images.

Many thanks to Red Millen, USMC (Ret.), of the Marine Corps Legacy Museum, Charles Bisch, Brig. Gen. Richard Natonski, USMC (Ret.), and Gregory Beck for gracious help and encouragement, especially with photography.

For several years, Dr. Charles Cureton, Col. USMC (Ret.), has kindly offered advice and suggestions based on his extensive research and publications on the history of USMC uniforms. This informed communication has been invaluable. Equally appreciated are the copies of Uniform Regulations sent by Tom McCleod and the catalog of Hahn Badge Company insignia, sent by David Dougherty. Ray Cowdery provided the author, free of charge, the example of B004.

The well known artist Don Troiani and his colleague and author James Kochan, were most helpful in reconstructing the history and discovery of some quite rare very early nineteenth century ornaments in chapter 1.

Friends and colleagues here in Vicksburg, Mississippi, made important contributions. I will forever be appreciative of the significant amount of time Mike McCoy spent teaching me how to process all the digital images in this book. I took McCoy's advice to simply beat down the learning curve and do the image processing myself instead of trying to find outside help. The professional skills of Janean Shirly in editing the manuscript and providing a summary of writing problems, has been invaluable. To Paula Wright goes an expression of gratitude for the excellent job of typing and table construction. Mike Gatti was instrumental in providing regular professional technical computer support and Jean Cuevas generously gave of her time and expertise, helping me to best make use of computer spread sheet programs

To the brothers Barry and Gregg Bingham goes a sincere thank you for kindly taking me with them to the various military shows in the region. These trips were more than a pleasurable occasion; they were great education and networking opportunities. Similar thanks goes to Col. Richard Zales, USMC (Ret.), who considerately chauffeured me around the USMC Base Camp Pendleton, introducing me to civilian and military historical program staff, who in turn helped with important published sources in the libraries and museums of Camp Pendleton. The author is grateful to the Marine Corps Heritage Foundation for the award of a $500 grant specifically to offset costs for extensive layout work.

Last but not least goes a sincere statement of thanks to my artist wife, Elke. Her patience and support during the research and writing has been an invaluable resource and encouragement. She could always be counted on for sound advice in response to the writer's tendency to verbalize ideas that were not adequately thought out, before making an attempt to write. The verbalizing and feedback from Elke was especially helpful.

INTRODUCTION

At the end of WWII, as all the young soldiers, sailors, and marines were returning home, me, as a boy, would walk up and down the neighborhood alleys of the west bottoms of Kansas City, Missouri, scrounging through trash cans looking for all the "neat" military stuff being thrown away. The expendables of these veterans were my treasures. Little did I realize that this passion for scrounging old things would ultimately lead to a career as a professional archaeologist. I could easily talk relatives and friends out of this common and "unimportant" stuff. The small collection grew with the addition of USMC emblems given to me by my stepfather, who had served during the WWII/Korean War period.

The Marine Corps emblems issued to me in 1959 and other "expendable" emblems scrounged from "short-timers" at my first duty station added fuel to the collecting fire. Again, what fellow marines thought expendable were treasures to me. There was a tendency among those old "brown leather corps" marines to disdain the new emblems in preference to the old. The pattern 1936 emblems were gradually being replaced by the current pattern. I took great pride in wearing not only dad's emblems but his cut-down dress blue uniform, which still hangs in my closet today.

The sixties and early seventies in Southern California were the golden age of flea markets and a heyday for Marine Corps emblem collecting. It was easy to inexpensively put together a great collection. Apparently, Marine Corps emblem collectors in those days were few and far between. In retrospect, it has since become well known that there were really at that time only a few serious Marine Corps emblem collectors. In those days, before the hobby exploded into a big business, the few collectors usually knew, or knew of, each other. A lot of communication, trading, and reciprocity occurred.

John Driscoll's pioneer 1971 publication, *The Eagle Globe and Anchor 1868–1968,* had a profound impact on all who thought collecting USMC emblems was a wonderful and inexpensive hobby. For over forty years, Driscoll provided the only really useful publication on the subject, and an excellent guide to what might be available to look for. On the down side, Driscoll's book "was quickly followed by a dramatic increase in prices."[1] Those were the halcyon years of Marine Corps emblem collecting.

In 1991, a painful reality finally sank in. The wonderful "inexpensive" hobby of emblem collecting was simply becoming cost-prohibitive. A conscious decision was made that the passion for the subject would be better served as a research project, where my training and research experience as a professional archaeologist could be employed. With this decision, the passion for the subject not only increased but there was also a certain sense of liberation from the addictive preoccupation with collecting increasingly expensive things. Having the opportunity to examine, photograph, describe, classify, and date a very large number of Marine Corps emblems, using conventional archaeological research techniques and methods became far more important than feeding an insatiable drive to simply acquire and own these treasures. This research effort has provided something comparable to a sense of emblem ownership.

The goal of this project is to provide a two-volume set of books with 1:1 scale color photographs, including formal descriptions of as many Marine Corps emblems as possible. It is envisioned as an extension of the pioneering work of John Driscoll and includes everything from the earliest known metal insignia down to those of the present day. These are presented in chronological (date) and functional (use) order. The scope of the project focuses on the most important emblems that distinguish US Marines. With but a very few and notable exceptions, these are the metal emblems worn primarily, but not exclusively, on headgear or the collars or shoulders of uniforms.

I have attempted to grapple with answers to the following basic questions about each Marine Corps emblem. What is it and what was its function? What are the most significant things about it, including its historical context? When was it used and if known, when was it manufactured, and when was it discontinued or replaced? A critical consideration is to address the question, "what information supports these conclusions and interpretations?" This is a conscious attempt to distinguish this research from other works based largely or exclusively on unsubstantiated opinion.

The current effort does not attempt to cover other insignia, such as branch insignia, cloth insignia, or decorations, etc., even if they are exclusive to US Marines. Despite their vast number and variety, no real attempt has been made to cover more than a small sample of sweetheart pins. Sweetheart pins were meant for private purchase, usually as gifts, and not authorized for the uniform of US Marines. Only a few of the so-called sweetheart pins are included, such as those often purported to be authentic Marine Corps emblems. Marine Corps branch insignia and sweetheart pins would be appropriate subjects for future research.

A concerted effort has been made to include, in addition to authentic emblems, a number of emblems that are other than authentic USMC emblems (i.e., fakes, reproductions, re-strikes, counterfeits). There is a clear and pressing need for more objective information to help identify the alarming number of honest reproductions and more importantly, the dishonest fakes. This research employs the numismatic concept of the "Black Cabinet," where a systematic description of counterfeit coins has been historically used to more objectively discriminate counterfeits from authentic coins. I have used similar procedures to comparatively describe both the authentic as well as the non-authentic USMC emblems.

The research for this volume formally began in 1991, when a standard methodology for photographing and describing emblems was developed. Standard methods and techniques have been used to photograph and describe over 700 separate Marine Corps emblems that will be covered in two volumes. This population of emblems comes from a large number of museums and private collections from all around the country. The methodology and techniques for photographing, describing, analyzing, classifying, and dating, draw heavily on standard archaeological procedures.

Inspiration for this effort came directly from three seminal works. The first is of course John Driscoll's *Eagle, Globe and Anchor 1868–1968* (1971).[2] John pulled together the most comprehensive set of USMC Uniform Regulations outside those at the United States Marine Corps History Center, Quantico, Virginia (USMCHCQV). Besides providing a chronologically arranged inventory and photographs of all emblems available to him, Driscoll included a valuable summary of the most useful information contained in the almost impossible-to-acquire USMC Uniform Regulations. Driscoll's pioneering book laid the groundwork and motivation for all serious future research.

A second major influence came from two works by Dr. Albert L. Scipio. Dr. Scipio's two volumes on enlisted US Army collar discs are remarkable for thorough and scholarly research, credibility, and fully substantiated presentation. Dr. Scipio's academic background as a professional historian and writer is apparent in the exceptional quality of these publications. The first tells the collar disc story up to 1926.[3] The second publication brings the exceptionally large inventory of collar discs up to 1999.[4]

The comprehensive research on the eagle, globe, and anchor insignia done by Richard Long is a third major inspirational model for presenting thoroughly researched argumentation and fully substantiated conclusions.[5] Long's tireless combing of sources available in the National Archives and Library of Congress and elsewhere on the adoption of the first eagle globe and anchor and his fascinating presentation of the information he gathered, is simply masterful. John Driscoll, Albert Scipio, and Dick Long have all been especially generous in giving their time, research assistance, and much appreciated encouragement.

CHAPTER I

Earliest Emblems

(B001 to B022)

Prior to 1804, there were no known distinctive metal emblems specific to the US Marines. Possible exceptions were brass and white metal buttons, which in most cases may not have been distinct from naval buttons. In his unpublished mimeographed 1925 and 1932 manuscripts Edwin McClellan states in a footnote, "Up to the present there have been nowhere found any description of the device worn by the Continental Marines but from the earliest days of the Continental period, distinctive plumes, cockades, tassels, and epaulets were prescribed and worn, and served to distinguish Marines from other military men."[1]

There are many examples of naval type buttons from this period in the literature on American historical military buttons and it would be very appropriate for a book on Marine Corps emblems to include these. However, this research effort has failed to find any particular button type that could confidently be associated with USMC uniforms or from archaeological contexts prior to1804. Therefore no attempt was made in this inventory to include photographs of even good candidates for USMC buttons before 1804.

The tiny size of the Marine Corps compared to other branches of service using the same or similar emblems would make it unlikely that any such item would be associated exclusively with the US Marines. The same conclusion can be made regarding the known use of black leather cockades or any other devices also worn by the much larger US Army and State Militias of that time. Until there is a strong Marine Corps association demonstrated with such artifacts, their inclusion in this inventory would be both uncertain and arbitrary. The metal emblems of the USMC are the focus of this research.

B001

Earliest Dress Hat Plate

In his original 1932 mimeographed manuscript, of which only 200 copies were made, Marine Corps historian Edwin McClellan described the late eighteenth and early nineteenth century development of the Marine Corps uniform.[2] His research is based on correspondence and records available to him in the official Marine Corps archives. A radically edited version of McClellan's 1932 manuscript was reprinted in 1974 and is, when appropriate, cited here because it is a more readily available document.[3]

The first formal Marine Corps Uniform Order of March 25, 1804 was signed by Robert Smith, secretary of the Navy, and refers to a brass eagle and plate for enlisted men.[4] McClellan cites other vague references to "brass plates, die impressions and eagles" for headgear for enlisted men. In correspondence from Commandant Franklin Wharton to George Harrison dated February 19, 1805, Wharton is quoted as having written an order for enlisted men that included, "200 caps, plumes, bands, and eagles, I mean the square plate for these."[5] This strongly suggests that the plates were informally referred to simply as "Eagles." It is also an inaccurate statement, since there are no known examples of square plates, they were consistently rectangular, see figure I-1 below.

It is not until August 1, 1807, that McClellan cites Commandant Wharton's order for "500 caps and Octagon Plates."[6] This is the first clear and unequivocal reference to B001, see also figure I-1. Five hundred octagon plates would have been enough for the entire Marine Corps at that time, including both officers and enlisted men. Reference to officers using the same plate as enlisted men was not found in McClellan's work. It is also not at clear if there ever was an earlier square plate. In his research, McClellan found significant gaps in the surviving archival records. The missing correspondence for these early periods may never allow us to answer certain questions with confidence.

Figure #I-1
Marine private, ca.1812

On the basis of photographs, both published and provided by colleagues, the author is aware of three complete and four fragmentary examples of B001. All seven were recovered from excavated contexts. Complete examples include B001 in the New York State Office of Parks and Preservation, Waterford, New York. Another complete, but damaged, plate is in the collections of the USMCHCQV. The Quantico plate is wrinkled, giving the appearance of having been burned. It was purchased from Leland T. Smith in January 1986, who claimed it was excavated by Duncan Campbell at Sackett's Harbor.[7] A third complete, and better preserved, plate is in the private collection of the well-known artist Don Troiani. The Troiani plate was purchased from Norm Flayderman in 1996 and is thought to have been excavated from a fort in Florida.[8] The three complete plates are rectangular with clipped corners (eight-sided) and struck from very thin brass with a high copper content. All conform to the 1807 description for the enlisted cap or shako plate. With the exception of the Troiani plate, all the other complete and fragmentary plates were probably excavated, beginning in 1959, by J. Duncan Campbell at the Fort Tomkins, Sackett's Harbor War of 1812 battlefield site. It is not known exactly how many plates Campbell and Howell recovered from this site. It has been suggested that others have been preserved. Campbell donated B001 to the New York State Museum, where it was photographed and described by their staff for this inventory. Two of the four known fragmentary plates were donated by Campbell to the Smithsonian. A third fragment was sold by Campbell to Emile Stefanacci, who kindly allowed the author to photograph that fragment in 2002. The fourth fragmentary plate is with B001 in the New York State Office of Parks and Preservation.

That the octagonal plate dates to 1804 is probable but remains an open question because of vague, inaccurate, and confusing statements in the surviving Marine Corps records. Campbell and O'Donnel suggest the 1804 date for the octagon plates and cite Commandant Wharton's letter of August 24, 1804, that refers to prices paid to George Armitage of twenty-five cents for the large (B001) and six cents for the small plate (B005).[9] Both may have been worn up to 1821 or possibly as late as 1823 when brass eagles were introduced for both officers and enlisted men. Campbell and O'Donnell consider B001 to be the first documented US military metal cap insignia, even predating other US Army and militia metal cap insignia.[10]

The heavy brass rectangular plate B002 was donated to the Smithsonian Institution by J. Duncan Campbell and was considered by Campbell and Howell as a die sample for the Armitage 1804?/1807 cap or shako plate.[11] Rankin supports this die sample interpretation for B002.[12] On close examination, there are no discernible differences between the intricate designs of B001 and B002. The only subtle difference is that B001 and the other excavated octagonal plates on thin, high-copper-content brass, are a weaker strike than B002. The

B002

heavier B002 brass plate was probably subjected to multiple strikes to bring out more detail, perhaps to impress potential buyers of George Armitage's high-quality craftsmanship. The thickness of the brass and the quality of the strike may have been the reasons why Duncan Campbell and others classified B002 as a die sample. Unlike the more weakly struck examples of B001, the die sample B002 shows no indication of long-term burial. The weaker strike of the surviving excavated examples of B001 is expectable. It would be more efficient and economical for Armitage to strike his 1807 commission of 500 emblems on thin high-copper-content plates with as few strikes as possible. It may also be significant that Campbell and O'Donnell omit this heavy brass four-cornered die sample from their comprehensive book on headgear insignia.[13]

Campbell and Howell warned that copies of B002 were made prior to being donated to the National Museum (Smithsonian Institution).[14] Some foreshortened four-cornered brass reproductions of B002 were commissioned by Col. John Magruder, the former and long-since deceased director of the USMCHCQV. Before J. Duncan Campbell passed away in the fall of 2007, Kenneth Smith Christmas interviewed him by telephone. The purpose of the telephone call was to clarify some misinformation in the literature and to determine who commissioned the heavy brass reproduction of B002. Kenneth Smith Christmas was told by Campbell that, "Magruder had the heavy brass die made from the image on the thin (Fort Tomkins) plates—it is not original."[15] Col. Magruder probably assumed that Marines in the 1804 to 1820 period wore the foreshortened four-sided device (B002). The author is aware of at least three separate examples of the four-cornered heavy brass reproductions. It is not known how many of these reproductions were prepared, but more are very likely to surface. The only Marines known to have worn B002 are modern USMC historical interpretation specialists.

In addition to the brass reproductions of B002, cast versions, in hard rubber from two-piece molds, were also prepared for Magruder's USMC historical interpretation specialists. The purpose of these re-created uniforms was to foster an increased sense of pride in USMC history. According to retired USMC Maj. Rick Spooner, these hard rubber castings were prepared for Magruder about 1968 while Spooner commanded the Criminal Investigation Section at the USMC Base, Quantico Virginia.[16] A two-piece mold was used to cast hard rubber copies of a brass reproduction of the B002 plate then in the Smithsonian. The hard rubber copies were then spray painted gold and applied to the shakos in the kit of the War of 1812 USMC historical interpretation specialists. The reproductions of the four-cornered plates in brass or hard rubber that Col. Magruder had commissioned, can be seen in several late sixties, early seventies photos of USMC historical interpretation specialists.[17] More recently, USMC War of 1812 historical interpretation specialists, as well as other civilian reenactors, have been using B003, the eight-sided modern reproduction.

Mr. Ray Darida for many years has specialized in manufacturing excellent metal military insignia, primarily for sale as honest reproductions, especially for military re-enactors. Darida had a die cut based on an impression from an original die of B001 in the W. Stokes Kirk collection. In the late 1960s, Darida viewed the W. Stokes Kirk die collection, which contained virtually all of the Marine Corps emblem dies from 1804 to 1904.[18] From an impression taken from the W. Stokes Kirk die, Darida had a new die sunk for manufacturing the modern reproduction B003. Darida's reproductions are excellent die-struck pieces, reasonably priced and highly polished and finished to give a brand-new appearance. Unfortunately, dishonest dealers are known to alter Darida's insignia to make them look aged. These fakes are being distressed and artificially given a fake chemical patina or weathered look. The dishonest fakes regularly show up on the militaria market. The disreputable dealers often blatantly claim that they are authentic antique military insignia and consequently demand top dollar for something that in fact cost them very little. B003 can be purchased from S & S Firearms for a reasonable price along with no pretense of authenticity.

B003

There are some obvious features on B003 that can be readily distinguished from B001 and B002. The diesinker who prepared the die did not and perhaps could not have been expected to exactly reproduce the B001 device. Along with other minor discrepancies in details such as the very busy eagle feathering, the diesinker misinterpreted a minor flaw in the impression of B002 and added an extra star in the flag of B003. There are many other obvious discrepancies to be seen but the extra star in the Naugatuck Novelties reproduction is a clear giveaway (see figures I-2, I-3, and I-4). A careful comparison of details seen in the images of the original B001 from Sacketts Harbor, the die sample B002 donated to the Smithsonian by J. Duncan Campbell, and the modern

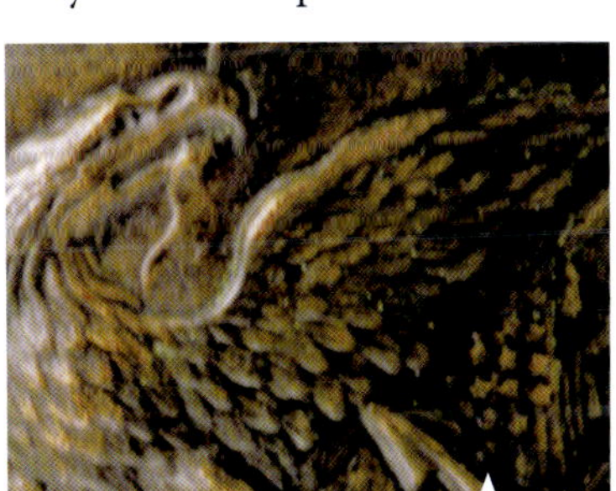
Figure I-2
B001 with twelve stars.

Figure I-3
B002 with same twelve stars.

Figure I-4
B003 with thirteen stars.

B004

reproduction B003 should be helpful to anyone wishing to discriminate the authentic devices from the modern fakes, which are often made to look old.

Ray Cowdery manufactured this fine reproduction on a thin copper alloy plate. The die may have been the work of Craig Nanos. B004 was kindly given to the author by Mr. Cowdery. It only roughly resembles the 1804/1807 shako plate (B001). These, like Ray Darida's insignia, were never meant by Cowdery to have been anything but obvious and honest reproductions of historically interesting emblems. Even a cursory comparison of details in the image of B004 will allow anyone to easily see that this is a modern reproduction. For example, note that B004 has only ten stars in the US flag. Cowdery may have struck only 1,500 examples of B004. The dies and trimming tools for B004 were later sold on the Internet and it is not known if they are currently being used to strike new devices. Characteristic of B004 is the handsome chocolate brown color, probably done chemically. Although an obvious reproduction, the B004 plate is known to be artificially aged and dishonestly offered on the Internet as the authentic 1804 USMC plate.

Early Oval Plates

B005

The best substantiated example of B005 is in the artifact collections of the USMCHCQV. B005 came from a well-documented War of 1812 battlefield site. According to acquisition records, it was found by Mr. George E. Whiting at "the White House Point" historical site in Virginia. It was here on September 3, 1814, that US Marines and sailors under Navy Capt. David Porter fought the British Naval squadron from the banks of the Potomac River.

Only three examples of this particular device are known to the author. These include a pencil rubbing of a broken and damaged specimen. George Mennegaux provided the author a reproduction of that rubbing.[19] Both George Mennegaux and Kenneth Smith Christmas had been informed that the plate in the rubbing had been excavated in the late seventies or early eighties at San Fernandino, near Saint Augustine, Florida.[20] The San Fernandino plate was sold in 1996 by a man named Guthman to Don Troiani.[21] If the information is correct, this plate may well be an artifact of the December 23, 1812, amphibious landing made by US Marines and US Army Infantry on the beach in the St. Mary's River, Florida. The landing was meant to put down a serious insurrection.[22]

Photos of a third plate are known. A copy of a photo by Everett Partridge was kindly provided to the author by John Stacey. This example of B005 is in much better condition than the two described above. There is a fine black and white illustration of the Partridge B005 plate in Campbell and O'Donnell.[23] No provenance information is provided on either photo.

This type of oval plate was interpreted by McClellan as an officer's cross belt or shoulder belt plate.[24] McClellan supported this interpretation by referring to correspondence, and records he researched in the Marine Corps archives describing a gilt officer's shoulder belt plate manufactured by George Armitage and cut, like B001, by his chief diesinker, Moritz Furst. McClellan also presents a black and white image of US Marine Lt. William S. Bush, wearing a large officer's oval shoulder belt plate with a small interior oval and impressed eagle design very similar to B005.[25]

Campbell and O'Donnell suggest that B005 is an enlisted cap plate but admitted that its purpose was still open to debate.[26] In their view, it is clearly an issue item for enlisted headdress or some sort of cockade device. Perhaps the thin strike on a flimsy brass plate seemed to them an inexpensive enlisted item rather than a fancier and usually more expensive officer item.

Based on new information found in the unpublished 1925 and 1932 McClellan manuscripts, there is some validity to both of the above interpretations. It is suggested that B005, in and of itself, is neither an officer's shoulder belt plate nor an enlisted headgear device. The thin plate B005 is too flimsy to serve the function of a shoulder belt plate. All three surviving plates are unleaded. For fastening purposes, four sets of double holes were drilled at the top, bottom, and at each side. Something much stronger in construction, such as B006, with substantial, hard soldered or brazed "puppy paw" brass attachments or holders, would better serve the function of a shoulder belt plate. The flimsy B005 device with the eight pierced holes suggests instead a decorative function with attachment by wires or sewn on with thread.

The original oil painting of Lt. William S. Bush that McClellan relied upon for his interpretation has recently been donated to the USMC Combat Art Collection. Figure I-5, is a color copy of the Bush portrait provided courtesy of Mr. Michael Miller, USMC University Special Collections. The painting clearly shows Lt. Bush wearing a large, dark-colored, perhaps bronze, oval-shaped, shoulder belt plate with a smaller oval-shaped plate, perhaps of gilt or silver, suggestive of B005 and applied to the center of the larger outer plate. The smaller inner oval may have been struck, as B005, from the distinctive die sunk by Moritz Furst and may have been richly gilt.

Figure I-5
Portrait of Lt. William S. Bush.

There exists another War of 1812 period portrait of US Marine 1st Lt. Charles H. Broom, wearing an all gilt shoulder belt breast plate device, significantly larger than B005.[27] Both the Bush and Broom portraits suggest that an officer's version of B005 was probably a decorative element within a larger, stronger shoulder belt breastplate.

Information found in Edwin McClellan's unpublished 1925 and 1932 manuscripts throws new light on the function of B005 as an enlisted man's leather cartridge box decoration. By itself, B005 makes more sense as a decorative item rather than a functioning shoulder belt breastplate. McClellan cites correspondence found in Marine Corps Archives dated July 15, 1816, between Johnston (probably 1st Lt. Albert Johnston) on the US brig *Niagara* and Commandant Major Wharton.[28] Johnson states, "I have a large quantity of clothing on hand, with the exception of Uniform Coats, Linen and fatigue overalls, and small plates for cartridge boxes."[29] In the same source eight pages later, McClellan mentions correspondence between Smith and Gale on September 25, 1819, "I have received from the Navy Store Keeper at Philadelphia ... 100 cartridge box plates."[30] This is consistent with other correspondence found by McClellan in the Marine Corps Archives that describe costs charged by Louis Armitage for supplying to the Marine Corps large plates (twenty-five cents) and small plates (six cents).[31] McClellan also refers to "... cap plates ... belt plates, small plates" found in Marine Corps correspondence.[32]

Finally, of the three known thin-stamped brass ornaments, one must consider the chances that all three of these would be officer's shoulder belt breastplates. Given at least an expected 20:1 ratio of enlisted men to officers in that time period, these surviving rarities are simply not likely to be elements of officer's shoulder belt plates.

The Bush and Broom portraits and McClellan's work clearly describe an officer's shoulder belt plate with a smaller element probably struck from the same die used to strike B005. A documented example of this type of compound officer's shoulder belt plate as depicted in the Bush and Broom paintings in either silver, gold, or in plain gilt would be a most welcome find. It is likely that B005 was struck from the distinctive die sunk by Moritz Furst and was used for inexpensive (six cents) enlisted cartridge box decorations and served as well as an element of a more expensive and fancier officer shoulder belt plate.

Clear evidence exists to indicate that the small plain brass oval plate B005 was used as a decoration for the leather cartridge boxes of enlisted Marines. These probably date back to 1804 and quite likely right up to or just after 1821. From two surviving portraits of Marine Corps officers, it can be inferred that the same Furst die was probably used to strike a smaller central decorative oval as part of a fancier, larger, and stronger metal oval plate that functioned as a compound shoulder belt breastplate for officers.

There is nothing in McClellan's manuscripts that accounts for this handsome cross belt plate from a private collection. It has a wonderful engraving style and respectable patina. McClellan's work consistently refers

B006

to plain oval-shaped brass cross belt plates for enlisted Marines. The extensive Marine Corps uniform research of Dr. Charles H. Cureton, who has combed Treasury Department and official Marine Corps archival sources, also categorically points to a plain, undecorated oval cross belt plate authorized for enlisted men of this time period.[33] Nevertheless, certain features of B006 are still intriguing. Details of construction, especially the strong, hard soldered or brazed "puppy paw" fasteners and reddish brass alloy are notable. This kind of engraving and construction can be found on oval belt plates illustrated in O'Donnell and Campbell and thought by them to have been made in England about 1790 to 1801.[34] This suggests the tantalizing possibility that B006 could be an unauthorized enlisted Marine cross belt plate that could date earlier than anything in this inventory. Lacking good documentation and other surviving examples, this plate should at least be considered an interesting anomaly.

B007

Like B002, Campbell and Howell also considered this plate a die sample and warned that reproductions were known to have been made prior to the acquisition of B007 by the Smithsonian National Museum.[35] One of these reproductions can be found in the holdings of the USMCHCQV. These modern reproductions were donated to or commissioned by Col. John Magruder for use by USMC historical interpretation specialists. Col. Magruder borrowed an original die to have these reproductions made. USMC historical interpretation specialists wearing B007 can be seen in USMCHCQV photographs dating from the late 1950s through the 1960s.

O'Donnell and Campbell quote a letter by Moritz Furst dated March 29, 1826, "I have begun the two dies for the breast plates, one for the Marin (sic) and one for the Army of the United States."[36] The plate intended for the Marines was not adopted.[37] The Marine Corps adopted instead a plain oval plate. The research of Charles Cureton is entirely consistent with this die sample hypothesis. Cureton found no evidence that the plate was ever sold to the Marine Corps or actually worn by Marines.[38] As with B002, the only Marines who have worn B007 are modern USMC historical interpretation specialists. In their research, Campbell and O'Donnell have also omitted this plate from consideration.[39] Figure I-6 is a photo, courtesy of Mr. Ray Darida, of an original die for B007 purchased by him from W. Stokes Kirk when that company went out of business. Darida informed the author that he has not used this die to strike modern reproductions.[40]

Figure I-6
Original Die for B007

Large Eagle Plates: Dress Hat

The best candidate, in the author's view, for the eagle plate that replaced the octagonal plate (B001), perhaps as early as 1821 or 1823 is B008. There may well be other good candidates. Documentation that the author has found regarding this change is not at all clear, and hopefully, will be clarified with future research. Campbell and O'Donnell consistently refer to the "1821" Army pattern eagle for a large variety of eagles with a three-inch and sometimes a five-inch wingspan.[41] Did the Marine Corps change to eagles occur at the same time (1821) or in 1823 when the Marine Corps adopted the bell crown shako?[42] The ornament B008 is a unique eagle on an essentially complete, well-preserved Marine Corps bell crowned shako in the private collection of Joe Musso, see figures I-7 and I-8. The shako has a brass Marine Corps button with thirteen six-pointed stars mounted on a black leather, two-tiered, cockade in front of a red pompon at the top of the shako.

B008

Figure I-7
USMC shako, 1824 to 1828.

Figure I-8
Enlargement of the Joe Musso dress hat.

B009

After examining several photos, Charles Cureton provided the author with his written comments.[43] Mainly on the basis of the construction and components of the shako, Cureton thought it probably dates between 1824 and 1828 and is not one of the Army shakos transferred to the Marine Corps in 1834.[44] Other key features in Cureton's estimation are: 1.) the seamed construction of the leather in the bell crown (see figure I-8), a feature that was changed to a seamless bell crown in 1828; and 2.) the red pompon. Yellow pompons replaced red ones when uniforms were changed from blue to green in 1834.

The distinct eagle of B008 is about the same size as those that Campbell and O'Donnell refer to as the Army 1821 pattern, e.g. B009, B010, B012, B013, B014, B015, but an eagle struck from this particular B008 die is not included among the large number of varieties they classify as the 1821 Army pattern. This suggests that the unique B008 may be a distinguishing feature for Marines not found on Army or militia headgear of this period. The same eagle does show up as a staff officer's cartridge box decoration of the Civil War period.[45]

The next best candidate for a Marine Corps eagle plate for shakos or dress hats is B009. The regulations of this period and what McClellan has to say about emblems are at best vague and at worst silent. McClellan continues to refer vaguely to correspondence mentioning "plates" (June 30, 1821) as well as "eagles" (January 1, 1824).[46] McClellan mentions official correspondence dated May 24, 1820, that officers would wear the same plates as enlisted men.[47] McClellan again reports Marine Corps Correspondence dating March 1821, "… cap plates similar to those worn by the men."[48] Does this refer to the earlier Armitage octagonal plate B001 or to eagles similar to the Army 1821 pattern?

Lacking specifics in the few examples of Marine Corps Uniform Regulations, the best information the author had to go by were the few surviving paintings and illustrations of the period and published sources about early American headgear and ornaments.

Even considering a certain amount of artistic license, B009, with a wingspan on the eagle of five inches, shares plausible similarities with the enlarged eagle depicted on the shako of a Marine private in 1825 painted by Charles R. Floyd (see Figure I-9). A large eagle plate is also evident in the painting *The Dance-Jack Tar Ashore* by an unknown artist depicting a Marine first lieutenant of the 1825 to 1830 period.[49] Campbell and Howell include B009 in their 1963 work.[50] They include both a three-inch and a five-inch wingspan version of B009 in their work.[51] They also describe these as a "fairly common stock pattern, similar to eagles worn by the Washington Blues of Philadelphia, the Marine Corps (after 1834) and others."[52] The large and small versions of B009 share a strong family resemblance, suggesting that the dies were prepared by the same diesinker. McClellan includes a photograph of the smaller eagle plate with three-inch wingspan on a shako identical to the Musso shako.[53] At least one very similar die variety, weakly struck on very thin brass plates, is known. Thin weakly struck eagles with iron wire attachments are efficient and cost effective features of early nineteenth century enlisted insignia manufacture, where multiple strikes enhancing greater details were reserved for more expensive officer's insignia.

Another example of B009 occurs on a shako in the collections of the USMCHCQV. Chenowteth and Nihart present an excellent image of a shako with B009.[54] The shako also conforms to Musso's figure I-7 and I-8. The eagle plate shares similarities with B009, but is clearly the five-inch wingspan version.

Figure I-9
Floyd painting of a Marine private, 1825.

B010

There is evidence that another type of eagle plate was probably worn by US Army, Militia, and US Marines. Campbell and Howell classify B010 as basically the Army 1821 pattern, but its refinement of design and manufacture compared to cruder, earlier eagle types suggests to them a date in the 1830s or 1840s.[55] Campbell and O'Donnell do not include an exact B010 in their work but list a very similar silver-plated eagle excavated from a Civil War battlefield site with a probable manufacture date of 1845 to1855.[56] A tracing of B010 appears in a 1900 cutting dies catalog by Jacob Gminder.[57] catalog illustrates many early, middle, and late nineteenth century dies for striking military insignia. There is good reason to think that many, if not most, of the Gminder dies still exist as part of the extensive Hahn Badges Company die collection in Baltimore, Maryland.[58]

Figure I-10.
Marine private, 1840-1841, Huddy and Duvall.

Again, considering a certain amount of artistic license, the Huddy and Duval picture of a Marine private dating 1840 -1841, (see figure I-10) seems to conform reasonably well to B010 and may have been the same three- to three-and-a-half inch wingspan Army eagle plate turned over to the US Marines along with castoff Army shakos in 1834.[59] McClellan mentions a Marine Corps Order dated November 4, 1834, directing that a brass eagle with a wingspan of three-and-one-half inches be worn on the uniform hat.[60] These sources are consistent with a later date for B010 than the earlier eagle plate with a five-inch wingspan.

Support for B010 having been used by US Marines as a shako ornament comes from a well-preserved shako found in the USMCHCQV that is identical in construction techniques to the distinctive Muso shako. The Quantico shako is missing side buttons, pompon, and brass eagle plate, but is identical in construction to the Musso shako. Although the eagle plate is missing, one can clearly see a stain left on the leather where the missing eagle plate had been attached for a very long time. The stain conforms very well to the distinct shape of the smaller three-and-a-half inch wingspan eagle B010. It is definitely not the larger five-inch wingspan eagle B009. This strongly suggests that both B009 and B010 were worn on USMC and US Army headgear as well.

B010 came from the collection of Joe Lowry, who began collecting in the early 1940s, long before the flood of modern reproductions appeared on the market. This device (B010) may have come out of W. Stokes Kirk or Francis Bannerman surplus. A careful comparison of the images of B010 and the modern reproduction B011 unfortunately reveals very little difference. Naugatuck Novelties manufactures B011. It was provided courtesy of Ray Darida. The only discernible differences are in the developed patina of B010, the weak strike showing less detail and the use of a different trimming tool. The stronger strike of B011 shows more detail, even though both B010 and B011 may have been struck from the same die or dies so similar that they appear indistinguishable. Different trimming tools are in evidence and may prove to be the best way to distinguish the modern reproduction from B010, especially if B011 had been purposely altered to look old. The modern reproduction is trimmed tightly while the possible nineteenth century surplus emblem (B010) clearly shows a loose trimming pattern. In a loose trimming, the cutting tool does not cut as close to the design as a tight trimming. A loose trimming pattern can easily be altered to appear tight, but a tight trimming pattern cannot be made to look loose. On the one hand, there is some question about the authenticity of B010; it may be authentic nineteenth century surplus. On the other hand,

B011

there is no question about the modern reproduction B011. The Naugatuck reproduction can be purchased for a reasonable price from S&S Firearms and perhaps others.

B012

The eagle plate B012 is unlikely to have been worn by Marines but cannot with certainty be precluded from consideration. It is a distinctive design not found in the literature. Note the three stars in the upper shield.

Because of the disparity in size of the tiny Marine Corps and the significantly larger US Army and State Militias at that time, it is probably not a US Marine item. For lack of certainty, however, it is included in this inventory.

B013

This distinctive eagle plate is probably one of the earliest of the 1821 types. It is weakly stuck on a very thin brass plate, reflecting the crude, pre-industrial revolution, simple drop hammer striking technology. It is unlikely to have been worn by Marines and is probably a US Army or state militia device. Nevertheless, it cannot automatically be eliminated as a possible cap ornament also worn by US Marines. It is illustrated in Campbell and O'Donnell as an eagle worn on the 1832 pattern chapeau of Gen. Thomas Jesup, US Army Quartermaster General 1818 to 1860.[61] This eagle plate also came from the Joe Lowry collection.

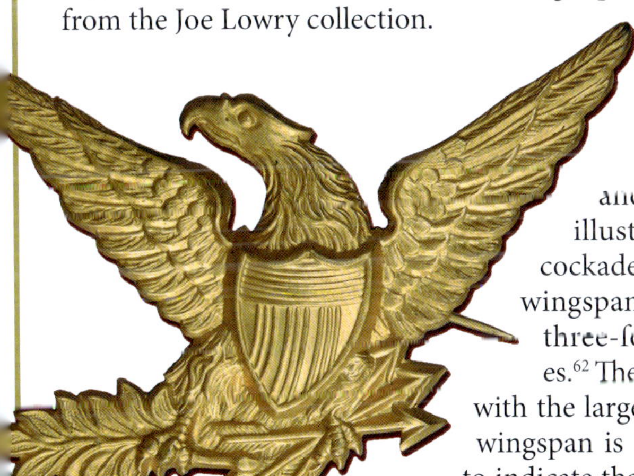

B014

Campbell and O'Donnell illustrate a small cockade eagle with a wingspan of one and three-fourths inches.[62] The style of B014 with the larger three-inch wingspan is so similar as to indicate that it is simply a larger version by the same diesinker, featuring a deep die strike characteristic of the 1850s. Earlier eagles were usually more weakly struck using shallow dies and thinner brass plates. B014 is more than likely an Army or militia eagle plate.

B015

This eagle device was struck on a very thin brass plate characteristic of the 1820s and is illustrated in Campbell and O'Donnell, who describe it as Army or militia 1830 to 1835.[63] Emerson illustrates B015 and describes it as a pattern of the Army 1832 cap eagle, similar to the 1821 pattern, but omitting the cut-out regimental numbers.[64] The B015 device is silver-plated copper. It was stamped from a die, then was trimmed by hand. It is included in this inventory for comparison. Unlike Marine hat eagles of this period in yellow metal, this is the silver color characteristic of US Army infantry hat eagles. The author has found no reference to this device in brass but it still remains a possibility.

The dress hat eagle plate B016 with a three-inch wingspan also came from the Joe Lowry collection and may have been bought from W. Stokes Kirk or Bannerman nineteenth century surplus. It could have had a long period of use, beginning in the 1830s and continuing right up to the Civil War.

B016

Emerson describes B016 as the Army 1832 pattern.[65] It is also illustrated and described as US Army infantry dating 1832 to 1851 in Howell and Kloster.[66] Campbell and Howell classify B016 as a US Army infantry cap device 1834 to 1851.[67] Campbell and O'Donnell classify B016 as possibly the last three-inch wingspan eagle device worn on light artillery dress caps in 1864/1865.[68] Campbell and Howell reiterate this interpretation.[69] LaFramboise also concurs with the others.[70] Since B016 is described consistently by so many researchers, it must have been used by many over a long period. With all these interpretations, no one so far has suggested that B016 was ever worn by US Marines in the period 1835 to 1857.

B017

B017 is manufactured by Naugatuck Novelties. Ray Darida kindly provided this emblem. The die for striking B017 was purchased from W. Stokes Kirk before they went out of business about 1970.

A noticeable difference between B016 and B017, besides the obvious newness of brass and soldering, is the stronger strike of B017 or use of a less worn die copy, seen especially in the feather pattern of the eagle's left wing and the lines in the shield. The ornament can be purchased for a reasonable price from S&S Firearms.

A close comparison of B016 with the modern reproduction B017 clearly indicates different die strikes and trimming tools. Again, there is some question about B016 being authentic nineteenth century surplus, but no question about B017 being a modern reproduction.

B018

Later Very Small Eagle Ornaments

This small eagle plate came out of the collection of Jack McCord. It may be an officer's small chapeau eagle ornament worn on a black leather cockade as described by McClellan from correspondence dating May 1821.[71] Small brass eagles were worn on black leather cockades by Marine, Army, and militia officers. Such a device is depicted in the painting dating ca.1827–1834 of Brevet Lt. Col. John Marshal Gamble on the cover of McClellan's 1974 publication and is illustrated again on page 39.[72] Jacob Gminder's 1900 catalog of dies illustrates a small eagle die that conforms to B018.[73] This further substantiates a probable early nineteenth century date for B018. Campbell and O'Donnell illustrate a wide variety of small cockade eagles, but not B018.

This small brass eagle attached to a die struck thirty-four-point black leather cockade was recently transferred from the Smithsonian Institution to the USMCHCQV. The eagle and cockade were donated to the Smithsonian Institution by Maj. J. Duncan Campbell. Since Campbell's collecting specialty was not US Marine insignia, he was known to have donated authentic Marine Corps items to the Smithsonian Institution and to others. The actual B019 is illustrated and described in Emerson, who identified it as the chapeau device worn by US Marine officers because of the distinctive shape of the leather cockade.[74] Even though the small brass eagle was worn by US Army and Militia officers, Emerson concluded that this device had to be worn by Marines. The distinctive shape of the leather cockade conforms to cockade illustrations for Marines in McClellan and is unlike the circular shape of Army cockades of that period.[75]

Campbell and O'Donnell illustrate an example of the B019 eagle along with its actual die block from the Bruce Bazelon collection.[76] The die block is stamped with the maker's name, H. Jacobus/Philada. Consequently, they date the die block after 1860 since that was the year that Jacobus started his business. Even though they date the die after 1860, Campbell and O'Donnell point out that, "This style of eagle dates from the 1830s." McClellan describes small brass eagles worn on the officer's dress chapeau as early as 1821.[77] B019 is a Marine officer's dress chapeau ornament possibly dating as early as 1821. B019 and the eagle illustrated in Campbell and O'Donnell have a distinctive trimming pattern suggestive of hand trimming and quite different from the trimming pattern of known modern reproductions.

B019

B020

This small chapeau type eagle plate is a modern reproduction of B019 manufactured by Naugatuck Novelties. Using an original W. Stokes Kirk die, an impression was made that served as the basis for preparing the Naugatuck die. Comparing the modern reproduction B020 to B019 and the photo in Campbell and O'Donnell, one can see that the modern reproduction B020 has a different trimming pattern and clear indications of a stronger strike or a less worn

B021

die than B019. The bright brass and new solder characterize the reproduction sold by S&S Firearms. Caution is recommended when trying to discriminate between altered reproductions and potentially genuine nineteenth century eagles.

Naugatuck Novelties also manufactures this reproduction of a small officer's brass chapeau cockade eagle of a style dating from the 1830s. The die and trimming tools for the original 1835 to 1840 eagle, which the reproduction B021 is based on, is illustrated in Campbell and O'Donnell.[78] The reproduction can be purchased from S&S Firearms. The author has not had the opportunity to closely compare an original eagle with the reproduction, but B021 shows some areas that are trimmed tighter than the illustrated eagle in Campbell and O'Donnell. Once more, extreme caution is recommended regarding authentic versions of an emblem that is rarely encountered. At least one other modern reproduction of a small eagle for officer's cockades is known. Who is manufacturing this modern reproduction is not known and the type is not included in the literature.

B022

This tiny eagle plate is a modern reproduction sold by the Fall Creek Corporation. It corresponds well to a very small eagle plate illustrated in Campbell and O'Donnell that they date ca.1835–1845.[79] It will be a challenge to the serious collector to tell the difference between altered modern reproductions of B022 from an original of this cockade eagle. Besides the obvious newness, the modern reproduction B022 has some indications of a different trimming pattern that may prove helpful in discriminating the modern reproduction from the original illustrated in Campbell and O'Donnell. Serious collectors are advised to avoid a tightly trimmed modern reproduction. More high-resolution photos of good nineteenth century insignia would be useful in dealing with this vexing problem.

Early Nineteenth Century die striking technology employed very simple machinery, involving a heavy hammer, raised by manual labor and simply dropped on the dies. This primitive process required thin brass plates. To bring out greater detail, the thin plates had to be struck with multiple blows. All of this was quite labor intensive and time consuming and explains why early Nineteenth Century metal insignia were characteristically thin and lacked sharp detail and significant relief.

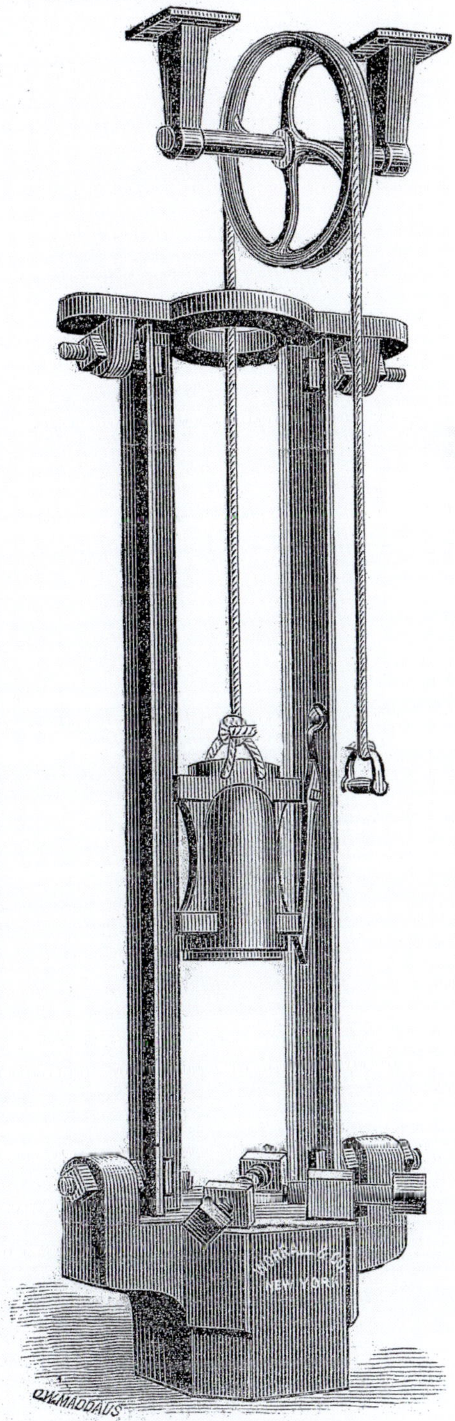

Figure I-11.

CHAPTER II

Emblems from about 1839 to 1859

(B023 to B037)

The headgear emblems worn by officers and enlisted Marines of this period are poorly documented. The 1833 Uniform Regulations are silent on the subject of headgear emblems. The 1839 Uniform Regulations are very skimpy and offer only a few tantalizing clues. After the three-inch brass eagle plate in chapter 1 was dropped, what was worn and exactly when it was worn are problematic questions. The uncertainty of the following discussion of emblems begs a greater research effort. Despite the paucity of information in the Uniform Regulations, there are hints that Marine Corps Headquarters correspondence and especially Treasury Department records of emblem procurement could throw important new light on the subject. The following order of discussion should be considered more of a simple heuristic device than a confident chronological ordering of the subject. Some of the variations described below will ultimately require new interpretations.

The German Script "USM" Cap Emblem

Headquarters correspondence dated January 23, 1840, describes officer brass belt plates with a gold wreath and raised German text letters of silver within the wreath.[1] These distinctive officer belt plates are depicted in photos of the period. The same order describes the unique wreath and German script USM pattern of the belt plate as, … "the same pattern and dimensions as the work on the fatigue cap.[2] Figure II-1 is an enhanced copy of the German text letters illustrated in the 1840 Marine Corps Headquarters Order.

Figure II-1
USM in German script.

During this research, no photos or examples of this officer's fatigue cap ornament B023 could be found. Figure II-2 is the author's interpretation of the shape and size of the B023 fatigue cap ornament. The interpretation is based on the above information as well as an illustration in the 1852 Uniform Regulations of the belt plate of the same design with similar silver German style letters surrounded by a gold wreath. Whether B023 was struck of metal or exclusively embroidered in gold and silver thread is not known nor specified in the Uniform Regulations. What is known is that the commandant ordered that B023 be discontinued for wear on the officer's fatigue cap in 1845.[3] Joel Thacker claimed this device was worn on both officer's and enlisted full dress caps from 1840 to 1859 and on officer's fatigue caps for only a few months when replaced by the wreath and anchor B028.[4] Unfortunately, Thacker cited no specific documentation to substantiate his interpretation.

Figure II-2
B023
Author's interpretation of the officer's fatigue cap ornament, 1839 to 1845.

B024

The ornament B024 is a modern and fanciful reproduction of an officer's fatigue cap device probably made in Pakistan. It consists of gold embroidered thread for the wreath and struck false embroidered white metal letters "USM." The style of the letters is closer to Roman script rather than German script as specified in the 1839 Uniform Regulations. Each metal letter is individually attached by a pair of single strand wires to a navy blue wool and roughly oval-shaped ground or cartouche. The cartouche shows no evidence of attachments or ever having been sewn to a fatigue cap.

B025

A private collector stated that this modern reproduction was made in Pakistan and thought to have been commissioned by a colleague to resemble the officer's 1845 fatigue cap ornament. Such obvious reproductions were made simply to give some idea of what the originals may have looked like. It minimally follows the scantily worded 1839 Uniform Regulations. The letters "USM" are made of silver embroidered thread but not in the style of specified German script. The wreath is embroidered in gold-colored thread. The reverse of the roughly shaped and crudely trimmed navy blue wool ground contains yellow thread and a black rubber-like adhesive. There are no obvious aging features, no attachments, or evidence of ever having been sewn to anything.

B026

Another modern reproduction was purchased from Fall Creek Suttlery, Whitestown, Indiana. The seller stated that it had recently been made in Pakistan. The wreath is made of gold-colored non-magnetic metal embroidery thread. The silver letters USM are also made of non-magnetic metal embroidery thread and only vaguely resemble the style of those illustrated in the 1839 Uniform Regulations. Characteristic of modern Pakistan embroidered insignia reproductions are the totally anachronistic gold-colored white plastic sequins instead of metal sequins as used in the mid-nineteenth century. This handsome creation is embroidered on a black felt oval. A fine outer gold embroidered oval surrounds the wreath and letters. Sandwiched between the black felt ground with the embroidery is another, smaller, interior black felt oval to give strength to the construction. Glued and sewn to this construction is a black cotton reverse.

Several examples of attempts to age such reproductions by applying stains and caustic reagents to make the embroidery look corroded have been seen by the author. The result is that the metal gold and silver thread looks corroded but the gold color on the sequins is damaged, exposing a base of white plastic or resinous material. Small samples of the metal thread and plastic sequins were tested by burning in a candle flame.

B027

The B027 device should not be confused with B023. It is a more modern strike using dies and trimming tools under high-pressure machinery characteristic of the industrial age and post Civil War period. The more modern and high pressure machinery produced harder strikes and high definition of details on relatively thick brass and white metal elements, compared to early nineteenth century ornaments struck with cruder, less powerful machinery, on relatively thin, often hand-trimmed brass plates. Emerson illustrates several US Army post-Civil War ornaments with this particular and distinctive wreath.[5] There are many examples of this distinctive wreath for the US Army insignia that Emerson dates primarily between the Civil War and 1905, including one for US Army hospital stewards that has the same style of Roman letters "US" in white metal. Emerson dates these Civil War ornaments to 1882.[6] The wire attachments predate the adoption of screw post attachment by the US Army in 1896.[7] The meaning of the "USM" letters is unknown. Other examples of late nineteenth century or later brass wreaths with the letters USM that are of an even more modern style than B027 have been seen by the author.

Gold Fouled Anchor in a Gold Wreath

A device with a gold fouled anchor within a gold wreath replaced the B023 type emblem on the officer's fatigue cap in 1845. This device is described in the Uniform Regulation of 1839: "… 5. Cap, blue cloth … with a foul anchor of gold, in a gold wreath in front."[8]

B028

The officer's fatigue cap emblem B028 is the only probable example of the 1845 pattern device examined in this research. Cureton includes an excellent photograph of 1st Lt. Josiah Watson with what appears to be an embroidered version of this ornament.[9] The size of B028 and the device on Watson's fatigue cap compare favorably in marked contrast to most of the undersized modern reproductions. The 1839 Uniform Regulations and the 1840 changes do not specify that B028 should be struck or embroidered. The wreath and anchor of B028 are struck brass, the cable is made of two strands of twisted silver wire. The anchor, cable, and wire loop attachments are soldered to the reverse of the wreath. The wreath is distinctive in that the leaves on the right and left sides are quite different, indicating a wreath composed of two different plants.

Because B023, see figure II-2, had silver letters in a gold wreath, a question arose at the time as to whether the anchor in B028 should be silver or gold. Commandant Archibald Henderson's order in response to this question states, "… The foul anchor is to be made of gold."[10] Furthermore, Henderson's

B029

Order of July 15, 1851, states "The position of the foul anchor in the gold wreath in the undress cap should not be horizontal but in the position of the anchor on the uniform cap."[11] It is not at all clear that Henderson's order specifying a diagonal anchor refers to the large officer and enlisted dress hat ornaments B032-B033 or the enigmatic B031. One example of an embroidered horizontal anchor inside a gold embroidered wreath, which may be the unauthorized device that the Commandant's order refers to or more than likely a US Navy officer's cap ornament of that time period has been seen by the author.

This modern reproduction was probably made in Pakistan and according to the present owner, was commissioned by his close colleague. It features an embroidered anchor and wreath in silver and gold thread, respectively. The color of the anchor thread is not consistent with Henderson's very specific order of March 27, 1850. The ground is of black wool material. The design is possibly based on the anchor-in-wreath device for the officer's fatigue cap illustrated in the 1852 Uniform Regulations. The wreath and ties approximately follow that design.

This distinctive officer's rectangular eight-sided dress hat or shako ornament is known only from an 1840 Huddy and Duval print.[12] The illustration depicts two US Marine officers, one standing and one seated. The seated officer's dress hat or shako has a unique rectangular shaped device, see Figure II-3.

Figure II-3
US Marine officers, 1840, *United States Military Magazine.*

Figure II-4
B030
Enlargement of Figure II-4.

B030 vaguely resembles the more complicated plate B031 that is illustrated in the 1852 Uniform Regulations. It may be an earlier version of B031 or an inaccurate artist's rendition, with its widest dimensions top to bottom rather than side to side as in B031. The design of an eagle perched on a diagonal anchor and thirteen stars above is similar in both devices, but B030 is obviously missing the shield and wreath elements of the more complicated B031, see figure II-4.

Figure II-5
B031 as illustrated in the 1852 Uniform Regulations.

An actual example of this plate (Figure II-5) has never been seen by the author, but Ray Darida recalled having seen the original die in the W. Stokes Kirk collection at that place of business some forty years ago before they closed shop.[13] The excellent line drawing illustration of the B031 seen in figure II-5 depicts the plate itself and the plate attached to a lieutenant's cap.[14]

Another rather impressionistic line drawing of B031 (Figure II-6) depicts two Marines wearing eight-sided plates that conform roughly to B031. This illustration dates 1853.[15] It is not certain when, or even if, this ornament was actually adopted. It is placed here following B030 because of its strong similarity to the emblem known only from the Huddy and Duval painting that must date sometime before 1841. It seems unlikely that both of these period illustrations are the product of artistic license or mistaken interpretation.

Cureton and Sullivan state that B031, although illustrated in the 1852 Uniform Regulations, "… had never gone into actual use."[16] Presumably this conclusion is based on the absence in surviving quartermaster records of orders for or receipt of this plate. An alternative interpretation by Todd is that B031 was strictly a plate for an officer.[17] The illustration of B031 (Figure II-5) from the 1852 Uniform Regulation is described specifically for officers, not enlisted Marines. This interpretation is not consistent with Figure II-6 showing enlisted marines wearing what the 1852 Uniform Regulation categorically describes as an officer item. Additional documentation for B030 and B031 would be very welcome. A very fanciful and modern reproduction of B031 embroidered in bright yellow and silver thread on a black or navy blue, eight-sided background, is known but has not been included in this inventory. Even if attempts were made to artificially make it look old, the elements embroidered in bright cloth thread and the unauthorized silver anchor make it an obvious modern reproduction. No attempts to pass off "faked" versions of this obviously modern reproduction are know by the author.

Figure II-6
B031 Uniform of the Marine Corps of the United States Navy [sic].
Gleason's Pictorial Drawing Room Companion

Eagle on a Cocked Anchor

The next group of brass emblems for the uniform hat is quite distinct. The design features a large eagle facing to its right and perched on a large diagonally oriented anchor leaning in the opposite direction. The design is a larger but simplified version of the more complex designs of B030 and B031. There are excellent surviving photographs of both officer and enlisted marines wearing the general B032/B033 type. In keeping with well-established convention, the officer's emblem may have been made by multiple strikes to bring out details and then gold plated while the enlisted versions were probably single strikes in plain brass. The author has never seen the B032/B033 type gold plated with multiple strikes; only emblems struck in plain brass.

B032

There is some uncertainty about the dating of B032/B033. Charles Cureton dates this type back to 1846.[18] Campbell and O'Donnell date this type from 1852 to 1859, perhaps because B031 is prominently illustrated in the 1852 Uniform Regulations. In addition, good photographs of B032/B033 exist that seem to date between 1852 and the appearance of the 1859 Uniform Regulations.[19] The dating uncertainty raises questions about what replaced what and when, as well as the less likely possibilities that more than one type of emblem may have been worn concurrently or that the 1852 Uniform Regulation illustrates an emblem (B031) that was never worn.

B032 was struck from a different die than B033. This fact is pointed out by tick marks on the images of both. Note the position of the ironwork on the anchor stock where the stock contacts the cable. The B032 die variety is far less often seen and came from a private collection. It was found over forty years ago in an old cavalry feed bag at a W. Stokes Kirk surplus store.[20] The die and trimming tools for B032 were not seen at that time by Ray Darida in the W. Stokes collection. Only one other example of B032 has been examined by the author. According to Smithsonian acquisition records, this second example was also acquired from the W. Stokes Kirk collection in 1959. Unlike the modern restrikes, B032 has a healthy patina and iron (magnetic) wire attachments soldered to the reverse. Iron wire attachments were typical of mid-nineteenth century productions in contrast to the usual single strand brass wire attachments soldered to the reverse on modern reproductions.[21] Tick marks on B032 point out obvious differences between B032 and B033. This author knows of no modern reproductions using the original die that struck B032.

There is a very real problem in recognizing genuine surplus that ended up in inventories such as W. Stokes Kirk and Francis Bannerman. The problem is well illustrated by the confirmed occurrence of B032 in the old W. Stokes Kirk collection. At least one known original die for striking the very similar B033 design adds to the problem of recognizing emblems struck from original dies or very good copies of original dies. A concerted effort has been made in this research to point out ways to objectively distinguish modern restrikes and reproductions from authentic emblems, when that is possible. There are, however, plenty of cases where distinguishing authentic emblems from unauthentic emblems is problematic.

The far more frequently encountered die variety for this group is B033. As described above, Ray Darida acquired an original die for B033 from W. Stokes Kirk.[22] The author was told by Darida over ten years ago that for fear of damaging the original Stokes Kirk dies, he was generally not using them for mass production.[23] Since his productions of B032 are now plentiful and reasonably priced by sellers such as S&S Firearms, it is assumed that a very good copy of the original die is now in use. B032 has been advertised for at least the last five years in the S&S catalog as a restrike from an original die. Several years ago, Darida explained to the author that he burnishes and polishes his productions so that they have a bright, "brand spanking new" appearance.[24] Unfortunately, it is very common to see Naugatuck Novelty reproductions on the militaria market blatantly advertised as authentic nineteenth century US Marine insignia.

B033

According to Darida, dies for B033 and other early emblems were, more than forty years ago, loaned by W. Stokes Kirk to Col. John Magruder, director at that time of the USMCHCQV.[25] As with other early Marine Corps emblems such as B002 and B007, the borrowed dies were used to make restrikes for historical interpretation specialists at various USMC bases. There is, to this author's knowledge, no easy way to confidently identify the earlier Magruder restrikes from potentially authentic W. Stokes Kirk or Bannerman surplus.

The problem of correctly identifying dishonestly doctored-up versions of B033 and other emblems in this study is vexing. For the above stated reasons, and before paying premium prices for frequently encountered and highly questionable examples of B033, the infrequently encountered B032 would be a safer choice. A good rule of thumb for serious collectors would be to avoid the uncertain in favor of emblems for which there are no known examples of restriking from old dies or production with close copies of old dies. Nevertheless, one cannot in every case be certain that the plentiful examples of B033 are always modern restrikes or reproductions. Someone at some time struck emblems from the original die for B034 before Ray Darida rescued that die from the W. Stokes Kirk collection. Some of these strikes were probably genuine nineteenth century surplus, a few were known to be struck for Col. John Magruder's USMC historical interpretation specialists, most are modern reproductions from a very good copy of the die that struck B033.

There are variations in the trimming of B033 that are unlike the more complete trimming pattern in the two examples of B032 that the author is aware of. Ray Darida did not get the original trimming tool when he acquired the die from W. Stokes Kirk and for many years laboriously trimmed his productions by hand with a jeweler's saw.[26] The incompleteness of the trimming of the Darida productions using his laborious trimming method may help to distinguish some of his restrikes from authentic nineteenth century surplus trimmed more completely with the lost original trimming tool. Naugatuck Novelties now uses a new trimming tool to trim their more recent productions of B033. It is not known if this new trimming pattern is any different from those authentic W. Stokes Kirk or Bannerman surplus items trimmed with the lost trimming tool.

B034

The untrimmed plate B034 was graciously given to the author by Ray Darida more than ten years ago. It was one of only a few pieces that were struck at that time from the original die. Darida also kindly provided the author with a copy of a photograph of the original W. Stokes Kirk die (see Figure II-7). It is included to show that B034 was categorically struck from that die. The flaws seen between three and four o'clock on the plate B034 correspond to the pits seen on the original die in Figure II-7. Darida suggested that these pits in the die may well be rust damage to the die as a result of the great Boston fire of 1872 that damaged the building where these dies were stored.[27] There is no reason to think that a great number of these plates were struck from the original B034 die; the author greatly appreciates having an example of this restrike to include in this research.

Figure II-7
Original Stokes Kirk die for B033.

This modern reproduction was purchased from S&S Firearms. Presumably it was manufactured by Naugatuck Novelties. It is evidently not a restrike from the original die (Figure II-7), but is struck by a very good copy of that original die. However, B035 does not bear a one-to-one relationship with B033 and B034. Tick marks point out some of the more obvious differences. Note, for example, the differences in the thickness of the cable of B035 compared to B033 and B034. It is as if the cable where it crosses the anchor shaft is mashed down and spread out. In keeping with the black cabinet concept, as discussed in the introduction, it is recommended that serious buyers, sellers, and collectors closely compare an actual example of B035 to expensive emblems of this type for sale, purportedly as rare and authentic mid-nineteenth century US Marine emblems. A black cabinet comparative emblem of B035 would be a good investment to give assurances that one is not buying a fake.

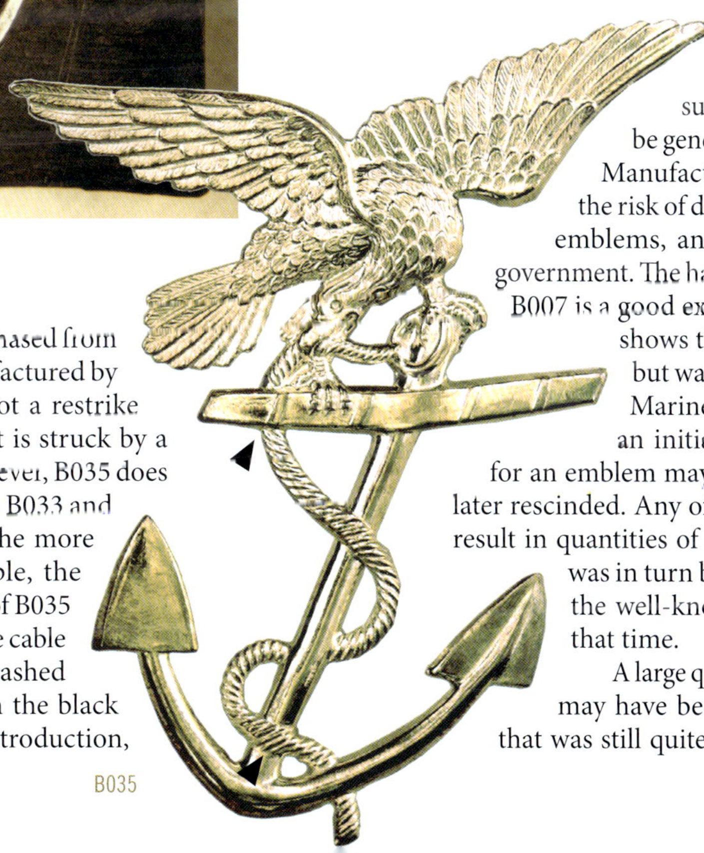

B035

Flowing Script USM Cap Ornaments

B036

The questionable ornaments B036 and B037 are the brass letters "USM." They have a distinctive flowing script writing style. B036 and B037 are struck from separate dies. The differences are indicated on the images of each by tick marks. B034 has reinforcement segments between the letters to give more strength to the arrangement of the thin, frail letters. During this research no period photographs or illustrations could be found of Marines, either enlisted or officers, wearing this particular emblem. The type is not included in any Uniform Regulation. The same is to be said of any mention or description in any Marine Corps correspondence or orders that the author is aware of.

An example of B036 was acquired by Col. John Driscoll from a surplus store in the 1950s well before the proliferation of modern reproductions of this emblem.[28] B036, unlike the modern reproduction B037, is attached with two iron (magnetic) "U"-shaped wires instead of the brass wires common with reproductions. The well-known late nineteenth century surplus dealers often bought great quantities of genuine surplus that included obsolete insignia that had been replaced by changes in the Uniform Regulations. Large quantities of surplus insignia could also be generated for other reasons. Manufacturers may have taken the risk of designing and producing emblems, anticipating sales to the government. The handsome cross belt plate B007 is a good example, documentation shows that it was prepared for, but was never accepted by, the Marine Corps. In other cases, an initial Marine Corps order for an emblem may have been placed and later rescinded. Any of these situations could result in quantities of unneeded surplus that was in turn bought for a pittance by the well-known surplus dealers of that time.

A large quantity of B036 emblems may have been acquired as surplus that was still quite plentiful as late as the

1950s and 1960s. Nevertheless, there is no convincing evidence that the emblems B035/B036 were ever worn by Marines or purchased by the Marine Corps. Until further support such as period photos and illustrations, or written documentation is forthcoming, this has to remain an open question. The existence of significant quantities and varieties of seemingly authentic insignia surplus at places like W. Stokes Kirk and Francis Bannerman's stores explains how John Driscoll and other collectors bought their examples of seemingly authentic nineteenth century surplus. The availability of so much genuine surplus prior to the explosion of recent reproductions was a collector's dream and may explain why so many of these items continue to show up. Being authentic surplus is one thing, having been purchased for and actually worn by US Marines can be a totally different situation.

Instead of the script USM devices B036, B037 Cureton and Sullivan state that quartermaster records indicate that enlisted Marines, sometime before 1859, wore a forage cap device with the block letters 'USM' in brass.[29] The only period illustration known so far is dated 1857 and shows an enlisted Marine wearing a forage cap with the block letters USN, which Cureton and Sullivan attribute to a printing error. This seems plausible, but raises the gnawing question of artistic license or fallible artistic interpretation of block letters rather than flowing script. The artist's interpretation of the eagle on the cocked anchor device (B032 or B033) in this same illustration is certainly not accurate. A citation of the specific quartermaster records bearing on this issue would be most welcome for throwing new light on the question of use by enlisted Marines. The author is aware of one example of a block letter USM ornament that is a modern reproduction.

B037

Several years ago, the author purchased this emblem from S&S Firearms, but it was manufactured by Naugatuck Novelties. It was advertised as struck by one of the original dies that Ray Darida acquired from the W. Stokes Kirk Company, see Figure II-8. The original force had been lost and Darida had to have a new steel force made in order to strike emblems using this die.[30] B036 has been laboriously trimmed very closely using a jeweler's saw. One can purchase these from S&S Firearms for reasonable prices, but they are now being offered untrimmed.

Figure II-8
B036 Original W. Stokes Kirk die.

CHAPTER III

Enlisted and Officer Emblems: Civil War Period

(B038 to B068)

Dress Hat Plates

The documentation for emblems of this period is greatly improved compared to earlier information. With the appearance of the more explicit text and superb line drawings in the 1859 Uniform Regulations, the task of identifying emblems from this period was made much easier. In addition, the availability of an increasing number of period photographs has thrown important new light on a complex subject. Many more examples of Marine Corps emblems have survived from the period largely as a function of the increase in the number of Marines who served at this time.

Large Size 1859 Pattern Shield, Wreath, Bugle, and Letter "M" Dress Hat Emblem

One of the most important finds in this research was an extremely well-preserved 1859 pattern enlisted full dress uniform hat ornament that conforms very well to the device illustrated in the 1859 Uniform Regulations.[1] Unlike most of the emblems in this work, there is no question about its age or authenticity. More importantly, one can rule out that it was thrown together by early surplus dealers or collectors. This cannot be confidently said about many of the emblems in this study. Probably the only collector of B038 was a sailor named H.R. Brown.

B038 lay in the mud of the Yazoo River in west central Mississippi for 102 years. It was among a huge collection of extraordinarily well preserved artifacts recovered by the US Park Service. It is now on display at the Vicksburg National Military Park. The ironclad USS *Cairo* was sunk by Confederates hidden ashore on December 12, 1862. The confederates used a pull cord attached to an artillery friction primer and ignited an anchored and submerged five-gallon glass demijohn filled with black powder. The explosion of the improvised mine blew a huge hole in the unarmored wood below the waterline on the starboard side. The *Cairo* sank with miraculously no loss of life in just twelve minutes.

Examination of *Cairo* muster rolls shows that no Marines served on board. According to the recollections of the now deceased Mrs. Margerie Bears, who catalogued the *Cairo* collection, B038 was associated with a complete enlisted Marine dress hat found inside a sailor's small wooden locker box in the forward starboard hold in a section where enlisted sailors stowed their personal gear.[2] All the metal parts were very well preserved, but the leather and cloth elements, although recognizable, were in a bad state of preservation.[3] Other items preserved in this wooden box indicate that the owner was Seaman H.R. Brown, who enlisted in the Navy March 24, 1862. There is no H. Brown or R. Brown listed in the USMC muster rolls from 1858 to 1862.[4] How this USMC dress hat ended up in a sailor's locker box in the *Cairo* in 1862 is intriguing. Dress hat ornaments, like firearms, were considered company property and were required to be turned in at the end of an enlistment.[5] The fact that five pocketknives, each with different carved initials, also ended up in seaman Brown's wooden box is even more fascinating.

Thanks to the excellent preservation medium of the Yazoo River mud, we have a remarkable example of exactly how the brass bugle and white metal "M" were attached to the larger shield in December 1862. Small brown isosceles triangular-shaped leather strips were used to hold the bugle and "M" by wedging the leather strips into a system of soldered brass wire "U"-shaped loops. This is fully corroborated in the 1859 Uniform Regulations describing an attachment

B038

system of "eyes and rings with leather strips."[6] This attachment system probably survived up to the adoption of the screw post attachment and is a very practical method of assembling and disassembling the elements of the device for polishing and at the same time protecting the rest of the dress hat. Anyone who has ever stood a Marine Corps personnel inspection could especially appreciate this convenient and efficient way of keeping brass bright.

The *Cairo* dress hat ornament conforms very well to both the text and line drawings of the 1859 Uniform Regulations. Like most of the examples of complete 1859 pattern dress hats that the author has seen, and as specifically described in the 1859 Uniform Regulations, there was no red leather circle behind the white metal "M" inside the brass bugle. Both the text and the drawings in the 1859 Uniform Regulations clearly describe the red leather circle inside the brass bugle for the enlisted undress cap (kepi) ornament only. This issue will be discussed in reference to other emblems in this chapter where red leather circles have been inappropriately put inside the brass bugle, probably by nineteenth century surplus dealers or early collectors who may not have been aware of the distinction between the undress cap (kepi) device and the dress hat ornament.

The shield, wreath, bugle, and white metal "M" elements for B038 are all struck from dies different from the other uniform hat plates in this chapter (B039 through B042). When one considers only the shield and wreath patterns, B038 is distinct from all the others. It has also been the author's experience that B038, the US *Cairo* plate, is seldom encountered while the second type of wreath and shield pattern is far more common. Only one other example of the B038 device is known to the author. The disparity in the frequencies of these two main types is consistent with USMC Quartermaster records of uniform hat plates delivered by manufacturers.[7] Cureton and Sullivan document that only two manufacturers delivered uniform hat plates in 1859. James S. Smith and Company delivered a total of 850 plates, while Horstmann Brothers and Company delivered only 150 plates. It would stand to reason that the small order would more than likely be B038, just as the larger order delivered by James S. Smith Company would likely be the more common second type shield and wreath (B039-B042).

B040

B039

All the elements of this ornament, including the shield, wreath, bugle, and white metal letter "M" are struck from dies different than B038. This ornament was probably manufactured by James S. Smith and Company. B039 and minor variants of this type are far more common. Many examples of B039 apparently ended up in the inventories of the late nineteenth century surplus dealers. There are many differences between B038 and B039, but the most obvious are seen in the segmented stars in the shield and the shape and more rounded edges of the leaves in the wreath. A comparison of the white metal "M" on B038 and that on B039 clearly shows obvious differences as well.

This arrangement of the 1859 pattern shield, wreath, bugle, and white metal "M" elements is the same as B039, except for two important features. The brass bugle is a distinct false embroidered pattern (see B051). The shield and wreath are gilded and polished, suggesting an officer's version of B039. This interpretation is in keeping with the convention of a fancier treatment for officer's emblems that were typically given multiple strikes to bring out additional details. The officers' devices were gilded and polished, while enlisted emblems were single die strikes on brass plates without gilt.

B041

The shield and wreath in this assemblage are struck from the same dies as B039, B040, and B042. What distinguishes this emblem is a bugle struck from an entirely different die and a brass Roman style "M" inside that bugle. The block Roman style "M" is a known motif for Confederate States Marine Corps buttons manufactured with back-marks HB&T Manchester (Figure III-1).[8] B041 may be a construct from common nineteenth century surplus elements that may or may not have anything to do with Confederate Marines. The button in Figure III-1, does not correspond exactly one to one with the "M" in B041, yet the possibility exists that the brass Roman style "M" was a designation for Confederate States Marines.

Figure III-1
Block M Confederate Marine Corps button back marked, HB&T Manchester.

To the author's knowledge, there is no known evidence, including photographs, of Confederate Marines actually wearing this particular device. Donnelly pointed out that "No copies of Confederate Marine uniform regulations seem to be in existence …,"[9] and, "… no cap ornament or Corps insignia has been located."[10] On one hand, it seems likely that given the severe supply problems faced by the South, Confederate Marines may simply have been forced to make do without dress caps. On the other hand, Donnelly presents an 1864-dated clothing allowance for Confederate Marines that includes one dress cap and three fatigue caps and three pompons.[11] This allowance is essentially equivalent to the 1859 enlisted US Marine clothing allowance.[12] In the same source, Donnelly cites Confederate Marine regulations regarding the officer commanding the Marine guard on war ships having the exclusive use of a storeroom, where arms and other company property such as "uniform caps, pompons etc., were kept."[13] That these documents mention uniform caps and pompons is one thing; whether Confederate Marines actually wore dress uniform caps with a distinctive brass ornament such as B041 are separate questions, begging answers based on more convincing information.

A formal written inquiry about B041 was made to the Museum of the Confederacy at Richmond, Virginia. The gracious response of the museum curator was that they had no knowledge of Confederate Marines wearing such a device.[14] This still leaves the tantalizing possibility that some Confederate Marine detachments had opportunities to use emblems captured from Federal sources during the war, especially early in the war, or purposely copied or put together Confederate versions of the 1859 dress hat arrangement. This, however, does not seem to be a very likely explanation for the significant number and variety of Roman style block 'M' brass letters on 1859 pattern shields and wreaths that have shown up on the market. A more likely explanation is that most, if not virtually all of these emblems, were put together by early surplus dealers or early collectors from mix-and-match authentic surplus. Some of this surplus may have been intended for sale to the Confederacy but never really worn by Confederate Marines. Another possibility is that such a mix and match of surplus had nothing to do with the Confederate States Marine Corps. New information on the above conjectures will be most welcome.

The shield and the wreath of B042 are the same as B039 and B040. What is distinctive is the anachronous white metal eagle globe and anchor ornament B143, probably dating ca.1881 to 1905. The B042 ensemble, when purchased, was mounted on a thin wooden shield painted flat black. The shield and wreath lack the brass loops characteristic of the

B042

Cairo specimen and are attached to the wooden shield by single strand brass wire attacments. These single strand brass wires are characteristic of late nineteenth and early twentieth-century surplus. Much of the glut of this War between the States surplus was probably unfinished. B042 is flat and not curved to fit snuggly against the front of the hat like B038. It seems likely that surplus dealers like Francis Bannerman and W. Stokes Kirk soldered single strand brass wires to these unfinished emblems as a cheap and expedient means of attachment. According to Ray Darida, W. Stokes Kirk put together these black wooden shields with various artifacts to appeal to potential buyers.[15] These wooden shields with various artifacts mounted on them can also be seen in old Bannerman catalogs. On the back of the B042 wooden shield was a glued paper with the typed statement, "Shield and wreath used on regulation Marine Corps drums." Published photographs and Marine Corps Uniform Regulations up to 1917 corroborate the use of the 1859 shield and wreath with a much later white metal, eagle globe and anchor device.[16] One photo dating 1926 clearly shows the Civil War shield and wreath attached to drums of China Marines.

A very small number of the B042 shield and wreath devices were also used by the US Marine band drum majors from 1963 to ca.1975. The Director of Marine Corps Museums, Col. John Magruder, not without some reservations, recommended that a brass shield and wreath with the current (1955 pattern) emblem be attached to the front of the Marine Band drum major's busby.[17] Magruder's letter suggested that either the large 1859 or the smaller 1875 shield and wreath be considered. Jack MCord said to the author that Col. John Driscoll, author of *The Eagle Globe and Anchor 1868 to1968*, while still on active duty, had a lot to do with the adoption of the larger 1859 shield and wreath on the drum major's busby.[18] Photographs provided to the author by the USMC Band indicate that drum majors in the mid-1960s wore the current enlisted emblem.[19] Drum majors up through about 1975 wore the current officer's eagle globe and anchor on the 1859 shield and wreath (see Figure III-2). Drum Major Carroll removed the shield and chain from the bearskin sometime in the mid-1970s. He felt the bearskin busby was over decorated.[20]

Figure III-2
B042 Shield and wreath with current officers dress cap emblem, worn briefly by Marine Corps Band drum majors.

Despite the documented use of B042 on Marine drums up to at least 1926 and then again by drum majors of the Marine band, many, if not most of these B042 devices that appear on the market today, were probably put together by dealers or collectors using common items bought from available surplus. The number of surplus items and unfinished findings had to far outweigh the few sets that were actually used by a few Marine bandsmen in the twentieth-century.

B043

Reduced Size Civil War Period Dress Hat Emblem

On July 23, 1861, Commandant John Harris expressed his written opinion that the 1859 pattern brass full dress hat ornament (B038/B039) was too large and thereby directed that it be reduced in size by twenty-five percent (Figure III-3).

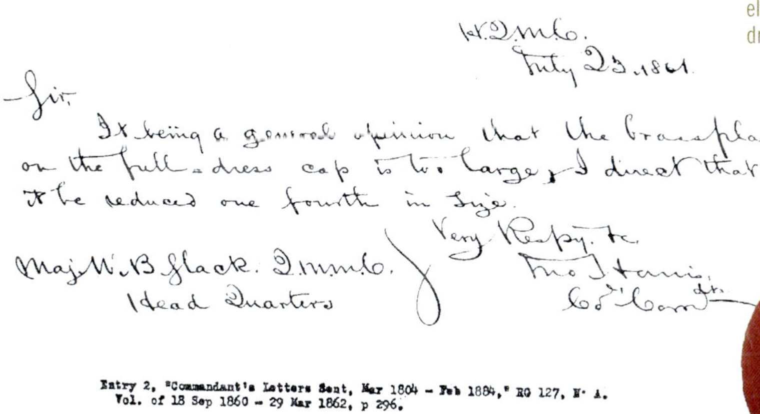

H.Q. M.C.
July 23, 1861.

Sir,
It being a general opinion that the brass plate on the full-dress cap is too large, I direct that it be reduced one fourth in size.

Very Respy. &c.
Jno. Harris,
Col. Comdt.

Maj. W. B. Slack, Q.M.M.C.
Head Quarters

Entry 2, "Commandant's Letters Sent, Mar 1804 - Feb 1884," RG 127, N. A.
Vol. of 18 Sep 1860 - 29 Mar 1862, p 296.

Figure III-3
Commandant's order reducing the size of the full dress uniform cap ornament.

Allowing sufficient time for a contractor to respond to the order and produce the new emblems, it had to be late 1862 or even into 1863 before B043 could have been issued to enlisted men or purchased by officers. A survey of images available and especially considering the superb group of photos in Cureton and Sullivan[21] and Sullivan,[22] B043 can be seen along with B038 and B039 in several images of Civil War Marines. B043 gradually replaced the two earlier and larger dress hat plates. A particularly well-known Civil War photo of a Marine sergeant and five privates at the Washington Navy Yard shows the sergeant wearing the earlier large size and the lesser ranks wearing the 1862 reduced-size device.

The image of B043 shown here was put together by Ray Darida from separate elements that he found at a W. Stokes Kirk surplus store many years ago. Figure III-4 shows all the elements that Ray Darida pieced together from the W. Stokes Kirk inventory. The author has also had the opportunity to examine and photograph two other examples of B043 that were a part of the Smithsonian Institution holdings that have been recently transferred to the USMCHCQV. The former Smithsonian examples of B043, according to Smithsonian acquisition records, were also acquired from W. Stokes Kirk. All, including the shield, bugle, and letter "M" are struck from the same dies and do not have a red leather circle inside the bugle (see Figure III-5).

Figure III-4
B043 with associated bent and bush elements on dress hat.

Darida and Donnelly mention three different contracts for manufacturing enlisted dress caps 1859 to 1861.[23] The first contract was with Wm. J. McCoy on October 21, 1859. The second contract was with James Riley and dated October 4, 1860. The last contract was with Bent and Bush of Boston dating

Figure III-5
B043 on Dress Hat.

B044

Tracings of the reverse of the shields of B043 and B044 (Figure III-6) illustrate differences in the pattern of rectangular slots where the bugle and letter "M" elements were attached by loops and eyes to the Naugatuck Novelties reproduction shield. Brass wire loops were soldered purposely to the B044 bugle in a different and higher position than that found on B043.[27] This pattern probably distinguishes some B044 modern reproductions from the B043 shield from W. Stokes Kirk surplus.

Enlisted Fatigue Cap Ornaments

In one respect the 1859 pattern enlisted undress or fatigue cap ornament was different from the bugle and white metal "M" elements of the 1859 full dress or uniform cap ornaments B038 and B039. The fatigue cap ornament included a red leather circle in the center of the bugle highlighting the white metal old English "M." This is clearly stated in Uniform Regulations.[28] B045 has a healthy patina and other features indicating that it is authentic nineteenth century surplus likely from W. Stokes Kirk, Francis Bannerman, or other inventories. The B045 bugle is very close but not exactly the same as the die that struck B039. Tick marks point out some important differences. B045 is not struck from the same die that produced the Naugatuck Novelties reproduction B046.

B045

This bugle and white metal "M" for dress headgear was dropped in 1875, except for Marine Corps buglers who continued to wear such a device as seen in photos on the 1898 campaign hat as late as 1901.[29] Perhaps most of the authentic nineteenth century surplus of B045 may have been US Army rather than the Marine Corps because of the much larger size of the US Army infantry, using the same device from 1872 to 1875.[30] Emerson states that the US Army infantry dropped this device in 1875, which resulted in a surplus of that emblem.[31] This Army surplus, as in the Marine Corps, was also put to good use as a distinction for US infantry and US artillery buglers.[32]

B046

Naugatuck Novelties manufactures B046. It is sold at reasonable prices by S&S Firearms, who claim to have all the equipment necessary to stamp these.[33] It is struck from a copy of the die that struck B045. They do not, however, bear a one-to-one correspondence (see tick marks). They are commonly offered as authentic 1859 to 1875 emblems by unknowing or dishonest sellers. Close examination of the details of B045 and this reproduction is advisable. That is the bad news; the good news is that B045, because of its close similarity to B046,

September 28, 1861. The enlisted dress cap illustrated in Darida and Donnelly clearly shows the later, reduced size plate B043 with Bent and Bush manufacturer labels in the cap. It seems entirely possible that B038 and B039 were manufactured by Wm. J. McCoy and James Riley.[24] Darida and Donnelly state that with the exception of two contracts in 1873 and 1874, the company of Bent and Bush of Boston was the main contractor for the enlisted dress cap with B043 from late 1862 to 1875.[25]

This modern reproduction is struck from a die copied from the W. Stokes Kirk elements that Ray Darida put together for B043. It is a very good copy, but does not exactly correspond one to one with the models for this copy that came from the W. Stokes Kirk collection. The most obvious difference is that the modern reproduction is a strong strike showing more detail than the emblems that came out of the W. Stokes Kirk collection. To be even more confident in identifying expensive, authentic emblems, the serious collector would be advised to acquire, for comparative purposes, an example of the modern Naugatuck Novelties reproduction. Real 1862 to 1875 pattern reduced size dress hat emblems are certainly uncommon. In contrast, B044 is readily available. Some are purposely altered and dishonestly offered as authentic 1862 to 1875 emblems. Collectors should be cautious. Many examples of B044 use green leather-like triangles to attach the brass loops simply because the red color material was not available to the manufacturer when these were produced.[26]

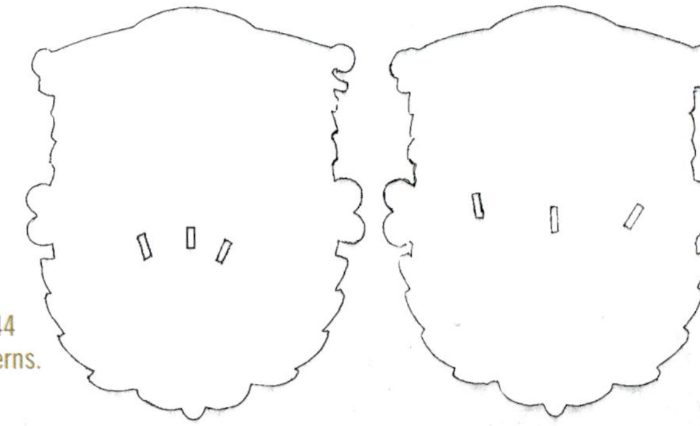

Figure III-6
B043 and B044
aperture patterns.

can still be found at reasonable prices. The difficulty of distinguishing the two may have tended to keep prices reasonable for the nineteenth century surplus.

A modern reproduction, manufactured by Naugatuck Novelties and currently for sale by S&S Firearms and perhaps others, it is a very good copy but does not bear one-to-one correspondence with the bugle in B043. Tick marks point out some critical differences. In general the modern copy shows details that are not present in B043, which was struck from a different or more worn die. This is a good example of "less is better." In terms of detail, the modern reproduction is a better and more detailed strike than those from nineteenth century surplus (B045). However, for the seller and collector interested in authenticity, an investment in nineteenth century surplus, even if questionable, should still be preferable to buying an obvious modern reproduction.

B047

Officer's Fatigue Cap Emblems

The next twenty emblems (B048 through B068) are classified as officer's emblems 1859–1868. All are false embroidered brass stampings or cloth or metal bullion embroidered emblems. The most authentic emblems are presented first, followed by problematic emblems and, finally, the more obvious reproductions. For recognition and identification, the emblems are grouped by overall similarity.

The officer's false embroidered brass- and gold-plated undress cap ornament B048, missing the white metal "M" in the center, was purchased by Enrico Saccone of Santa Barbara, California, sometime before 1976.[34] The device was part of a substantial collection including two officer's uniform coats, an 1859 dress hat with wreath, plate, and brass net acorn, an officer's sword and other items once belonging to an unnamed officer, whose family (descendants) sold the collection to Saccone. Ultimately, B048, along with a superb epaulette set (B067) in the original metal box, with white gloves and leather stock, were acquired as a group by the USMCHCQV (see Figure III-8).

B048

B048 is larger than most of the enlisted devices discussed in the first part of this chapter. It conforms reasonably well to other larger kepi ornaments commonly seen in the literature. Published photos, especially those of both Cureton and Sullivan, document a very wide variety of officer's undress hat ornaments. Despite many possible matches, nothing in the published photographs can be unquestionably matched to specific emblems in this chapter. Nevertheless, the many photos that have been published clearly corroborate the wide variety of officer's kepi and enlisted devices in terms of their style, size differences, and construction methods and materials. These variations include brass and silver struck devices and a wide variety of embroidered devices in both cloth and metallic thread.

In keeping with the photographic indications of a very wide variety of officer's War between the States period undress cap ornaments, B049 is quite unlike B048. Besides being much smaller, it is embroidered in gold bullion thread on a red velvet-like ground. B049 is missing the white metal "M" but like B048 is also pierced in the center of the red cloth ground where that "M" element would have been attached. The reverse consists of cotton cloth and loose cotton threads glued to a paper-and-cotton backing. The smaller size of this device is not in compliance with the specifications of the 1859 Uniform Regulation, requiring it to be the same size as the enlisted fatigue cap ornament.[35]

B049

Nevertheless, small size officer ornaments like B049 can be seen in many War between the States period photos. The surviving photos of Marines of this period clearly indicate wide variation in the size and lack of uniformity of both enlisted and officer fatigue cap ornaments.

The struck false embroidered brass bugle with a red wool center and cut silver letter "M" is attached to a navy blue wool cartouche (oval-shaped ground). The cartouche or ground is of compound construction and includes a stiffening material such as leather or cardboard neatly sandwiched between the navy blue wool and a cotton backing very neatly sewn together. Although the device does not show obvious features of a modern reproduction, it is problematic for several reasons.

B050

It does not strictly conform to the line drawing or text description in the 1859 Uniform Regulation describing the officer's undress hat ornament. The regulation makes a clear distinction between the officer's ornament being embroidered and the enlisted counterpart being of yellow metal.[36] That nonconformity may have been overlooked by an interpretation of the language of the regulation "gold embroidered bugle" to accommodate false embroidered struck brass bugle ornaments. But also problematic is the mounting of the brass bugle and letter 'M" on a navy blue ground or cartouche instead of following the uniform regulation specification for red cloth backing, as seen with B048 and B049. That inconsistency may have also been within the range of variation tolerated for officer's undress cap devices at that time, but in terms of existing photos of Civil War headgear, a variant such as B050 has yet to be found.

There is no discernible difference between B050 and the untrimmed plate B051 thought to have been struck from an original and dated die. A careful examination of blown-up images of all three (B050, B051, and B052) indicates very little discernible difference. The question of authenticity for B050 remains and will be revisited when discussing B051 and B052.

B051

The untrimmed plate B051 was photographed when it was in the collection of Jack McCord. It has a heavy patina and a somewhat weak strike compared to the modern Naugatuck reproduction B052. The untrimmed plate clearly shows "WHH&S" and "April 59" and the word "KEY." Ray Darida stated that he struck these from an original die that he procured from W. Stokes Kirk.[37] It is still an open question as to how many modern restrikes have survived compared to those struck in the nineteenth century and ending up in the inventories of surplus dealers. No clear differences can be seen between B050 and B051.

The author is grateful for having been given (by Ray Darida) several modern Naugatuck Novelties reproductions, including B052. A careful comparison of blown-up images of B052, B051, and B050 indicates that the modern Naugatuck reproduction (B052) is struck from a copy of the original W. Stokes Kirk die. Although extremely close, B052 does not exactly correspond one to one with B050 and B051. Besides the sharp details of the modern die, tick marks point out other differences seen between it and B050 and B051 struck from the original die. Caution is recommended for serious collectors and sellers attempting to distinguish authentic nineteenth century surplus from modern restrikes and the even more common and very similar modern reproductions. The bright and shiny Naugatuck Novelties reproductions have been known to be altered and distressed to look authentic by dishonest sellers.

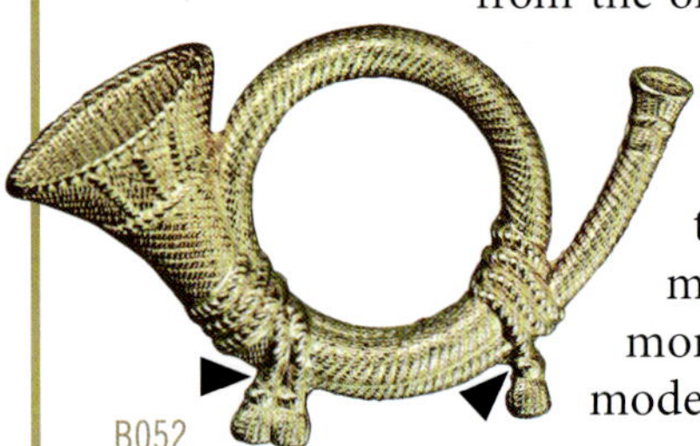

B052

Characteristics that dis-tinguish the modern reproduction B053 by Naugatuck Novelties are: the large size of the brass bugle, the false sequins, and the false embroidery. There is no known use of this type emblem by US Marines. Campbell and O'Donnell classify B053 as a modern restrike of an 1861 militia insignia.[38] Included in the same Campbell and O'Donnell reference is a photo of the original 1861-dated steel die now in the collection of Ray Darida. B053 is probably struck from a modern copy of a die for US Army ornaments of the 1851 pattern. This device is for sale at reasonable prices by S&S Firearms. Unfortunately, these have also been known to be altered to look old and stuck on red or navy blue cloth backgrounds and offered as authentic US Marine Officer's undress cap emblems.

B053

The author purchased this highly polished and lacquered ornament from S&S Firearms. It was probably manufactured by Naugatuck Novelties and struck from a copy of an original die from the W. Stokes Kirk collection. In both shape and size, this false embroidered device is distinctive. This device has shown up on the market artificially aged and purported to be a genuine officer's ornament. Ray Darida refers to it as a US Army type of false embroidered bugle.[39]

B054

This distinctive design with highly polished and lacquered false embroidered brass bugle was made by an unknown manufacturer and purchased by a collector colleague in 2007. Key features are a distinct bugle and crude stamped white metal "M" on an artificial red leather (leatherette) circle. The interior of the bugle is untrimmed with a single rectangular slot pierced in the center (twelve to six o'clock) to attach the white metal "M."

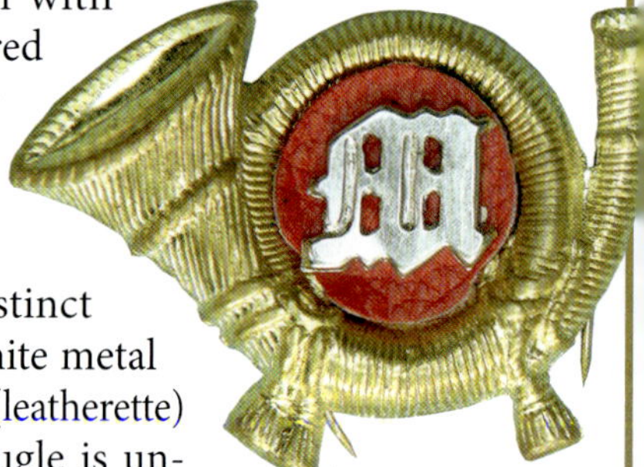

B055

Campbell and O'Donnell refer to this officer's false embroidered bugle as a non- regulation commercial item worn by militia infantry ca. 1855 to 1865.[40] It has a healthy patina on both the brass and

B056

solder points for the two missing brass wire attachments. There are no indications of it being a modern reproduction. Whether it is strictly a US Army or militia item or was also worn by Marines is an open question. The ornament came from the Jack McCord collection, which was started long before the plethora of reproductions came on the scene. A photo of a very similar minor variant of B056 is included in Cureton and Sullivan.[41] To complicate the question of enlisted versus officer use, the ornament is on a fatigue cap interpreted to be enlisted; perhaps this is just another example of mixing officer and enlisted items.

B057

The false embroidered bugle B057 is distinct from B056. It was damaged and repaired sometime in the past by soldering. It conforms well to a bugle device that Campbell and O'Donnell refer to as "primarily a militia device worn by all ranks."[42] In support of the interpretation that it is not a USMC item are the words "60th Regt" scratched in the reverse of the bugle bell. There was no 60th Regiment of Marines during the Civil War.

Officer's Embroidered Fatigue Cap Emblems

The next group consists of emblems embroidered in metallic or gold-colored cloth thread. With one exception, they are embroidered on a red cloth background as specified and illustrated in the 1859 Uniform Regulation. Most of this group, to say the least, are questionable: some are categorically modern, altered reproductions. None conform closely with the excellent illustration of the officer's undress cap ornament in the 1859 Uniform Regulation, (see Figure III-7). This last observation is not unexpected, given the great variation known in Civil War period embroidered officer emblems. A couple of these embroidered fatigue cap ornaments are questionable, most are at best obvious modern reproductions and at worst, reproductions purposely altered to look old.

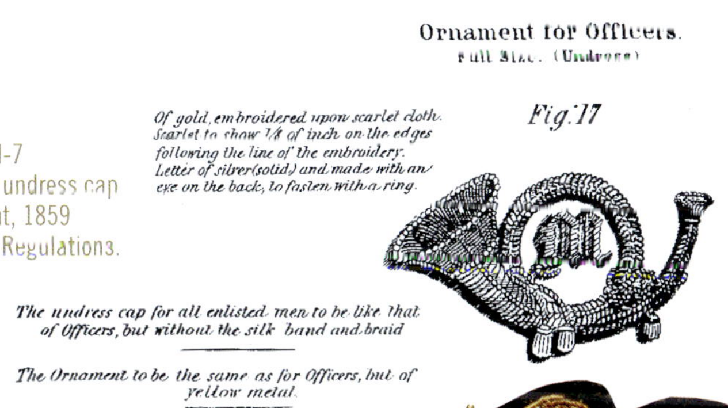

Figure III-7
Officer's undress cap ornament, 1859 Uniform Regulations.

A handsome undress cap bugle ornament in gold embroidered metallic thread with a red leather inner circle and a stamped (not solid silver) white metal "M" as in B042 and B043, is attached to an enlisted man's 1859 pattern kepi. The cap and ornament are illustrated in Chenoweth and Nihart.[43] The owner, Rick Spooner, thought it may be an officer's device attached to an enlisted man's undress cap lacking the specified silk band and quatrefoil.[44] The officer's gold braided cord is also much later than the Civil War period. This mismatch of anachronistic officer and enlisted elements is puzzling and suggests the possibility that it may have been put together from surplus items by someone who may not have been aware of the mixed elements. The bugle is embroidered on a non-regulation navy blue ground instead of the regulation red background. It is possibly one of a great variety of authentic officer's ornaments and has no obvious indication of being a reproduction.

B058

This device was purchased inexpensively by a respected Marine Corps emblem collector in the late 1970s.[45] It is a superb gold thread embroidered bugle on an obviously aged red wool background. The metal embroidery, which is turning black, does not match any of the modern Pakistan reproductions described later in this chapter. The stamped white metal Roman style "M" has a frosty silver finish and also does not match modern reproductions. The quality of workmanship seen in the intricate sewing of brown burlap to the reverse suggests the possibility that it was an undress cap device for officers of the Confederate States Marine Corps. An alternative interpretation is that someone stuck a later cast Roman style "M" to an authentic embroidered USMC officer's bugle device. Such a construction could have been done by a late nineteenth century surplus dealer or collector or an earlier Confederate States Marine Corps officer. The sequins added to the gold thread embroidery are definitely metal, not plastic, as in modern reproductions. This suggests that it is at least a nineteenth century surplus construction and possibly a Confederate Marine officer's ornament.

B059

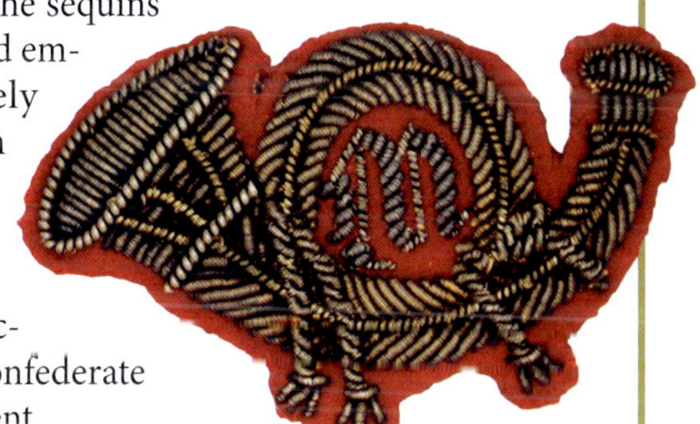

B060

Two very similar examples of this device are currently at the USMCHCQV, one is more moth-eaten than B060. They are finely embroidered in metallic gold-colored thread (bullion) and do not exactly correspond one to one in the shape of the embroidery or the shape of the red wool ground. Both have a backing of white batting sewn with yellow thread. A gold-colored embroidered "M" is found in the middle of the bugle of this pair. A gold embroidered "M" is not consistent with the 1859 Uniform Regulations, which specify a solid silver "M," but this may have been a contemporary aberration that was tolerated or perhaps a later reproduction.

B061

The gold metal thread embroidered bugle on an oval-shaped red wool cartouche with a gold embroidered letter "M" seems highly unlikely to be an authentic officer's undress cap ornament of the War between the States period. This device, found in the Quantico collections with no provenance, is sewn to a backing of navy blue burlap-like material with dull gold colored thread. On the reverse is a rectangular white paper sticker with the text "WDL #4 USMC." A device so deviant from the Uniform Regulations seems more likely to be some kind of reproduction. In the USMCHCQV collections are four other variants of B061 that do not conform to USMC officers kepi devices with red cloth centers.

The next two emblems (B062 and B063) on first appearance seem very similar, but on closer examination reveal some critical differences. B062 conforms extremely well with the 1859 Uniform Regulations including its size, the shape of the red wool backing, and the solid silver "M" in the middle of the embroidered bugle. The silver "M" also conforms very well to the silver "M" in the epaulette set B067, for which there is no question about authenticity. The metallic gold-colored thread embroidered bugle is very close to the device illustrated in Cureton and Sullivan.[46] The cut silver letter "M" is attached by two silver wires to a backing of tan cotton material. B062 is the best candidate in this inventory for an authentic Civil War period officer's fatigue cap device.

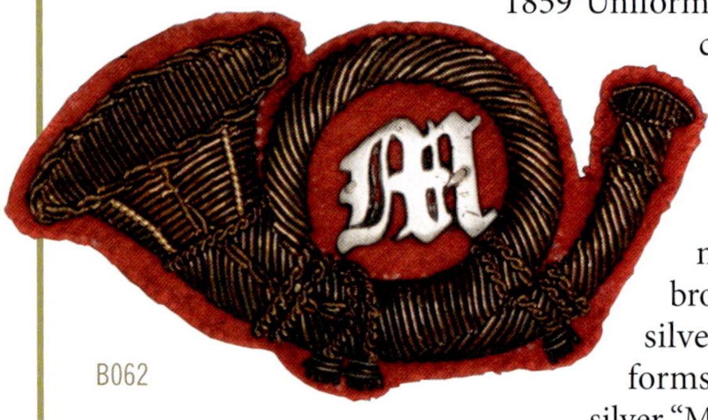

B062

Three important features distinguish B062 from the very similar B063 close up. The embroidered bugle is similar, but unsurprisingly, not exactly the same. The red wool background is quite similar in shape but the white metal "M" is struck in a false embroidered pattern. Ray Darida said he produces reproduction false embroidered bugles like these (see B064).[47] More importantly, the embroidered bugle B063 includes sequins. The sequins in B063 are made of an unknown material. When the author photographed and described B063 in 1997, he was unaware of the plastic sequin issue. An answer to this sequin question on other examples of B063 would be most welcome today.

B063

Two other examples of B063 from other private collections have been examined. One example was found to be thoroughly distressed by what appears to be an acid-like reaction that heavily corroded the metal threads, giving them an aged appearance. The reagent used also distressed and faded the red wool backing and removed the gold color from the sequins, exposing a white-colored plastic base. Plastic sequins were not invented until much later than 1861 to 1865. These fakes are being offered as authentic and very expensive emblems by dishonest or unknowing sellers. The best advice to collectors is to be very cautious with purported officer's Civil War period ornaments and avoid plastic sequins.

The next three emblems are unquestionably modern reproductions, probably made in Pakistan. They are bright and shiny with no pretense of age or authenticity. The author purchased these from several honest sources who sold them up front for what they were. One known vender is Falls Creek Suttlery, Whitestown, Indiana. Nevertheless, they can and have been altered to look old. There have been recent offerings on the Internet of purported authentic devices like B063 that have obviously been distressed to look old. Although obvious fakes, they are an important part of the black cabinet of reproductions. A prudent selection of these by serious collectors and sellers offers an objective way to identify many fakes and artificially aged reproductions.

B064

The modern reproduction B064 was purchased by the author at a gun show in January 1997. It consists of a red wool background with a metallic gold-colored embroidered bugle with gold-colored plastic sequins. A small sample of a sequin was cut away and tested by burning in a candle flame. Another small sample of the metallic gold embroidery thread was also tested and did not burn in the same candle flame. The reverse consists of two layers of navy blue cotton batting sewn and glued to the red wool background. The white metal false embroidered letter "M" is attached by a single strand of doubled-over brass wire soldered to the back of the letter "M." This white metal letter "M" device is currently made by Naugatuck Novelties, while the rest of the B064 emblem was reported by the seller to have been made in Pakistan. A US Marine officer's embroidered undress cap device conforming very well to the reproduction B064 has been advertised in the S&S Firearms catalog since 2002.

Differences between the modern reproductions B064, B065, and B066 can be seen in the pattern of embroidery, the overall size, the color of the gold embroidery thread, the shape of the red wool background, and the different dies used to strike the white metal "M." The method of construction and the elements used, including plastic sequins, are the same.

B065

Figure III-8
B048 and B067 with associated artifacts from an unnamed first lieutenant.

These ornaments, probably made in Pakistan, likely employ hand-operated embroidering machinery that accounts in part for these variations. The above emblems are probably only a small sample of the varieties of modern reproductions that exist.

A third variant of a modern reproduction of the Civil War period embroidered officer's undress cap ornament was bought by the author in 2002 from a military goods dealer in Virginia. The main differences are seen in the details of the embroidery and the comparatively fat shape of the bugle. The false embroidered white metal "M" is the same as B065, but is struck from a different die than B064. Everything else, including plastic sequins, conforms to the materials and method of construction of B064 and B065.

B066

Officers's Epaulette Ornaments

Along with B048, Enrico Saccone donated to the Marine Corps History Center this superb set of solid silver officer's epaulette ornaments attached to the original epaulettes and in their original metal storage box. Other items once worn by an unnamed first lieutenant can be seen in Figure III-8. This set conforms to the specifications contained in the 1859 Uniform Regulations except for being oversized.[48] The set dates from the relatively short period 1859 to 1869. Interestingly, epaulette ornaments in the 1859 Uniform Regulation were to be the same size as the embroidered bugle worn on the undress cap. The silver old English letter "M" is attached to the epaulette by two single-strand wires.

The final item in the War between the States chapter is another all-silver right epaulette device also dating no earlier than 1859 and dropped in 1869 when the officer's epaulette device was radically changed. B067 is struck in silver and comparable in size to undress cap ornaments B050 and B051, as the Uniform Regulations specify.[49] Ray Darida found this device at a gun show in Baltimore, Maryland, in the early 1960s.[50] It was struck from the same die that struck B050 and B051.

B068

B067

CHAPTER IV

Enlisted Emblems: Post-Civil War Period

(B069 to B079)

The period between 1865 and 1875 saw significant changes in the emblems worn by US Marines. Enlisted men and officers continued to wear the large brass shield, wreath, and bugle devices on dress hats up to 1875. The most significant change was the adoption of the first eagle, globe, and anchor ornament for the undress (fatigue) hats for officers in late 1868 and enlisted men in late 1869.

Largely as a result of the superb research tasked by US Senator Paul H. Douglas through the Commandant of the Marine Corps to Richard Long, then curator of history and fine arts at the USMCHCQV, the story of the first eagle, globe, and anchor emblem is now well-known.[1] Richard Long, using sources in the Library of Congress, the National Archives, Marine Corps Headquarters, and elsewhere, painstakingly put together the fascinating story of the adoption of the first eagle globe and anchor emblem. Senator Douglas wanted the story to be thorough.

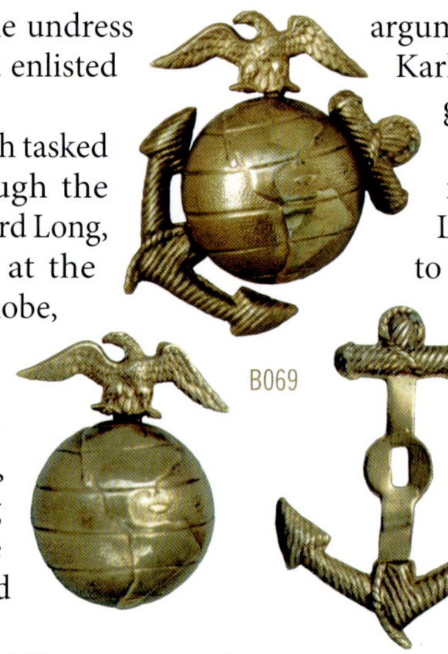

B069

Although seldom encountered, the 1868 pattern eagle globe and anchor devices are very well documented, thanks largely to Dick Long's thorough research. The publications of Driscoll,[2] Long and Wyckoff,[3] and Magruder,[4] rely heavily on Long's research. The Magruder publication relied on Long's research notes but failed to give him credit. Nevertheless, these significant publications cumulatively tell the full story, which will not be repeated here. The famous eagle, globe, and anchor emblem has remained basically the same since 1868.

By November 19, 1868, both Commandant Jacob Zeilin and the Secretary of the Navy, Gideon Welles, had approved the new eagle, globe, and anchor design that had been recommended by a committee of Marine Corps officers. These officers were specifically tasked by Commandant Zeilin to select a new device from among several submitted.[5] Once approved, officers were immediately authorized to purchase the new emblem through private purchase. For lack of a contract and funding, enlisted men had to wait.[6] It was not until sometime after the new fiscal year (July 1869) that a contract for enlisted emblems could be issued. An initial order for 2,000 emblems went to Boston contractors Bent and Bush.[7] Since Jacob Gminder is included in this document, he was somehow a party to this procurement.

All of the above-cited publications are recommended reading for those interested in more information. There is, however, one aspect of this story that deserves mentioning here. An ongoing debate still persists regarding who should be given credit for having designed the first eagle globe and anchor emblem. On one hand, there is a claim, not without substantiation, that George C. Reid, aide de camp to Commandant Jacob Zeilin at the time of the adoption, designed the emblem. On the other hand, there exists the plausible argument that the prominent Washington, DC, jeweler, Karl Wilhelm Breuninger, originated the first eagle globe and anchor emblem. Long and Wyckoff as well as Magruder have taken the position that neither argument has been categorically proven. Long and Wyckoff suggest that there may be validity to both claims.[8]

The enlisted version of the 1868 pattern was to be the same as the officer's ornament but struck from simple brass instead of silver and gold.[9] It is of compound construction consisting of five separate elements including attachment prongs. A thin brass asymmetrical eagle element is soldered to a thicker brass rectangular tab curved to fit and then soldered to the inside of a thicker brass globe. This unique means of attaching the eagle to the globe is a distinctive feature common to late nineteenth century officer's emblems made by Karl Breuninger (see Figure IV-1). An entirely separate and thin brass anchor is attached to a rectangular and thicker two-prong brass element. The rectangular attachment tab is doubled over and soldered to the center and inside of an equally thick globe (see Figures

Figure IV-1
Rectangular tab attaching eagle to globe.

Figure IV-2
B069 Reverse.

Figure IV-3
B069 Reverse showing heavy globe and attachments.

IV-2 and IV-3). The rectangular tab for attachment was drilled at one end, perhaps serving an anti-twist function, if sewn to the fatigue hat. The eagle and anchor are struck from much thinner cartridge gauge brass plates. Enlisted men were probably issued the new device about September of 1869. Quartermaster correspondence states that enlisted men were allowed one emblem per year, should it be lost or damaged, the Marine was charged fifty cents.[10] B069 can be identified in photographs of this period.[11] The measurements of B069 conform to those described in the letter from the board of officers to Commandant Zeilin.[12]

B069 was deemed unsatisfactory by Quartermaster William Slack, "the device of multiple pieces, the eagle and anchor are too fragile."[13] Headquarters correspondence clearly indicates that some in the Marine Corps wanted a less fragile emblem struck from a single piece of brass.[14] Perhaps the initial Bent and Bush order of 2,000 emblems of five separate elements were all or most of all that were ever produced. This might explain why B069 was short lived (1869–1875) and is rarely seen today. The author is aware of only four complete and one incomplete examples of B069. One complete but damaged example was excavated about 1982 along with a USMC button with Civil War period back-marks from Fort Lincoln, one of the ring of federal fortifications that protected Washington, DC, during the Civil War.[15]

B070

The mystery emblem B070 is very unusual, with a huge eagle sitting on a vastly undersized plain globe without cartography and an equally and disproportionately small anchor oriented in the wrong direction for a cap device. It has very little wear, but exhibits heavy tarnish and some green patina. Attachments are three single-strand inverted "U"-shaped brass wires soldered to the reverse. The style of the eagle seems older than the more modern appearing anchor. This is the only example of this device that the author is aware of. It came from the private collection of a well-respected and long-time collector. There is no known or convincing explanation for this emblem. It has been suggested that it could be a prototype that may have been offered for consideration but never documented or accepted by the Marine Corps.[16]

B071

In 1875, the Marine Corps dropped the enlisted and officer's 1859 pattern dress hat with large brass shield, wreath, bugle, and white metal letter "M" and replaced it with a new style full dress hat with a smaller brass shield with a very distinctive small, white metal eagle, globe, and anchor emblem.[17] Figure IV-4 is a photo purported to date 1881 that shows an early B071 device on the 1875 pattern shield attached to the white cork helmet. This research has identified four distinct varieties of the 1875 shield and two die varieties of the small eagle, globe, and anchor device. The emblems are struck in brass but have at least two different white metal finishes. The small 1875 eagle globe and anchor has measurements comparable to the first 1868 pattern.[18] Appendix A, Figures 1 and 3 graphically illustrate the measurement of both the 1868 (B069) and 1875 (B071) devices.

Figure IV-4
B071 with Type I shield on white cork helmet adopted sometime after March 17, 1881.

The distinctive 1875 pattern eagle globe and anchor B071 was the first emblem to replace the 1868 pattern. It is attached to the 1875 type I brass shield. The B071 shield is distinguished, among other things, by the flat stars and a unique six-pointed element at the very bottom of the shield. The shield is struck from cartridge gauge brass. The eagle, globe, and anchor emblem is also struck from the same gauge brass and nickel-plated. The 1875 Uniform Regulations specified that the enlisted eagle, globe and anchor was to have been nickel-plated brass while the officer's device was to be solid silver on a highly gilt shield with multiple strikes.[19] Attachments were two conventional brass wire loops. Two eyes or rectangular apertures were cut into the shield for neatly attaching the eagle globe and anchor by wedging removable triangular strips of leather into the wire loops, locking

B072

the eagle, globe, and anchor to the brass shield. The small shield and white metal emblem were removed from the white cork helmet and dropped along with the 1875 pattern dress hat in 1892.[20]

The eagle, globe, and anchor on B072 has a healthy patina and although struck from the same die as B071, it is struck from cartridge gauge brass and not nickel-plated. A plain brass ornament was worn on the fatigue cap or so-called kepi. B072 was found by Ray Darida at Peace Costumes in Boston in the early 1960s, while the shield came from W. Stokes Kirk store in Philadelphia about the same time.[21] Brass ornaments were not worn on the brass shield. The photo of B072 with a brass ornament is a mismatch of an enlisted fatigue cap emblem on an enlisted dress hat shield. Nevertheless, the type II shield is clearly distinguished, among other things, from the Type I shield by the segmented stars and the distinct six-pointed star at the bottom of the shield. There are other minor differences in the two dies for B071 and B072.

There is excellent, independent information regarding both the dating and function of B072. Three examples of B075 were recovered by divers from the wreck of the USS *Huron* off Nags Head, North Carolina. The *Huron*, a US Navy alert class screw steam gunboat sank in a storm November 24, 1877, with the loss of over 100 lives. Of the three specimens of B072 recovered, one still had remnants of the blue wool material of a USMC fatigue cap (kepi). From a compartment of the *Huron*, the divers recovered many other USMC artifacts, including the leather bill of a fatigue cap. Because the underwater recovery of artifacts from a US Navy ship is illegal, lawyers for the US Navy demanded and received the artifacts from the USS *Huron*.

A third variety of the 1875 shield is easily seen in comparison to B071 and B072, especially in the pattern of parallel lines at the top of the shield and the broad six-pointed star at the bottom of the shield. It is possible that Ray Darida bought this variety from the W. Stokes Kirk inventory in the early to late 1960s.[22] There are two "U"-shaped brass wire attachments soldered at six and nine o'clock on the reverse. Two other wires, now missing, were once soldered at twelve and six o'clock on the reverse. This type III 1875 shield is less often encountered than the other two varieties described above.

B073

B074

The author photographed and described this most unusual type IV variation from the Joe Lowry collection in 1997. Joe, now deceased, bought this device attached to an 1875 dress hat with manufacturer markings "Bent and Bush, Washington Street Boston." It had a black, not red, pompon! It is the only example that the author has seen where an old-fashioned and large wreath is attached in a one-piece construction to the smaller 1875 shield that in and of itself already has another smaller wreath. Joe thought that it might be an officer's dress hat ensemble because of the extra gilt and fine detail of the strike. The brass eagle, globe, and anchor emblem is struck from the same die as B075 but according to the 1875 Uniform Regulations, it should be nickel-plated for enlisted men and silver for officers.[23] This is another example of a mismatch of fatigue cap and dress hat elements. Perhaps the enigmatic B074 is a transitional piece or a prototype that was never adopted or documented. This anomaly certainly deviates significantly from the 1875 Uniform Regulations.

B075

The brass eagle, globe, and anchor B075 is the same device found on the B074 shield and wreath. Close comparison with B071 and B072 clearly indicates that B075 was struck from an entirely different die, although its measurements remain essentially the same. Distinctions can be readily seen in the beak, wing feathering pattern, and crest of the eagle. The pattern of the cable under the anchor stock is also different. There is no reason to question the authenticity of the two die varieties of eagle, globe and anchor ornaments represented by B071, B072, and B075.

These two die varieties are far less commonly encountered than the wide variety of later types for which B079 is representative. This later and larger white metal emblem (B079) is referred to as the "squat legged eagle type" and will be discussed in chapter 8. It is often seen in later nineteenth century photographs with later artifact contexts. Most 1875 brass shields are associated with these later eagle globe, and anchor emblems and far less often with B071, B072, and B075. In view of this patterning and the scarcity of B071, B072, and B075, they are the original 1875 pattern. It is not known how long these were used or if one replaced the other or exactly when they were replaced by those later designs (similar to B079) and covered in later chapters. It is possible that B071, B072, and B075 were replaced in 1881 by the subsequent "squat legged eagle" design when the white cork helmet was first adopted. In keeping with the 1875 Uniform Regulations, B075, an all brass eagle, globe, and anchor struck from a single piece was worn on the enlisted undress (fatigue) hat.[24] B075 is of conventional construction with two "U"-shaped brass wire loops soldered at the anchor stock and anchor crown reverse.

B076

Brass eagle, globe, and anchor devices found on the 1875 pattern brass shield for enlisted dress hats were probably mistakenly put together by collectors or surplus dealers unknowingly mixing full dress cap and fatigue (undress) cap elements.

The next two emblems (B076 and B077) are modern reproductions manufactured by Naugatuck Novelties. They were given to the author by Ray Darida or purchased by the author from S&S Firearms. They are close copies of the B072 shield, eagle, globe, and anchor device, but are distinguishable from the other above-described insignia (see tick marks). They are often honestly offered for sale as reproductions but there are also many dishonest vendors who routinely alter them to appear aged and stressed and offer them for sale as authentic and expensive USMC emblems, dishonestly purported to date 1875.

The shield of B072 and the eagle, globe, and anchor ornament for B071/B072 were used as models to make copies for the dies used to strike B076. These struck reproductions are very close to their models but do not correspond one to one. In general the modern reproduction shield does not have the distinct, sharp lines displayed on shield types I, II, and III (B071, B072, and B073). Instead lines on the modern reproduction are less distinct and less sharp. The intersections of lines, especially lines forming right angles in the B076 shield, tend to appear as curves rather than sharp right angles, see B076 tick marks. The Naugatuck Novelties B076 eagle, globe, and anchor is struck in brass but has a white metal finish, perhaps nickel plated. When manufactured they are highly polished, giving them a brand-new appearance. They are sold as honest reproductions especially to military re-enactors by S&S Firearms and perhaps others. Increasingly, altered versions are showing up, especially on the Internet. These routinely are not presented as reproductions but as authentic emblems. With some attention to detail, one can avoid these dishonest and purposely altered fakes. To the author's knowledge, the other types of 1875 pattern shields (B071, B073, and B074) are not currently being reproduced. The same can be said for the eagle, globe, and anchor ornament B075. Until there is evidence that these types are also being reproduced, it would be advisable for the serious collector and dealer to emphasize items not known to be currently reproduced.

The same die used to strike the Naugatuck Novelties B076 is used to strike B077, but in plain brass. It is also highly polished, giving it a brand-new appearance on both the obverse and reverse. Although the eagle, globe, and anchor devices (B076 and B077) are close to their B072 model, obvious differences can be seen especially in the crude feathering pattern of the eagle's right wing, its huge beak, and smaller crest compared to B071 and B072 with their neat, regular feather pattern on the eagle's right wing, a strong crest, and six lines of latitude instead of five (see tick marks B072, B076, B077). The author has no difficulty seeing these obvious distinctions displayed on altered fakes routinely offered as authentic emblems on the Internet.

Included here is this mismatched set of an over-sized brass (Army type) bugle with a type II (B073) shield. It was found in the Smithsonian collection and was purchased from the W. Stoles Kirk collection shortly after that company went out of business. The anachronistic mix was probably put together from disparate elements of nineteenth century surplus. The oversized bugle has two single-strand brass wires soldered to the reverse and crudely forced into pieced holes in the shield despite the presence of neat, rectangular apertures characteristic of the 1875 pattern USMC shields. There was probably a great deal of mixing and matching of surplus elements or findings by both collectors and dealers

B077

B078

B079

using genuine and plentiful surplus that still turns up on the militaria market today. There are no known or dated photographs of this mismatched device.

The red and blue painted type II shield (B072) has a nickel-plated eagle, globe, and anchor emblem. The white metal ornament is the first of a large variety referred to as the "squat-legged" eagle type. They are clearly larger than the 1868 and 1875 patterns (compare B079 with Figures 1, 3, and 5 in appendix A). Presumably this type dates later than the smaller ones described above. These are known in several distinct varieties and alloys and will be discussed in more detail in chapter 8. The general squat-legged eagle type is recognizable in many photographs dating from the mid 1880s to about 1904. Poorly focused photographs of this general type do not allow accurate identification of known varieties. It is not known exactly when the "squat-legged" eagle type first appeared, perhaps as early as 1881 or as late as 1892. The majority of 1875 pattern shields (Types I-III) showing up on the market today are associated with a variety of these squat-legged eagle, globe, and anchor emblems (B079).

The 1875 type II shield (B079) with eagle, globe, and anchor was, when purchased by the author, mounted on a wooden shield painted flat black with three US Army and one USMC button mounted in the four corners of the wooden shield. Surplus dealers were known to make up these painted arrangements of military artifacts to appeal to buyers and promote sales. These wooden shield arrangements can be seen in old Bannerman catalogs. There is no reason to think that the red and blue paint was applied as some kind of special Marine Corps function, such as officers or bandsmen emblems, as some have suggested.

Two sets of single-strand brass wires were used to attach the shield and the eagle, globe, and anchor device to the wooden shield. The painting and the soldering of single-strand brass wires for attachment purposes suggests something that surplus dealers would do to items in their inventory. This was probably meant to simply give the item more sales appeal. Single-strand wire attachments do not conform to the Uniform Regulation regarding a system for attachment with "eyes and rings and leather strips."[25]

CHAPTER V

Officer Emblems: Post-Civil War Period

(B080 to B090)

This chapter covers the brief period from 1867 to approximately 1875. In addition to authentic officer's undress hat emblems and probable nineteenth century surplus items, modern reproductions of these items based on investment castings and strikes from dies copied from original emblems or fanciful creations, are included as well.

While still on active duty with the Marine Corps and in the process of writing *The Eagle, Globe, and Anchor 1868–1968*, Col. John Driscoll found B080 in a warehouse at a railroad siding at the Marine Corps Base Quantico, Virginia. The emblem was among uniform items once belonging to Col. Henry Clay Cochrane.[1] Col. John Magruder, then director of the USMCHCQV, had been tasked by Commandant Lemuel Shepherd to put together artifacts for a Smithsonian Institute Marine Corps exhibit. As part of the commandant's tasking, Magruder specifically solicited uniform items from families of prominent Marines. These families quite likely included descendants of Henry Clay Cochrane.

The Magruder solicitation for artifacts was apparently so successful that the artifacts flooded in at a remarkable pace and it took several years to properly accession and identify what had been donated. Kenneth Smith Christmas shared with the author the formidable challenge he faced as a new museum curator at the Marine Corps History Center. It became the job of Kenneth Smith Christmas and Linda King and the small museum staff to properly accession and identify this huge backlog of acquisitions.[2]

B080 is a rare example of the first officer's 1868 eagle, globe, and anchor emblem. There is no known cutoff point for when B080 was no longer worn. It may have simply been slowly phased out as older officers who purchased these left the service. The eagle is cut from solid silver plate and given a great deal of individual jeweler's attention, such as hand engraving of details of the intricate feathering pattern and silver soldering of the distinctive Breuninger rectangular tab attaching the eagle to the inside of the silver globe. The anchor is embroidered in gold thread on a navy blue oval-shaped cloth ground and conforms quite well to the description contained in the Marine Corps Headquarters correspondence cited in chapter 4. In all likelihood, Lt. Henry Clay Cochrane is wearing B080 on an undress cap in an excellent photo of him dating 1874 (see B080 in appendix C-1).

John Driscoll kindly provided the author with his original black and white prints and negatives of B080 used for his 1971 publication. From these Driscoll originals, colored images were prepared on the computer for this publication. Regrettably these images and Driscoll's notes are all that we have of the Cochrane emblem today. It turned up missing at the USMCHCQV during an inventory made about 1990.[3] The black and white print (Figure V-1) is an original Driscoll photograph of the distinctive reverse of the Cochrane emblem. This black and white photo of the reverse of B080 may some day help to identify the missing Cochrane emblem. Hopefully, this exceptionally rare emblem may one day be returned to the Marine Corps History Center where both its public appreciation value and research potential could be better served.

B080

Figure V-1
Original black and white photo of B081, reverse side.

A completely different silver eagle and globe with separate gold continents is seen in this variant of the 1868 officer's undress cap ornament. The superb craftsmanship is comparable to B080. It is likely that officer's emblems at this time were highly variable.

Privately purchased officer emblems could have been made and sold by any competent jeweler. It looks like B081 may have been repaired by silver soldering the eagle to the globe by reattaching the eagle with two overlapping hand-cut small silver plates.

B081

The metal eagle and globe did not start out life with the gold metal thread embroidered anchor sewn to a navy blue oval cloth ground. The current owner purchased the B081 eagle and globe separate from the gold embroidered anchor on the navy blue cartouche. The embroidered anchor in B081 is the very same anchor B089, photographed and described by the author ten years earlier in the George Mennegaux collection. Typical of these gold embroidered anchors is that no two seem to be exactly alike. This individuality is probably a function of the labor-intensive, hand embroidering tools used in their manufacture. For attaching the silver eagle and globe to the cloth ground of B081, two single-strand silver wires were soldered to a circular silver plate attached to the back of the globe. This system of silver plates holding everything together seems to be either an elaborate repair job or perhaps the original construction. After all, emblems were meant to be seen from the front. If a repair job, it may have originally had the distinctive Breuninger rectangular tang holding the eagle to the globe. With the attachment of this silver plate, there is no way to tell if the distinctive Breuninger tang is attached to the inside of the globe.

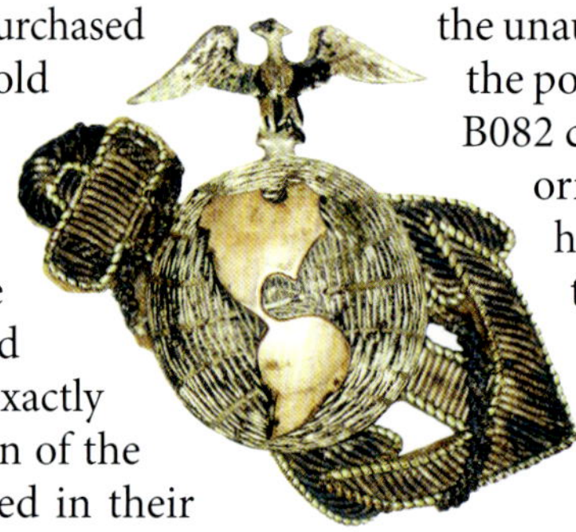

B082

B083

This emblem is more than intriguing. According to acquisition records, it was donated to the USMCHCQV by the family of George C. Reid. As with B080 and B081, the metal work in solid silver and gold shows superb craftsmanship. Unique, chased lines radiate from the center of the globe. The silver eagle is identical to the eagle seen on post-1869 epaulette devices. For example, see B119, an epaulette device worn by Julian C. Smith and donated by his widow to the USMCHCQV. It is also an element of the left epaulette device worn by Lt. W.R. Brown.[4]

The anchor of B082 is a unique style and embroidered with gold-colored metal thread, then sewn to white cloth backing with a probable interior layer, perhaps cardboard, for stiffening. The compound construction is sewn together with tan thread. The sewn construction has two single-strand brass wires for attachment. This brass wire attachment method suggests that it is more likely an epaulette device rather than a cap ornament, which was usually sewn on.

Most importantly, the anchor size of B082 is much closer to the anchor size specified for the 1869 epaulette device[5] than it is to the 1868 officer's undress cap, compare Figure 1 and Figure 2 in appendix A. This line drawing graphically shows what the uniform regulations required for the epaulette ornaments and the cap ornament. Thus B082 is either an aberrant undress cap emblem with an over-sized anchor oriented incorrectly or a right epaulette ornament with an unauthorized gold embroidered anchor. To add to this perplexity, there are known photographs showing officers wearing undress cap ornaments with the anchor facing the wrong direction. At the same time, there are plenty of known examples (chapters 7 and 11) of unauthorized epaulette ornaments, particularly epaulette emblems that are undersized and not all silver.

Given this uncertainty, the author leans slightly toward the unauthorized epaulette explanation, but leaves open the possibility that Cureton and Sullivan suggest; that B082 could be the very first 1868 pattern undress cap ornament, possibly designed by George C. Reid himself.[6] The problems with non-conformity with the Uniform Regulations were persistent well into the latter part of the nineteenth century. The order by the commandant in 1869 for the new epaulette device also expressed his dissatisfaction with deviation and lack of uniformity with the officer's cap ornaments.

The identification of B083 is problematic. Long and Wyckoff describe how the commandant, on May 2, 1867, approved a design for an emblem for the officer's fatigue cap.[7] The measurement's in the commandant's order and described by Long and Wyckoff are far closer to the measurements for B083 than they are to any emblem depicted in appendix A. The approved device was to be a silver globe with gold continents of the Western Hemisphere and gold lines of latitude surmounted by a silver eagle. This emblem was to be worn on a red cloth ground. Eleven days later, an order

Figure V-2
Original die for B083.

was issued informing all stations of the Marine Corps that the device would be available for purchase at Horstmann and Brothers, Philadelphia. By June 5, 1867, the commandant surprisingly revoked this order.[8] This leaves the tantalizing possibility that B083 could be unfinished Horstmann and Brothers surplus or brass emblems struck from an original Horstmann and Brothers die.

Ray Darida purchased the original die for B083 from W. Stokes Kirk (see Figure V-2). This die may have been commissioned by Horstmann and Brothers to P.H. Jacobus, whose name appears on that die. Whether or not B083 was manufactured by Horstmann and Brothers in response to the commandant's ill-fated order, the most significant fact is that this brass unfinished device was probably never worn by USMC officers.

The B083 emblem is die struck brass with a gilt finish that is both worn and corroded, suggesting some legitimate aging. Two "U"-shaped wire attachments are soldered to the reverse behind the eagle and at the bottom of the globe. Other varieties are known with thin, flat tabs, rectangular in cross section, instead of round wire attachments. Another variant was cut out using a piercing tool that left an opening between the eagle's legs. This suggests a possible nineteenth century strike using the original die and original, but now lost, trimming and piercing tools.

The exact age of this investment casting in silver is unknown. It purportedly came from the estate sale of a collector and former Marine named Hollisman who died in 1969 or 1970.[9] The model for the mold was probably B083. It displays the clear features of a casting such as rounded edges instead of the sharp, right-angled edges of a die-struck piece. Casting also leaves muted effects making details look worn. The lines of latitude and longitude and cartography are also muted and not sharp. Other casting flaws such as pits and cracks are especially evident on the reverse. A grinding tool was used to erase some of these more obvious flaws. It is punch marked ".925" on the reverse of the globe. Two thin tabular-shaped attachments (rectangular in cross section) are soldered to the reverse of the globe at twelve and six o'clock, respectively. There is no supportable reason to think that this casting is an original 1867 Horstmann and Brothers die struck device.

Naugatuck Novelties produces B085. If it is struck from a new die based on the original W. Stokes Kirk die (Figure V-2), it is not at all apparent. The author has not been able to see any appreciable differences between B083 and the modern Naugatuck Novelties reproduction B085. A close comparison of greatly magnified details of images of B083 and B085 shows no clear distinctions. It is as if the Naugatuck Novelties modern reproductions were struck from the original die rescued from W. Stokes Kirk, or the new die is so close that there are no

B084

B085

B086

B087

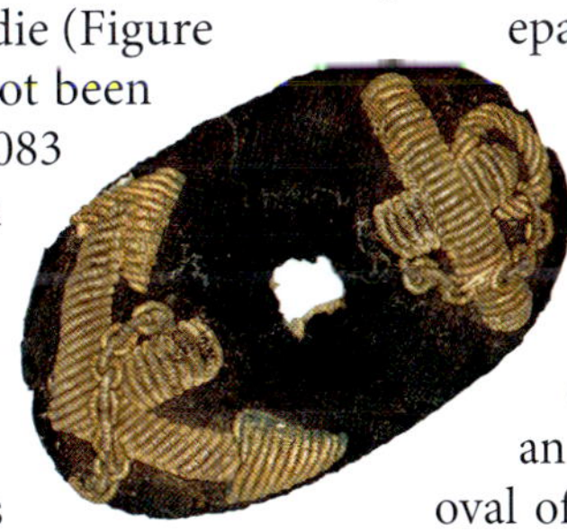

B088

discernable differences. The only difference that the author noted was the means of attachment. B085 has two relatively heavy single-strand brass wires soldered to the reverse, while B083 has two lighter and inverted "U"-shaped brass wire attachments soldered approximately at the same position. The author bought B085 from S&S Firearms.

The only obvious distinctions between the Naugatuck Novelties reproduction B085 and B086 is in the white metal alloy used to make the restrike and the use of an old, gold-colored paint on the continents. The gold paint is chipping off. Only about a dozen of these handsome white metal, gold-painted emblems were made by Naugatuck Novelties.[10] These were made expressly as gifts to friends and were not sold. Chenoweth and Nihart[11] mistakenly include B086 in their book as an example of the ill-fated 1867 officer's undress cap ornament that was revoked. For many years, B086 with its handsome red cloth backing has been on exhibit at the Globe and Laurel Restaurant in Triangle, Virginia. It is displayed there as the handsome modern restrike that it is.[12]

Ray Darida bought this white metal emblem at Pease Costume shop in Springfield, Massachusetts, in the late 1960s.[13] Its measurements, shape, white metal alloy, and construction technique conform better to specifications and measurements in the 1868 and 1875 Uniform Regulations rather than to later regulations. Compare Figures 1 and 3 (1868 and 1875 emblems) to later and larger officer emblems illustrated in appendix A. The distinctive eagle is struck from brass and silver or is nickel-plated. The globe with strange cartography is possibly struck from solid silver plate. A single flat white metal tab is folded over and soldered to the inside center of the globe. This folded, flat metal tab is similar to the attachment used for the first enlisted and officers eagle, globe, and anchor devices. Ray Darida pickled and burnished B087 to improve its appearance. An "L"-shaped white metal tab is soldered to the back of the eagle and top of the inside of the globe for attaching these two separately struck elements covered in chapter 7.

B087 could have served multiple purposes, as an officer's undress cap ornament or as a Corps device for decorating each flank corner of the saddlecloth as first mentioned in the 1875 Uniform Regulations.[14] In addition, the same or extremely similar white metal eagle, globe, and anchor ornaments are associated with the silver epaulette emblems covered in chapter 7.

The gold embroidered anchor B088 in the USMCHCQV is quite similar but does not correspond one to one with B080, further emphasizing the individuality of these embroidered anchors. The metallic gold thread of the anchor is embroidered to a navy blue wool ground cut to form an oval. To this wool oval is sewn a slightly smaller oval of cream-colored burlap material. A paper oval is glued to the burlap material to stiffen the construction.

B089

This anchor, embroidered in gold-colored metallic thread to a navy blue wool cartouche, was meant to be sewn to an officer's undress cap. The pattern of the design, especially the cable fouling, is distinctive. The embroidered anchor B089 is the very anchor seen with B081. The author photographed and described B089 through the courtesy of George Mennegaux back in 1999. It was not until this chapter was drafted ten years later that these embroidered anchors were recognized as being the same. This supports the authenticity of both B081 and B089 even though B081 was put together quite recently. Their inclusion shows details not seen in the individual photographs of each alone. Note the cut in the center for attaching the officer's silver eagle and globe ornament. It is unclear when these embroidered anchors attached to a white metal eagle and globe device were discontinued. They were probably worn no later than 1892. Well- dated photographs or written documentation about this change would be a welcome addition to this research.

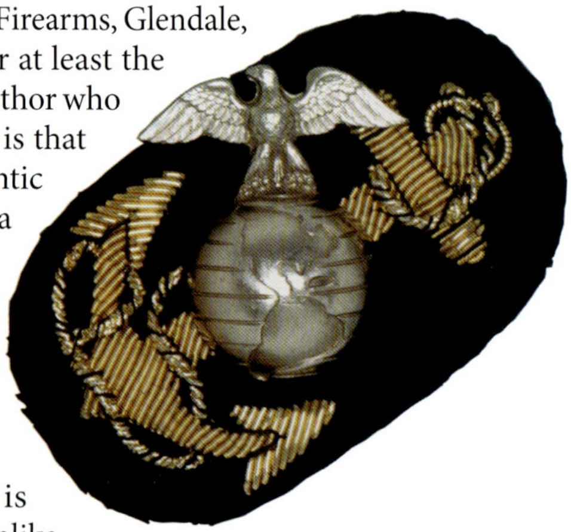

B090

The author purchased B090 from S&S Firearms, Glendale, New York, where they have been sold for at least the last eighteen years. It is unknown to the author who actually produces these. The main point is that B090 only vaguely resembles the authentic officer emblems described above. It is a handsome creation in white metal applied to a modern Pakistan embroidered anchor on a navy blue cloth cartouche. The eagle is obviously modeled from a late WWII officer's cap device. The globe is also modeled from the same Hilborn and Hamburger officer's cap device, but is interestingly struck in reverse (intaglio). Unlike the late WWII Hilborn and Hamburger officer's cap emblem, the continents and lines of latitude of B090 are not raised but sunk into the globe.

CHAPTER VI

Officer Emblems: Late Nineteenth Century

(B091 to B114)

From 1875 to approximately 1904, officer's emblems became even more diverse than earlier. In addition to jewelers making highly variable creations, new uses for emblems came into being. Besides a wide variety of dress and undress cap devices, the eagle, globe, and anchor was worn on the white cork helmet and is first mentioned in the Uniform Regulations for wear in the corners of the officer's saddlecloth.[1] Another significant change that added to this variation was the adoption, for the first time, of officer's dress collar ornaments beginning in 1877.[2] With the exception of one more common stamped type, it is the author's impression that almost no two sets of these superb collar sets are exactly the same. Another example of this diversity is the ornament that was worn on the commandant and staff officers' full dress chapeau. Even more emblem uses and varieties will be discussed in later chapters.

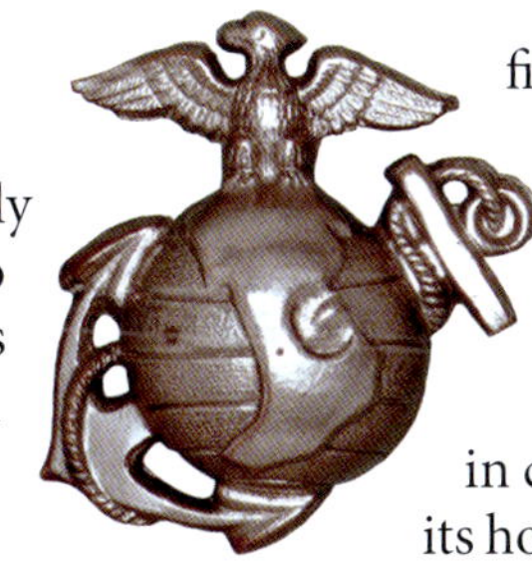

B091

With approximately twenty enlisted Marines to every officer in those days, it is understandable why officer's emblems are less often encountered. This infrequently seen white metal ornament (B091) may be silver- or nickel-plated, but definitely has a brass base. It is not cut from solid silver as described in the 1877 addendum to the 1875 Uniform Regulations. It is exceptionally well struck, suggesting multiple strikes to bring out details. It is struck from the same die that struck the less frequently encountered enlisted brass versions B074 and B075. The device has the conventional inverted "U"-shaped, single-strand soldered brass wires for attachment. The measurements conform to those described for the 1875 pattern officer's eagle, globe, and anchor struck from silver plated brass (see Figure 3, Appendix A).

B092

In addition to the four types of enlisted reduced size 1875 pattern brass shield for the dress hat described in chapter 4, a fifth type, B092 exists. It was recently acquired by the USMCHCQV and came from the collections of the Smithsonian Institution. It was photographed for this research by the Smithsonian staff. Several distinctions include a unique floral element at the base of the shield. This fifth type shield has yet to be found in association with headgear artifacts of enlisted Marines and may have been exclusively an officer's ornament. Extra rich gilt is evident along with sharp details, indicative of multiple strikes to bring out more details in the design. Compared to the four types of enlisted shields in chapter 4, B092 is more dramatically curved in both its horizontal and vertical dimensions to make it fit neatly against the front of the dress hat. Heavy brass loops with eyes, similar to British loop and cotter pin attachments, are brazed, not soldered, to the reverse. All these features are characteristic of the extra effort that manufacturers typically put into the more expensive officer's dress hat ensemble.

Approximately fifty percent remains of an extra rich gilt that indicates that B093 is an officer, not enlisted, shield. It is the same Type II shield (B072) seen in chapter 4. Other officer's 1875 pattern dress hat ornaments are known to have been struck using at least Types I (B071) and III (B073) dies. B093 was purchased by the author as part of a grouping containing an authentic Civil War period embroidered US Army Infantry officer's bugle ornament on a crude reproduction of an 1875 USMC dress hat. Single-strand brass wires were soldered to the reverse of B093 at three and nine o'clock, respectively, further indicating a mismatch of authentic surplus and unfinished findings put together to suggest old military headgear. It is impossible to say if such a creation was done by early surplus dealers or early collectors, probably the former.

The anchor ring and stock of B094 are broken off. The ornament is struck from a single plate of brass. The eagle and globe are silver-plated; the anchor and continents are gold-plated. The measurements of B094 conform well to the documents already cited that describe the 1868, 1875, and 1892 pattern officer's undress cap emblem. These measurements remained the same for all three patterns (see Figures 1, 3, and 5, appendix A). For several reasons B094 was

B093

B094

Figure VI-1
Emblem illustrated on the cover of *Aldrich*, 1875.

probably manufactured closer to 1868 than 1892. Note the unusual short, uncoiled cable at the anchor crown. This is a seldom-seen feature. It occurs with the first 1868 eagle, globe, and anchor for Marine enlisted men and shows up on the ornament illustrated on the cover of Aldrich's 1875 *History of the Marine Corps*.[3] Also, see Figure VI-1. This distinct feature was later replaced by a coiled cable and eventually anchor flukes would no longer touch the globe (see Figures 7 and 9 appendix A).

The means of attachment for B094 by two brass wires soldered to the reverse suggests a possible alternative use as an undersized and unauthorized silver and gold left epaulette device. The undress cap ornament explanation seems more likely, despite the two single-strand brass wires for attachment. This is the only example of this particular emblem the author has seen. The anchor and globe designs are unique; the eagle is very similar to B095 and eagles on other epaulette ornaments of this approximate time period. Ray Darida bought this device from Norsid Insignia Co., New York City, in the late 1960s.[4]

The most distinctive feature of this silver-and gold-plated brass undress cap emblem is the huge anchor relative to the globe. The eagle and globe are struck from a single plate of brass. The proportionally oversized anchor compared to an undersized globe is struck from a separate brass element. Anchor lengths of 1½-inches remained the standard in the Uniform Regulations from 1892 to 1904. Nevertheless, undress cap emblems with these relatively huge anchors are seen in old photographs dating about the turn of the twentieth century (see, for example, B095 in appendix C-1 (Officers Photo Database). B095 is one of the earliest, if not the earliest, example covered in this research of a USMC officer's undress cap emblem with a screw post for attachment. Emerson dates the first use of screw posts on US Army cap insignia to 1896.[5] If the Marine Corps also made this change about that time, it would be consistent with photographic evidence in appendix C-1 (Officer Photo Database) listing Lt. Newt Hall wearing the undress cap device with the distinctly oversized anchor and undersized globe. Hall was commissioned in 1897 and he is quite likely wearing his commissioning emblems in the photo. The same photo of Lt. Newt Hall wearing an emblem consistent with B095 also appears in Chester Hearn.[6]

The style of the B096 eagle is especially unusual and shares a family resemblance to the style of eagle in the 1877 pattern dress collar set B106. These eagles could be from the same manufacturer. It is silver- and gold-plated bronze that is extremely worn, with some corrosion. There is a sufficient amount of the silver and gold plate remaining to confirm its original use as a cap ornament. The eagle, globe, and anchor are struck from a single plate. The cable consists of two strands of silver-plated, fine-gauge brass wire. The means of attachment is a drop-in "C"-type clasp and pin assembly. The combination of proportionally oversized anchor and undersized globe suggests a date similar to B095. Up to 1900, by regulation, the anchor and globe remained the same size as specified in 1875, but at some point these oversized anchors appeared, at first with the older and smaller globe, then by 1904 with a larger globe as well. Compare the 1875 pattern (Figures 3, 5, and 7) with the standardization that occurred in 1904 and seen in Figure 9, appendix A.

B095

B096

There is little question about the function of B097. It is associated with a 1905 pattern unnamed officer's undress cap with trademarks Jacob Reeds' Sons in the USMCHCQV collections. The eagle and globe are struck from separate solid silver plates, with hand finishing touches such as chased lines of longitude and eagle feathering. The anchor is struck from brass, gold-plated, and showing considerable wear. There

B097

Figure VI- 2
B097 on 1905 officer's dress cap.

is some damage to the two-strand, silver-plated brass wire cable. The continents are cut from a thin but solid gold plate. A hinged drop-in "C"-type clasp-and-pin assembly was the means of attachment. All these features, including the characteristic "Breuninger" type eagle and distinctive silver tag used to attach the eagle to the inside of the globe, strongly suggest another Breuninger creation, even if there are, as usual for this period, no manufacturer's back-marks. A comparison of the handcrafted cap emblems in this chapter indicates, not surprisingly, that no two are exactly alike (see FigureVI-2).

One cannot be certain if B098 is an officer's undress cap emblem with an over-sized anchor and lacking a fouled cable or an unauthorized silver and gold leaf epaulette ornament. The size of the globe is closer to an undress cap emblem than to the measurements of the globe on an epaulette device specified in the Uniform Regulations. Compare B098 with Figures 2, and 3, appendix A. To find a set of B098 in both port and starboard or clearly identified in old photos could better answer this question.

The craftsmanship of this emblem is extraordinary, consisting of a solid silver eagle and globe and hand-cut, thin but solid gold continents. The anchor appears to be a gold plate over an unknown metal alloy. At some time in the past, B098 was converted to jewelry by permanently soldering the eagle, globe, and anchor to a silver oval plate with a drop-in pin assembly (not depicted). This jewelry conversion hides many features of the original construction of the emblem, including its original means of attachment. The eagle style, the exquisite hand finishing, especially the hand engraving pattern of the feather pattern and the distinctive silver tag that connects the eagle to the globe (see Figure IV-1), support the conclusion that both B097 and B098 came from the jewelry operations of Karl Breuninger (see appendix B, Dick Long photograph of Wm. Breuninger emblems).

Since there are no traces of gold plate remaining on the anchor or continents of this fancy variant of a possibly nickel-plated squat-legged eagle, globe, and anchor emblem, it is assumed to be either an officer's dress hat emblem, perhaps as early as 1881 or later. A less likely explanation for this white metal emblem is an undersized left epaulette ornament. It is not included with other squat-legged eagle varieties because of the special features suggesting an officer's emblem. The most obvious fancy features are the well-struck highly detailed feathers and the unique cartography that depicts major river systems. These attributes suggest more effort went into cutting the die as well as the multiple strikes made for detail definition. Three heavy bronze wires soldered to the reverse at the anchor stock, the eagle's back, and the reverse of the lower anchor fluke suggest a possible alternative use as a left epaulette ornament. B099 was "found in storage and not accessioned" in the USMCHCQV collections. These were evidently mass-produced with dies on thin brass plates, then probably given nickel plating. They

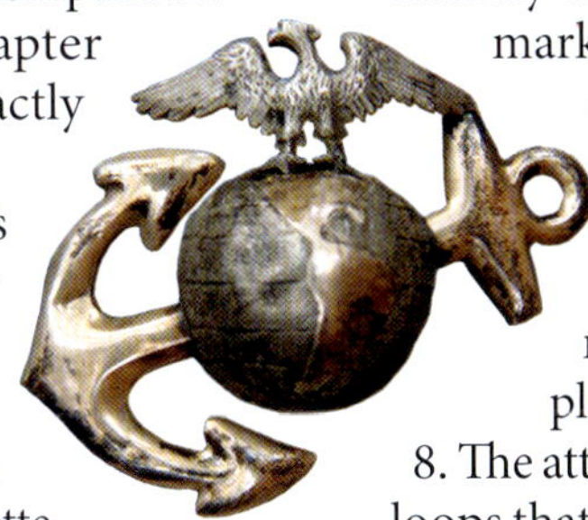

B098

B099

B100

lack the jeweler's hand tool finishing effects characteristic of solid silver emblems. Several have been seen by the author but in numbers far fewer than their counterparts for enlisted Marines to be covered in chapter 7.

Although there is a strong resemblance to emblems described later in chapter 8, B100 as well as B099 are officer's versions of the squat-legged eagle ornament struck from entirely different dies with very distinct features (see tick marks). The most obvious difference can readily be seen in the shape of the continents and details of the eagle's wings as well as the slender, curved, almost "S" shape of the eagle's body. The alloy may be German silver and is quite unlike the more commonly encountered and lustrous nickel-plated brass and chrome-plated emblems in chapter 8. The attachments are two "U"-shaped non-magnetic wire loops that comfortably fit into the rectangular slots pierced into the 1875 dress hat brass shield.

The date and exact function of B100 are uncertain. They have to post date 1881. David Sullivan, using an original copy of the 1875 Marine Corps Uniform Regulations with careful annotations on subsequent changes and reports, clearly dates the adoption of the white cork helmet for officers and enlisted men as March 17, 1881.[7] The annotations further specify that the first white cork helmets originally did not include the 1875 pattern small shield (B092) and white metal device (B091). Attaching the 1875 pattern small shield and white metal eagle, globe, and anchor to the white cork helmet had to happen sometime after March 17, 1881, and before 1892. Therefore the photograph (Figure IV-4) of a white cork helmet with B071 or B091 on an 1875 small shield has to date sometime after March 17, 1881, and the appearance of the 1892 Uniform Regulations of July 14, 1892.

Another example of B100 is attached to a white cork helmet presently in the USMCHCQV (accession #1975.87). The Quantico cork helmet with B100 is associated with Capt. William Rowles Brown and was transferred from the Smithsonian collections (#22415). Brown was commissioned in 1861 and as a captain probably wore this particular cork helmet sometime after 1881 to September 5, 1892, when he retired.[8] Another example of B100 is known to exist in a private collection and is neatly attached by inverted "U"-shaped loops to the rectangular apertures of an 1875 pattern, with an extra gilt, strongly curved, brass shield, also for an officer's dress hat.

The above date for B100 is consistent with the unique features and low frequency of occurrence compared to other similar emblems. The author's research has encountered very few examples of B100 compared to the other far more commonly encountered emblems in chapter 8. This pattern of occurrence probably indicates a brief period of use and/or low frequencies of manufacture. These German silver emblems may have been exclusively officer items as opposed to the other nickel-plated brass emblems specified for enlisted Marines in chapter 8. During this research it has not been encountered in association with enlisted headgear.

The modern reproduction in silver by Joe Weingarten using investment-casting procedures is offered for reasonable prices as an honest museum quality reproduction. Weingarten did not realize, until the author mentioned it, that the model he used to make the casting was a seldom seen variety. The lustrous silver alloy is quite unlike the dull German silver alloy used for B100 and is also twice as heavy as the thin struck B100. Attachments for B101 are inverted "U"-shaped silver wires at the center of the anchor stock and anchor crown reverse. This is an excellent single piece investment casting in silver, not a compound construction of several elements. It displays obvious features of investment casting that distinguish it from die-struck emblems. These casting features are especially evident on the reverse and include irregular, rounded edges, instead of clear, sharp, even edges. There is some muting of details and evidence of investment casting flaws such as globs and pits not seen in the clear, sharp details produced by a die-struck emblem subjected to tremendous forces in the striking of the die.

B101

No B102 in inventory. Only known through period photographs.

When an emblem can be documented to have been worn, but no examples were available for photographing and describing in this research, that emblem and information regarding it has been included in this inventory. Perhaps examples of these may one day show up. One of these, by definition, would have to be one of the rarest USMC emblems ever produced. The first mention of the commandant's special undress hat emblem was described in the 1892 Uniform Regulations.[9] Presumably the 1875 pattern officer's undress cap emblem is what was referred to as the emblem for the cap of the commandant, "The ornament to consist of a Corps device set in a wreath of gold acorn leaves." Later Uniform Regulations correct the curious wording "acorn leaves" with "oak leaves."[10] Only five Marines would have ever been authorized to wear this special device during its brief period of use (1896 to the mid-1920s). An example can be seen in Figure VI-3, and was published by Tulkoff in 2010.[11]

Figure VI-3
Commandant Charles Heywood wearing oak wreath device.

First Officer's Dress Collar Emblems 1877

There is little difficulty identifying the diminutive 1877 pattern officer's dress collar emblems, especially those made of solid silver and solid gold or gold-plated. They are highly variable and the smallest of all officer's collar emblems (see Figures 4 and 6 appendix A). The sample presented, however, does not give an adequate representation of the remarkable diversity of these first officer's dress collar emblems. In addition to the variety discussed below, other variants are known from photographs sent to the author or seen on the Internet. For lack of comparable descriptive information and for photographic proprietary reasons, all of these emblems could not be included in this inventory. Collectively, these variants clearly demonstrate the diversity of the officer's pattern 1877 collar emblems.

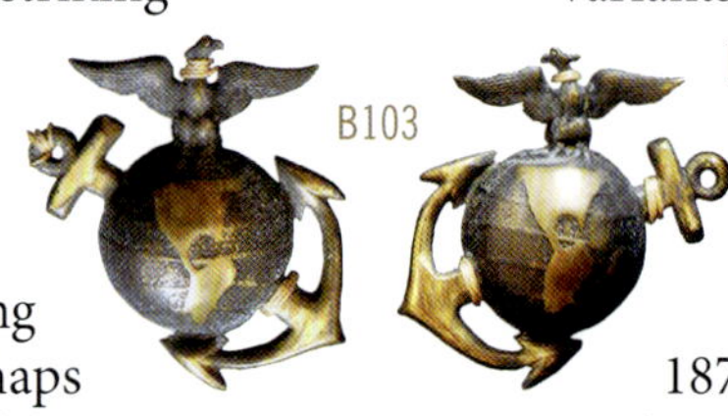

B103

Why was there so much diversity in the first officer's collar emblems? A contributing factor was certainly the lack of clear guidance to the manufacturers. Neither the Order of 1877,[12] nor the 1892 Uniform Regulations,[13] specify what metal they were to be made of. As a result, some manufacturers probably read between the lines and went "whole hog" producing a smaller and matching collar emblem along the lines of the more explicit requirements for the silver and gold undress cap device. Others may have interpreted the skimpy wording, "To be one half the size prescribed for the epaulette,"[14] to mean that the new collar ornaments should, like the epaulette ornaments, also be all silver, as specifically required for the 1869 pattern epaulette ornament. This confusion is not really cleared up until the more explicit 1904 Uniform Regulations specified silver and gold elements for the officer's collar ornaments.[15]

The set (B103) was worn by the well-known Marine officer Maclane Tilton and was recently transferred from the Washington Navy Yard to the USMCHCQV. A very unusual feature of this set is that the ornaments are sewn with gold thread to Tilton's dress coat collar. Tilton's collar ornaments were among a lot of his artifacts donated to the Marine Corps by his family. His dress coat and the B103 set were for years on exhibit in the Time Tunnel at the old Marine Corps exhibit at the Washington Navy Yard. In addition to the exquisite hand engraving of details, the set is made from solid silver and solid gold elements. Because the set is sewn to the coat collar, one cannot examine the reverse of the set without causing damage. Nevertheless, it is safe to say that even though they are not exactly the same, these ornaments conform extremely well to the Breuninger dress collar set photographed by Richard Long in appendix B.

The second set of distinctive 1877 pattern dress collar ornaments was also probably manufactured by Karl Wilhelm

B104

Breuninger. The distinctive hand engraving of the details of the eagle and the lines of latitude are Breuniger traits. Note by contrast the raised lines of latitude on B103. Another Breuninger feature on B104 is the separate silver rectangular tang attaching the eagle to the globe. The hand engraving of eyes on both sides of the eagle's head and the turning of the head forty-five degrees is a clever way of giving a three dimensional effect. The attachment is a multiple construction hinged pin and drop-in "C"-clasp assembly. Even though B103 and B104 are similar, they are also quite different. The B104 set did not start out life together. They were put together by Jack McCord in 2002. Jack made a deal with another knowledgeable collector friend, Emile Steffanacci, which resulted in complementing his right collar ornament with Steffanacci's left collar ornament.

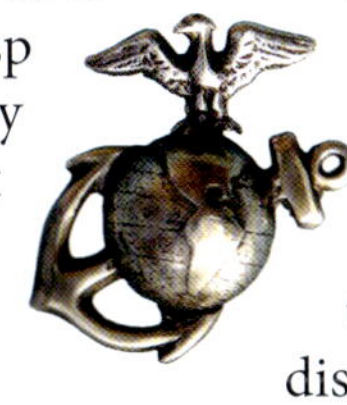

B105

The modern investment casting in silver is, like B101, the work of Joe Weingarten. An authentic 1877 pattern left collar emblem, B104 was used as the model for the Weingarten casting of B105. The comments on recognizing the modern investment casting B101 apply equally well to B105. Of most importance is the obvious single piece casting instead of the reassembly of separately struck eagle, globe, and anchor elements and rectangular tag attaching the eagle to the globe on B104 (See Figure IV-I).

B106

The diminutive size, the skilled jeweler's craftsmanship and finishing touches, the solid silver of the globe and eagle, the elaborate and intricate hinge pin and drop-in "C"-type latch-and-pin assembly and considerable variation in the measurements and weights of the port and starboard emblems of the B105 set, indicate that they were probably manufactured closer to 1877 than later on when mass-produced officer emblems became more common. Note also the family resemblance of the eagle and shape of continents to the cap ornament B096. The lack of obvious wear and a residue of clear lacquer still adhere to the aperture in the anchor ring, suggesting the set may not have ever been worn.

B107

There are several unique features of the right dress collar emblem B107. Its date of manufacture is also probably 1877 to about 1892 and perhaps a little later. Dates of manufacture and dates of use should not necessarily be considered the same. This is the only example of this distinct type the author has seen. It is struck on a single rather thick, solid-silver base. The anchor and continents are gold-plated. The asymmetrical eagle and anchor arms touching the globe are features that would soon be discontinued. A hinged drop-in pin assembly with a "C"-type latch is the means of attachment. Other interesting features are the sponge-like finish for the oceans and the line-tooled six lines of longitude. As is usual for this time period, there are no manufacturer's marks.

B108

On first appearance, the officer's right dress collar ornament with the distinct and separately struck eagle, globe, and anchor as well as the distinctly archaic shaped anchor flukes touching the globe suggest a Karl Breuninger production. The superb jeweler's craftsmanship, exhibited by hand-engraved lines of longitude and solid gold continents also suggest a Karl Breuninger production. It was attached to the collar by a hinged pin with a drop-in "C"-type catch.

B108 is certainly a mix of features, suggesting that it may be transitional. The eagle wingspan as well as the size of the globe and anchor is much closer to the requirements for the 1904 dress collar emblem than the 1877/1892 pattern. Compare B108 with Figures 4 and 10 in appendix A that illustrate the size differences spelled out in the Uniform Regulations.[16] A final indication that B108 may be transitional is the absence of the distinctive Breuninger tang attaching the separately struck eagle to the inside of the globe. B108 has a silver eagle hard-soldered to the top of the silver globe as specifically stated for the first time in the 1904 Uniform Regulations.[17]

The next three emblems were probably struck from the same die or very similar dies possibly prepared by the same diesinker. The differences are mainly a function of different alloys for the planchettes used and some definite variation with trimming and possibly piecing tools as well. The design of this group corresponds very well with items 4024 and 4025 in a 1900 catalog of Jacob Gminder dies.[18] Gminder illustrated this catalog with drawings of the outlines of his large inventory of cutting dies. Whoever may have been manufacturing these, they were apparently using Gminder's dies. One or more of these dies may still exist in the Hahn Badge Company die collection in Baltimore, Maryland.

These thin single-piece stampings of simple construction ushered in the era of less expensive mass-produced Marine Corps emblems. Collectors interviewed by the author, such as Jack Driscoll[19] and Ray Darida,[20] recall seeing great numbers of these on hand in surplus stores well into the 1960s. When these and other emblems became obsolete around 1904, great quantities may have been sold to surplus dealers. This would help explain their showing up in significant numbers even today.

Evidence of cutting and trimming tools that left a lot of extra flash can be seen in B109 and B111. What is highly unusual about B109 is that it seems to be struck from a thin, solid gold plate. The eagle and globe are silver-plated. Where the silver plate has worn away, one can see the untarnished gold underneath. After all these years, one would expect a less expensive brass base to show tarnish. Another feature that suggests extra quality is a brazed screw post attachment. This type of emblem usually has two simple, flat rectangular tabs soldered to the reverse of the globe as collar attachments. This was a crude, inexpensive, means of attachment to the collar that would soon be replaced by more sophisticated, less damaging, and more comfortable means.

B109

The B110 set in white metal is either nickel- or silver-plated brass. The set is trimmed tightly and neatly, leaving little flash. The more conventional rectangular flat tabs soldered to the inside of the leaded-in globe are the means of attachment. Their function was either as an officer's white metal collar ornament or as undress coat collar emblems for enlisted men of the USMC band for the brief period 1892 to 1900. The ambiguity and lack of specificity in the Uniform Regulations regarding metal used for officer's collar ornaments could have resulted in manufacturing these in white metal for officers or bandsmen. The short-lived enlisted bandsmen eagle, globe, and anchor collar ornaments were replaced in 1900 by small white metal or gold lyres, depending on one's rank in the band.[21] See Figure VI-5 that depicts USMC enlisted bandsmen wearing small white metal eagle, globe, and anchor emblems on their undress coat collars in 1901. It would seem likely that enlisted bandsmen

B110

B111

B112

Figure VI-4
USMC bandsmen on tour, 1901.

would have been issued the less expensive (fifty-five cents a pair), mass-produced emblems such as B110.

The 1904 Uniform Regulations first mention radically new specifications for emblems. The regulation first mentions bronze officer emblems for the new khaki cap and field hat.[22] Prior to that, officers wore their silver and gold cap and collar ornaments on their new khaki uniforms and in a few photographs the officer's dress cap ornament can be seen on the pattern 1898 campaign hat. It is curious that B111 is struck in bronze. In all respects the set is struck from the same die as B109 and perhaps B110, but is unusual for having a screw post for attachment. Perhaps some manufacturers produced unauthorized emblems for sale to Marine Corps officers using the older Gminder dies rather than retooling to meet the new 1904 requirements. If so, they apparently did not sell very many. The author can recall having seen only two examples of this pattern struck in bronze.

The set B112, although very similar, may be struck from a die variant of B109, B110, and B111 or, alternatively, may be trimmed by a different trimming tool. The great similarity indicates that perhaps at least two dies may have been prepared by the same diesinker. What is most unique is that the B112 pair is struck in solid silver. The attachments are two pointed, flat, rectangular tabs. A solid silver set of this design suggests that it is an officer's undress coat collar set or, less likely, a set to be worn on the undress coat of enlisted bandsmen 1892 to 1900. Since there were more officers than bandsmen during this period, it would suggest most of these distinct stamped silver sets were worn by officers. The white metal collar emblems purchased by the USMC Quartermaster for USMC enlisted bandsmen at forty-eight cents a pair in 1900 were not likely to have been silver, but a less expensive white metal alloy.[23]

The literature basis for identifying B113 is curious. It is identified by Cambell and O'Donnell as a French design for hats, belt plates etc. from 1861 to 1865.[24] Emerson describes this small eagle emblem as a US Army enlisted man's cap device adopted in 1872.[25] If they are correct, then this is a highly unusual example of the Marine Corps adopting a US Army enlisted man's insignia for wear by the commandant and staff officers from about 1875 to 1900. An alternative possible explanation is that the Marine Corps adopted B113 as a commandant and staff officer's full dress chapeau ornament simply because it was also worn on US Army officer chapeaus. The 1875 Marine Corps Uniform Regulation describes the staff officer's chapeau as "same as the present United States Army pattern with plume of red cock feathers."[260] Plate VI of that regulation includes an illustration clearly depicting B113.

B113

It seems more likely that the Marine Corps was using B113 in the same way that it was used as a US Army staff officer's chapeau ornament. The omission in the 1875 Uniform Regulation of any description of the commandant's yellow plume version of the full dress chapeau and the inference in Plate VI that the chapeau was worn by field officers compounds the confusion. Confusion about the yellow plume for the commandant and the red plume for staff officer full dress chapeaus was finally resolved in the 1892 Uniform Regulation.[27]

The full dress chapeau with B113 illustrated in Figure VI-5 was described and photographed in the USMCHCQV. Accession records indicate that this chapeau was worn by Capt. William Rowles Brown. This has to be an accession information error. W.R. Brown was a line officer during his entire thirty-one-year career.[28] He would never have been authorized to wear a full dress chapeau, let alone one with the yellow commandant's plume. The chapeau in Figure VI-5 was once in the collections of the Smithsonian Institution and was probably among the items donated by the family of Commandant Charles Grymes McCawley. Sometimes it took several years before these donations could be properly accessioned. By that time, information on the item may have been mixed up or limited to "found in storage." The chapeau with B113 may well be the very chapeau that Commandant MacCawley is holding in the excellent portrait by Norris (see Figure VI-6).

The tarnished eagle chapeau ornament B113 has two single-strand brass wires for attachment. Six-pointed stars are a unique feature of this ornament. The example of B113 found in Campbell and O'Donnell also has six-pointed stars.[29] Emerson illustrates a minor variant with five-pointed stars.[30] The author is not aware of any modern reproductions that match the details of this distinctive ornament.

There are many differences between the Naugatuck Novelties modern reproduction (B114) struck by a copy or perhaps a restrike from an original die rescued from the W. Stokes Kirk Company. Besides details of the eagle feathering and floral patterns in the wreath (see tick marks), the most obvious distinction is the number of points on the stars. The modern reproduction or restrike B113 has five-pointed stars. The attachments are also two single-strand brass wires. Not all five -pointed star varieties can be confidently identified as modern reproductions, since there is every reason to think that at least two dies were used to strike these in the latter part of the nineteenth century. As a rule of thumb, and given the choice between the examples of B113 and B114, it would be safer to go with an emblem for which there are no known modern reproductions or known restrikes.

Figure VI-5
B113 on commandant's full dress chapeau.

B114

Figure VI-6
Brig. Gen. Charles Grymes MacCawley, commandant. 1876–1891

Chapter VII

Officer Emblems: Turn of the Twentieth Century

(B115 to B134)

With the exception of two undress cap ornaments and one dress collar ornament of this time period, chapter 7 describes the seldom-encountered staff officer's shoulder knot emblems 1900 to 1904 and various officer's epaulette ornaments. The obvious diversity and richness of this small sample of emblems probably reflects only a fraction of the variation that was actually produced by the craftsmen and jewelers at a time before less expensive emblem mass production technology became prevalent.

B115

Staff Officer's Shoulder Knot Ornaments 1900-1904

The officer corps at this time consisted of line officers who basically commanded all the shipboard and shore-based units of the USMC and staff officers with specialized duties other than commanding US Marine line units. These duties specifically involved the Adjutant and Inspector's Department, the Quartermaster's Department and the Paymaster's Department. Staff officers in the 1900 Uniform Regulations were authorized the distinction of wearing a special silver and gold eagle, globe, and anchor device on their shoulder knots.[1] Line officers at that particular time did not wear the eagle, globe, and anchor on their shoulder knots, only their insignia of rank. The critical feature of this special emblem was its intermediate size between the undress cap and dress collar ornaments worn by all officers.[2] Measurements are the best way to distinguish the rare staff officer shoulder knot ornament. The distinction can be readily seen in the line drawings to scale in Figure 8 Appendix A. Compare the measurements for the staff officer shoulder knot ornament (Figure 8) with cap ornaments (Figures 3, 5, and 7) with 1877 and 1892 dress collar ornaments (Figures 4 and 6). One can immediately see the distinctive intermediate size of the special staff officer's shoulder knot ornament.

That these are seldom seen is primarily a function of numbers. During the period 1900 to 1904 the average number of line officers in any one year was only twenty. The average number of staff officers during this same period was less than 10% of those few line officers. Therefore, line officer emblems can be expected to be encountered in numbers at least ten times greater than the special staff officer's shoulder knot emblems. Lacking information on the owner of emblems, measurements are about the only way one can confidently identify the seldom encountered staff officer's shoulder knot emblem.

This rarely encountered emblem consists of a solid silver globe and eagle and solid gold, hand-trimmed continents with a gold-plated anchor. It is clearly intermediate in size between the officer's collar and cap ornaments. Compare B115 to the scaled line drawings Figures 4, 5, and 7 in appendix A. The distinctive style of engraving on the eagle and globe and the silver tag attaching it to the inside of the globe are characteristic Karl Breuninger features. The drop-in "C"-type latch and intricate hinged pin assembly are the means for attachment. Somewhat unusual is the very thin two-piece anchor shaft rather crudely soldered to the inside of the globe.

B116

Another wonderful piece of handcrafted military jewelry, B116 has line tool engraving on a solid silver eagle and globe and a very thin solid gold anchor. It has hand-trimmed solid-gold continents. The superb hand engraving is manifested especially in the lines of latitude and the eagle eye engraved on the reverse. The silver eagle is hard-soldered to the top of the silver globe. This and other features are typically not Karl Breuninger touches and suggest another manufacturer. The silver pin assembly is of complex construction. It has a hinged pin and a two-piece ball-shaped locking latch very unlike the simple drop-in "C"-type catch. B116 is an excellent match in most respects to Figure 8, appendix A.

It is odd that this right staff officer's shoulder knot emblem was purchased with other artifacts associated with Arthur Stokes. The lot is in a private collection that includes an expert rifle badge inscribed "Arthur Stokes" and dated "1910." Stokes was commissioned April 2, 1904.[3] He served as a line officer his entire career but evidently wore B115 as part of an oversized dress collar set long after it was discontinued as a special staff officer's shoulder knot device in 1904.[4] This would be an early example of recycling an obsolete emblem as well as a statement about a casual interpretation and enforcement of Uniform Regulations.

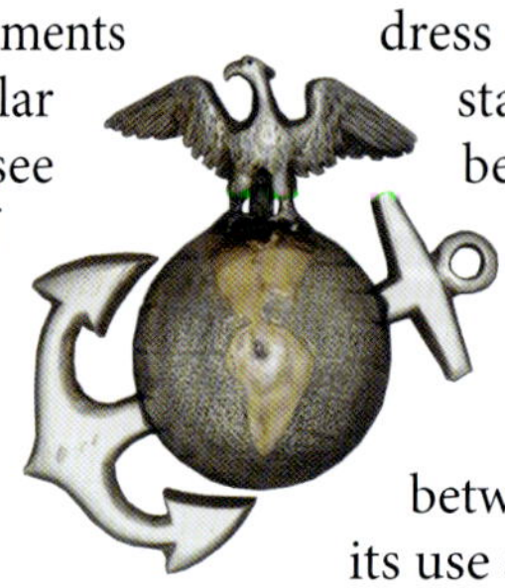

B117

A third solid silver and solid gold left eagle, globe, and anchor device is also intermediate in size between the cap and collar emblems of that time, indicating its use also as a staff officer's shoulder knot ornament. It is probably a Karl Breuninger creation with the characteristic silver tag connecting the typical Breuninger eagle of cut silver to a solid silver globe with hand-trimmed, thin solid gold continents. Typical also of this time period is the intricate silver hinged pin assembly and "C"-type drop-in catch. B115, B116, and this emblem also share a feature that seems to distinguish emblems of this period in contrast to later dress emblems. The anchor arms are more "U"-shaped than the "C"-shape seen typically in emblems after 1904. These "U" shaped anchor arms on collar emblems can often be seen in photographs dating around the turn of the twentieth century and worn by officers commissioned before that time. Also noteworthy is the unusually thin and simple anchor stock.

There is a strong family resemblance between B118 and the other Karl Breuninger type emblems described above. These similarities can be easily seen in the distinctive hand chasing and engraving of the solid silver eagle on both the obverse and reverse and the characteristic silver tag for attaching the eagle to the globe. The silver tag is last mentioned in the 1900 Uniform Regulations. The 1904 Uniform Regulations state "hard solder the eagle to the hemisphere."[5] The complex silver pin assembly with hinged pin and a drop-in "C"-type catch are also typical Breuninger features.

B118

What distinguishes B118 from the emblems described above are its modern proportions. Comparing the image of B118 with the to-scale line drawings in appendix A, the best match is clearly Figure 10, the 1904 pattern for the officer's dress collar. It is far too small for the staff officer's shoulder knot ornament and corresponds very well instead to the increased size of officer's collar ornaments that occurred in 1904. B118 is clearly transitional in maintaining earlier features that seem to drop out after the radical emblem changes of 1904. These 1904 changes essentially established the modern proportions for both officer's and enlisted men's emblems that have basically remained unchanged since that time.[6] The 1904 changes represent a watershed for identifying emblems both before and after that date. Those emblems dating before the 1904 changes are far more challenging to identify and date.

Officer's Epaulette Emblems after 1869 to 1904, and Even Later

The best description of the officer full dress epaulette emblem is found in the Commandant's Order dated November 29, 1869.[7] The order states, "... there will be substituted for the Silver Bugle worn by officers of the Marine Corps on the epaulette, an ornament of the same design as that at present worn by officers on the fatigue cap, except that the anchor be of plain silver." The requirement for a plain silver anchor is explicitly spelled out but what was left unsaid is also significant. One has to literally read between the lines with this vague wording, which only implies, but does not explicitly state, that the 1868 fatigue cap requirement for gold continents also applied to the 1869 epaulette emblems. This vague and skimpily worded order had some serious consequences.

The Commandant's 1869 Order for the new epaulette ornaments also lists five specific measurements. These measurements were used for the to-scale drawing (Figure 2 in appendix A, 1869 Epaulette Ornament).

Instead of clarifying the vague 1869 requirement for an epaulette ornament with gold continents, the Uniform Regulations of 1875 only exacerbated the problem by stating that the epaulette be, "Gold, with solid crescent, device of the Corps in silver, placed within the crescent."[8] The subsequent 1892 Uniform Regulations and 1896 revisions are both completely silent on the epaulette ornament. The 1900 Uniform Regulations compound the problem by reiterating that the epaulette ornaments shall be, "all silver."[9] Since no measurements are mentioned in the 1875, 1892, or 1900 Uniform Regulations, one has to assume that the 1869 Order was still in effect. This lack of specific guidance is probably the main reason why epaulette emblems prior to 1904 and even later are extraordinarily varied in size, styles, elements of their construction, and metal alloys used. For example, even though the Uniform Regulations after 1875 categorically specify that epaulette emblems be all silver, gold elements (closely following the 1869 Order) are routinely encountered, even up to and well after WWI.

The 1904 Uniform Regulations spelled out explicitly new requirements for the "all silver" epaulette ornament including highly explicit measurements greatly simplifying the challenge of identifying and dating epaulette emblems from that point on. The epaulette ornament turned out to be one of the longest-lived Marine Corps emblems. Even though the full dress uniform and epaulette were dropped from the 1922 Uniform Regulations, the full dress epaulette reappeared in the 1929 Uniform Regulations expressly for the uniform of the aide-de-camp to the president and officers detailed for duty at the White House. The pre-1904 epaulette emblems, as well as the distinctive post-1904 pattern, were used right up to the early 1950s and appear in illustrations in the 1929 Uniform Regulations.

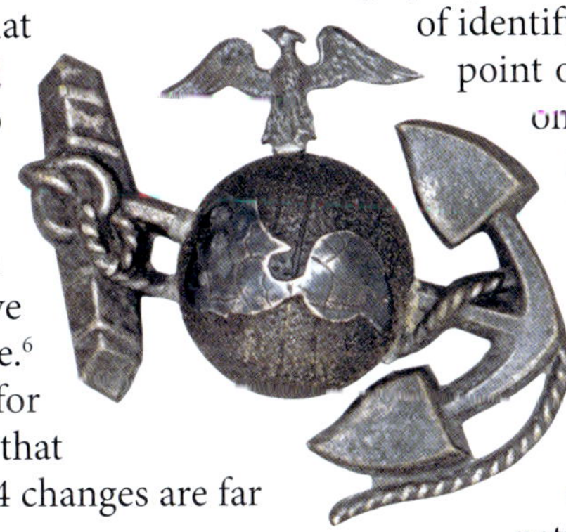
B119

Probably one of the earliest epaulette emblems in this group is B119. It has many early features. Compare the image of B119 with Figure 2 appendix A. The heavily tarnished device was among a collection of medals, insignia, and buttons donated to the USMCHCQV by the widow of Lt. Gen. Julian C. Smith. Smith was commissioned January 1, 1909, and retired from the Marine Corps December 1, 1946. He probably wore the emblem from 1909 until full dress epaulettes were dropped for almost all Marines in the early 1920s. It is a good example of an older style pre-1904 epaulette emblem.

B119 has strong similarities to an early epaulette emblem worn by W.R. Brown.[10] Another (B120) was worn by Commandant McCawley. The Brown and McCawley emblems were probably worn by those officers as early as 1869.

With the exception of an oversized anchor and the all-silver construction, B119 (a right epaulette device) conforms very well with the measurements in the 1869 Marine Corps Order. The solid silver eagle is struck from the same die that struck the eagle on B082 but unlike the Reid cap device, it is not hard-soldered to the solid silver globe; it is instead attached to the inside of the globe by a sharply angled silver tag. The unique design of the globe and engraved lines of latitude are strangely rotated ninety degrees. The die-struck, oversized anchor, is a single one-piece construction of silver-plated cartridge gauge brass and is a standard pattern commonly worn also by US Navy officers about the time of the Civil War. For attachment to the cloth of the epaulette, four single-strand wires or two inverted "U"-shaped wires were both known to have been used. The eagle on B119 is not facing the same direction as the anchor flukes. This inboard-facing convention for eagle heads and anchor flukes on emblems would not be mentioned until the 1904 Uniform Regulations. Old photographs of officers commissioned before this time show eagles heads facing outboard or sometimes in the same direction.

B120

The heavily tarnished left epaulette device (B120) was worn by Commandant Charles Grymes McCawley, probably from 1869 until his retirement in 1891. Figure VII-1 illustrates the complete McCawley left epaulette. B120 was photographed and described from the collection of the late George Mennegaux. The matching right epaulette worn by the eighth Commandant is illustrated in Magruder's 1968 *Marine Corps Gazette* article.[11] The matching set was once donated to the USMCHCQV at the time of Col. Magruder's solicitations of artifacts from the families of famous Marines. George Mennegaux showed the author a letter from Col. Magruder regarding a trade made for B120. The matching right epaulette device worn by Commandant McCawley is thought to have been recently transferred to the USMCHCQV from the Smithsonian Institution.

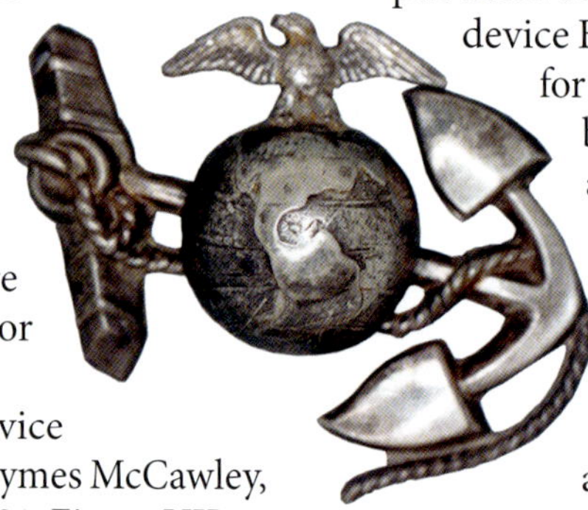

B121

Figure VII-1
B120 on left epaulette worn by Commandant Charles McCawley.

As the author was writing this chapter, colleagues from the USMCHCQV kindly sent photographs of a complete set of epaulettes in their original metal box. This set was worn by Capt. Edward P. Meeker, probably from 1869 until his retirement in 1893.[12] The Capt. Meeker set is exactly the same as the McCawley set. The measurements of the finely engraved solid silver eagle and die-struck silver globe conform extremely well to Figure 2, appendix A. The eagle is hard-soldered to the top of the globe. Both the distinctive eagle and globe are struck from dies entirely different from B119. The over-sized, single-piece anchor is silver-plated, cartridge-gauge brass. It is the same standard US Navy and USMC anchor as B119 and B121. The anchors of B119 and B120 are a port and starboard match.

The separately struck solid silver eagle and globe elements are the same device as B087 classified in chapter 5 as a possible officer's cap ornament. The B087 eagle and globe emblem was purchased separately from the stamped, silver-plated brass single piece anchor and cable. Ray Darida put these separate elements together as a right epaulette device B121. The measurement of the globe and eagle for B120 actually fit Figure 2 appendix A (epaulette) better than those measurements for the 1868 and 1875 cap ornaments. Therefore the actual functions of B087 and B121 are open to question. The B121 anchor could have been used as a US Navy officer's ornament or a USMC officer's epaulette ornament, since they are known to have been struck in port and starboard pairs. The means of attachment are two inverted "U"-shaped brass wires leaded in on the anchor stock reverse and two on the reverse of the anchor flukes. Long, pliable, pointed wires could be positioned more effectively and securely.

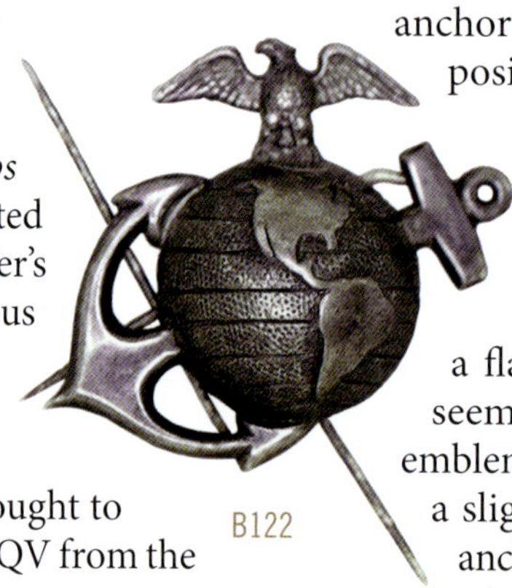

B122

The single-piece eagle, globe, and anchor struck from solid silver is unlikely to be anything other than a left epaulette device because of the absence of a cable and the presence of three long silver pins to accommodate attachment to a flat epaulette. This means of attachment would seem both cumbersome and dysfunctional for a cap emblem. The measurements for B122 and B123, despite a slightly oversized globe and a slightly undersized anchor, still best fit Figure 2 in appendix A (epaulette). The eagle bears a strong family resemblance to B121, B123, and B124 but on close comparison there are indications that different dies, or at least different trimming tools, were used, perhaps by the same manufacturer. The anchor flukes attached to the globe are features that were changed sometime after the 1892 Uniform Regulations (see Figures 7 and 9 in appendix A). This is the earliest example of an emblem in this research with a back-mark. B122 is stamped "SILVER" on the anchor crown reverse.

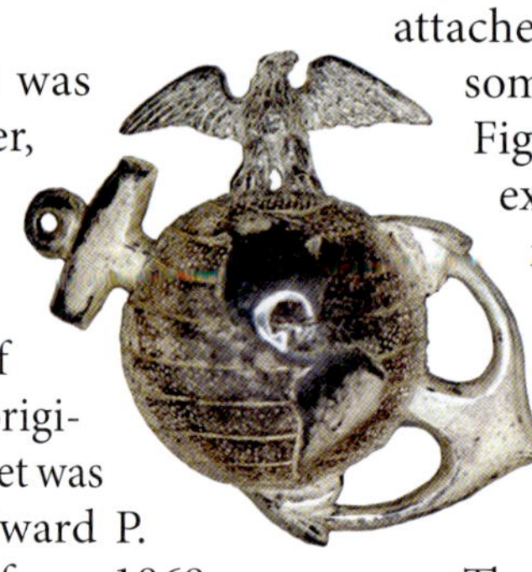

B123

With the exception of the frosted silver finish and the position of the three shorter attachment wires without points, B123, a right epaulette device, is a good match for the left device B122. The eagle, globe, and anchor are struck from a single piece, apparently using the same die set as B122. Unlike B122 from a private collection, B123 was "Found in Storage" with no provenance information at the USMCHCQV.

The most unusual feature of the white metal (silver?) separately struck eagle, globe, and anchor is the fact that it has been chemically darkened to a brown color. This suggests a transition emblem, where an earlier die was used to strike in white metal an undersized eagle, while later dies conforming to the measurements specified in the 1904 Uniform Regulations were used to strike both the globe and anchor. Compare B124 with Figure 9 in Appendix A. The chemical coloring would comply with changes in the 1904 Uniform Regulations adopting the first bronze emblems for the officer's field hat and khaki cap.[13] With the exception of the undersized eagle, the measurements for B124 conform to those in Figure 9 in appendix A (1904 officer's cap). The globe for B124 was struck from the same die that struck B122 and B123. The anchor is quite similar but the flukes are no longer touching the globe and more in keeping with the 1904 changes. Further indications of the transitional nature of this emblem are the Breuninger type tag attaching the eagle to the globe, a feature dropped in the 1904 Uniform Regulations. The eagle on B124 does not comply with the 1904 Regulation that states, "eagle to face away from the anchor ring."[14]

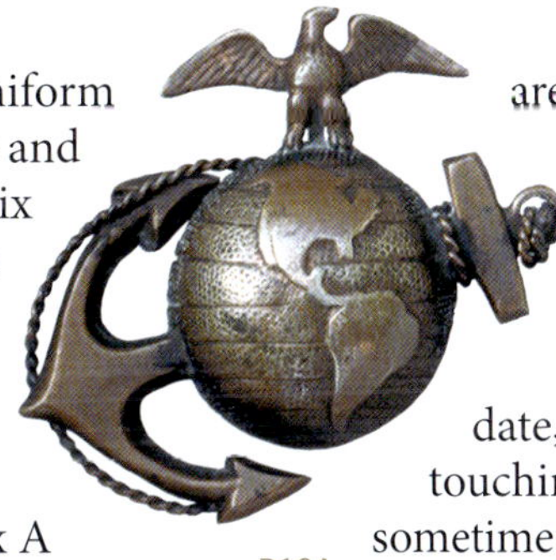

B124

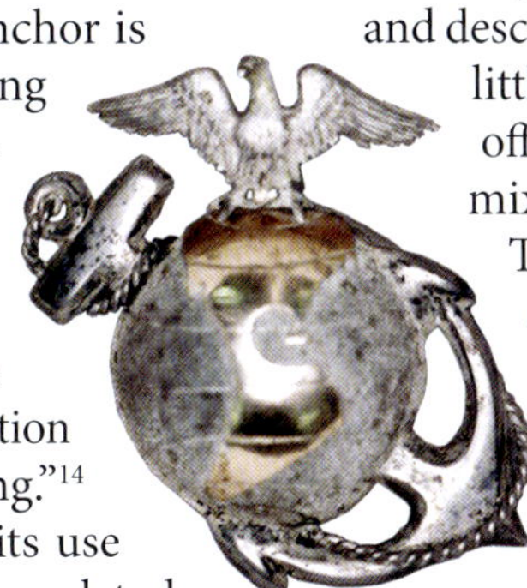

B125

Several anomalous features of B125 make its use uncertain. It has solid-gold continents and a silver-plated two-strand brass wire cable. In addition, the size of both the globe and anchor are all characteristic of a post-1904 officer's dress cap emblem. If it were worn as a dress cap ornament, the anchor orientation is certainly wrong, but not totally unheard of. Compare B125 to Figure 9 (1904 dress cap) and Figure 2 (1869 Epaulette) in appendix A.

B126

Despite these dress cap features, the anchor orientation suggests an unauthorized right epaulette device with an oversized globe and gold continents. Adding to the uncertainty are the three silver-plated, single-strand wires typical for attachment to an epaulette. Whether it was used as a cap or epaulette ornament might be open to question but it clearly displays all the key features of a Karl Breuninger creation, including the distinctive engraving on the eagle and globe with three-dimensional effects evident on the eagle's head and talons, as well as the distinctive silver attachment tag for the eagle. Perhaps as a sales strategy, Breuninger's craftsmen purposely mixed cap and epaulette features so that their emblems could reasonably pass as either cap or epaulette ornaments.

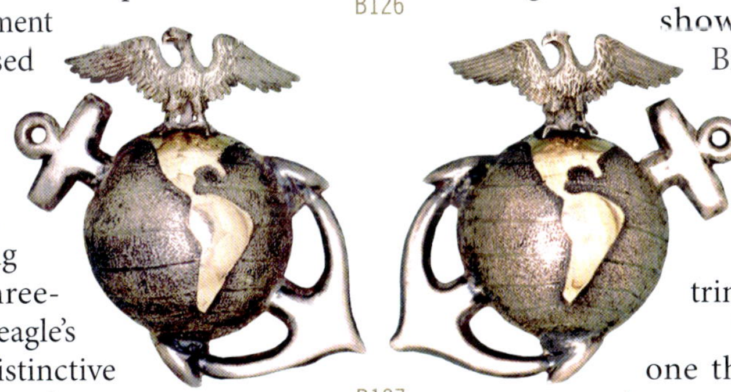

B127

With the exception of the eagle being slightly undersized, the globe and anchor on this typical Karl Breuninger creation with superb hand chasing of details conforms very well to all requirements for an officer's cap emblem post-1904 (see Figure 9 in appendix A). The solid-gold continents, the gold-plated anchor, and the silver-plated, two-strand copper wire fouled cable are perfectly consistent with features of a cap emblem rather than epaulette ornament. B126 includes the Breuninger silver tag attachment for the eagle and has both a broken pin back and three wires for attachment, suggesting a repair job. The overall measurements indicate a post-1904 date, but both the style of the anchor arms and flukes touching the globe are earlier features that were dropped sometime between the 1892 and 1900[15] Uniform Regulations.

The port and starboard pair of emblems photographed and described from the George Mennegaux collection leave little doubt about being anything other than a superb officer's epaulette set, despite the fact that the set is a mix of both epaulette and dress cap measurements. Three sets of silver double wires soldered to the reverse serve as the attachment method. They display all the characteristic features of a Karl Breuninger epaulette set: hand engraving of eagle parts and lines of latitude, silver attachment tag for the eagle, three-dimensional eagle head and talons, and hand-cut solid-gold continents. The set exhibits the 1892 pattern of anchor flukes touching the globe and the pre-1904 pattern of eagle heads not facing inboard. The set was most likely manufactured during the 1890s or perhaps earlier. Such silver and gold epaulette sets were known to be worn up through at least the mid-1920s and possibly later.

The left epaulette ornament B128 was also photographed and described through the generous assistance of George Mennegaux in 1999. It is essentially the same as the B127 Breuninger set also from the Mennegaux collection. It is included in this inventory to show the variety produced by the Breuninger craftsmen. Although the same dies were probably used, there are plenty of individual finishing effects seen particularly in the solid silver eagle, the details of the globe, and especially the hand-trimmed solid-gold continents.

This epaulet set (B129) is the only one this author has ever seen. It was photographed and described from a private collection. The port and starboard emblems were attached to the original epaulettes of an unknown first lieutenant. The

B128

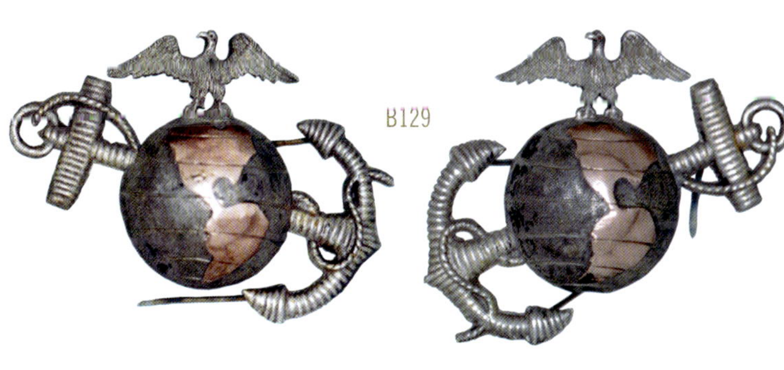

B129

set came in the original tin case and conforms exceptionally well to both the text and measurements of the 1869 Order. In comparing B129 with Figure 2 in appendix A (1868 Epaulette), they are an excellent match, suggesting that at least one manufacturer was producing epaulette emblems closely following the measurements specified in the 1869 Order. It further suggests that the set was manufactured before the confusion brought on by the 1875 and subsequent Uniform Regulations that contradicted the 1869 Order. The stylistic treatment of the silver anchors is also distinctive. The set is unique for its highly unusual false embroidered pattern seen on the anchors.

B130

The eagle and globe are struck from the same dies that produced B081, the 1868 pattern officer's undress cap ornament in chapter 5. There is no reason to think that B129 or B081 are Karl Breuninger emblems. In addition to the entirely different dies used, the details of construction are quite different. For example, the unique anchors for the B129 set are compound constructions. The upper part of the silver anchor shaft is attached to the lower part of the silver anchor shaft by a thin, rectangular brass connection. The hand-cut solid-gold continents are attached to the globe through an aperture in the silver globe with a copper strip soldered to the inside of the continents and globe. These unusual features of construction and unique dies indicate a manufacturer other than Karl Breuninger.

B131

The all-silver right epaulette emblem (B130) conforms well to the measurements for Figure 9 in appendix A (Officers Cap and Epaulette ornament post-1904). Separate globe, eagle, anchor, and continents were struck from solid silver and are in excellent condition, showing no significant wear and tear. The device exhibits excellent hand engraving of finishing details. The oceans are depicted by a handsome incised sand grain pattern. The style of the eagle is unique and never seen before by the author. Note that the separately struck continents are applied to the globe in reverse, as if the craftsman was not familiar with the cartography of North and South America. This incorrect cartography has been noted in other foreign-made officer emblems such as those made in China. Typical of the time period is the absence of manufacturer back-marks. The means for attachment are also unusual. Two flat, rectangular-shaped silver tabs with points were used. This emblem was "found in strorage" at the USMCHCQV with unfortunately no further information.

B132

Besides being in a wonderful state of preservation, the B131 set on the original full dress epaulettes and in its metal box was photographed and described in the extraordinary collection of George Mennegaux. The port and starboard set is entirely consistent with the 1904 requirements. Compare B131 left and right with Figure 9 in Appendix A (Dress Cap and Epaulette 1904). This is the only set of this distinctive type that the author has seen. The set is a rarity not only because it is a seldom seen type, but because of its ultra rare informational context. It is associated with 1st Lt. Reginald F. Ludlow, who was commissioned May 5, 1907[16] and died on active duty January 3, 1913.[17] This five-year window dating its use can in all probability be condensed to an even shorter period when Ludlow probably purchased the set in Japan before coming off sea duty in February 1910. Ludlow died in the US Marine Hospital Key West Florida of illness contracted in the line of duty. The epaulette set was acquired by George Mennegaux through the family of Lt. Ludlow from Wisconsin.

The metal box for the epaulette set is marked "K. Kusafugi, Yokahama." The right emblem seems to be struck from a different die than the left emblem. It is odd that the continents of the left emblem are correct, while those of the right emblem are reversed (flipped 180 degrees) just like the reversed continents of B130. Although the eagle and globe seem to be mirror images of each other, the anchors are not. These peculiar features of construction indicate a high level of laborious craftsmanship, so unlike the mass production technology that would soon follow. Three silver wires serve as attachments for each emblem.

B132 is another rarity by virtue of also being identified with a particular Marine, William E. Smith, commissioned July 23, 1900, and last appearing in the Muster Rolls in August 1903.[18] The well-preserved set was photographed and described from a private collection. The die seems the same as B134 and B136 enlisted cap ornaments of the squat-legged eagle type described in chapter 8. The strike is excellent for detail definition. The squat-legged eagle-type emblems for both officers and enlisted men are peculiar in being larger than the 1875/1900 cap pattern (Figures 1, 3, 5 and 7) and smaller than the 1904 cap emblem (Figure 9 in appendix A).

Unlike the enlisted emblem, B131 is struck from a thin solid-silver plate and displays a fancy compound hinged pin assembly with six separate elements and a "C"-type drop-in catch. The pin and catch assembly are soldered on the reverse at six and twelve o'clock.

The most striking feature of this set is the superb job of converting two left cap emblems into a port- and starboard-matching epaulette set. The anchor and cable from one left cap device was carefully cut away and repositioned with silver solder to the globe and the underside of the eagle's right wing to create a mirror image of the left ornament. Both eagle heads still face to their right. The requirement for the heads to face inboard does not appear in the Uniform Regulations until 1904.

At first glance, B133, another right epaulette ornament, looks very similar to the other squat-legged eagle right epaulette emblems such as B132. However, B133 is struck as a single piece from a thicker solid-silver planchette from an entirely different die, presumably a port-and-starboard die set. The fine details suggest multiple strikes. The evidence for different dies is pointed out with tick marks. Attachment to the epaulette was by means of two double silver wires.

B133

The epaulette set B134 was photographed and described through the courtesy of the late Jack McCord. The set is struck from solid silver from a single die for a cap device. The die is entirely different from the dies used for B132 and B133. The continents are gold-plated in keeping with the 1869 Order on epaulettes but ignore the subsequent contradictory post-1875 Uniform Regulations requiring all silver. The same clever conversion by cutting and soldering elements of a left or cap emblem, turning it into a right epaulette emblem, is seen in B132. Two flat rectangular and pointed tabs attached to the reverse anchor crown and anchor stock serve as attachments.

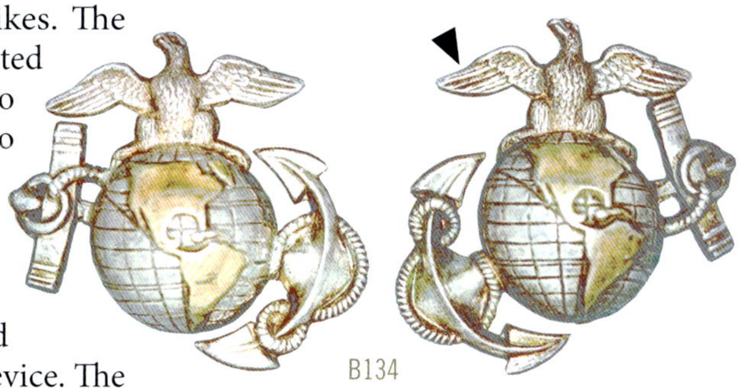

B134

CHAPTER VIII

Enlisted Emblems: Late Nineteenth Century

(B135 to B143)

The varieties of the squat-legged eagle design (B135 to B143) for enlisted emblems share several features. Both the brass and white metal versions are struck from thin cartridge gauge metal. Attachments are two inverted "U"-shaped wires (cap) or single- and sometimes double-strand wires. The latter attachment method is common for enlisted shoulder boards. The emblems in this chapter have to date sometime after 1881. The squat-legged eagle type is first confidently recognized in a photograph dating after 1889 (see B099, appendix C-1, White, Harry Kidder). Sometime after 1881 with the adoption of the white cork helmet the requirement for white metal ornaments for the Marine Corps at least doubled. No dated photographs could be found so far that clearly supports a more exact date.

By 1892, with the adoption of the enlisted shoulder board with nickel-plated brass eagle, globe, and anchor ornaments, the requirement for emblems would again dramatically increase.[1] It seems more likely that these important uniform changes creating increases in emblem procurement were the potential occasions for introducing the distinctive varieties seen in chapter 8. The earlier and smaller pattern 1875 emblems such as B071 and B075 covered in chapter 4 were replaced by the later and larger squat-legged eagle types covered in this chapter.

B135

B135 is the brass version of B143 in white metal. Both are struck from the same die and share a distinctive pattern of many small secondary feathers in the wing of the eagle (see tick marks) and single-strand brass wire attachments, even though the 1875 Uniform Regulations specify brass loops.[6] An obvious flaw can be seen where the lower anchor fluke is connected to the globe with flash. This flaw is possibly a result of a faulty trimming tool. It is curious that B143 in white metal is one of the most common emblems that the author has encountered in this research. B135, B137, and B143 are all struck from the same die.

Figure VIII-1
The original die for B135. It was purchased from the W. Stokes Kirk Company by Ray Darida, who kindly provided the author this image. Ray labeled his picture, "die for the 1892 cap emblem."

Enlisted Cap Ornaments, 1892? to 1898

The two following brass emblems (B135 and B136) are interpreted as enlisted undress cap (so called kepi or fatigue cap) and 1898 to1904 field hat ornaments because of their thin, brass construction. This pattern would radically change later. The author has seen this type emblem on the Mills woven cartridge belt buckle. These are contrary to the uniform regulations for enlisted equipment.[2] The 1892 Uniform regulations describe a plain brass plate for the white leather waist belt. There is no mention of an eagle, globe, and anchor device on the Mills woven cartridge belt.[3]

Brass emblems were required for the enlisted undress cap in the Uniform Regulations of 1875[4] and 1892.[5] The dress hat for officers and enlisted Marines was dropped in 1892, but at the same time, pairs of nickel-plated brass emblems were adopted for enlisted shoulder boards and were worn until 1905. The coming and going of different die varieties (both white metal and brass enlisted emblems) with different functions during this time period present an especially complex and challenging puzzle.

Figure VIII -2
Marine Corps Pvt. James Spillane, who served for the brief period of August 1893 to June 1894.[7] Ray Darida provided the author a copy of Spillane's medical discharge dated June 28, 1894. Spillane is wearing the 1892 pattern undress cap with an emblem that generally conforms to B135 or B136.

Figure VIII-5
Enlarged image of the brass wire attachment of B135 to campaign hat.

Figure VIII-3
1898 pattern campaign hat with B135.

Another example of a brass emblem worn on the 1898 pattern campaign hat can be seen in a photo published by John Stacey.[9]

Figure VIII-5 shows how the single-strand brass wires were bent into a "U"-shape to better lock the emblem to the felt material of the hat. The photo also clearly shows the buildup of an old *in situ verdigris* on the wires and felt. This verdigris buildup indicates that the emblem had been there long before it was purchased by Kenneth Smith Christmas in the early 1970s.

Despite numerous examples of white metal emblems on USMC headgear seen in museums and various publications, it is the author's contention that brass emblems such as B135 were the authorized emblems for enlisted dress and undress caps as well as field hats prior to 1904. Figures VIII-3, VIII-4, and VIII-5 depict the brass emblem B135 on a pattern 1898 field hat. This particular campaign hat was purchased in the early 1970s at a flea market in Pennsylvania for eight dollars.[8] It is now in the collection of Gen. Richard Natonski USMC (Ret.). All three photos are the courtesy of Richard Natonski.

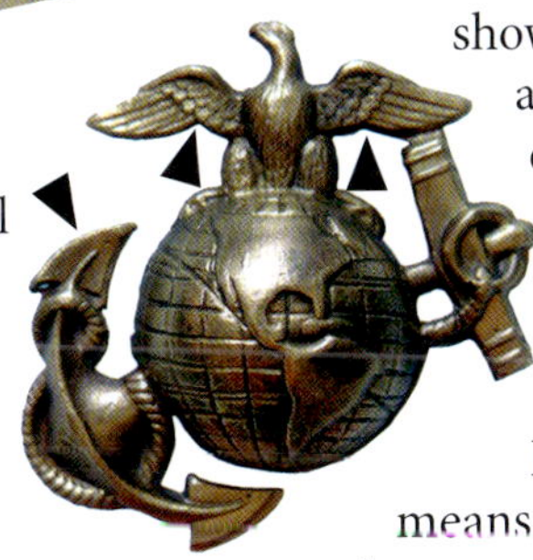

B136

The thin brass emblem B136 struck in brass is a far less often encountered die variety than B135 (see tick marks that distinguish the two). Like B135, two single strand brass wires were the means of attachment, not the inverted "U"-shaped brass loops and eyes specified in earlier Uniform Regulations. The most obvious distinction is the pattern of the eagle's secondary wing feathers. They are fewer, larger, and more even. Tick marks also clearly show differences in the design of the anchor flukes and fouling of the cable on the upper fluke.

B137

In comparing B135 with B137, one essential difference is the attachment method using eyes and rings with leather strips for B137 instead of single- or double-strand brass wires. These inverted "U"-shaped wire loops on B137 are a seldom-encountered magnetic iron alloy. According to Ray Darida, the unusual magnetic wire attachments are earlier than the far more common brass wire attachments.[10]

A second distinction is the black lacquer finish over what is probably plain brass or perhaps bronze, instead of nickel- or chrome-plated brass. Several examples of darkened B137 emblems have been encountered in this research, suggesting that the older, thin, obsolete emblems of brass may have been purposely darkened to attempt to recycle them to accommodate the 1904 Uniform Regulation. The 1904 changes specified, "A Corps device of the same pattern and dimensions in dull-finished bronze will be worn on the field hat and the khaki cap cover."[11] The regulation implies, but does not explicitly spell out, a thicker bronze emblem equivalent to the undress brass hat emblem of gilders metal #14 first specified in the 1900 Uniform Regulations.[12] This significant change will be taken up in chapter 10. The vague and inexplicit language in the regulations may account for so many darkened emblems of the older thin stampings.

Figure VIII-4
B135 enlarged.

Examples of B137 are also known to use brazed screw posts instead of wire attachments, perhaps another attempt to respond to the 1900 and 1904 Uniform Regulations. The author has also observed varieties of B137 without the flash between the lower anchor fluke and globe. These may have been struck and trimmed before the trimming tool was damaged.

B138

The device B137 is struck from brass and may have been nickel-plated but is severely worn and corroded. It is struck from the same die as B135. It is another example of the earlier thin, so-called stamped, emblems having a screw post soldered to the inside of the globe instead of the far more common and conventional wire attachments, which on this emblem show no evidence of ever having been attached. What is most striking about this emblem is a silver devil dog element soldered to the center of the globe. This distinctive devil dog motif first shows up during the WWI period. The author is in agreement with the owner, Paul Stine, who interprets this as a WWI novelty item comparable to the multitude of sweetheart pins produced during and after WWII.[13] When purchased, the ornament had a late Ching dynasty Chinese cash coin with a square hole in it, serving as a washer for the screw post and nut.

B139

The thin enlisted cap devices with wire attachments (B135 through B139) were probably sold to the Marine Corps by William Horstmann. Quartermaster records examined in this research identify no supplier of enlisted cap ornaments other than Horstmann for the period 1892 to 1898. Horstmann charged the Quartermaster in 1895 and again in 1896 three cents each for these thin brass ornaments with wires for attachment.[14] What is most significant about this group of thin, inexpensive enlisted cap ornaments is that the last Quartermaster order was filled in the spring of 1898. After that, a new heavier enlisted cap device was adopted. That story will be covered in chapter 10.

For at least the last six years, B139 has been advertised at reasonable prices in S&S Firearms catalogs as a reproduction "1892 forage cap and campaign hat ornament."[15] These reproductions are manufactured by Naugatuck Novelties and struck from an original die or most likely, a copy of an original die from the W. Stokes Kirk Company collection.[16] With the exception of the trimming flaw (flash) on the lower anchor fluke and the attachments, they seem indistinguishable from B135 and B137. At least three patterns of attachments are known. Double- and single-strand wires of brass are soldered to the reverse in the middle of the anchor stock and anchor crown. Some of these reproductions have inverted "U"-shaped brass wire loops. The B139 reproduction is also known in a dark brown finish vaguely simulating the 1904 enlisted field hat ornament B167 or B168. Buyers should be cautious of B139, especially when purposely altered to look old.

1892 to 1905 Enlisted Shoulder Knot Emblems

With the possible exception of use as earlier enlisted or officer dress hat or white cork helmet ornaments, the next group of emblems (B140 to B143) was mainly used on the enlisted shoulder knots, see Figure VIII-6. The sample shown here is representative but incomplete. Many die varieties for these white metal emblems were produced in very large quantities. Enlisted shoulder knots are known in port and starboard matched pairs as well as sets with two left emblems. A National Archives photo published by Charles Cureton clearly shows a sea-going sergeant sitting at the mess table of the USS *Galena* about 1900 wearing a left emblem on the right shoulder board of his dress uniform.[17] This is photographic corroboration that enlisted shoulder knots were not necessarily port and starboard matching sets.

It is the author's impression that the port and starboard sets that appear on the market today are definitely in the minority. The 1892 Uniform Regulation specifies only a, "... Corps device on the center of the pad."[18] Some manufacturers evidently read between the lines and went the extra step to produce port and starboard matching pairs.

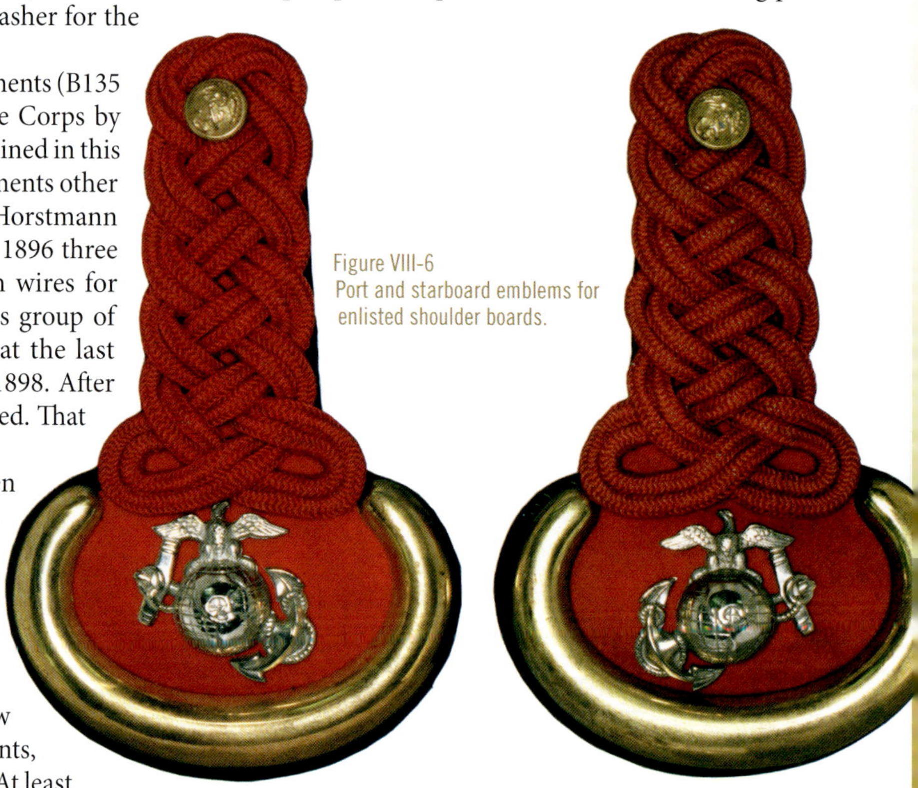
Figure VIII-6
Port and starboard emblems for enlisted shoulder boards.

B140

One cannot be certain about this emblem struck from a silver alloy, not silver- or nickel-plated brass. It was described and photographed in the Jack McCord collection and could have been attached to the brass shield of an officer's dress cap worn up to 1892. Since it is silver, it was probably not an enlisted ornament for the dress hat or shoulder knots. Tick marks indicate some distinctive features, including fewer large and quite even secondary feathers on the eagle's wings and an unusual "S"-shaped curve to the end of the fouled cable. The white metal inverted "U"-shaped wire attachments suggest an ornament attached through the two rectangular apertures of the brass shield for the dress hat, but since B140 is also known to occur in port and starboard pairs, it could be an officer's epaulette device that essentially ignores many of the requirements specified in the 1869 Order on officer's epaulettes. The author is unaware of epaulette ornaments with this kind of attachments.

B141

Tick marks point out features that distinguish B141 from similar emblems in this chapter and attest to the great variety that this sample touches upon. Note the eagle wing feathering, the shape of the end of the fouled cable, and the shape of the lower anchor fluke. It is struck from cartridge gauge brass and nickel-plated, thus conforming very well to an enlisted dress hat emblem (1875 to 1892) or left shoulder knot ornament. The original attachments of this device were double wires soldered to the reverse center of the anchor stock and anchor crown, further indicating an original use as a shoulder knot ornament. These wires are broken off and in their place a screw post was soldered to the inside and center of the globe, rendering it dysfunctional as a shoulder knot ornament. The use of white metal ornaments of this type with screw posts is enigmatic. Screw posts became common with brass cap ornaments but there is no reason to think that cap ornaments after 1897 were white metal. Other examples of B140 in white metal are known with two single-strand wire attachments or with two inverted "U"-shaped loops. This variety of attachments indicates use as an unauthorized hat emblem and shoulder knot ornament.

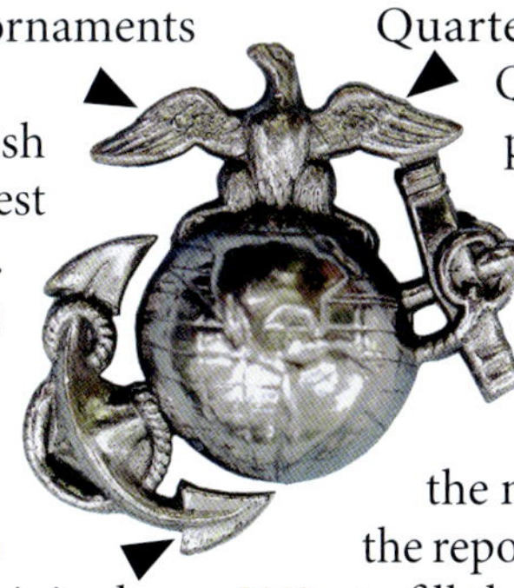

B142

Struck from white metal, not a brass base, this device seems likely to have been used as a left shoulder knot emblem. Tick marks point out indications of a die different from others in this chapter. The most obvious features are the fewer and larger secondary eagle wing feathers. The means of attachment is a neatly soldered drop-in "C"-type pin assembly soldered to the mid- anchor stock and mid- anchor crown reverse. There is no indication of earlier wire attachments common with enlisted shoulder knots.

The last of this group of enlisted white metal emblems (B143) is one of the most common emblems that the author has encountered in this research. It is a nickel-or perhaps chrome-plated version of the plain brass B135. These emblems are characteristically shiny with essentially no corrosion and to the author's knowledge, never occur in port and starboard pairs. The description of B135 applies to B143 in every respect, except for the white metal plating. Consistent with their common occurrence on the market today, especially on the Internet, was the observation of Emille Stefanacci, who recalled seeing, in surplus stores in the 1950s and 1960s, cardboard boxes full of these in pristine condition.[19]

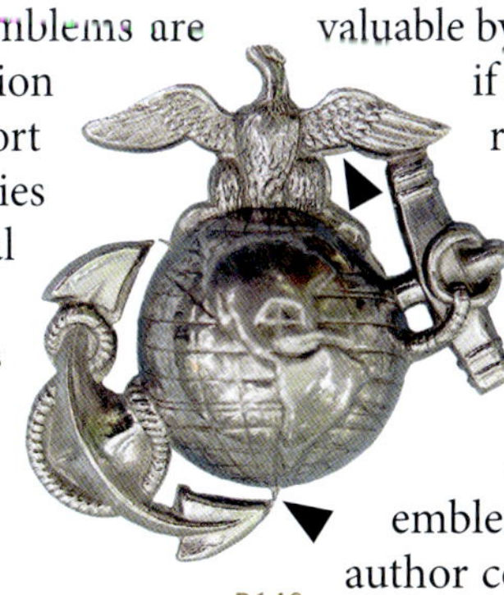

B143

Why B143 and many of the emblems in this chapter are still so plentiful is intriguing. White metal emblems like these served several functions. Every time a new use was adopted, it created an increased procurement demand. In addition, the Marine Corps between 1875 and 1905 increased from 1,980 to 7,011 Marines.[20] According to the Commandant's Annual Reports to the Secretary of the Navy from 1897 to 1901, perhaps more than 500 pairs of these white metal emblems were purchased by the Quartermaster.[21] The small numbers received by the Quartermaster each year (see table VIII-1) were probably the minimum number of pairs needed to assure that all enlisted Marines were issued a set. With the increasing number of enlisted Marines for that five-year period, there would be a shortfall of shoulder knot pairs. Those turned in by Marines discharged were probably insufficient to meet the needs of the new Marines recruited. It is likely that the reported numbers of pairs annually received were meant to fill that shortfall.

TABLE VIII-1	White Metal Emblem Pairs Received Compared to Numbers of Enlisted Marines by Year	
Year and Emblem	Pairs Received	Enlisted Marines[22]
1897	49	3,735
1898	80	3,481
1899	200	3,066
1900	200	5,240
1901	204	5,694

The Question of Function for White Metal Enlisted Shoulder Board Emblems

The function for these white metal emblems, like B141, is exacerbated by their fairly common occurrence with headgear on both the open market and in published photographs. The 1900 Uniform Regulations clearly specify brass emblems for both the dress cap and campaign hat.[23] Initially, the author assumed that these white metal hat ornaments were simply stuck on headgear by collectors or dealers because they are far more plentiful than the appropriate brass emblems of this time period. In other words, it was the old ploy of making the item more valuable by sticking a common emblem on the old cover, even if it did not belong with it. This no doubt has happened regularly simply because these white metal emblems are so plentiful compared to far fewer well-preserved examples of headgear from that period.

Nevertheless, there remains the gnawing uncertainty that some of these plentiful white metal emblems may have been recycled and used, especially on campaign hats, at times when brass emblems may have been in short supply. What made the author consider this possibility was finding a white metal emblem (B142) on the 1898 pattern campaign hat worn by Smedley Butler in a collection of his uniform items donated by the Butler family to the Smithsonian Institution and recently transferred to the USMCHCQV collections. Whether this emblem is actually Butler's or may have been unknowingly stuck on his field hat by museum personnel, perhaps for exhibit purposes, remains an open question.

By 1905, practically all white metal emblems for enlisted men suddenly became obsolete. Since shoulder boards were issued as company property, each Marine was required to return them when discharged.[24] This meant that in 1905 all these white metal emblems became surplus and probably went up for sale. It is reasonable to think that aggressive surplus dealers like Francis Bannerman or W. Stokes Kirk bought this glut of surplus where it remained in their inventories in significant quantities right up to their going out of business as late as the late 1960s and early 1970s.

Some interesting exceptions to the 1905 obsolescence of these white metal emblems are known. Thin, nickel- or chrome-plated brass enlisted emblems such as those discussed were recycled as ornaments attached to the drums of Marine bandsmen. They show up in old photographs at least up to 1926. A good example is illustrated in the 1913 Uniform Regulations.[25] Another example can be seen in appendix C-1 (B042).

CHAPTER IX

Helmet Plates and Saddlecloth Ornaments: Post-1892

(B144 to B157)

The 1892 Uniform Regulations first mention the adoption of the black felt helmet for enlisted Marines.[1] The officer's version is described as well.[2] Figure IX-1 depicts the officer's version. The helmet style may have been largely influenced by the German "Picklehaube," a style of military headgear that gained popularity after the success of the Germans in the Franco Prussian War. It replaced the earlier 1875 pattern dress hat for both officers and enlisted Marines. With this change to a black felt helmet came an unusually large and very distinctive eagle, globe, and anchor emblem. For enlisted Marines the new ornament was fired gilt brass. The same design was used for the officer's emblem but instead of ordinary brass, these were to have an eagle and fretted silver Western Hemisphere. The continents of North and South America and the anchor (but not the cable) was to be gold.[3] This distinctive enlarged eagle, globe, and anchor helmet device for both officers and enlisted Marines lasted only fourteen years. Nevertheless, several distinct varieties of this device have been identified.

Also included in chapter 9 are saddlecloth ornaments for officers that were modeled on the pattern 1892 enlarged helmet device. Although these large saddlecloth ornaments were used much later in time than the helmet device, they are included in chapter 9 because of their strong family resemblance to the 1892 helmet device. Prior to 1904 and up to at least 1916, the silver-and-gold helmet plate was also used to decorate the corners of the officer's navy blue dress saddlecloth. Although the black felt helmet and its enlarged ornament were dropped in 1905, a bronze field saddlecloth ornament was adopted in 1904.[4] The 1912 Uniform Regulations again mention the bronze field saddlecloth and the silver-and-gold dress saddlecloth ornaments.[5] The 1917 revisions to the 1912 Uniform Regulations still described silver-and-gold Corps devices sewn into the corners of the officer's dress saddlecloth.[6] The same 1917 revisions first mention the russet or tan leather eagle, globe, and anchor ornaments worn on the officer's field saddlecloth. It is not until the appearance of the 1922 Uniform Regulations that dress saddlecloth eagle, globe, and anchor ornaments of scarlet leather are described for the corners of the officer's dress saddlecloth.[7] These rare and distinctive scarlet leather dress saddlecloth ornaments are again described in the Uniform Regulations of 1929.[8] They were finally dropped sometime between 1929 and the appearance of the 1937 Uniform Regulations.[9]

B144

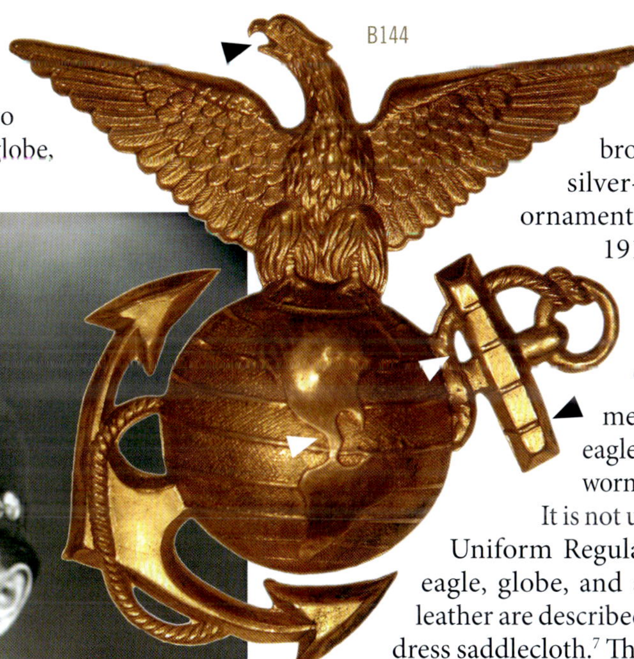

Figure IX-1
Marine band leader William Santleman.

The enlisted ornaments in this chapter include three distinct types struck in brass from three different dies. Officer's helmet ornaments include the prescribed silver-and-gold emblems struck from the same three dies. The chapter also includes additional types that may have only been prepared for officers.

The author identified B144, the enlisted helmet plate ornament, in the private collections of at least three reputable Marine Corps emblem collectors of long standing. It was also described in the collections at Quantico and the Smithsonian Institution. It is classified as Type I. The distinguishing features are indicated by tick marks in the color B144 photo. These include; but are not limited to, a cartographic rendition of Central America shaped like the letter "C" reversed, or counter "C." Type I also has an open beak on the eagle and an opening under the upper anchor stock and above the cable and upper anchor shaft. A screw post is the usual means of attachment but the type is also known less frequently with two brass wire attachments. The examples that the author examined are struck from quite thin brass (0.60 to 0.80 mm) and have a strong curvature. They often, but not always, have small anti-twist pins soldered to the tips of the eagle wings. The curvature of the eagle wings and set pins serve to lock the device to the shape of the felt helmet.

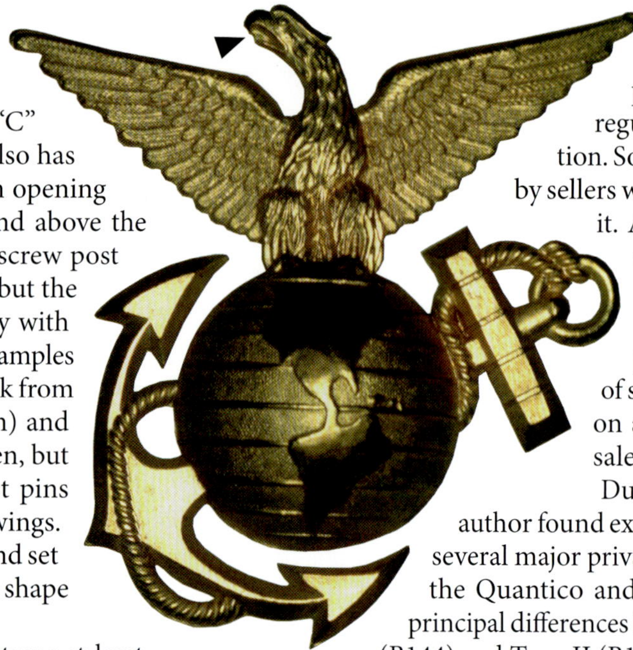

B145

Naugatuck Novelties manufactures at least two varieties of a handsome reproduction of the B144 Type I helmet plate. The die used is a modern copy of the original die for B144 rescued from the W. Stokes Kirk collection by Ray Darida, more than forty years ago. Ray Darida kindly provided the copy of the photo of the original 1892 die (see Figure IX-2). The key features that distinguish B145 from B144 are also illustrated by tick marks. The most obvious of these differences is the thick brass plate used. It is almost twice as thick as B144 and weighs almost twice as much, or more, than all the known varieties of B144. Besides the thick, heavy brass, one can immediately see the closed eagle beak and the absence of piercing between the upper anchor stock and the cable above the anchor shaft. Unaltered Naugatuck reproductions typically have neither the curvature, nor set pins soldered to the reverse of the eagle wings tips as described for B144. There are at least two varieties of B145. An earlier emblem has a single screw post and the lower anchor fluke does not touch the bottom of the globe. A later variety has two screw posts with the lower anchor fluke attached to the globe. Both of these varieties are probably struck from a modern copy of the original die.

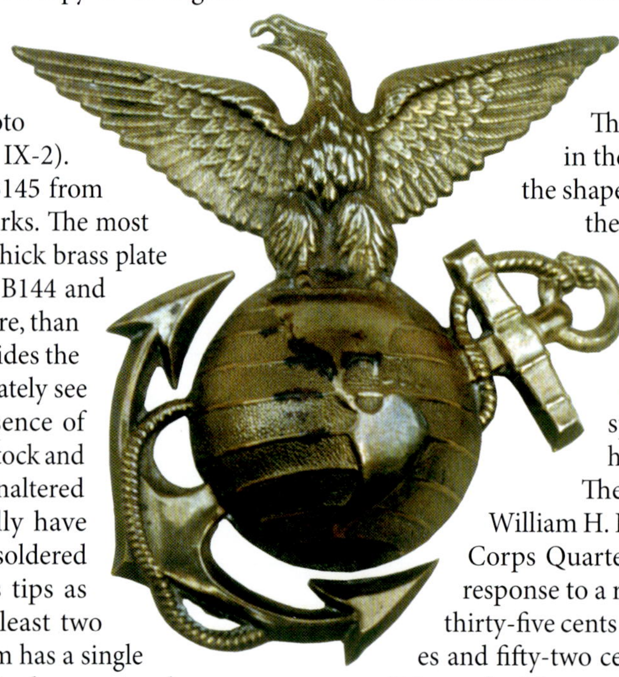

B146

Figure IX-2
Original die for B144.

Since at least 1973, B144 has been offered for sale as a reproduction for reasonable prices by S&S Firearms. Nevertheless, these continue to be one of the most often encountered offerings that, either in ignorance or dishonesty, purport authenticity. At best it is regularly offered as an honest reproduction. Sometimes it is offered as questionable by sellers who may actually be uncertain about it. At worst, it is all too often dishonestly offered as an authentic 1892 to1904 emblem. It is often seen for sale on what seems to be authentic period headgear. This is the old ploy of sticking an inexpensive reproduction on authentic headgear to increase the sale value of the combination.

During the course of this research, the author found examples of the Type II helmet plate in several major private and public collections, including the Quantico and the Smithsonian collections. The principal differences between Type I enlisted helmet plates (B144) and Type II (B146) are pointed out with tick marks in the photos. An obvious distinction is the "C" shape of Central America. Note also a thicker pattern to the feathering of the upper wing. These are differences in the dies not just the different trimming and piercing tools. There are other subtle differences seen in the eagle heads and fathering as well as the shape of the anchor flukes. A screw post is the usual means of attachment for B146, but two brass wires are occasionally seen on the earlier emblems.

Through the generous sharing of information found in the research of Alec Tulkoff, there exists corre-spon-dence about the pattern 1892 helmet plate in the National Archives.[10] The correspondence was between the William H. Horstmann Company and the Marine Corps Quartermaster at Philadelphia and was in response to a request for a proposal listing prices of thirty-five cents each for 1,200 old style helmet devices and fifty-two cents each for 1,200 helmet devices of #20 metal with screw posts and set pins. It is not known exactly which type this correspondence refers to, but it would seem most likely that these were the far more common Types I and II (B144 and B146). This information corroborates the change from an earlier helmet device struck of thinner brass with two wire attachments that dated prior to May 26, 1898. After this date, a heavier and more expensive ornament was adopted. The modern reproduction B145 is struck from an even heavier brass sheet than either B144 or B146. A simple test will distinguish the authentic pieces from the modern reproductions. When both are held in one's hands, the modern reproduction will be obviously heavier than either B144 or B146.

This is also consistent with the 1896 date for the US Army's change to a screw post for their hat insignia.[11] The Marine Corps seems to have made the same change about this time. The 1898 description in the Horstmann proposal for providing the new helmet ornament of the thicker metal #20 may have served the function of providing a stronger, more efficient, solder point for the new screw post attachments. The change to screw posts for emblems struck from thicker brass also correlates to the advent of the new 1897 pattern enlisted dress cap with a metal grommet for attaching an emblem with a screw post.[12]

A third type of enlisted helmet plate for this period is far less often encountered than the two above types. Type III (B147) is especially close to B146. See tick marks pointing out key distinctions in the three dies. Although extremely close to Type II (B146), Type III (B147) has incised ironwork on the anchor stock, not the raised ironwork seen in Types I and II. The tick marks also show differences in the eagle feathering, anchor flukes, continents, and other details indicating different dies. These differences may simply be minor die and trimming tool variations, or alternatively, indications of different manufacturers using unique dies. However, no manufacturers other than William Horstmann have been found in Quartermaster records up to 1904.

One example of B147 has three flat and pointed double brass tabs soldered to the mid- anchor stock reverse, the mid-anchor crown reverse, and the eagle breast reverse. A second attachment method is known using a long and pointed brass pin coiled like a safety pin at the top of the pin and soldered to the eagle neck reverse along with a short "U"-shaped brass wire soldered to the center of the globe reverse, see Figure IX-3. This combination of long coiled pin and short two-prong wires allowed a locking effect of the brass emblem to the helmet. This attachment method probably came before screw posts. The thin plate also suggests a date before 1898 but another Type III officer's helmet plate (B150) was manufactured with the later screw post attachment. Whether or not helmet plate Types I, II, and III were made by the same or different manufacturers, is essentially an open question. It is known that Type III is associated with Karl William Breuninger and that William C. Horstmann provided at least two varieties of helmet plates.

Enlisted helmet plates types I, II, and III were also manufactured for officers with the prescribed gold and silver features. A Type I helmet plate (B148) is the officer's version of B144 with the Counter C-shaped Central American cartography. The screw post, set pins, and heavier #20 gilders metal, indicate the post-1898 William C. Horstmann emblem mentioned in the 1898 Quartermaster correspondence.[13] The emblem is struck in brass with a silver-plated eagle and globe that has a distinctly frosted appearance to the finish. The continents, anchor, and cable appear to be gold-plated. The attachment could not be examined at the time it was photographed and recorded because the device was mounted under glass at Rick Spooner's superb emblem exhibit at the Globe and Laurel restaurant in Triangle, Virginia. Obvious distinctions between this emblem and the modern reproduction are described under B144 and B145.

The modern reproduction of the Type I officer's helmet plate is struck from the same Naugatuck Novelties die used to strike B145. It is the same in almost all respects to the plain brass version B145, except that the finish of the eagle and globe has a rather flat, thick painted quality rather than a thin frosty silver plate. Also, the lower anchor fluke is attached to the globe, not separated from the globe like B148. All the other distinguishing features pointed out for B145 also apply to B149.

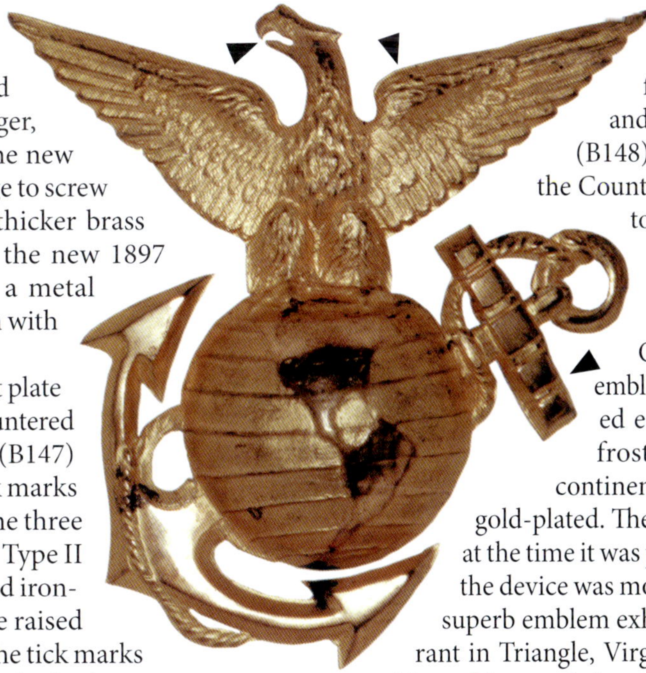

B147

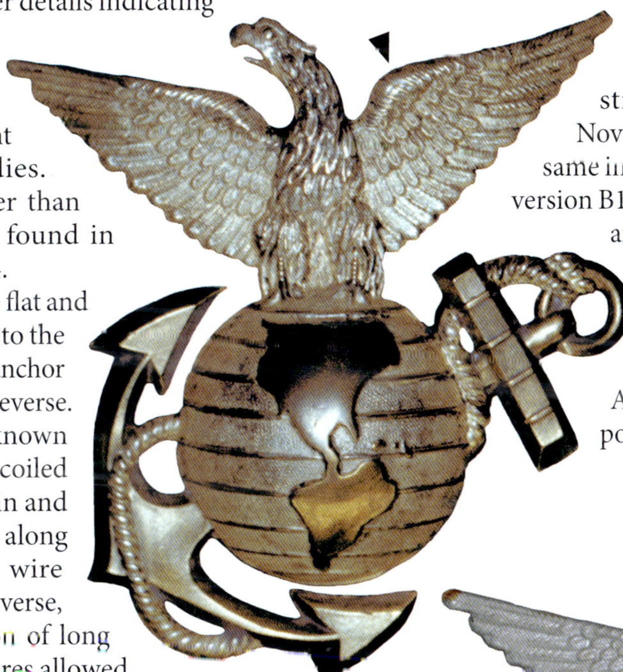

B148

B149

Figure IX-3
B147 reverse.

B150

B151

B152

Figure IX-4
B152 on Col. Cochrane's dress helmet.

The officer's version of the Type II helmet plate is B150. Note the distinctive "C"-shape to the Central American cartography as well as other features pointed out with tick marks. Unlike the silver finish of the Naugatuck Novelty reproduction B149, B150 has a silver finish more like B148. This silver finish or plate has a thin frosted appearance instead of a flat, thick, silver paint look. Note also the open beak and raised iron work on the anchor stock. The screw posts on this and other examples of B150 observed in the author's research indicate a post-1898 date. B150 can be seen on the helmet worn by William H. Santelmann (Figure IX-1). This photograph probably dates to 1898, when Santelmann was appointed nineteenth director of the US Marine band.

An unexplained variation of the Type II helmet plate is this all-white metal, perhaps nickel-plated B151 emblem. There are no traces of gold color on the anchor, cable, and continents as required by the Uniform Regulations. It has a good patina and does not appear to be modern plating. The original attachment method included three sets of double-strand wires. These were removed and replaced by a single-strand "U"-shaped brass wire soldered to the inside and center of the globe. This enigma might simply be an unfinished finding or a conversion for some unknown function. The lack of curvature suggests a dress saddlecloth rather than helmet ornament.

Col. Henry Clay Cochrane wore this emblem and associated dress helmet with red buffalo hair plume, and it is now a part of the collection of USMCHCQV (see Figure IX-4). The heavily tarnished solid silver eagle and gold-plated anchor, cable, and continents conform to Type III emblems struck from the same die as the B147 enlisted emblem.

According to Richard Long, Type III B152 was manufactured by Karl William Breuninger. Richard Long, while interviewing a Breuninger family descendent, got permission to photograph the group of Breuninger-made officer emblems seen in appendix B.[14] The officer emblems shown to Long were in a small metal candy box. They had come down through the family as examples of Karl Breuninger's work. Long had this photo taken as a part of his research that resulted in the critical publication on the first Marine Corps eagle, globe, and anchor emblem, which appeared in the United States Naval Institute *Proceedings*.[15]

By far the most distinctive helmet plate in this chapter is B153, an oversized solid silver Chinese-or Japanese-made emblem. Like B151, it does not conform to the requirement for silver and gold elements. There are no traces of gold. In addition to it being an excellent strike, it exhibits skilled handcrafted effects, such as engraving and special enhancing of details. Both the emblem and the four long attaching wires, silver soldered to the reverse eagle wing tips, anchor stock and anchor crown, are solid silver with a good patina. The unique ornament is not curved, suggesting the possibility of use as a dress saddlecloth ornament instead of a helmet plate.

B153

The most interesting and unusual features of B153 are the four Chinese or Japanese characters contained in two rectangular back-marks or chop marks stamped into the reverse of the emblem at the anchor crown (see Figure IX-5). Dr. John Brunner and his colleague Jim Zakhar, both knowledgeable in reading Chinese, kindly provided a translation of the four characters as "Zhu Yin Yi Bao."[16] Brunner and Zakhar translate this to mean, "vessel treasure made of pure silver." They were inclined to think that this particular set of characters may be Japanese. B154 was purchased in Southern California by Mark Kasal, along with a group of other US Marine items. The extremely well made, all-silver emblem could have simply been a theatre-made officer's helmet plate or more likely a flat dress saddlecloth ornament that for some reason did not conform to the Uniform Regulations. Alternatively, all the gold plate may simply be worn away. This seems unlikely in view of the lack of obvious wear on any of the details of the emblem.

In the US Marine Corps photographic collection at the Washington Yard in July 2003, an excellent black-and-white print was found of a large unique eagle, globe, and anchor device that was presumably an officer's helmet plate (see B154 black and white photo). The print had on the back the attribution, "Cap ornament designed by Mr. William Breuninger," Defense Department Marine Corps #515357 RWM." This photo is the only example of this particular device the author has encountered.

B154

Figure IX-5 Chinese or Japanese back-marks on B153, reverse.

It bears some faint similarity to another black and white photo of John Phillip Sousa's band director's baton surmounted by a similar large eagle, globe, and anchor device that was donated to the USMCHCQV collections by Sousa's daughters. The emblem on Sousa's baton may be one of a kind. The black and white photo of B154 may be an example of one of the emblems from a group of photos that were especially prepared for the Louisiana Exposition at the 1904 World's Fair in St. Louis. The 1904 Louisiana Exposition photos that included Marine emblems have not been found, despite recent efforts to locate them at the National Archives.[17]

Officers wore B155 in the corners of the field saddlecloth from 1904 until at least 1917. Joseph H. Pendelton in a 1913

National Archives photo is seen mounted with the field saddlecloth and the bronze emblem conforming to B155 or perhaps a minor variant (see B155 appendix C-1). Photographs confirm that these bronze saddlecloth ornaments were not worn in port and starboard pairs as B156. Four brass wire attachments were soldered to the reverse of the eagle wing tips, the anchor crown, and the anchor stock. This is a more practical attachment method than the dysfunctional 1898 screw post. Double brass wire attachments in a "U" shape are also known. In over twenty years of research, the author can only recall having seen one other example of the bronze saddlecloth ornament. This second example was Type III (B152) with incised ironwork on the anchor stock.

First mentioned in the 1917 Uniform Regulations, B156 is a port and starboard set of russet-colored leather field saddlecloth emblems, see Figure IX-6. They were worn in the rear corners of the field saddlecloth until about 1937 when they were dropped from the Uniform Regulations. They can be seen in period photos well into the mid-1930s. Jacob Gminder, in his circa 1900 die catalog, mentioned that his dies were used to make both metal and leather items.[18] The backs were padded with grey felt and sewn to the saddlecloth. The B156 set was removed from the original saddlecloth before it was purchased by Ed Wages.

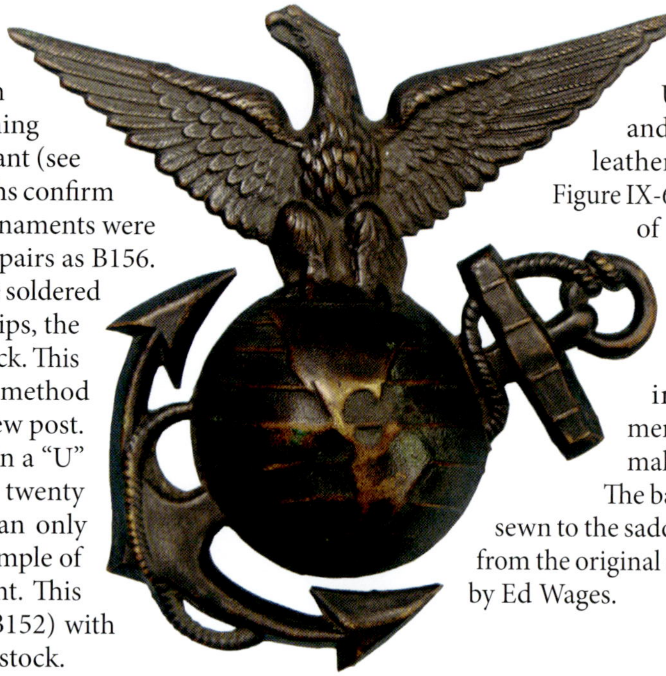

B155

B156

B157

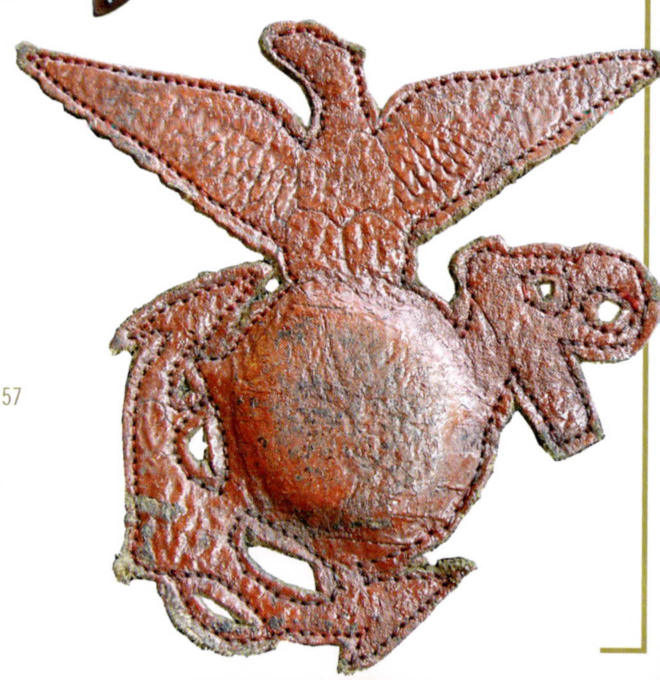

The date of the adoption of the officer's dress saddlecloth ornaments of red leather is uncertain. B157, from the collection of John Driscoll, is one of only two examples of the red leather dress saddlecloth emblem set that the author has encountered. The B157 set was photographed on the dress saddlecloth of navy blue cloth trimmed with red leather. It is included in this chapter even though it may actually date post-WWI. Prior to the red leather ornament, the silver-and-gold helmet plate was attached to the corners of the dress saddlecloth. The author is aware of at least two photos showing the silver-and-gold helmet plate on the dress saddlecloth, but has not found a single photograph clearly showing the red leather port and starboard set.

Figure IX-6
B156 Field saddlecloth ornaments worn by Gen. John Lejeune.

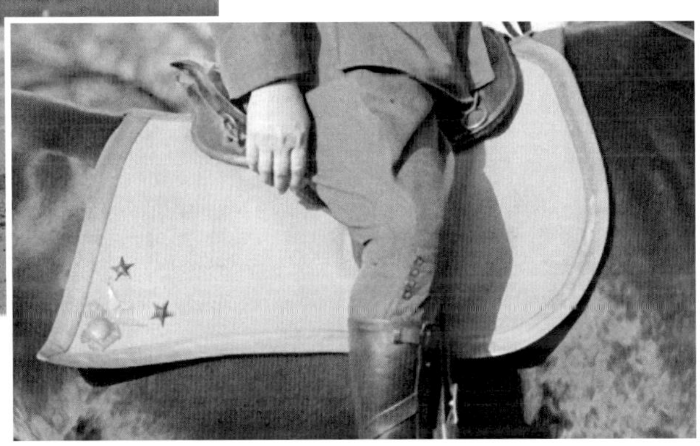

CHAPTER X

Enlisted Headgear Emblems: Early Twentieth Century

(B158 to B172)

This chapter includes a wide variety of enlisted ornaments worn first on the new 1897 pattern cap and then the 1898 campaign hat. Other varieties in this chapter were worn on the subsequent dress, undress, full dress, and khaki headgear of enlisted Marines described in the 1900, 1904, and 1908 Uniform Regulations. An excellent description of this evolution of Enlisted Marine headgear with superb photos can be found in Tulkoff.[1] Unlike the earlier thin emblems with wire attachments described in chapter 8, the devices in chapter 10 were first struck in 1898 from the heavier gauge gilders metal #14, first specified in the 1900 Uniform Regulations.[2] In addition, all headgear ornaments after 1898 have, for attachment purposes, a brazed screw post (usually thirty-two turns per inch). These important emblem changes are consistent with the changes in the pattern 1897 enlisted cap, which has an eyelet specifically for attaching an emblem with a screw post.[3] Issuing the new cap began approximately concurrent with the first issues of the new emblem in 1898. After 1898, enlisted headgear emblems of gilders metal #14 with screw post attachments became the standard issue

This classification is probably inadequate for describing all the known variations. The use of different trimming and piercing tools, as well as worn-out dies and normal wear on the emblems, make it difficult to define formal types based on objective criteria. It was relatively inexpensive for a manufacturer in those days to prepare new dies, piercing and trimming tools to replace or supplement older worn or broken tools and dies. All these factors may help to explain the known wide variation seen in emblems at this time. Finally, it is known that the William Horstmann Company was not the only manufacturer selling enlisted emblems to the Marine Corps in the time period covered by chapter 10.

The classification used is an effort to define types based on explicit die and alloy variations with a consideration of some of the fascinating modifications performed by Marines themselves on the emblems as originally manufactured. Associations with other datable artifacts such as dress caps and uniform lots, can be helpful but are often problematic and have to be viewed with caution since anyone can stick anything on an old cap to increase its value. The uncertainty of dating emblems from this period means that the actual dating may not strictly follow the succession of the B numbers in chapter 10. Some of the emblems in chapter 10 continued in use but in small numbers up through WWI. It is likely that the new types of enlisted cap ornaments covered in subsequent chapters began appearing perhaps as early as 1912, and later when the significant Marine Corps uniform changes initiated in 1912 were eventually implemented.

The first of three distinct types of enlisted emblems for this period share a strong family resemblance to earlier thin emblems with wire attachments covered in chapter 8. The William Horstmann Company may have provided the lions share of the first three distinct types. These have been graphically and collectively referred to by some in the emblem collecting community as the "squat-legged eagle" emblem. Although they display strong similarities, a closer examination indicates a pattern of at least three distinct die variations, possibly more. Old photographs are almost always sufficiently out of focus to prevent confidently identifying the details of cap emblems. Nevertheless, the overall similarity of B158, B159, and B161 certainly suggests a single manufacturer.

On the basis of Quartermaster records copied by Alec Tulkoff from the National Archives for the year 1898 and shared with the author, it is clear that the William Horstmann Company was the sole provider of both cap and helmet ornaments that year.[4] The data summarize the numbers received. The total cap emblems received exceeds the end strength of enlisted Marines in 1898.[5]

Wm. Horstmann Co.
Cap Emblems and Helmet Plates Received
Quartermaster Receiving Records
1898

Date	Cap Ornaments	Helmet Ornaments
9 April	2	
26 May	1,200 old	1,200 new
4 June	300	
11 June	988	
16 June	2,175 new	
18 June	1,212 old	
28 June	145	
9 July	145	
TOTAL	4,967	2,400

To avoid potential confusion with other emblems with similar "squat-legged eagle" features, B158, B159, and B161 are referred to instead as the Samar Types I, II, and III. Besides having a strong family resemblance, they are distinct from other similar "squat-legged eagle" emblems in chapter 10.

Of all the emblems included in this chapter, B158 Samar Type I is the only emblem so far that has good documentary evidence of a Marine who actually wore it and when. Accession records at the USMCHCQV indicate that B158 was donated to the Quantico collection by the immediate family of Pvt. Charles R. Morgan, who served in the Marine Corps briefly from January 1900 until September 1902.[6] USMC muster rolls document Morgan's service on Samar and Cavite Philippine Islands from April 1901 until his early discharge in September 1902. This is a rare example of an emblem with a documented brief window of use by an identified Marine. The Samar Types I, II, and III (B158, B159, and B161) are representative of a common type and in all likelihood were manufactured exclusively by William Horstmann. One or more of the three types may well represent the bulk of the 5,483 cap emblems issued in the year ending June 30, 1899.[7] The Marine Corps Quartermaster in 1899 paid William Horstmann eleven cents each for the new cap emblem of guilders metal #14 with the new screw posts. Horstmann's charge for the older thinner cap emblem with two wires for attachment (B135 and B136) in 1895 was three cents.[8]

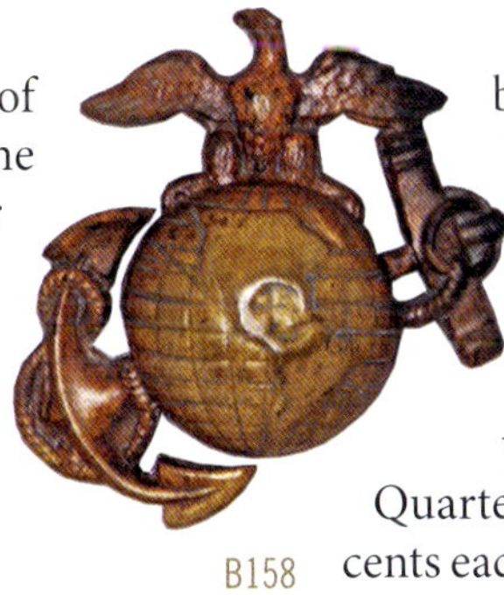

B158

The most distinguishing features of B158 are the few large secondary feathers in the eagle's wings and only two rows of secondary feathers on the eagle's left wing.

With the Industrial Revolution came dramatic increases in the power of machinery. Steam power replaced the earlier, primitive, manual labor, drop process. By the end of the Nineteenth Century, even more powerful electrical presses, such as the coin press in Fig. # X-1, gave insignia manufacturers greater efficiency and speed. Emblems of heavier gauge and displaying greater detail and higher relief were the result. The electrically driven press in Fig. # X-1 could strike over 1,000 items an hour at a striking pressure of 200 tons. This extraordinary pressure produces so much heat that the press operators has to wear gloves to protect their fingers when handling newly struck coins.

Figure X-1
Late Nineteenth Century High-Powered Die Press

Figure X-2
B158 and B159 enlarged.

B158 is known to be an element of at least one enlisted belt plate.[9] Uniform Regulations 1875 to 1904 do not describe the enlisted brass belt plate. Presumably, they were plain brass as depicted in the illustrations of the 1875 Uniform Regulations. Nevertheless, brass belt plates with an emblem of the Samar Type have periodically shown up on the market. A few belt plates with emblems have also been seen in photos of this period. A good example can be seen in Driscoll.[10]

The Secretary of the Navy Annual Reports for the years 1898 through 1901 give quantities of cap emblems received, issued, and on hand at the end of each fiscal year.[11] The data clearly reflect increased cap emblem procurement to meet the increased number of Marines during the Spanish-American War to 1901. These data also substantiate increased cap emblem procurement to meet the shortages exacerbated by the adoption of the field hat in June 1898 and first issued to Huntington's Battalion in Cuba without emblems.[12] By July of 1900 the authorization of only one cap emblem was changed specifically to meet the need for a second emblem for the new campaign hat.[13] The uniform allocations were again modified in 1904, authorizing up to six emblems for up to six field hats, if necessary.[14] The field hat had obviously replaced the 1897 pattern cap in its overall importance.

Enlisted Cap Ornaments Received, Issued; and On Hand: Annual Report, Secretary of the Navy

Fiscal Year	1898	1899	1900	1901
On hand July 1	not reported	2,286	2,783	633
Received from contractors	7,000			
Received from all sources	7,058	6,623	3,333	9,336
Total issued	5,887	6,126	5,483	8,463
On hand 30 June	2,286	2,783	633	1,506

Several minor features indicate that a different die was used for striking the B159 Samar Type II emblem, see Figure X-2. Such close similarity in the dies suggests that the probable manufacturer was William Horstmann. It is not known if they were used contemporaneously. Other manufacturers may have been supplying the Marine Corps with emblems at this approximate time period, but not with anywhere near the quantity supplied by Horstmann. As a rule of thumb, it is assumed that there will be greater variation seen in emblems that are made by different manufacturers. Of literally hundreds of B158 and B159 emblems the author has seen, none were back-marked.

Many examples of customized, or salted, emblems are known from this time period. B160 is simply a modified version of the emblem struck from the Type I Samar B158 die. The usual treatment to give a salty appearance was to cut the left wing of the eagle away from the upper anchor stock and bend both wings upward to give it a swept wing effect. The bending invariably stresses and distorts the details, especially the feathering and wing shape of the original die-struck pattern. The author has never seen an example of a die-struck emblem with upswept wings that was not clearly a cut and stressed modification. To the author's knowledge, no known die-struck examples with upswept wings exist. There is a wide range of ingenious modifications, including hand stippling of the oceans as well as grinding and polishing effects to give the emblem a distinctive salty appearance.

The enlisted cap and pre-1904 campaign hat emblem B161 is referred to as Samar Type III. It is struck from the same, or an extremely similar, die used to strike the thinner enlisted cap emblems in Chapter VIII. Having more than one die would facilitate increased production. Recycling the die used to strike the soon-to-be-obsolete white

B159

metal Horstmann shoulder knot emblems would be another way to increase production or replace worn-out dies. The obvious difference between B161 and the thinner versions in chapter 8 is the heavy gilders metal #14 and the thirty-two turns per inch screw post. Note the distinct pattern of many small secondary and tertiary feathers of the wings of the eagle. These obvious differences, unlike the more subtle differences between B158 and B159, do not have to be enlarged to be easily seen. Given the previously cited Quartermaster correspondence from 1898 and the Commandant's 1900 Report to the Secretary of the Navy, this minor die variety sharing strong family resemblance to the Samar Types I and II is probably also a William Horstmann production.

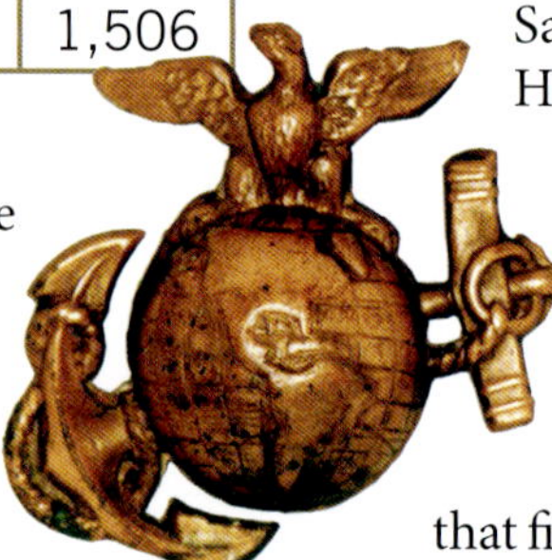

B160

The extreme similarity of B158, B159, and B161 indicates that they are minor variants adopted by the Marine Corps in April of 1898 and convincingly described in Quartermaster correspondence.[15] The Assistant Quartermaster in Philadelphia wrote the Quartermaster USMC in Washington stating that five different cap ornaments had been received from the William Horstmann Co. and that, "Nos. 1 (sic) and 2 are the same quality of metal, No.1 being polished and No.2 plated; Nos. 3 and 4 are the same metal with the same change; No.5 is very much finer grade and will cost more; Nos. 3 and 4 will cost about the same as our present standard. It is struck from No.14 gauge gold (sic) metal, you will notice that the post is much heavier and the thread coarser … I recommend the adoption of Nos. 3 or 4."[16]

B161

Assistant Quartermaster Prince again wrote the Quartermaster on May 12, 1898, stating, "It is the opinion of this office that the No.3 cap ornament had been definitely adopted, and was to be bid for at once."[17]

Compared to the three Samar Types of enlisted cap and campaign hat emblems, everything about B162 is different, indicating in all probability another diesinker and a manufacturer other than William Horstmann. Most noticeable is the shape of the eagle wings, the distinctive shape of the continents, anchor stock, and large anchor crown. It is a type very seldom encountered by the author, suggesting low numbers manufactured probably before 1904. B162 is the actual emblem chosen by John Driscoll for his Figure 34 on page 29 of *The Eagle Globe and Anchor*. Since none are known in bronze this would further suggest a date of manufacture before the 1904 bronze emblems made their first appearance.

B162

Another highly distinctive type of enlisted dress cap and campaign hat emblem is B163, referred to here as the "Deep Feathers Type" because of the excellent strike and the high relief of details, especially seen in the extremely well-struck feathers. Fortunately, an example of B163 is known to be

B163

associated with a lot of items that appeared on eBay. The diverse lot included uniform items, photos, and documents including sergeant chevrons worn by Lewis A. Laws, who enlisted on December 31, 1903.[18] Laws made sergeant before his discharge on December 31, 1907. Lots of diverse items associated with an identified Marine and corroborated by USMC muster rolls are a more reliable means of dating emblems than simple association with old Marine Corps headgear.

The B163 the "Deep Feathers Type" is also associated with a variety of enlisted undress and full dress headgear dating 1897 to 1912. Some of these associations may be dubious, but it is improbable that all are anachronistic associations.

A die variant of the deep feathers enlisted dress cap emblem can be seen, especially in the eagle wings of B164. At first it was thought that this variation was simply the function of a different trimming tool rather than a different die. But the details of the eagle wing feathering categorically indicate a different die. B164 has fewer primary feathers and other clear differences that could not simply be the result of using a different trimming tool. By comparison to B163, the B164 die variety is seldom encountered and to date is not known to occur in the post-1904 bronze emblems.

B164

In keeping with the assumption that radical differences in design probably indicate different manufacturers, B165 has hardly anything in common with the other enlisted emblems in chapter 10. It is referred to as the "Lazy M Eagle Wing Type." B165 has shown up on the 1905 pattern and later enlisted headgear. One specimen, found in the collection of Joe Lowry, a long-time reputable collector who started collecting at the end of WWII, has a "Made in England" back-mark on an applied rectangular tab. It is quite likely that B165 is the emblem sold to the Marine Corps Quartermaster by J.R. Gaunt and mentioned in the Index of Quartermaster Correspondence files in the National archives.[19] The actual J.R. Gaunt letter was reported missing in 1997 and could not be located in a search conducted again in 2010. Without the actual correspondence, all we know is that J.R. Gaunt sold enlisted dress cap emblems to the Marine Corps in the 1907 to 1908 time frame. A second example of B165 that recently surfaced in the collection of Michael Manifor has the same rarely encountered "Made in England" back-mark on a raised rectangular tab on the anchor crown reverse. B165 has to be considered the enigmatic J.R. Gaunt production mentioned in the index of USMC Quartermaster Correspondence. Since it is also known in bronze (B171), it is quite likely to have been a small purchase item for the USMC Quartermaster after 1904.

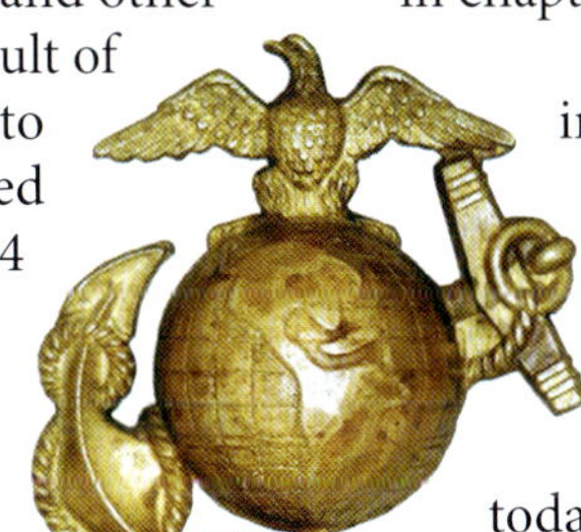

B165

There is no reason to think that the Marine Corps ever contracted for cast enlisted cap emblems at this or any other time period. B166 is obviously a casting where something close to B165 was used as the model. It is included in this inventory to show the obvious differences between a casting and a die-struck emblem. B165 was not simply used as the model for casting B166. Note the differences especially seen in the cartography of the two emblems. The absence of a screw post and the presence of a clasp type pin assembly for attachment are common characteristics of sweetheart pins.

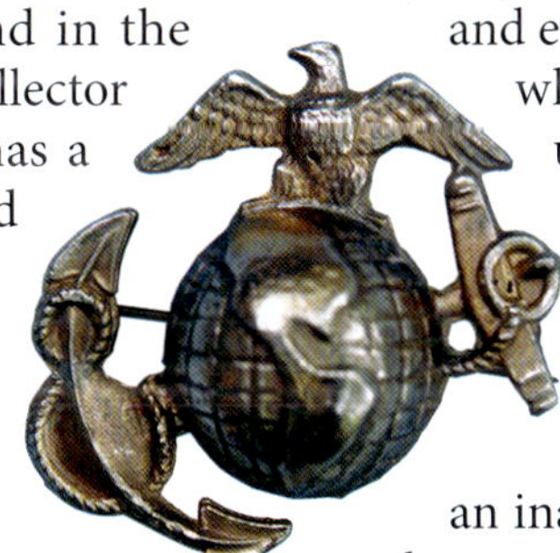

B166

White Metal Emblems on Enlisted Headgear

Before moving on to enlisted bronze service cap and campaign hat emblems, it would be appropriate at this point to revisit a subject that was introduced back in chapter 8. The issue of white metal emblems that commonly occur on enlisted headgear needs to be discussed in the context of important uniform changes that occurred in the period 1897 to 1912. A discussion of the problem of white metal headgear emblems is more appropriate here in chapter 10.

Up to 1904, the Uniform Regulations were explicit in specifying or implying brass emblems exclusively for all caps and field hats. It seems unlikely that a mix of white and yellow metal elements would have been authorized on enlisted headgear at any time. A more likely explanation for the common occurrence of white metal emblems appearing today on enlisted headgear is that the huge surplus of white metal emblems made obsolete by 1905 has probably over the years been mistakenly put on authentic headgear by surplus sellers, collectors, family members of old Marines, and even museum curators, etc., without realizing that white metal emblems were inappropriate. Being unaware of the proper function of white metal emblems, it is perhaps understandable that emblems so similar in all respects, except the alloy, would be mistakenly put on headgear by many including ill-informed or dishonest sellers hoping to get top dollar for an authentic cap with an inappropriate emblem. Old black and white period photos only add to the problem; one cannot readily distinguish white metal from brass in these photos.

Consider the facts that the white metal emblems were both obsolete and abundant and no longer needed by the Marine Corps after 1905. That is also the case with the 1897 and 1904 patterns of all types of enlisted caps. Tulkoff clearly describes the interesting evolution of enlisted headgear between 1898 and 1912.[20] All these obsolete varieties of headgear probably went on the surplus market just as the earlier glut of white metal emblems did when the new enlisted caps and field hats were adopted in 1912.[21] These major changes in enlisted headgear meant that enlisted Marines were eventually issued the new 1912 pattern cap and field hat while the obsolete varieties of headgear, as with the obsolete white metal emblem, were added to the redundancy of unneeded government surplus on the market.

There is no reason to think that this was the same case with the brass and bronze cap emblems discussed in chapter 10. On the contrary, there is very good reason to think that the older brass and bronze emblems continued to be used up to their exhaustion in the supply system and even beyond that time by some old salts who hung on to their old emblems. This observation on white metal emblems and the various enlisted caps becoming obsolete but not the earlier brass and bronze emblems helps to explain why the emblem types covered in chapter 10 continue to commonly show up in photographs and on later headgear right up to and even after WWI. Given this pattern in uniform changes, many obsolete caps would have ended up in surplus inventories and collections without their original emblems simply because the emblems, unlike the expendable caps, were not obsolete and continued to be worn on new headgear. A large number of obsolete white metal emblems available and a large number of obsolete caps available without emblems would present the opportunity for many collectors, surplus dealers, and even museum curators to expediently use what was easily available and put these common white metal emblems on surplus headgear lacking emblems.

An interesting alternative explanation for at least some white metal emblems has to be considered. The dramatic increase in the size of the Marine Corps at the time of the Spanish-American War and the numerous uniform changes of the period before 1912 would have created a need for more emblems. The increased requirement would have produced critical shortages of emblems. Emblem shortages may have made it expedient for Marines to use whatever was available. The more plentiful white metal emblems may have been recycled to meet the shortage of brass emblems, especially on the new campaign hats. This expedient might apply to some cases, but certainly not to the preponderance of old headgear with white metal emblems seen today on the emblem market and in museums.

What made the author consider this latter possibility was finding a white metal emblem (B143) on the 1898 pattern campaign hat worn by Smedley D. Butler during the Chinese relief expedition. The campaign hat with emblem (Smithsonian #C168) was donated by Mrs. Butler along with a collection of her husband's uniform items.[22] These Butler items were transferred from the Smithsonian Institution to the Marine Corps History Center Quantico in 2006.[23] Whether this B143 emblem is actually Butler's is an open question. Officers bought their dress hat emblems. These by comparison to enlisted cap emblems were quite expensive. It is conceivable that Smedley Butler chose to put a less expensive, readily available white metal eagle, globe, and anchor emblem on his 1898 pattern campaign hat instead of his more expensive silver and gold expertly crafted dress cap emblem. On the one hand, the author is aware of at least one photo from this same time period clearly shows the more expensive silver-and-gold officer's emblem on his field hat. On the other hand, there are plenty of old photographs proving that some officers wore enlisted emblems, especially on field headgear. The uncertainty about white metal emblems on campaign hats forces one to keep an open mind. The unauthorized and expedient use of enlisted white metal emblems on campaign hats by a few does not detract from the separate issue of so many white metal enlisted emblems inappropriately put on other enlisted caps of this period.

B167

In 1904, the Marine Corps adopted bronze buttons as well as bronze emblems for both officer and enlisted field hats (campaign cover) and khaki cap covers.[24] Prior to this change in the Uniform Regulations, buttons, emblems, company letters, and battalion numbers were made of brass. B167 is the service version of the B158 Samar Type I but struck in bronze instead of brass. As with the B158 emblem in brass, B167 in bronze, was most likely manufactured by William Horstmann.

The less frequently encountered bronze service cap emblem B168 appears to be struck from the same die as the "Many Small Feathers" Samar Type III brass emblem B161. Note the distinct pattern of many small feathers in multiple rows on the eagle wings and the characteristic shape of the head and neck of the eagle. Unlike the earlier thin-stamped B137 with two wire attachments described in Chapter VIII, B168 is struck from a heavier bronze plate with a screw post attachment. The bronze plate categorically dates the emblem post 1904. This heavier bronze plate may also be a correlate of hard soldering screw post attachments to the inside center of the globe. It is curious that B168 weighs twice as much as the thin-stamped B137 in chapter 8, but is only about half the weight of the other bronze emblems in chapter 10. Despite these variations, it is clear that two, possibly all three, Samar types were produced in both brass and bronze.

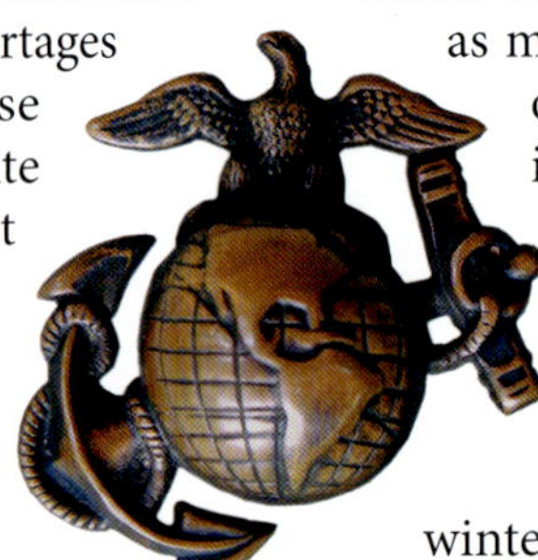
B168

B168, along with the other bronze emblems in this chapter, would have typically been worn with the field hat, summer service khaki, and later winter service green caps at least up through WWI. It is likely that new enlisted service cap ornaments were brought into service about 1912 or 1914, certainly by 1917. Unlike the 1905 pattern caps and 1898 pattern field hats that became obsolete in 1912, the enlisted cap emblems covered in chapter 10 continued to be worn on the new headgear for as long as supplies lasted. There is nothing in the Uniform Regulations of this period that indicates that enlisted cap emblems were company property that had to be turned in at the end of a Marine's enlistment. Because of their relative expense, the large enlisted helmet plates 1892 to 1905, the earlier plates worn on the dress hats 1859 to 1892, as well as enlisted shoulder knots, were government property, not the property of the Marine.[25] In fact, Marine Corps Orders state that enlisted Marines who shipped over were allowed to wear the older emblems that had been issued to them.[26]

The deep feathers bronze emblem B169 is simply the bronze version of B163 struck in brass. This emblem was first worn on the khaki cap and campaign hats, and then was adopted for use on the enlisted service greens uniform that was ultimately issued sometime after 1912. It is not uncommon to see it associated with uniform lots up to and possibly beyond WWI. It is curious that a service bronze emblem conforming to B172 shows up in a photo of John Lejeune wearing the pattern 1898 campaign hat. The photo probably dates about 1904 to about 1910; see B169 in appendix C-1. The focus of this photo is not clear enough to tell if the emblem is actually B169 or an officer's version of B169 with applied continents. There are no known B169 emblems with applied continents. It is more likely that the photo depicts a not unknown example of an officer wearing an enlisted cap emblem. A single example of B169 is known from some 31 later bronze eagle, globe, and anchor enlisted cap emblems found by Gilles Lagin, George Bailey, and others from America Expeditionary Forces (AEF) 1918 French battlefields context.[27]

B169

B171

Missing from this inventory is a bronze version of the B164 gilt variant with short eagle wings. Since all the dies for the emblems described in chapter 10 seem to have been used to strike both brass and bronze emblems, B170 quite likely exists. Therefore, a "B" Number has been assigned as a placeholder. The author would greatly appreciate having the opportunity to include B170 in an update of this publication.

As with other upswept eagle wing varieties, B171 is a purposely modified example of the unaltered B169. It has been customized by cutting, bending, and stippling to give it a salty appearance. Characteristic of all the enlisted emblems of this time period, there are no back-marks. It is plain bronze with no indication of a lacquer finish.

B172

The final emblem in chapter 10 is the bronze service version of the brass B165. It has a dark brown lacquer finish. The date of its first appearance is unknown. It is probably the J. R. Gaunt emblem mentioned in the lost 1908 Marine Corps Quartermaster correspondence. As expected, this type was gradually replaced by the extremely common enlisted emblems of the 1912 to WWI period. One example of B172 was found in the recent AEF 1918 French field collection of emblems found by Gilles Lagin, George Bailey, and others.[28]

CHAPTER XI

Officer Emblems: Early Twentieth Century

(B173 to B193)

The emblems of this period worn on the officer's dress cap are chronologically divided into two groups. The first and smallest group, B173 to B176, based on information from the Uniform Regulations and especially early photos of identified Marine officers, are dress cap emblems with a date of manufacture from approximately 1898 to probably no later than 1904. The second and largest group, B177 to B193, share the distinct and well-documented features of dress cap and epaulette devices that first appear in the explicit 1904 Uniform Regulations.

A Period of Significant Change and Extraordinary Variety

The year 1904 is the watershed of officer emblems. The significant changes in details and measurements spelled out that year basically defined all officer's cap, collar, and epaulette emblems from that date on. It is usually an easy matter separating officer emblems that were manufactured after 1904. It is not easy to determine the period of use of cap and epaulet emblems, since many emblems continued to be used by officers throughout their career. As a corollary to this, one should also be cautious in remembering that all emblems with the distinct 1904 features are not necessarily that old.

Figure XI-1
Gen. Alexander Vandergrift.

Consequently, the dating emphasis in this classification is placed on specifications and important changes in the Uniform Regulations complemented by useful photographs that can be identified and dated. The dating scheme presented here does not necessarily correlate one to one with the actual period of use. With the exception of the post-1926 service collar ornaments and the full dress epaulette ornaments, there was really no requirement for officers to stop wearing their old emblems until 1965.[1] Consider also that a date according to Uniform Regulation specifications is not the same as a date of manufacture and nowhere close to those cases where emblems were worn throughout an officer's career. Figure XI-1 shows Commandant Alexander Vandergrift wearing what is likely his 1909 commissioning dress cap emblem in a photo dated no earlier than January 1944.

This chapter introduces a significant variety of officer emblems for a relatively short period. It should be a good representative sample but is admittedly and woefully incomplete. Manufacturers during this period were known to have offered to Marine officers a variety of options. These options ranged from very expensive to inexpensive and help to understand the great variety of officer's emblems that continue to appear on the market today. Below are excerpts from the catalogs of just two manufacturers. Copies of these catalogs were kindly provided to the author by Ray Darida. If this level of variation is evident with just two manufacturers, one can only imagine the amount of variation among all known manufacturers of this time period.

Excerpt From
V.T. Blackinton Price List, ca.1918

Miscellaneous Insignia

Plate No. Style No. Article Price

1. 100 MC Marine Corps Officers Cap Device
Bronze .50 Ea.
Gold and Silver Plate .50 Ea.
Sterling Silver 1.50 Ea
Bronze with superimposed continents .75 Ea

Gold and Silver Plate with superimposed continents .75 Ea
Gold and Sterling with superimposed continents 4.85 Ea

4. 200 MC Marine Corps Officers Collar Devices
Bronze .60 Pr.
Gold and Silver Plate .60 Pr.
Sterling Silver 1.50 Pr.
Bronze with superimposed continents 1.00 Pr
Gold and Silver Plate with superimposed continents 1.00 Pr
Gold and Sterling with superimposed continents 5.75 Pr.

For 5c extra the above insignia would be in genuine fire bronze.

Excerpt From N.S. Meyer 1918 Catalog[2]

Marine Corps Insignia

Officers Cap Device EachOfficer's Collar Device Pair

No. 306 – Bronze $ .75 No.301—Bronze $ .85
F306 – Fire Bronze .85 F311 – Fire Bronze 1.00
RB306 Real Bronze 1.50 RB 311 – Real Bronze 1.75
Gold and Silver Plate .85 P311- Gold and Silver Plate 1.50
S 306- Sterling Silver 1.50 S311 – Sterling Silver 1.75
G306 –Solid Gold and Silver 5.00 G311- Solid Gold and Silver 6.00

The author gave up trying to put together a comprehensive inventory of this diversity. The extraordinary variety known has implications for serious collectors and sellers. Unlike the rigid standardization of emblems today, there was at this time period, on the part of the Marine Corps, a tolerance of wide variation. This tolerance was also extended to a lesser degree to enlisted emblems. This earlier tolerance for diversity was somewhat curtailed in 1937 when some standardization was attempted. The traditional tolerance of the old days was brought to an end with the adoption of the current style of Marine Corps emblem with precise specifications and rigid uniformity. This story will be taken up in volume 2.

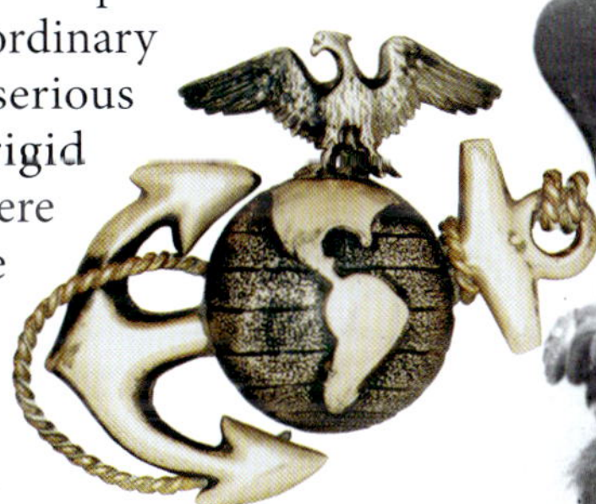

B173

B174

Breuninger and Similar Late Nineteenth Century Officer Dress Cap Emblems

The solid silver and solid gold dress cap ornament B173 is a masterpiece of the military jeweler's art. The style of the eagle, especially the superb hand chasing, engraving and stippling, strongly suggests the craftsmanship of Karl Breuninger. Compare B173, especially the eagle, with the known Breuninger-made emblems illustrated in appendix B. The details of the separate elements show wonderfully intricate hand craftsmanship. The continents seem to be cut by hand from a thin sheet of solid gold. The hand engraving is exquisite and can be seen in the fine details of the eagle feathers and especially the remarkably artistic touch of hand engraving eyes on both sides of the eagle's turned head, giving it a sensational three-dimensional effect.

B173 was photographed and described through the courtesy of a colleague who preferred to remain anonymous but had put together one of the most extraordinary collections of Marine Corps emblems the author has ever encountered. The emblem was on a dress cover purchased from the John Twiggs Meyers estate.

A characteristic feature of Breuninger-made officer's cap emblems for dress caps was the rectangular tab that attached the free-standing eagle to the inside and center of the globe (see Figure IV-1). Another archaic feature characteristic of officer emblems seen in photos of this period is the shape of the anchor arms, more like the letter "U" turned on its side rather than the letter "C." The means of attachment for B173 was a silver drop-in pin assembly, which is the more common attachment for cap emblems of this period, despite a few known examples of screw posts after 1898.

A date of manufacture between 1900 and 1904 is based not only on similarity to dated photographs where this general type can be recognized, but more importantly on the dimensions and measurements summarized in appendix A. B173 conforms best to Figures 5 and 7, rather than the post-1904 Figure 9.

Figure XI-2
Smedley D. Butler, B174.

Photos of emblems manufactured before 1904 give the immediate impression of a huge anchor. This is just an illusion because of the relatively smaller globe and eagle compared to the increases in the size of the globe and eagle that were established after 1904.

A good example of the diversity in these very early twentieth century officer dress cap emblems of skilled craftsmanship, B174 is probably also from the shops of Karl Breuninger. There is obvious similarity to B173 in the eagle, the globe, and the rectangular attachment tag. It is also solid silver and solid gold construction. The continents also seem to be cut by hand from a thin sheet of solid gold. The pattern of hand engraving and stippling differs significantly from B173, suggesting the work of more than a single craftsman. The emblem in Figure XI-2 worn by Maj. Smedley D. Butler in a photo dated 1910 conforms very well to B174.

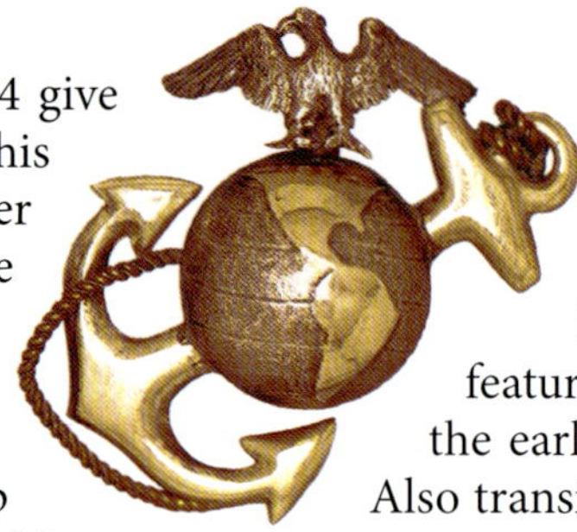

B175

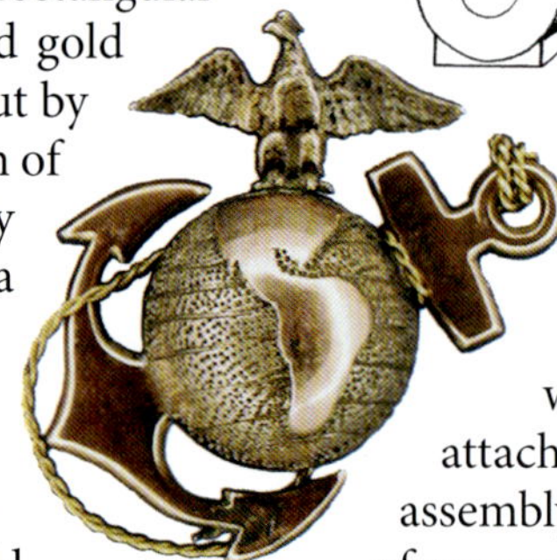

B176

Another exceptional feature of craftsmanship is the compound construction of the solid gold anchor. It consists of two separate pieces, a semi-round upper element and a flat gold sheet on the bottom. The bottom flat sheet on the reverse is pierced with a hole that indicates clearly that it is solid gold not gold-plated. Unlike B173, the means of attachment is a very long silver screw post hard-soldered to a rectangular bar that is in turn attached to the inside of the silver globe. The bar with the attached screw post is surprisingly intricate, consisting of two layers. The top layer with attached screw post is silver, but under it is a gold layer. The two layers are clad together. The cable is gold-plated, two-strand brass wires.

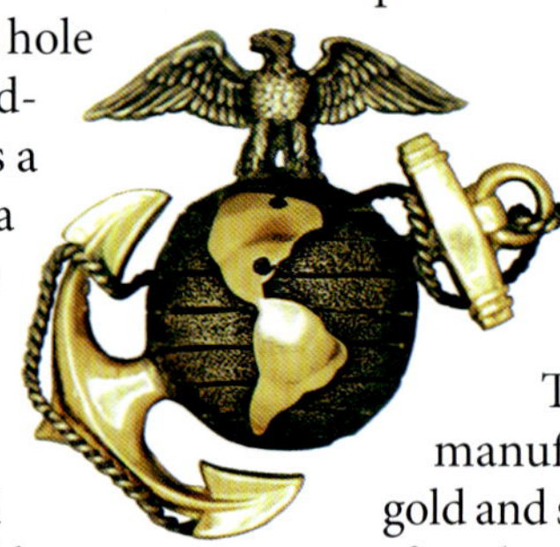

B177

A third and distinct variety of the turn-of-the-century Breuninger type silver and gold dress cap emblem is B175. It has, in addition to the distinctive Breuninger rectangular silver bar attaching the eagle to the inside of the globe, a large anchor with a distinct shape. These features differ significantly from both B173 and B174. Like B173 and B174, it displays many handcrafted features such as engraving and chasing seen especially in the hand-engraved lines of latitude and the extremely long eagle beak. Unlike B173 and B174, the means of attachment is a screw post.

The author has examined other variants of B173 and B174, but these are not included in this photographic inventory. Most of the variants have pin assemblies for attachment and show wide variation in the anchor, anchor stock, and fluke shapes indicative again of individual hand-craftsmanship. Further examples of these very late nineteenth and very early twentieth century emblem variations can be clearly seen in early photos. It is almost as if no two emblems were exactly the same.

Stylistically, B176 is unlike the probable Breuninger emblems described above. The shapes of the eagle, anchor, and continents are so different as to suggest another manufacturer or diesinker. It displays exquisite workmanship in crafted details on solid gold and silver. The anchor consists of two separate elements welded together. A bottom flat silver element is attached to a raised upper element in solid gold, giving it a hollow and half-rounded effect. A transitional feature is the eagle hard-soldered to the globe without the earlier Breuninger rectangular tag for attachment. Also transitional are the measurements of the anchor and globe, which conform more to the 1904 specifications than the earlier emblems with their relatively large anchors and reduced size globes (see appendix A, Figures 5, 7, and 9). As with most officer cap emblems of this period, the attachment is by means of a simple drop-in silver pin assembly, see Figure XI-3. Also characteristic is the absence of any maker's marks. Because of the archaic features and especially the "U"-shaped anchor arms, it is included in the pre-1904 group.

Figure XI-3
Drop-in pin assembly, B176.

Early Bailey, Banks & Biddle Dress Cap Ornaments

Typically the most expensive emblem that a manufacturer offered was a dress cap emblem of solid gold and silver. B177 is a superb example of the craftsmanship of Bailey, Banks, and Biddle. There exists a considerable variety of dress cap emblems of this style with and perhaps without BB&B back-marks. The distinctive BB&B style emblem can be identified readily in some old photos. These were probably started in 1904 in response to the important changes spelled out in detail in the Uniform Regulations dated that year.[3] Solid gold (10 and 14K) and silver dress cap emblems are described in the BB&B 1907 catalog with princely prices of eight and ten dollars, respectively.[4] B177 displays several handcrafted effects including uniquely shaped continents, probably hand cut. Note the uncomplicated (straight) cable between the anchor flukes and the aperture between the eagle's legs. These handcrafted features distinguish this early BB&B creation from their later productions that continued up to WWII and probably even later. These later quite distinctive BB&B officer's dress cap emblems should not be lumped with those in this chapter and will be taken up in volume 2.

This research has not found an earlier example of manufacturers using a back-mark. Hallmarks were not required until the National Gold and Silver Stamping Act of 1906 and then only for emblems with gold karat marks. Hallmarks were additional steps in the manufacturing process and involved additional expense. The requirements of the 1906 National Gold and Silver Stamping Act were a way to guarantee the content of gold and silver items. The hallmark was also a

National Gold and Silver Act of 1906

Prior to this law (US Code, Title 15, Chapter 8) US Marine Corps emblems as well as other manufactured items using silver and gold were simply stamped "Gold" and "Silver." Some items in fact were alloys containing very little gold or silver. The 1906 law imposed strict standards and made it illegal to stamp items only with the words "Gold" and "Silver." After 1906, gold items were described with a karat mark, such as 10, 14, or 24K. A silver item could be described as "Sterling" or "Sterling Silver" only if it was 0.925/1000 parts pure silver. If a manufacturer opted to stamp a karat mark, they were required by law to accompany that karat mark with a registered trademark or the name of the manufacturer of the piece. This law generally separates the pre-1906 emblems marked "Silver" and "Gold" from emblems manufactured after 1906.

means of advertising the notion that BB&B was producing the Cadillac of officer emblems. A comparison of the quality of emblems from this period supports this idea. The fact that B177 is back-marked "Sterling" on the eagle right wing reverse indicates a date after 1906.

B178

Given the post-1906 "STERLING" and "BB&B" back-marks, this dress cap emblem was produced by Bailey, Banks, & Biddle sometime after 1906. B178 conforms very well to the illustrated cap ornament seen in Bailey, Banks, and Biddle's 1907 catalog,[5] (see Figure XI -4). Very thin layers of gold are laminated over a brass anchor and over a Sterling silver globe to form applied continents. The very thin lamination indicates a higher degree of craftsmanship than simple gold and silver-plating of a brass base metal. The incised BB&B back-mark has a distinct archaic lettering style. B178 has a fine two-strand silver wire cable and a complex silver clasp type pin assembly for attachment. Originally, this well-worn emblem had a screw post attachment and an anti-twist pin. Both of these were later cut away and replaced with the complex rolling type catch and pivoting pin assembly, (see Figure XI-5). An unusual feature is the complex fouling and unconventional placement of the cable in front of, rather than behind, the eagle and globe.

Figure XI-5
Roll type catch and pivoting pin assembly.

B179

A third variety of the superb early BB&B officer's dress cap emblem also shows many hand-crafted effects in the solid gold and silver construction, the hand-trimming of the super thin gold sheet used for the distinctive applied continents and small "C"-shaped silver links attaching the silver eagle to the silver globe instead of the more conventional hard-soldering specified in the 1904 Uniform Regulations.[6] B174 is also unusual for having a solid gold or gold-plated cylinder to attach the fine two-strand silver wire cable to the lower anchor fluke reverse. These cable attachment cylinders are usually a less expensive alloy. The lines of latitude are hand-engraved. The letters of the BB&B hallmark are stylistically different from B178. They are raised rather than incised. The number 792116 is crudely scratched by hand below the BB&B maker's mark on the anchor crown reverse. The significance of this curious number is unknown. B179 conforms to the dress cap emblem illustrated in the 1912 Uniform Regulations.[7]

Figure XI-4
1907 B178 BB&B catalog

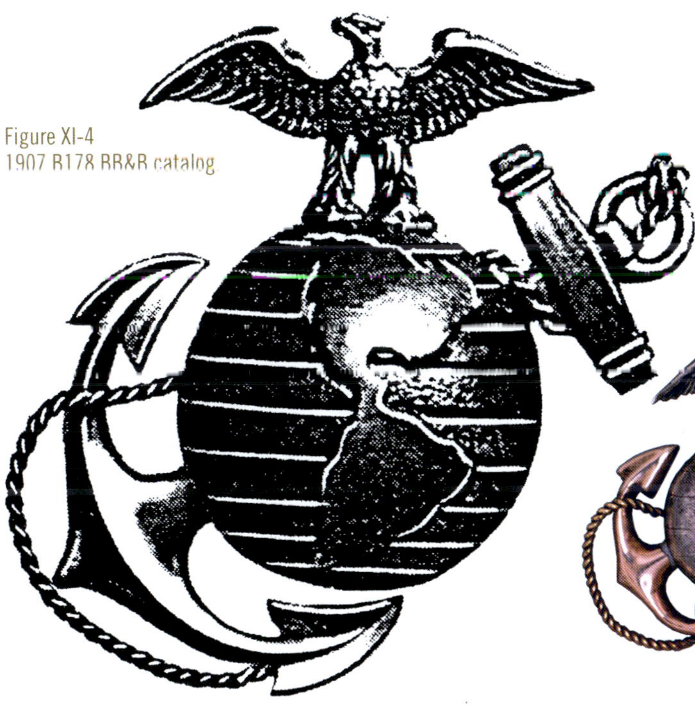

Early Questionable Manufacturers

The group B180, B181, and B182, despite many differences, shares the similarity of an eagle with an obviously large beak and large talons quite unlike the BB&B dress cap emblems. The officer's dress cap emblem B180 is the only one of this distinct type the author has encountered. It is a curious mixture of pre-1900 and post-1904 features. A colleague acquired it along with a matching set of dress collar ornaments (B213) from the estate of Frank J. Schwable, USMC 1900 to 1935.[8] It may well be Schwable's 1900 commissioning set. It has a pre-1904 broad rectangular tag attaching the freestanding eagle to the inside of the globe just under the North Pole

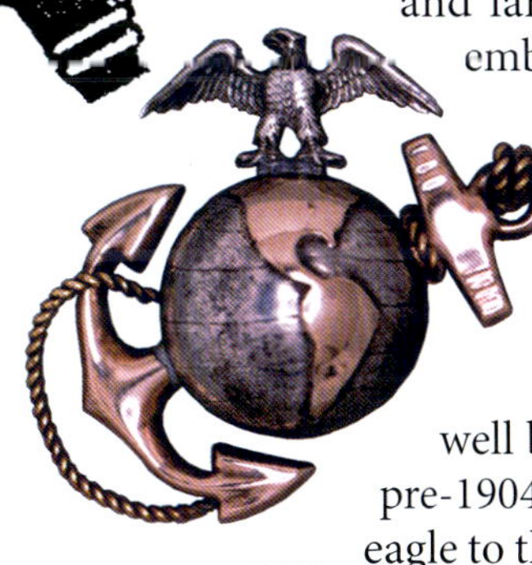

B180

and unlike the earlier Breuninger tag. B180 is entirely different from the earlier Breuninger type dress cap emblems. Several hand-engraved features are evident, such as the lines of latitude and the stippling pattern for the oceans. The hollow anchor is a two- piece construction of both silver and gold similar to B174 and B176. The uniquely shaped continents are gold-plated on the silver globe. Another pre-1904 feature is the more "U"-shaped anchor arms. The absence of back-marks leaves an open question as to who manufactured this distinct dress cap emblem with distinctly shaped gold anchor, continents, and a silver screw post.

B181

The BB&B emblems above, as well as B180, are struck from entirely different dies than B181. Even though the eagles on B180 and B181 are a close match, they are not from the same die. The differences can be seen in the details of the eagle and especially the shape of the continents. With no back-marks, the manufacturer is unknown but the strong similarity to B180 suggests the same manufacturer. B181 is the dress cap version of B195 in bronze. A probable example of B181 can be identified in a photo of James E. Mahoney dating 1904 (see B181 in appendix C-1). Some handcrafted features are also exhibited on B181, such as the fine stippling pattern of the oceans, the solid gold continents and the two-strand fine silver wire cable. The type was probably produced from 1904 to possibly as late as 1937, or perhaps even later. Because of strong similarities, especially in the eagle, the earlier B180 and especially B181 can easily be mistaken for the far more common and later Hilborn and Hamburger back-marked emblems that will be described and explained in volume 2. B181 and the later Hilborn and Hambuger officer's cap emblems are definitely struck from separate dies.

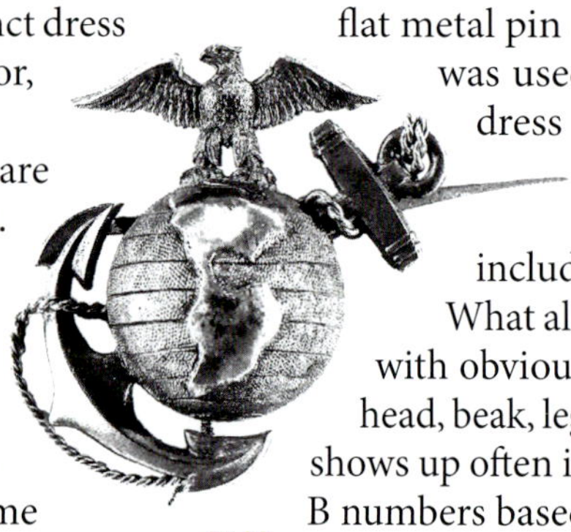

B182

One of the rarest emblems known is the commandant and staff officer gold and burnished chapeau ornament. With only four or possibly five commandants and a relatively small number of staff officers authorized to wear this unique emblem, only a few would have been manufactured. These are first described, but only for the commandant, in the 1900 Uniform Regulations.[9] The author has never had the occasion to see or photograph one. They are described for wear on the full dress chapeau of the commandant as well as staff officers in the 1904 Uniform Regulations.[10] The full dress chapeau (see Figure XI-6) is last mentioned in the 1917 revisions to 1913 Uniform Regulations.[11]

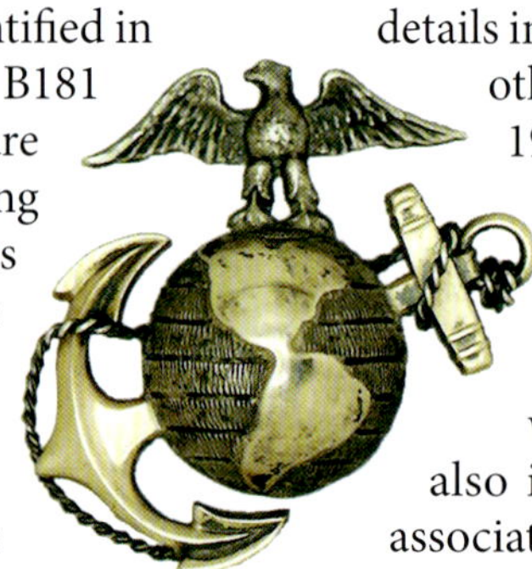

B183

John Driscoll fortunately photographed the only known example of the commandant and staff officer chapeau ornament that the author is aware of. This is Figure 44 in *The Eagle Globe and Anchor*.[12] John Driscoll provided an original print of his Figure 44 and graciously shared his original black and white photo print (B182) with the author. B182 is struck from the same die as B181, but has a unique means of attachment. A long flat metal pin attached to the upper anchor fluke reverse was used to pin the device to the cloth of the full dress chapeau.

A third and large group of very early twentieth century officer dress cap ornaments include B183, B184, B185, B186, B187, and B188. What all have in common is a distinctive silver eagle with obviously asymmetrically shaped wings, a distinct head, beak, legs, and talons. The asymmetrical wing pattern shows up often in old photographs. These are given separate B numbers based on differences found in other details such as construction and shape of the continents, anchor, and other details in engraving, finishing touches, and alloys used. The other feature in common is their dating as early as 1904 up through the WWI period. These should not be mistaken for many later emblems with an asymmetrical wing pattern that post-date WWI and will be covered in volume 2.

A late collector colleague bought B183 along with a dress collar set B221 in an estate sale that also included uniform items and a dress white cap associated with John Twiggs Myers USMC 1895 to 1935.[14] B183 has the pre-1906 "Silver" and "Gold" back-marks. The applied gold-plated continents have a very distinctive shape. That recognizable shape is known on other emblems with the pre-1906 back-marks and conforms very well to the later B184 back- marked "J.R. Gaunt." Five variants have been observed with only very minor difference. All had the shark's tooth engraving for oceans, screw post attachments, and a straight, uncomplicated two-strand silver wire cable, but with minor differences in the position of the fouled cable. As is usual with early officer's dress cap emblems, B183 does not have a maker's mark but in view of the strong similarities seen with the device in Fig. XI-10, it may be a J.R. Gaunt production. An asymmetrical wing officer's cap device is also illustrated in Bunkley.[15]

A minor variant of B183 is known from the collection of another colleague who acquired the emblem from the estate of Brig. Gen. Percy Archer USMC 1903 to 1937.[16] Only minor differences are evident in the shape of the applied continents, the lay of the cable at the anchor stock, and smooth oceans without the line tooling. This variant further supports the pre-1906 date as well as the extraordinary variation in handcrafted finishing techniques.

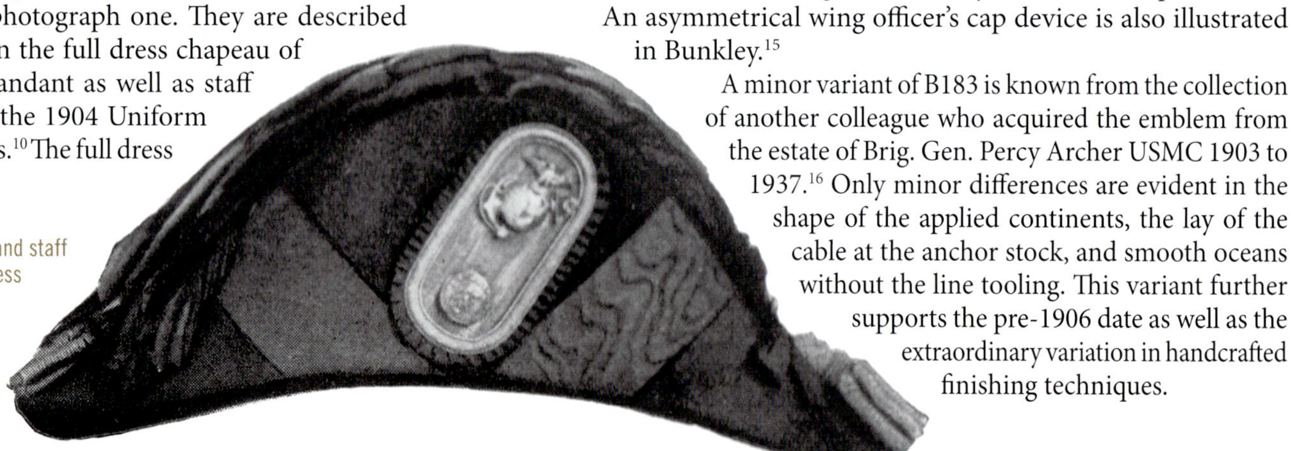

Figure XI-6
Commandant and staff officer's full dress chapeau.[13]

J.R. Gaunt and Son back-marks on the anchor crown reverse and a "Sterling" post-1906 back-mark on the left eagle wing reverse distinguish B184 from B183. The "Sterling" back-mark indicates a later date than B183. Only minor differences can be seen between B183 and B184, such as the lay of the fouled cable at the anchor stock and the size of the aperture between the legs of the eagles. The overall similarity between B183 and B184 further indicates that J.R. Gaunt manufactured both emblems.

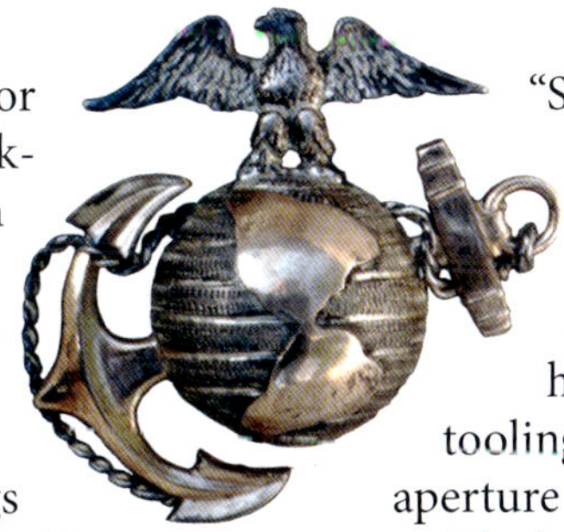

B184

The solid gold and silver elements show special craftsmanship on this pre-1906 dress cap emblem marked "Gold" and "Silver." B185 has unusually shaped continents probably cut by hand and an odd configuration of the fouled cable at the anchor ring and stock. As with all the other Asymmetrical Wing Type cap devices, it has a screw post for attachment. It was purchased by a collector colleague from the estate of Robert Oswald Burwell, who was commissioned in June 1915 and resigned from the Marine Corps in January 1920.[17] This is an unusually narrow window of time and use by a known Marine Corps officer. There is another known example of B185 associated with a 1912 pattern dress blue cover in the USMCHCQV.

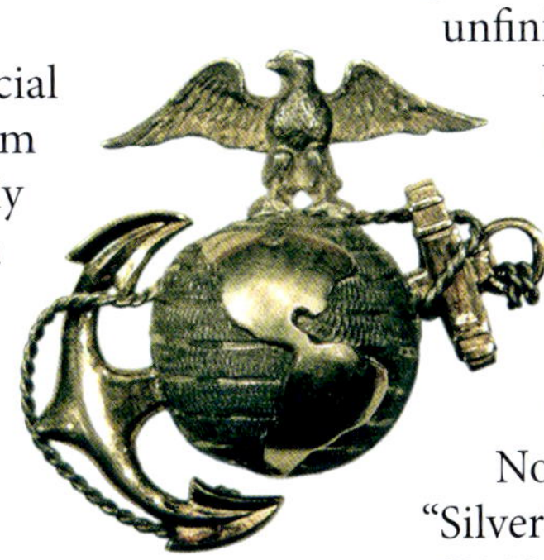

B185

B186 is another variant of the Asymmetrical Wing Type officer's dress cap emblem that also probably dates prior to the implementation of the 1905 US Stamping Act. It shows strong similarity to others of this type, except for the distinct shape of the struck continents and line tool engraving, giving a very fine shark's tooth pattern to the oceans. The anchor and continents are gold-plated, while the eagle and globe are solid silver with a screw post and anti-twist peg on the eagle throat reverse. With these unique features and a lack of maker's marks, the manufacturer is uncertain.

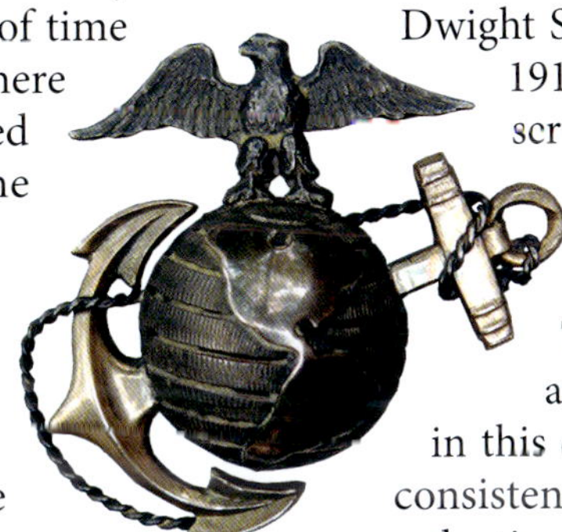

B186

The degree of handcrafted effects on B187 is impressive. The main elements, solid silver eagle and globe and solid gold anchor, are essentially the same as the other Asymmetrical Wing Types. The differences are in the details of skilled finishing techniques. Note the hand-engraved lines of latitude and the superb shark's tooth pattern of the oceans, obviously done by hand with a line tool. The solid gold continents were applied before the superimposed shark's tooth pattern was engraved. Drill holes were used to indicate the Gulf of Mexico and the Arctic Ocean. The "Silver" and "Gold" back-marks indicate a manufacturing date prior to the US Stamping Act. B187 has a screw post attachment and cylinder for attaching the two-strand, silver-plated brass wires of the cable.

B187

Another example of B187 with the pre-1906 "Silver" and "Gold" back-marks has been observed in another private collection. The eagle, globe, and anchor are the same as B187, suggesting that the same dies were used to strike both B186 and B187. The differences are in the details of the handcrafted finishing techniques, such as the line tooling and use of a different trimming tool, leaving no aperture between the eagle's legs.

The last of the Asymmetrical Wing group has distinctly shaped struck and gold-plated continents and a smooth unfinished surface for the oceans on a white metal globe. It does not include the same degree of handcrafted finishing touches so characteristic of earlier officer cap emblems in this group. It is probably one of the first officer dress cap emblems produced by more efficient mass-production techniques avoiding additional expensive, inefficient, as well as labor-intensive hand-crafted workmanship. None have been seen by this author with pre-1906 "Silver" or "Gold" back-marks.

B188 has most often been observed in post-WWI contexts but has been identified in a photograph of 1st Lt. Dwight Smith (see B188, appendix C-1) dated July 20, 1914.[18] Officer's Asymmetrical Wing Type dress and service cap ornaments are often seen in WWI period photos but for reasons of poor focus cannot be confidently identified as any particular Asymmetrical Wing emblem described here. The author has seen more examples of B188 than any of the other Asymmetrical Wing Type emblems in this chapter. This observation of high frequency is consistent with the switch from hand-crafted to mass production technology that clearly became evident with the dramatic increase in the size of the Marine Corps by WWI.

Ray Darida provided the author a black and white print of some forty-seven WWI period US Army and Marine Corps Insignia. That photo, from the W. Stokes Kirk collection, was thought to be a V.H. Blackinton, Attleboro Falls, MA, salesman's sample board (see Figure XI-6). B188 is also known with S.N. Meyer back-marks.

The Blackinton association with B188 is also supported by its illustration in a V.H. Blackinton advertisement dating about 1927.[19] B188 is clearly identifiable in the line drawing Number 1094. In that 1927 advertisement, the price for a B188 dress cap ornament was only $1 compared to $4.85 charged by Blackinton in 1918 for a solid gold-and-silver dress cap emblem with applied continents. Another V. H. Blackinton advertisement in the American Rifleman also clearly illustrates B188 (Figure XI-8). Although B188 was used by Marine officers long after World War I, it is included in this chapter because of its documented appearance before WWI.[20]

B188

Figure XI-7
V.H. Blackinton salesman's insignia sample board.

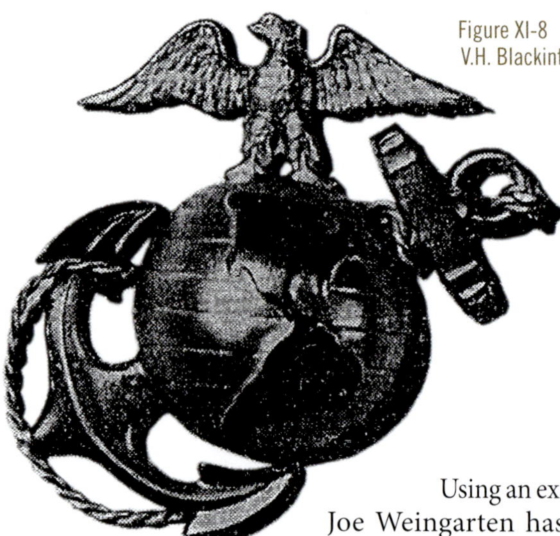

Figure XI-8
V.H. Blackinton advertisement.

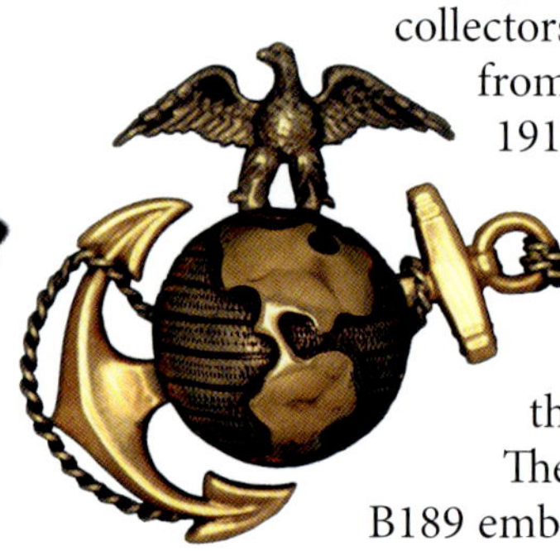

B189

Using an example of B188, Joe Weingarten has produced a handsome investment casting of that device in silver. Like B101 and B228, the investment casting of B188 is an obvious single piece reproduction. It is not a production of reassembled die struck elements.

The last distinct officer's dress cap ornament type that pre-dates the First World War is B189. It has a unique style eagle, anchor, and applied continents unlike anything in this study up to this time. Typical of other emblems of this period, there exists a great deal of variation not in the die-struck elements, but in the details of the handcrafted finishing touches. Variations are known in the hand-engraving and line tool effects, indicating the lines of latitude and oceans. B189 has a solid-gold anchor and applied continents and is stamped "10 K" on the center of the anchor crown reverse and "Sterling" on the center of the eagle's back, but no marks indicating the manufacturer. It has other silver elements for the screw post, the anti-twist peg, and a cylinder for attaching the single-strand silver cable, made to look like two strands, to the lower anchor fluke reverse.

This particular emblem came from the collection of the late George Mennegaux, one of the most respected long-time collectors of Marine Corps emblems. George bought B189 from the estate of Commandant Clifton Cates USMC 1917 to 1956. The emblem was attached to a dress blue cap of the 1936 to 1956 pattern. B189 is possibly the June 1917 commissioning emblem of Clifton Cates. It is well worn but entirely serviceable and was possibly used throughout the career of Commandant Cates.

There are several known varieties of the WWI period B189 emblem with, for example, different line tool effects for the oceans, such as the shark's tooth pattern or the dot-and-dash pattern. One variety had smooth oceans with no engraving. B189 should not be confused with the similar, but later, N.S. Meyer back-marked dress cap emblems. These later N.S. Meyer emblems can be formally distinguished from the earlier B189. The N.S. Meyer Company includes an excellent illustration of B189 in their 1918 catalog but these are not the same as the later and more common N.S. Meyer emblems (see Figure XI-9).[21] There is good reason to think that these later back-marked emblems did not appear until the mid-1920s and later. The story of the early and late N.S. Meyer officer dress cap emblems and how to differentiate them will be taken up in detail in volume 2.

OFFICER'S CAP DEVICE

Figure XI-9
Early N.S. Meyer service cap emblems.

Officer Epaulette Ornaments

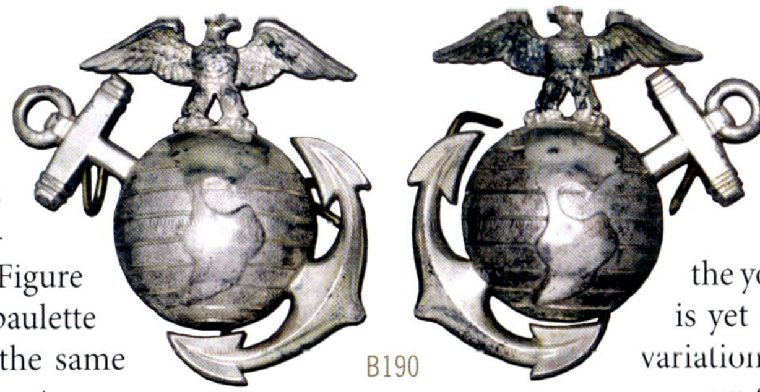

B190

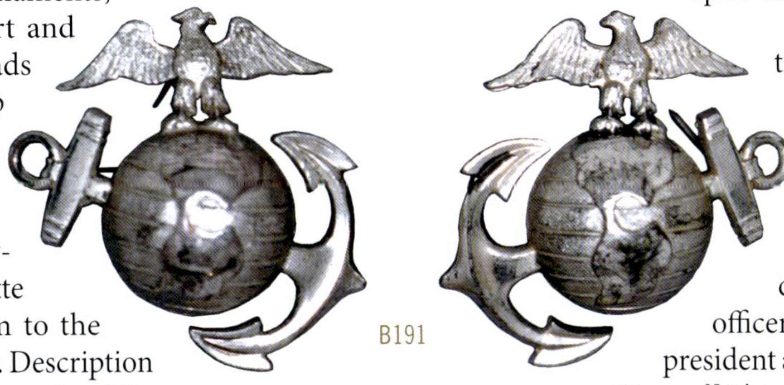

B191

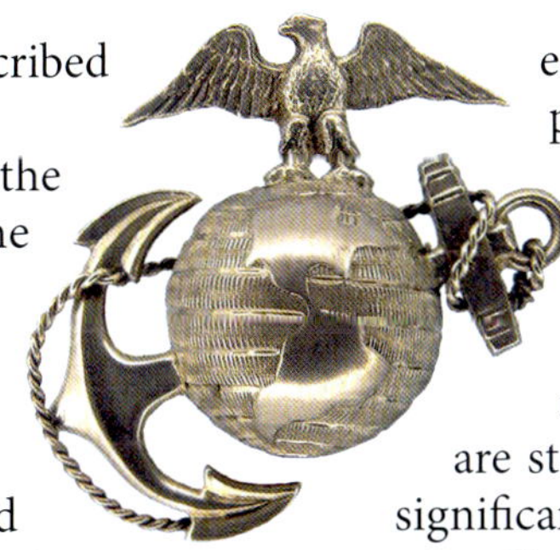

B192

The final group of emblems in chapter 11 conforms to specifications contained in the 1904 Uniform Regulations.[22] These are summarized by Figure 9 in appendix A. Officer's full dress epaulette ornaments were required to have the same measurements as dress cap ornaments, except they were to be in port and starboard pairs, with eagle heads facing inboard. Unlike dress cap ornaments with gold continents and anchor, epaulette ornaments were required by the Uniform Regulations to be all silver. However, a few silver and gold epaulette emblems that did not conform to the Uniform Regulations are known. Description of the anchor cable was simply omitted from the 1904 and 1912 Uniform Regulations that described epaulette ornaments.

The port and starboard set B190 is part of the USMCHCQV collections. Unfortunately, the acquisition records reveal nothing about donors or the Marine officer who wore this superb set. As with most epaulette emblems, the means of attachment is three brass wires soldered to the reverse anchor flukes and anchor stock. Hand craftsmanship, especially finishing touches, is evident. In the Quantico collections is another example of an all-silver B190 left epaulette ornament worn by Gen. John Lejeune before full dress epaulettes were dropped after WWI.

The main elements of B190, especially the distinct shape of the continents, are very similar to B191. This set is actually the silver epaulette version of the B181 dress cap emblem as well as the B195 service cap ornament in bronze. The manufacturer of B191 is uncertain but might be J.R. Gaunt. The J.R. Gaunt illustration (Figure XI 10) conforms well to B190.[23]

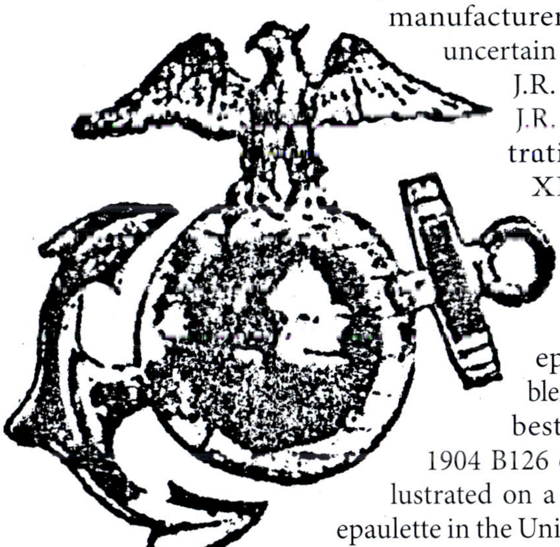

Figure XI-10
B189 In J.R. Gaunt advertisement.

It is curious that an epaulette emblem conforming best to the pre-1904 B126 or B127 is illustrated on a field officer's epaulette in the Uniform Regulations for 1912, 1917 (revisions) and 1929. In the same illustration, an epaulette emblem of the 1904 type such as B190 or B191 is also illustrated on an epaulette of a company grade officer.[24] This suggests that older officers were authorized to continue to wear their earlier epaulette emblems concurrently with the new 1904 pattern purchased by the younger (company grade) officers. This is yet another example of the tolerance of variation characteristic of the Marine Corps up to at least 1929.

Full dress epaulettes were discontinued sometime after 1918. Mention of full dress epaulettes and their emblems was dropped entirely from the 1922 Uniform Regulations but was reinstated in 1929 specifically for the full dress uniform worn only by Marine officers assigned as aide de camp to the president and officers assigned to the White House.[25] This tradition ended some time in the early 1950s, but would explain why B190 still appeared in the 1940 J.R. Gaunt Price List.

Very subtle differences can be seen between the B190 set and the B191 set. The latter was photographed and described from a private collection. The B191 set also does not have maker's marks. The eagle legs, wings, and breast of B191 are struck from different dies than B190. There is no significant difference in their measurements (see Figure 9, appendix A). Like B190, this set also has three wires for attachment purposes. These are soldered to the anchor stock and crown reverse and the eagle breast reverse. As with B190, the manufacturer is uncertain, but this set was probably made or sold by J.R. Gaunt. The illustration (Figure XI-11) conforms well to B191.[26]

Figure XI-11
Illustration of J.R. Gaunt epaulette emblem.

The left epaulette device B192 has the pre-1906 "Silver" back-mark and surprisingly has a screw post for attachment. There is no indication of attachment wires being replaced by the screw post. Compared to the simple and practical positioning of the emblem and mashing it down on the material of the epaulette thereby locking it in place, a screw post is impractical. An alternative possibility is that its function was actually a cap device that no longer has any trace of the original gold plate on the anchor or continents. The latter explanation seems less likely. No traces of gold plate were seen when examined closely in bright sunlight. Usually some trace of gold plate can be seen, especially in areas that were subjected to less wear.

Even without maker's marks, it is very likely that this emblem was manufactured by V.H. Blackinton because of the distinctive shape of the struck continents and the asymmetrical pattern of the eagle wings. By comparing B192 with B188, it can be seen that they are essentially the same with the exception of the line tooling of a shark's tooth pattern for the oceans seen on B192 and the smooth oceans on B188.

B193

The last emblem (B193) from a private collection is a solid silver right epaulette device with the conventional three brass wires on the reverse at the eagle back, anchor stock center, and anchor crown center. A close comparison indicates that B193 is the silver epaulette version of the J.R. Gaunt dress cap emblems B183 and the later B184. Compare B193 to the line drawing (Figure XI-10) taken from the 1940 J.R. Gaunt advertisement.[27] Note the similarities with all three eagles, anchors, and distinct shape of the applied continents. With the exception of a very minor difference in the shape of the continents, B193 conforms to the epaulette emblem illustrated in the 1912 Uniform Regulations.[28]

The same right epaulette emblem is also illustrated in the 1929 Uniform Regulations.[29] Such a minor difference in the shape of the continents is probably expected, given a range in variation and hand trimming of the applied continents by the J.R. Gaunt craftsmen. Left emblems of B193 have been seen in both the George Mennegaux and Mike Manifor collections.

CHAPTER XII

Officer Service Cap Emblems: 1904 through WWI

(B194 to B208)

The first four groups of service cap emblems parallel the same post-1904 four groups described in chapter 11. These correspond to the BB&B types, the Big Talon Big Beak types, the Asymmetrical Wing types and the Early N.S. Meyer types. Surprisingly, very few service cap emblems in chapter 12 turned out to simply be the service version of dress cap emblems described in chapter 11. This further attests to the great diversity of emblems that the various makers were selling to Marine Corps officers at this time. In addition to the four types that parallel those in chapter 11, four later types are also described. Most of these later types are probably from the WWI period. These have no counterparts in chapter 11. Modern reproductions of one distinct WWI officer's service cap emblem are included to show how these can be readily distinguished from the authentic emblem.

B194

B195

Bailey, Banks & Biddle Officer Service Cap Ornaments

The bronze service cap and field hat emblem B194 was struck using a die closest to the B178 BB&B dress cap emblem with similar struck continents. It conforms well to the cap emblem illustrated in the 1907 BB&B catalog.[1] It is also illustrated in the 1912 Uniform Regulations.[2] The continents are struck, not applied, and the oceans are depicted by a fine-grain sand pebble pattern. It has a dark brown lacquer finish on the bronze base metal. The BB&B back-mark is centered on the anchor crown reverse. A distinctive BB&B manufacturing technique can be seen on both B194 and the dress version, B178. The eagle is hard-soldered to the globe using small "C"-shaped, half circles of bronze metal as reinforcement points, giving more structure to the hard solder points where the eagle's talons contact the top of the globe. This clever BB&B feature has never been observed by the author on any other officer's cap emblem. Unlike the B178 dress cap device, B194 has a screw post for attachment.

B196

Big Beak Big Talons Type Cap Emblems: Unknown Manufacturer

The service version of the dress cap emblem B181 is B195 struck in bronze. The eagle, anchor, and globe with struck continents and a fine sand pebble pattern for the oceans are exactly the features seen on B181. The absence of a back-mark on both suggests a manufacturer other than BB&B. The unique cartography of North and South America is also unlike any BB&B productions in this study. For want of more information, B195, like its B181 dress cap counterpart, is simply classified as another example of the "Big Beak Big Talons Type." This emblem is early, see Figure XII-1; it probably dates as early as 1904 and should not be mistaken for the similar, but far more common, Hillborn and Hamburger back-marked cap ornaments of the late 1920s to at least WWII.

Figure XII-1 with blow up. Unidentified US Marine officer wearing B195; photo dated 1909.

Examples of B195 were photographed and described from two private collections. In one of those collections, B195 was just one of three insignia associated with Arthur Stokes.[3] Stokes was commissioned in 1904.[4] This small collection of Arthur Stokes insignia also included a rifle expert badge inscribed "1910." An illustration of B195 also appears on the cover of a 1912 copyright publication.[5] B195 conforms well with Figure XII-2. This same illustration can also be found in the National Archives.[6]

Although quite similar, the separate elements for the eagle, the globe, the anchor, and the applied continents of B196 are struck from different dies than those used to manufacture B195. The differences are most readily noticed in the eagle and anchor. A dress cap version of B196 is unknown but would be a welcome addition to future revisions of this work. The bronze alloy has a dark brown lacquer

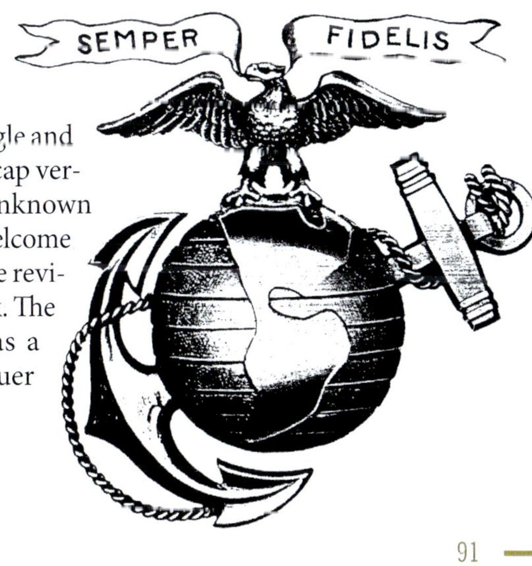

Figure XII-2
Old Style eagle, Globe, and anchor.

finish. The oceans are engraved by a line tool with a dot-dash pattern. The cable is a single-strand bronze wire made to look like two strands. The absence of hallmarks leaves the question of who manufactured it completely open. Although very similar, B196 should not be lumped with the later Hilborn and Hamburger emblems that will be discussed in volume 2.

Officer Asymmetrical Wing Service Cap Emblems: Different Manufacturers or Sellers

The following six officer's bronze service cap emblems are grouped as "Asymmetrical Wing Types." They all share a strong family resemblance, especially the unmatched shape of the eagle's wings. The six types are based on the use of different dies to strike separate elements or differences in the alloys used. Only one emblem is back-marked with "S.N. Meyer," but as with B188, an argument can be made that V.H. Blackinton manufactured several varieties of the Asymmetrical Wing Type.

As with their dress cap counterparts, the service versions of the Asymmetrical Wing Type cap emblems are commonly seen in WWI period photos, but can rarely be confidently identified with respect to the details used to distinguish these particular B numbers.

The service cap and field hat emblem B197 is the bronze version of the silver and gold B183 dress cap emblem. Both have distinctly shaped applied continents that have been identified in old photos (see B183, B197 in appendix C-1). B197 is also seen in the V.H. Blackinton 1927 advertisement and photo of a salesman's sample board (Figure XI-6 in the previous chapter). The emblem is finished with a dark brown lacquer and has a screw post attachment.

With the exception of different dies for the globe, the applied continents, and the anchor, B198 shares all other features with B197, including the strike of the eagle. Indications of different dies can be seen clearly in the anchor, especially in the spacing of ironwork on the anchor stock and the shape of the applied continents. Another minor hand-finishing effect is in the lay of the cable at the anchor ring. B198 has a different dark brown lacquer finish and a lazier anchor angle where it is attached to the globe. Except for the different dies, all these minor differences could simply be artifacts of hand-finishing techniques so common with officer emblems of this period.

B197 or its minor variant B198 are associated with a 1912 pattern winter service cap and uniform ensemble sold on eBay and worn by Emile Northenscold (see B198 appendix C-1). The pattern 1912 service green cap has to date no earlier than June 1918 and no later than 1926 when the new winter service caps were adopted. Northenscold, a former gunnery sergeant, was promoted provisionally to second lieutenant in France in June 1918.[7] The emblem B197/B198 is quite likely Northnescold's commissioning emblem. A second example of the B197 or B198 emblem is part of the battlefield collection of USMC emblems that Gilles Lagrin recovered from 1918 AEF battlefield sites in France.[8] A third example of B197/B198 was sold for $3,800 on eBay in December 2004. It was attached to a winter service green fore and aft cap with embroidered star associated with Brig. Gen. S.D. Butler and is probably the same emblem and cover seen in a well-known photograph of Butler taken in France in 1919.[9]

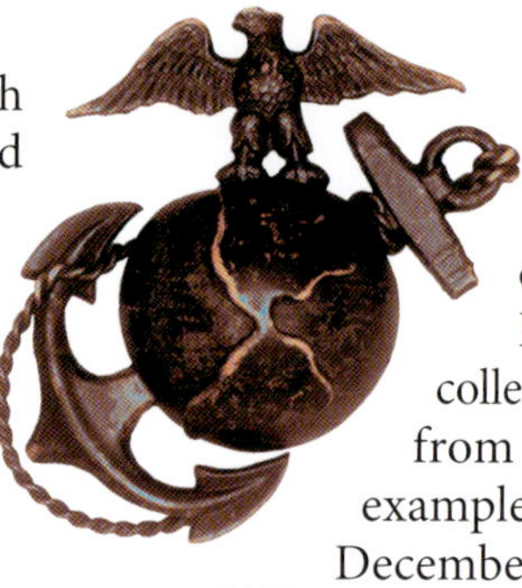

B197

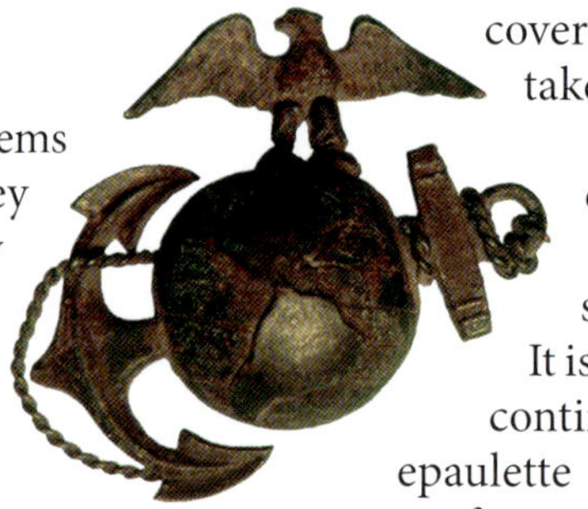

B198

B199

B200

The officer's bronze field hat and service cap ornament with screw post B199 is closest to the B191 silver epaulette set. Like the B191 epaulette set, the manufacturer or seller is also unknown. It is curious that the distinctive shape of the struck continents for B199 are the same as those for the epaulette sets B190 and B191, also with an unknown manufacturer. To complicate matters, the shape of the B199 eagle conforms well to the eagle illustrated in Figure XI-10 from the 1940 J.R. Gaunt catalog. Is it possible that manufacturers were subcontracting or sharing dies and/or fittings? Are all these variations simply within the range of variability of a single manufacturer/seller like J.R. Gaunt? There is no dress cap counterpart for B199 in this study. The future discovery of well-illustrated manufacturer catalogs would be most welcome for answering some of these perplexing questions.

An officer's bronze service cap emblem for which we have excellent provenience is the asymmetrical wing type B200. Maj. Gen. John Lejeune wore B200 on his fore and aft cover in 1918 and 1919 in France (see Figure XII-3). The cover with B200 worn by Gen. LeJeune was donated to the USMCHCQV by the Lejeune family at the time of Col. Magruder's solicitation for artifacts for a Smithsonian Institution Marine

Figure XII-3
B200 on fore and aft cover worn by Maj. Gen. John Lejeune.

Corps exhibit in the early 1950s.[10] The Lejeune cover with B200 was on display for many years in the "Time Tunnel Exhibit" in the Washington Navy Yard.

A dark brown lacquer finish, struck continents, and a screw post attachment are some of the features of B200. Although there seems to be do no discernable difference in the die strikes for B200 and the dress version B188 (chapter 11), Lejeune's emblem surprisingly has the highly unusual back-mark of "S.N. Meyer, Washington, DC." Simon N. Meyer produced military insignia from at least 1894 until 1930.[11] The B200 device was probably manufactured in response to the dramatic increase in demand for Marine Corps emblems that accompanied the equally dramatic 1917 and 1918 troop strength increases. This is another example of multiple manufacturers or sellers using the same dies. S.N. Meyer should not be confused with N.S. Meyer, manufacturer of B189, B203, and many post-WWI officer emblems of entirely different designs.

B201

The distinct struck continents of this asymmetrical wing officer's service cap device are very similar to B200, but struck from at least one different die for the anchor. Like B200, it has a smooth pattern for the oceans. The difference in the shape of the eagle wings is probably from bending after being struck. B201 is struck in a brass alloy and has a dark brown lacquer or chemical finish, a screw post attachment, and as usual for emblems of this period, no maker's marks.

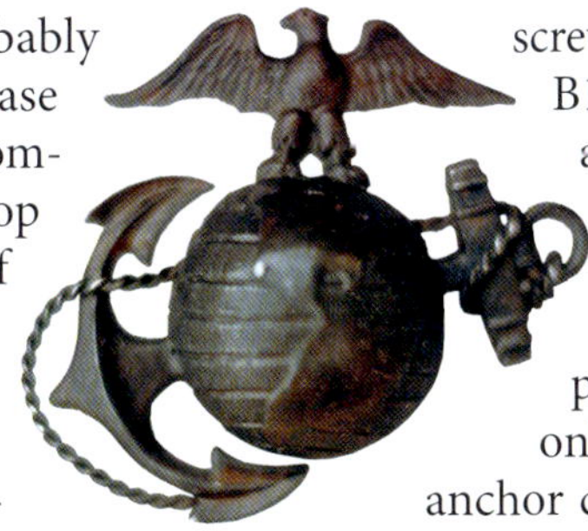

B202

Except for being struck in an alloy of silver and having a hand-engraved shark's-tooth pattern from a line tool for the oceans, B202 is extremely similar to B201. The "SILVER" back-mark on the anchor stock reverse places its date of manufacture before the provisions of the 1905 US Stamping Act took effect. A screw post is the means of attachment and the finish is a chemical process (liver of sulfate) that turns silver to a brown color. B202 is another indication that the asymmetrical wing types probably go all the way back to 1904. Both Blackinton and S.N. Meyer are both known to have manufactured or sold this type.

In the author's experience, this is the only occurrence of B202 encountered. This is in marked contrast to many less expensive, mass-produced brass asymmetrical wing emblem types with the distinct shape of the struck continents that occur on the market and have been identified often in old photographs. The high number of these less-expensive officer emblems is another likely artifact of the dramatic increase in the size of the Marine Corps during WWI, as well as a shift to less expensive, mass-produced officer emblems requiring less hand craftsmanship.

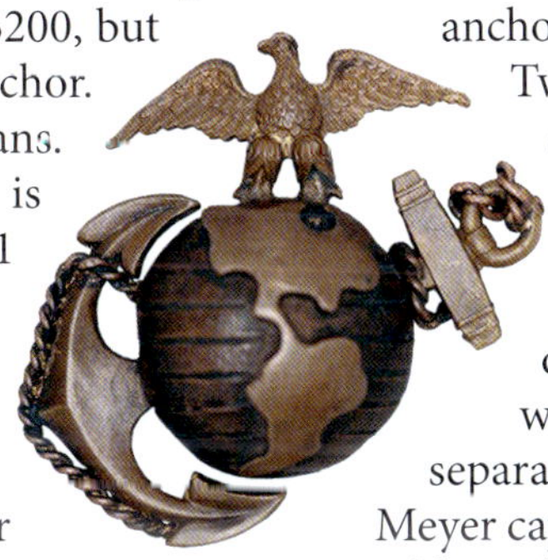

B203

Miscellaneous Types of Officer Service Cap Emblems of the WWI Period

The last service cap and field hat emblem that has a counterpart in the dress cap emblems covered in chapter 11 is B203. It features the same uniquely shaped eagle, continents, and screw post attachment method as the dress cap version, B189. The bronze has a dark brown lacquer finish and possibly a chemical finish with the sand pebble effect for the oceans. Because it has not been confidently identified in WWI photos, but is included in the 1918 N.S. Meyer catalog, it probably dates no earlier than about 1917.[12] The only back-mark on B203 is "Fire Bronze" on the anchor crown reverse. The absence of a manufacturer's hallmark is consistent with the dress cap version, B189. The cable has two strands of bronze wire attached to the lower anchor fluke reverse without the usual bronze cylinder. Two other examples of B203 are included in a collection of five bronze cap and collar ornaments from the estate of Julian C. Smith.[13] Smith was commissioned in 1909.

For this research, the WWI period B189 dress cap and the B203 service cap emblem, also without N.S. Meyer back-marks or shield, are separated from the later and far more common N.S. Meyer cap emblems that were manufactured in the 1920s and later (see B203 appendix C-1). These later N.S. Meyer cap emblems with the distinctive back-marks and logo were not manufactured until some time in the mid 1920s and later. In other words, very few N.S. Meyer emblems like B189 and B203 can be substantiated to date back to WWI; the vast majority of the distinctive N.S. Meyer emblems with back-marks are post-WWI. This story will also be taken up in Volume II.

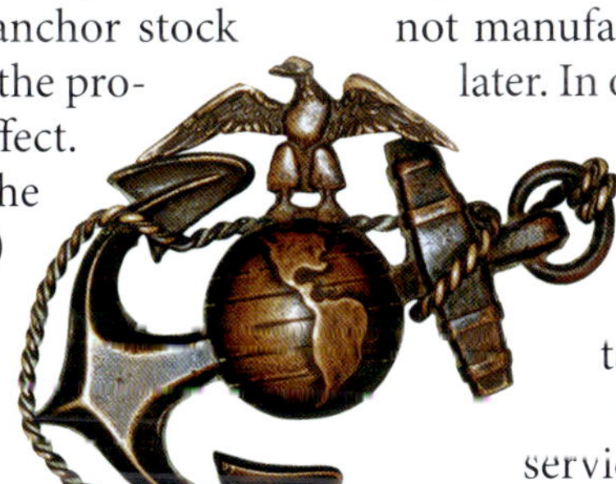

B204

One of the most spectacularly unique officer's service cap emblems is the French-made emblem B204. The eagle style is reminiscent of Napoleonic eagles. The author is aware of only three examples. These were apparently contracted to an unknown French manufacturer by the AEF Quartermaster in 1918. Both service collar and service cap emblems for officers were produced in France during the latter part of WWI. This French emblem was probably produced to meet the US Marine Corps emblem shortages in the AEF. The author has never seen another die variety or one made for dress caps in silver and gold. The pressing need in France during WWI was for service emblems, not dress cap emblems. B204 was found in France in 1998 and ultimately bought by George Mennegaux at an Ohio gun show.[14] The author had the privilege of photographing and describing B204 through the courtesy of George Mennegaux in September 1999. Another example of B204 is in the collection of Gilles Lagin, who found it in France in other than a battlefield context.[15] A third example known to the author was sold on eBay in 2002.

The separate elements of B204: eagle, globe, and anchor, are struck in two bronze plates of different thicknesses. The three struck elements, however, are thin compared to the extremely thick and heavy one-piece modern investment casting reproduction B205. The anchor of B204 is relatively large and thick compared to the undersized globe and eagle. The finish is either a thin dark brown lacquer or a chemical change to turn the natural bronze to a dark brown color. There is an extremely long screw post with a very small 60 mm thread size and an unusual four-pointed, star-shaped nut. The cable is of a two-strand bronze wire construction with some minor variation in its configuration and lay as seen in the two known examples of B204. This variation would be expected given the finishing work of hand craftsmen. The cable has a very unusual "C"-shaped bronze attachment that is hard-soldered to the lower anchor fluke reverse. The author is aware of no known photographs of AEF Marines clearly showing B204.

B205

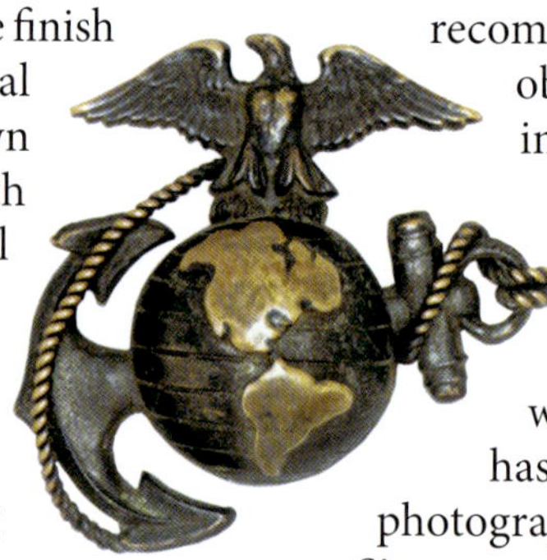

B206

B207

The large, thick, heavy bronze and obviously cast modern reproduction B205 only vaguely resembles the die-struck French emblem B204. The cast reproduction is significantly smaller than the authentic French-made B204, but is almost twice as heavy. There exists a variant of B205 with a two-strand cast bronze cable. The thick, heavy single-piece reproduction B205 displays all the telltale features of investment casting, completely lacking the obvious features of a thin die-struck emblem produced by a high-pressure die-striking method that is essentially the same traditional process used to mint coins at the US Mints. High-pressure die-striking brings out the finest details in emblems. Even the cleverest investment castings usually do not show the same degree of fine details. The details of an investment casting are characteristically muted and often display flaws such as irregular pits and protuberances. In addition, clear edge rounding is a function of trapped air brought into the mold by the flowing molten metal. The reverse of B205 especially reveals the thickness and edge rounding of an investment casting. At the same time, B205 shows the complete lack of thin, sharp perpendicular edges that are a function of a super high-pressure male die forcing the malleable bronze metal plate efficiently into every detail of the underlying female die, including the sharp perpendicular edges of that die. This edge clarity is especially obvious in die-struck emblems. The sharp edges can be seen along the 360 degrees of the reverse circle of the globe.

The author is not aware of who is actually manufacturing B205 or many of the other known modern emblem reproductions. Despite the fact that a few dealers, such as George Peterson of National Capital Historic Sales, are forthright about selling reproductions, the problem is that others are not being honest about modern reproductions and prefer to keep buyers in the dark with excuses like "let the buyer beware."

The vast majority of modern investment cast reproductions of Marine Corps emblems are readily distinguishable with some basic education of what to look for. A close examination of the obvious differences between B204 and B205 should be very helpful in dealing with this serious reproduction problem. It is further recommended that every serious collector and dealer obtain some representative examples of modern investment casting for comparative purposes.

The bronze service cap and field hat emblem B206 for officers is stylistically one of the most distinctive emblems found in this research. Every element, eagle, globe, and continents as well as anchor, has a unique style. This distinctiveness has been easily recognized in several old and dated photographs of known officers (see B206, appendix C-1). Since some of these officers did not serve in the AEF (e.g., Challacombe and Livingston, and at least one, Ridderhoff, never left the United States), this clearly suggests a stateside manufacturer/seller rather than an AEF theatre-made emblem, such as B204.[16]

B206 is struck from a fairly heavy planchette. Unlike other officer emblems, the eagle and globe are struck from a single piece of bronze instead of an eagle hard-soldered to the top of a separately struck globe. The means of attachment is also unusual in having a screw post brazed to a rectangular bar and soldered to the globe circle reverse. Even the lay of the cable is unusual, with a wide sweep from the midsection of the reverse of the eagle, anchor, arms, and flukes. Some collectors and dealers have begun referring to B206 as the "Pete Ellis Type" because it is clearly identified in a well-known 1918-dated photo of Col. Pete Ellis in winter service greens.[17] There is also no question about the matching service collar ornaments (B247) of the same distinct style. One collar ornament of this style appears in a publication dated 1921.[18] There is a known variant with struck, rather than applied, continents. The absence of back-marks and the lack of photographic evidence before 1918 indicate an unknown manufacturer/seller. On the basis of photographic evidence, they were essentially gone by ca.1930. The author has never seen these struck in gold and silver for dress use.

Another extremely unusual style and rarely encountered officer's service cap and field hat is the bronze ornament B207. The emblem has an eagle with a very unusual feathering pattern, a slender, gracile anchor, an oversized globe with continents so strange it is as if the craftsman was ignorant of the cartography of North and South America. Also odd for this particular time is the lack of a screw post for attachment. A complex rolling catch-type pin assembly was used instead. The emblem looks polished or burnished and is finished with a dark brown lacquer. The cable is not original, but was replaced using two-strand US Army sword handle wire. This is the only occurrence of this type of service cap device the author has encountered. It is back-marked with the characteristic logo of the William Link Company of Newark, New Jersey.[19] The logo consists of two joined chain links with the letter "W" in the middle between the two links (see Figure XII-4). Bazelon states that William Link probably did not produce military insignia before WWI and was out of business by 1930.[20] B207 is another likely example of a very unusual style of emblem possibly made in small numbers and only during the emblem shortage brought on by the dramatic increase in Marine Corps officers 1917 to 1919. The author is aware of only one other example of the unusual Link emblem for service or dress caps.

Figure XII-4
Link hallmark.

Ray Darida provided the author a photo reproduction of a rare manufacturer's catalog that illustrates B208. Although the reproduction is poor quality, there is no doubt that this Ronson catalog put out by "The Art Metal Works" of Newark, New Jersey illustrates B208, as item 8804, see Figure XII-5. The Ronson catalog probably dates 1918 or 1919, for it includes many WWI insignia including the US Army Tank Corps collar disc that was adopted May 7, 1918.[21]

B208

The unique shape of the eagle, the anchor, and the lay of the cable of B208 are distinctive. Since B208 was illustrated with a set of smaller bronze collar emblems, it must be assumed that the set was an advertisement for officer emblems, even though it lacks many of the fancier features characteristic of officer emblems. Enlisted Marines were not authorized collar emblems at this time. B208 is a bronze alloy with a black lacquer finish and a screw post for attachment. There are no back markings. With the exception of the uniquely shaped anchor and the single strand wire cable made to look like two strands, B208 shares a die-struck eagle and globe characteristic of enlisted dress and service cap devices that were manufactured in the 1920s and 1930s by V.H. Blackinton of Attleborough, Massachusetts. These will be described in volume 2.

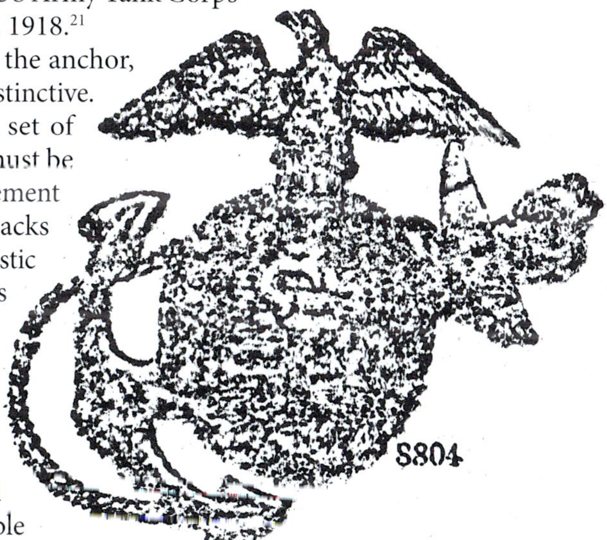

Figure XII-5
B208 illustrated in a 1918/19 Ronson catalog.

It is quite likely that B208 was another example of a manufacturer producing and selling a few emblems that could pass for officer's service cap emblems at a time when the vastly increased number of USMC officers created a pressing need for more emblems than were available from conventional sources. That these rarities were short-lived is probably a function of the Marine Corps being dramatically reduced in size after WWI, thereby reducing the need for emblems that were produced from other than the usual procurement sources. The author is aware of only one other example of B208.

CHAPTER XIII

Officer Dress Collar Emblems: 1904 through WWI

(B209 to B232)

As with officer dress cap emblems for this same period, dress collar ornaments were also offered for sale by manufacturers in an amazing variety of options. For a period of about a dozen years, this research documents some twenty-five emblem variations from at least five distinct groups of officer dress collar ornaments. The major groups in this chapter roughly parallel the officer's dress and service cap emblems in chapters 11 and 12. Dress collar emblems are presented in a similar sequence considering chronological criteria as well as formal die and alloy variations. Dress collar emblems in this chapter and service collar emblems in the following chapter can usually be readily distinguished from earlier emblems by their clear conformance to the 1904 Uniform Regulation specifications (see appendix A, Figure 10). Beyond these specified measurements other criteria were developed to separate collar emblems dating up through WWI from a myriad of officer collar emblems dating after WWI. These criteria will be discussed with reference to emblems by their B number.

B209

B210

B211

The dramatic increase in the size of the US Marine Corps in WWI was accompanied by the adoption of mass-production technology that accelerated the demise of hand craftsmanship in the manufacture of officer emblems. There is no surprise in finding that the most common officer emblems of the WWI period were mass-produced and that those produced by skilled craftsmen still show extreme variation. This inventory has to be only a sample, hopefully a representative sample, of the variation manufactured at that time. Some photographs confirm that very rare distinct types not covered in chapter 13 were in fact worn by US Marine Corps officers, but have never been observed by the author.

Bailey, Banks & Biddle Dress Collar Emblem Group

The first of three variants of dress collar ornaments with Bailey, Banks & Biddle back-marks is the B209 officer set. The distinctive eagle, anchor, and rectangular-shaped anchor stock of B209 are clearly illustrated in the 1912 Uniform Regulations.[1] Except for the shape of the continents, B209 conforms to the collar emblems illustrated in the 1907 Bailey, Banks & Biddle catalog.[2] The eagle and globe are solid silver. The anchor and the separate continents are gold-plated. On the anchor stock reverse appears the back-mark "BB&B G. Filled," indicating manufacture before the requirements of the 1906 US Stamping Act took full effect. The means of attachment is a screw post brazed to the mid-anchor shaft reverse. Handcrafted effects can be seen in the uneven pattern of the hand-engraved lines of latitude and the irregular positioning of the applied continents. Other minor variations in the shape of the continents are known.

Unlike B209, there is no indication on B210 of wear or gold-plating on brass. Both the continents and the anchor are solid gold construction. The anchor, rather than being rectangular in cross section, is tapered at both ends as if carefully struck in a separate die or cast in a gold mold. Both the anchor and continents are extremely thin. The shape of the continents conforms well to the shape seen in the 1912 Uniform Regulations.[3] B210 also conforms well with the emblem illustrated in the 1907 BB&B catalog.[4] Another indication of special craftsmanship is the intricate rolling catch for the pivoting pin assembly, very similar to Figure XI-5. The pin assembly is also highly unusual, being both short and oriented vertically from the eagle back down to the mid-anchor shaft reverse. An archaic style of the BB&B hallmark appears on the anchor crown reverse. Another characteristic finishing touch is the careful bending of the eagle wings, giving them a three-dimensional effect, instead of the simple flat look as struck in the die without aesthetic bending. Both B209 and B210 have a sponge pattern for the oceans, but others are known to have shark's tooth line tool patterns for the oceans. The slight taper on the ends of the anchor stock indicate that the die used for B210 is different from the one used for B209. One variant is back-marked "20 K," with applied continents over struck continents.

The most obvious and unusual feature of B211 is the incorrect facing of the eagle heads. They face outboard instead of inboard and away from the anchor ring as first specified in the 1904 Uniform Regulations.[5] Photographs of Marine officers dating prior to WWI are occasionally known to show this old fashioned feature not conforming to the Uniform Regulations. This reflects both the handwork done by individual craftsmen, as well as the variation tolerated when there was no specific requirement for the eagle head to face inboard prior to 1904. Like B210, the anchor and continents are solid gold. The eagle and globe are solid silver. The left and right gold continents do not match, and are another indication of intricate hand craftsmanship. The set has a nice even sponge pattern as a finishing touch for the oceans. B211 is back-marked BB&B 14K at the anchor arms reverse. The anchor is also struck from a different die than B209 (see tick marks pointing out slight differences in the anchor crown and stock between B209 and B211). The means of attachment is a minor variant of the complex, roll-type catch (Figure XI-5) on a pivoting silver pin assembly. A variant of B211 is known with 10K back-marks and a short vertical pin back assembly with the more common, simple, drop-in catch for the pin assembly and eagle heads correctly facing inboard. The sample of BB&B back-marked dress collar emblems and variation is definitely incomplete.

According to a 1907 Bailey, Banks & Biddle price list, a pair of their dress collar emblems in 14K gold and sterling silver cost $8.00.[6] In that same catalog, BB&B prided themselves on their emblems being regulation and of improved models. BB&B also noted their moderate prices for 10K and 14K gold emblems and the special care given to detail and finish in the tradition of their other fine jewelry.[7] The 1919 BB&B catalog also mentions that many of the sealed patterns with the USMC Quartermaster were BB&B productions.[8]

B212

The B212 solid gold and silver set, with the exception of some finishing touches, is very similar to both B210 and B211. The most obvious difference is the correct positioning of the eagle heads, conforming to the Uniform Regulations. Instead of a random sponge pattern for the oceans, B212 has a hand-engraved dot-dash pattern using a line tool. This irregular pattern of engraving, seen best in the right ornament, was obviously done to accommodate the shape of the already applied gold continents. The separate elements for the eagle and anchor but not the globe and continents, are struck from the same die as B211.

Bailey, Banks & Biddle did not always include back-marks on their emblems. Applying a back-mark is an extra step in the manufacturing process and would therefore increase production effort and costs. The gold and silver of B212 looks solid, but without K and STERLING back-marks, the grades of the alloys are unknown. The gold could be an excellent gold plate. This is inconsistent with the other BB&B dress cap and collar emblems in this study and curiously does not conform to the 1906 US Stamping Act.

Another example of the B212 set from another collection is also known to be without back-marks. It has solid gold or perhaps gold-plated continents, anchor, and even a gold rolling catch-type pin assembly. An enigmatic feature on two other known examples of B212 is the neat hand engraving of the numbers: 194127-172 on one set and 749117-148 on another known set. The purpose of these hand-engraved numbers is unknown; perhaps they indicate a particular production run or subcontracting orders or perhaps some sort of pricing or inventory method.

Gen. Holland M. Smith B212 Set

There is only one US Marine Corps officer on active duty today that is authorized to wear an obsolete set of dress collar ornaments that are probably at least 100 years old. The set is a minor variant of B212 and was originally worn by Gen. Holland M. Smith. The only officer authorized to wear Gen. Smith's dress collar emblems is the Commander of the Silent Drill Team at 8th and I Streets, Marine Barracks Washington, DC. The set was donated by Thomas L. Krebs, a relative of Gen. Smith and a former USMC company commander in Vietnam. The intention of the donation was for the Gen. Smith set to continue to serve the Corps in a place of honor.[9] The donation was only accepted by Capt. Giles Kyser, at that time commander of the Silent Drill Team, under the provision that each succeeding commander of the Silent Drill Platoon would sign for and pass on to their successor the Holland Smith emblems in perpetuity. Each new Silent Drill Platoon commander is also required to read *The Fighting General*, the biography of Gen. Holland M. Smith. Inside the book is the following inscription:

> "To each of you who commands the Marine Corps premier platoon, the legacy of General Smith is handed down. With the emblems comes the responsibility to learn about the man who first wore them and gave them their place in the history of our Corps. To that end this book is dedicated to you and to the Marines who so superbly represent our Corps as a member of your platoon."[10]
>
> Semper Fidelis.
> James Giles Kyser
> Capt. USMC

At the request of the author, the Gen.Smith dress collar emblems were identified as a minor variant of B212 by Capt. R. Kyle Aldrich, then the commander of the Silent Drill Platoon in January 2006. Capt. Aldrich also provided the information about the emblems, the book, and the Kyser inscription.[11]

Dress Collar Emblems Where the Manufacturer Is Uncertain

The next two officer collar emblems, B213 and B 214, share obvious features, but are without manufacturer's back marks. B180 and B181 dress cap, as well as B195 and B196 service cap, emblems also have no back-marks and as such are probably not simply BB&B variants, despite some general resemblance especially seen in the eagle. A close comparison of the eagles and anchors of B212 and B213 and the BB&B back-marked emblems indicates that they are struck from different dies. Alternatively, it is possible, but seems less likely, that the following four examples of B213 without back-marks are simply emblems struck from other BB&B dies.

A colleague purchased the dress collar set B213 from the estate of Frank J. Schwable.[12] The dress collar emblems were worn along with the dress cap ornament B180 as a three-piece set worn by Schwable and may well be his 1909 commissioning set. Superb craftsmanship is exhibited in the solid gold and sterling silver construction, detailed sponge pattern for the oceans and hand-engraved lines of latitude. It is an example where the continents were first struck, and then an applied set was superimposed over the struck continents. A simple drop-in type silver pin assembly is the means of attachment.

B213

B214

In addition to the Col. Schwable set, three other examples of B213 without manufacturer marks are also known. No two of the three other examples of B213 are exactly alike. An example of B213 is on the dress blue uniform with major rank insignia worn by E.C. Long, who was also commissioned in 1909 and promoted to major in July 1918.[13] The second example of the solid gold-and-silver dress collar set B213 came from the estate of Robert M. Burstan.[14] Capt. Burstan was killed in France in 1918.[15] The third example of B213 was worn by Capt. Donald Duncan KIA Belleau Wood June 6, 1918, (see B213 in appendix C-1). This is also a case where four examples of a particular emblem without manufacturer's marks can be confidently dated to a relatively narrow window of time.

B215

The final variant of this group B214 is very close to B213. It is also without back-marks but because it is so similar to others in this group, it could be another BB& B emblem struck from variant dies and without back-marks. The shape of the applied continents over struck continents is unique and may be a function of hand cutting and trimming or using continent findings manufactured by others. Like B210, the anchor is extremely thin and tapered at the anchor crown, as if cast separately from the other struck elements in a gold mold and finished by hand. The hand-engraved lines of latitude and the hand-engraved negative fine sand pebble pattern for the oceans is also very similar to B213. Like most of the others in this group (B209 to B214), the attachment method is a simple drop-in pin assembly.

A variant of B214 has the same distinctively shaped, but gold-plated continents and displays hand engraving and finishing effects around the talons of the eagle. In addition, this variant has the short drop-in vertical pin assembly attached to the eagle back and the mid anchor shaft reverse.

Early N.S. Meyer Type Officer Dress Collar Emblems

The distinct type B215 appears in a 1918 dated N.S. Meyer catalog.[16] Figure XIII-1, from that catalog, illustrates the well-defined shape of the struck continents, the huge triple talons and the unusually slender neck and diminutive eagle head. The catalog also advertises a variety of options offered to buyers. This helps to explain the extraordinary variety of officer collar emblems at this time. Note also that the illustration depicts the archaic feature of the eagle incorrectly facing outboard.

The B215 set is also not a matched set that started out together. The left and right emblems are not mirror images of each other and show considerable variation in measurements and finishing touches such as the non-parallel positions of the lines of latitude. The left device, on close examination in bright sunlight, has no traces of gold plating, indicating that it may have been a staff officer's all-silver shoulder knot emblem 1904 to 1912.[17] An all-silver and matching right collar device is known, further indicating that the N.S. Meyer set was used for staff officer's

OFFICER'S COLLAR DEVICE

		Per Pair
No. 311	Bronze	$ .85
F311	Fire Bronze......	1.00
RB311	Real Bronze.....	1.75
P311	Gold and Silver Plate	1.50
S311	Sterling Silver...	1.75
G311	Solid Gold and Silver	6.00

Figure XIII-1
B215 in 1918 N.S. Meyer catalog.

shoulder knot emblems. The right dress collar ornament of the B215 set is also an unmarked white metal alloy but with gold-plated anchor and continents. Unusual features on the set are the weak and fine sand pebble pattern for the oceans and very slender anchors. The two known examples of B215 that the author is aware of have a roll-type catch in a pivoting pin assembly for attachment purposes. Many variants are known with applied continents of different shapes and wide variation in engraving patterns. For example, line tools creating a dot-dash and shark's-tooth pattern depicting the oceans are common. One very unusual set is known with engraved lines of both latitude and longitude. A colleague has a variant set of B215 with gold-plated anchor and continents that came from the estate of Col. Percy Archer USMC 1909 to 1936 (see B215 in appendix C-1).[18]

Officer dress cap emblems very similar to the N.S. Meyer B215 type with the well-known Hilborn and Hamburger back-mark were first manufactured well after WWI. It is not known how these later H&H productions are related to B215, but for reasons that will be discussed in volume 2, similar emblems with Hillborn and Hamburger back-marks are treated separately. There is no reason to think that Hillborn and Hamburg back-marked emblems were manufactured as early as WWI.

B216

B217

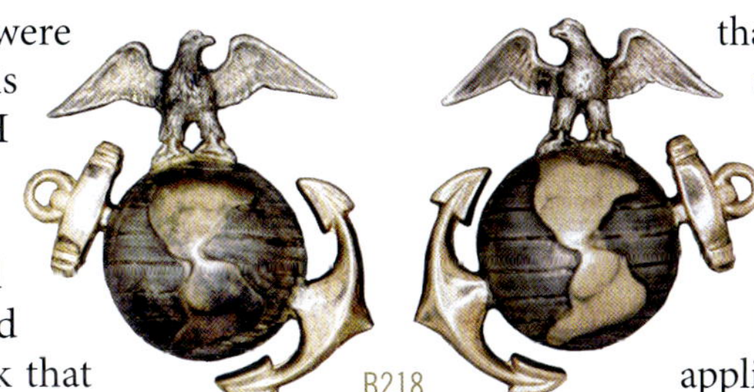

B218

Bent Neck Eagle Group

The most difficult group of officer dress collar emblems to classify with respect to function, date, and possible manufacturer were the variants B216 to B228. This group is referred to, for heuristic purposes, as the "Bent Neck Eagle Group." This selection is undoubtedly only a sample of many similar officer dress collar emblems. This is the most variable group of officer collar emblems from the period of 1904 to WWI. Later variants date after WWI through and even after WWII. What distinguishes them as a group is the distinctive eagle with a neck and head bent at a diagonal of almost forty-five degrees. In addition, the wings are quite slender and sharply pointed. The legs of the eagle are pronouncedly spread and form a triangular aperture. The anchors of the group seem essentially the same, but there is significant variation in the shape of the applied and struck continents and other finishing touches such as engraving and other conventions for depicting of the oceans. There are also various attachment mechanisms.

Examples of this group categorically date right back to 1904. One is depicted in an illustration in a 1907 Francis Bannerman catalog.[19] Several emblems in this group are back-marked by conventions that pre-date the 1906 US Stamping Act. The story of the group that post-dates WWI will be taken up in volume 2.

The dress set B216 shows excellent craftsmanship in line tool engraving of the irregular lines of latitude and the shark's tooth pattern for the oceans. The applied continents and anchor are an excellent gold plate. Back-marks only include the pre-1906 "SILVER." With no mention of "Gold," B216 is probably gold-plated. A simple drop-in pin assembly is the means of attachment.

Another example of B216 was described from the collections of the National WWI Museum at the Liberty Memorial in Kansas City, Missouri. The B216 right collar emblem was worn by Capt. Donald Duncan, KIA June 6, 1918, at Belleau Wood (see B216 appendix C-1). This example of B216 also had the pre-1906 "SILVER" back-mark. Another set of a minor variant of B216 has been observed that also includes the pre-1906 back-marking and superb hand finishing.

The USMCHCQV collections include the dress collar set B217 associated with Walter W. Wensinger, commissioned December 16, 1918. The dress collar set has gold-and-silver- plated anchor and applied continents of a unique shape. Like the above emblems of this group, it has the pre-1906 back-marks, "GOLD" and "SILVER." A very distinctive feature of the Walter Wensinger set is the Tiffany type catch and silver pivoting type pin assembly for attachment (see Figure XIII-2). The uniqueness of the Tiffany catch was first pointed out to the author by the well known, since deceased, Marine Corps emblem collector George Mennegaux. George was a retired jeweler from New York City. The shape of the continents on B217 is distinct from all others in this group. The set is heavily worn, but one can clearly see the line tooling producing a shark's tooth pattern for the oceans.

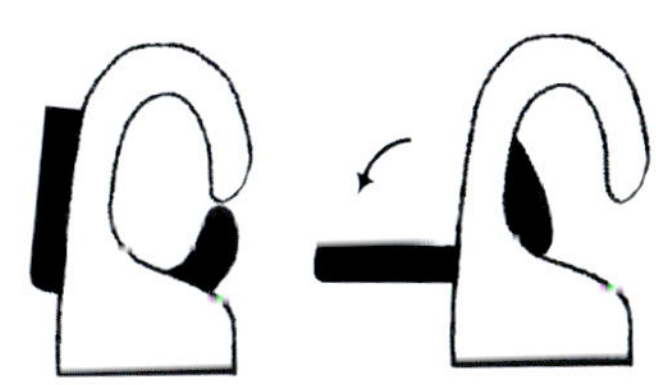

Figure XIII- 2
Tiffany catch.

A superb three-piece set of dress cap B185 and dress collar set B218 was photographed and described from a private collection. The set is associated with the estate of Capt. Robert Oswald Burwell, who was commissioned at Annapolis class of 1915 and resigned from the Corps in 1920.[20] This is another narrow window of time for the documented use of an emblem set. The only really unique feature is the shape of the handcrafted, gold-plated applied continents. The set shares many elements with others in the bent neck eagle group such as the shark's tooth line-tooled treatment for the oceans and hand-engraved lines of latitude and a rolling catch (Figure XIII-3) pin assembly.

With the pre-1906 "Gold" and "Silver" back-marks, the set could have been produced ten or more years before Burwell was commissioned. Without manufacturer's hallmarks, it is impossible to determine who may have made or sold the set. Another example of B218 with the pre-1906 "Gold" and "Silver" back-marks, with unevenly spaced and hand-engraved lines of latitude was sold on eBay.

B219

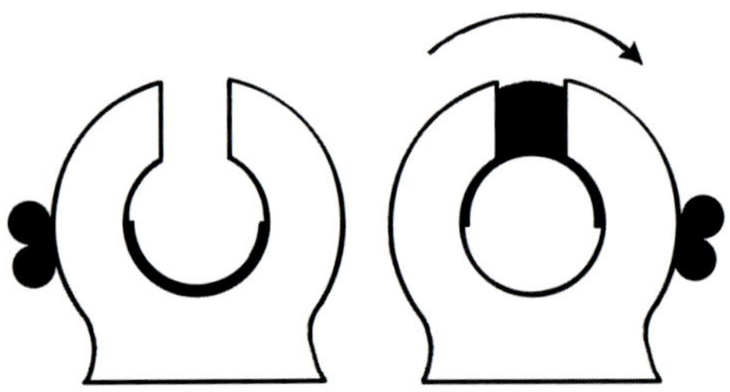
Figure XIII-3
Top-Loading
Rolling Catch.

The uniquely shaped solid-gold anchor, solid-gold, hand-applied continents, and the aesthetic bending of the eagle wings distinguish B219 from the B218 set. The bending of the wings for a more three-dimensional effect probably explains why WWI period black and white photos sometimes show officers wearing the bent neck eagle device with exceedingly long, thin, and pointed eagle wings. The "SILVER" and "GOLD" back-marks do not follow the 1906 legal requirements. The hand-engraved lines of latitude and the shark's tooth line tool engraving of the oceans display typical hand craftsmanship of this time period. Attachment was by means of a roll-type catch and silver pin assembly. A variant is known with a dot-dash pattern of line tooling for the oceans and the far less often seen Tiffany catch (Figure XIII-2). A set of B219 also lacking back-marks is known to be associated with Col. Percy Archer USMC 1909 to 1936.[21] As with the emblems of this group, the manufacturer could not be determined.

The unique shape of solid-gold continents applied to a solid-silver globe distinguish B220 from all of the emblems. The set has pre-1906 back-marks for "SILVER" and "GOLD" and exhibits a very thin solid-gold anchor tapered at both ends as if cast in a gold mold. This extra thin anchor, as well as the very lazy angle of the anchor where it is attached to the globe, is consistent with the early date of the set. The hand-engraved lines of latitude and shark's-tooth pattern for the oceans, as well as obvious differences in the measurements of the right and left emblems, are typical hand-crafted features. The screw post attachment is somewhat unusual, but not unknown with these very early twentieth century emblems.

The most unusual feature of the B221 set is the very peculiar shape of the solid- gold applied continents. At least one variant with this odd shape of the continents is known. Equally indicative of the jeweler's distinctive touch are the irregularly spaced and hand-engraved lines of latitude and shark's-tooth pattern line tooling obviously engraved after the continents had been applied. The back-marks "SILVER" and "GOLD" indicate production by an unknown manufacturer before or about the time of the 1906 US Stamping Act. The silver pin assembly consists of a variation of both the pivoting pin and a compound roll-type catch where the pin attaches to the side, not the top, of the catch (see Figure XIII-4). The set was purchased with uniform items associated with Brig. Gen. John Twiggs Myers USMC 1895 to 1935. The uniform items included the matching dress cap emblem (B183) on the general's dress white cover.[22]

Figure XIII-4
Side-loading, roll-type catch.
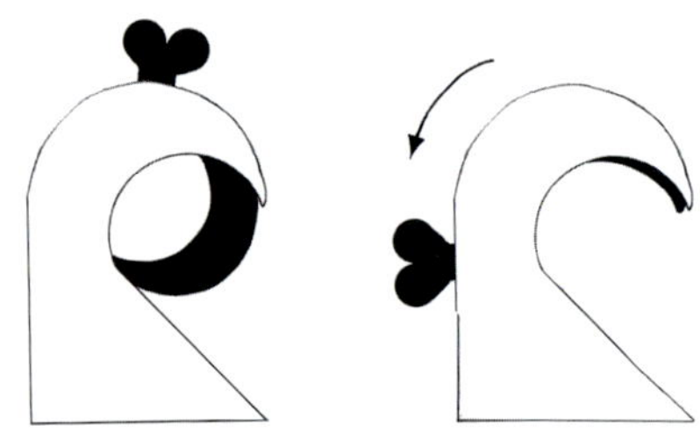

B220

Two examples of B221 are known, with the pre-1906 "SILVER" and "Gold" back-marks and a screw post for attachment. Not all early twentieth century dress collar emblems had pin backs.

B221

Compared to the collar emblems of the Bent Neck Eagle group, the right collar ornament B222 is a less expensive item, where corners were cut in the manufacturing process. It is probably the least expensive offering of V.H. Blackinton.[23] It is described as gold-and-silver plate, with no mention of superimposed continents. The sale price of B222 was only sixty cents a pair compared to $5 a pair for gold-and-sterling sets with superimposed continents. The anchor and distinctively shaped struck continents are gold-plated, not separate applied elements of solid gold. It still displays some hand-crafted finishing touches such as the engraved and uneven lines of latitude as well as a weak hand-engraved shark's-tooth pattern for the oceans. As with the above emblems, it also has the pre-1906 "SILVER" and "GOLD" back-marking convention and a silver pivoting pin assembly with the rolling catch where the pin is fed straight down, not on the side.

B222

Except for some details of hand finishing, the left collar ornament B223 is in all respects a fair match for B222. The craftsman positioned the anchor at a more acute angle than seen on B222. The hand engraving of the shark's-tooth and dot-dash pattern for the oceans is more complicated and vigorous than the weak engraving seen on the very similar B222. A well-worn matching set of B223 is associated with the dress blue blouse dated 1908 and

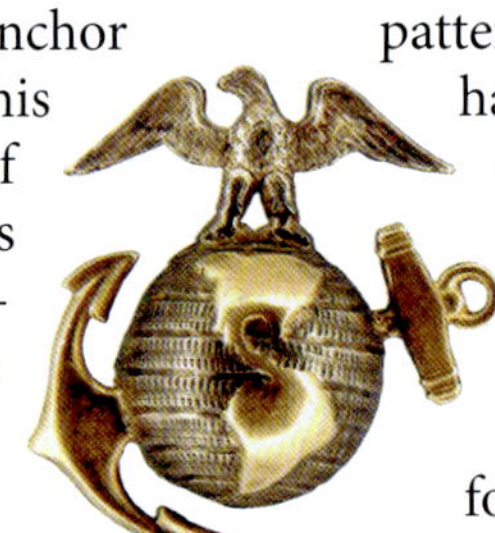
B223

identified to Capt. H.C. Snyder.[24] By 1912, Snyder had been promoted to major.[25] The dress blue blouse, with the B223 set and embroidered frogs across the chest, had by that time become obsolete. The Snyder dress collar set has the post-1906 "STERLING" back-mark. Other examples of B223 are known that vary with respect to finishing details, especially in the hand chasing of the oceans, the methods of attachment, and back-marks.

B224

Figure XIII-5
Blackinton catalog, ca.1932.

A matched set showing some wear, B224 is another likely set of V.H. Blackinton's less expensive dress collar ornaments with weak gold-plated anchor and struck continents. The means of attachment is a simple drop-in pin assembly. It can be distinguished from even less expensive sets by the hand chasing and finishing touches of uneven lines of latitude and the shark's-tooth pattern for the oceans. The set is back-marked with the pre-1906 "SILVER" and "GOLD" convention. It is also known without back-marks. Another feature of hand finishing is that the eagles and anchors are deliberately and cleverly bent to form a 360-degree disc, with the center of the globe forming the highest point with the eagle head, anchor ring, and crown forming the lowest points. Traces of a clear lacquer finish still remain.

B225

B226

The shape of the solid gold and applied continents of B225 is not really matched in this inventory. The set is in extraordinarily good condition and possibly never worn. The inclusion of pre-1906 back-marks with small fine-threaded screw post attachments is unusual, since screw posts of this type generally come later in time. Is this a very early screw post design or the continued use of pre-1906 back-marks after these were outlawed? The manufacturer is uncertain and variants with the same shape of solid gold continents are known, but with the dot-dash engraving for the oceans and the distinct Tiffany-type safety catch. Another example of B225 is known to have been converted to service collar usage by a chemical change that turns silver to a black color. With the shortage of officer service collar ornaments during WWI, converting dress sets to service use was not uncommon. A third example of B225 with the distinct applied continents is known with the very early twentieth century feature of the eagle head facing incorrectly.[26]

B227

Better documentation exists for identifying B226 than many of the Bent Neck Eagle types described above. It conforms well to the officer dress collar emblem #1090 illustrated in the ca. 1932 V.H. Blackinton Catalog (Figure XIII-5). At that time, #1090 was the bottom of the line set referred to as "Golden Ray," a mass-produced set with very little hand craftsmanship selling for $1.20 a set.[27]

Blackinton's cheapest dress collar emblems sold for only sixty cents a pair in 1918.[28] The catalog price data confirm the shift to mass production of inexpensive officer emblems to meet the emblem shortage and in response to a dramatic increase in the size of the officer corps. Further indication that B226 is a V.H. Blackinton production can be seen in Figure XIII-6. This advertisement appeared in *American Rifleman* in 1943.[29]

The service version of B226 is B239, which in addition to appearing in illustrated catalogs and advertisements, has been dated in photographs and uniform lots of WWI period officers. The common service version of B226 has also turned up in AEF French battlefield finds. All this indicates that B226 is the most common dress collar set of the WWI period.

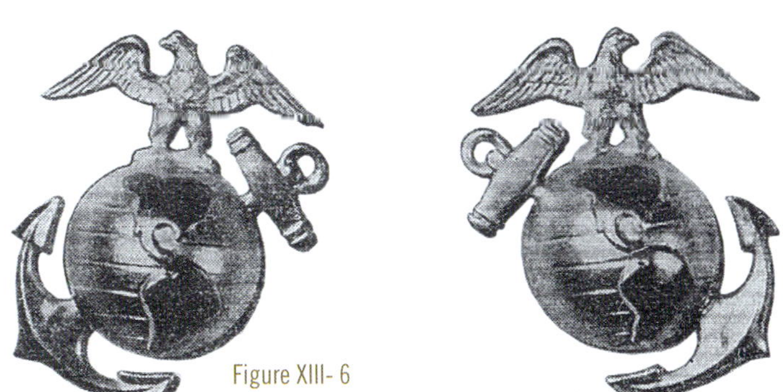

Figure XIII- 6
B226 Blackinton advertisement, 1943.

What clearly distinguishes B226 from the other Bent Neck Eagle Types is the lack of hand-crafted finishing touches and basic construction of the three elements: eagle, globe, and anchor, where essentially all details are from struck dies, without hand-engraving and other hand-crafted aesthetic touches such as applied continents. This is especially evident in the very fine and faint sand pattern for the oceans and die-struck lines of latitude. The lack of "SILVER," "GOLD," or "STERLING" back-marks suggests the use of some less expensive white metal or low-silver-content alloy as another measure to cut costs and increase production. The simple drop-in pin assembly is also consistent with a low-cost production. An example of B226 is known to have been converted from dress use to service by a chemical change or a dark brown lacquer.

Staff Officer Shoulder Knot Ornaments 1904 to 1912

The last of this highly diverse group is an all-silver emblem set that conforms to the 1904 Uniform Regulations and is best interpreted as the seldom-encountered staff officer's shoulder knot ornaments. For a very brief period (1900 to 1904), staff officers were authorized a distinct and intermediate size silver-and-gold set of emblems for shoulder knots. For the brief period 1904 to 1912, staff officers still maintained a special distinction from line officers by wearing all silver dress collar emblems on their shoulder knots.[30] After 1912, this special staff officer distinction was dropped. Both line and staff officers from that point on wore the same silver-and-gold dress collar emblems.

Consistent with the brief period of authorized use from 1904 to 1912 is the "SILVER" pre-1906 back-marks and the superb hand craftsmanship of B227. The engraving depicting the oceans was done with a line tool. The line tool effect was done as a distinct process after the continents had been struck. The line tooling obviously accommodates the shape of the exceedingly well-struck continents. The quality of the probable multiple strikes is also manifested in the superb details brought out in the anchor and especially the eagle feathering. Several hand-engraved lines also bring out details in the eagle. The engraved lines of latitude are not matching. The left ornament has ten hand-chased lines of latitude, while the right ornament has only nine. The silver pin is seated in a very unusual top-loading rolling-type safety catch with a special protective sleeve encasing the sharp tip of the pin, a feature no doubt designed for better protection and comfort. An example of B227 is known to have been converted to service use by applying a dark brown lacquer over the silver alloy. There is no good indication of who manufactured or sold the B227 set.

This excellent modern investment casting in solid silver is the work of Joe Weingarten. The original model for the casting is B226. Weingarten is up front and honestly advertises his high-quality work as museum grade reproductions and

B228

offers them for reasonable prices. The eagle, globe, and anchor are cast as a single piece and not as separate elements reassembled as in the original B226. Weingarten reproductions are highly polished with a simple drop-in pin assembly and "C"-shaped catch for attachment.

The most obvious features of the B228 casting are the muting of details and characteristic casting features discussed especially in chapter 12. Casting indications are especially evident on the reverse. The casting also leaves soft indistinct details, rather than hard clear details. This muting effect can be seen especially in the continents, lines of latitude, and eagle feathering. The fine, faint sand pebble texture for the oceans on the original model B226 is essentially muted in the casting, giving instead a smooth, rather than sandy, look. One can see a faint remnant of the original "STERLING" back-mark on the eagle right wing reverse. There is also a significant weight difference between the left and right emblems. This is the third example of a Weingarten investment casting discussed in this study.

B229

Miscellaneous and Unique Early Twentieth Century Officer Collar Emblems

One of the most distinctive officer dress collar ornaments encountered is in the collections of USMCHCQV. Two other emblems struck from the same die were described in two private collections. The most unique feature is a distinct eagle unlike anything seen on US Marine Corps emblems. It is reminiscent of the Mexican National symbol or a Napoleonic eagle of the First and Second empires.

The dress collar emblem B229 consists of two elements, an eagle struck from brass and a globe and anchor struck from a single and thinner sheet of brass. The combined eagle and globe element is silver-plated, while the anchor and continents are weakly gold-plated. Three rectangular-shaped bars or tags very similar to the Breuninger tags (Figure IV-I) serve to attach the thicker eagle element to a separate and thinner globe. Two other rectangular silver tags reinforce the thin anchor at its juncture with the equally thin globe. At the same time, these two tags serve as the base for a rectangular bar with a pivoting type drop-in pin assembly (see Figure XIII-7).

The second example of B229 came from the estate of Capt. Robert Oswald Burwell, USMC 1915 to 1920.[31] Burwell served from 1916 to late 1919 in the Caribbean at Santo Domingo, Nicaragua, and almost three years in Haiti before resigning in January 1920.[32] It is quite possible that the highly unusual B229 is a theatre-made emblem.

Figure XIII-7
Unique construction of B229.

It is curious that two other examples of this B242 die-strike in service bronze, are associated with two officers who also served in the Caribbean at about the same time that Burwell served there. At the same time, all three officers also served in the Washington, DC, area, where a local jeweler could have made these very unusual emblems.

B230

The next two emblems are also seldom seen and also have very distinct designs. Without manufacturer's marks or other indicators of age and manufacturer, they remain problematic. Because B230 is also known as a service collar ornament (B243), it is probably an officer's left dress collar ornament rather than an unusual and well-made silver-and-gold sweetheart pin. A firm date is not possible and this emblem may be from the period between WWI and 1926 rather than earlier. It is tentatively classified as belonging to the longer period 1904 to 1918 rather than the shorter period 1918 to 1926.

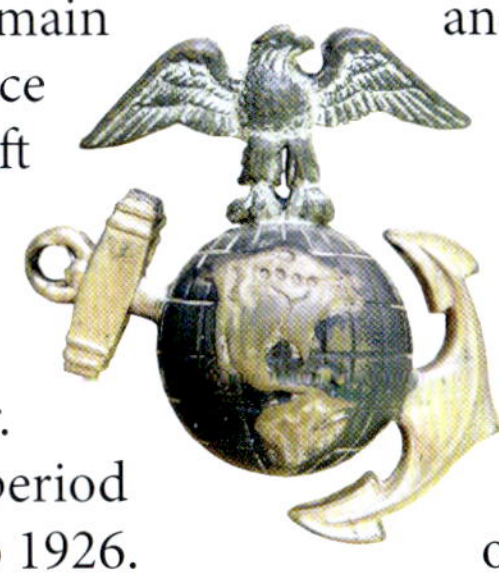

B231

The eagle, globe, and the anchor are struck from a single sheet of brass. This single-piece construction eliminates all the traditional handcrafted finishing touches. The thin gold-plated anchor and continents, as well as the thin silver plate of the eagle and globe are not of a high quality and wear easily, showing the brass base metal underneath. The lack of back-marks and the simple drop-in pin assembly are also consistent with a low-end mass-produced emblem of the WWI period.

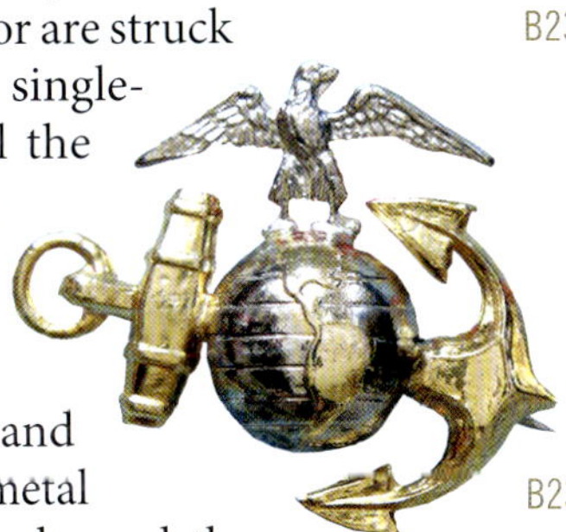

B232

Another distinct and highly unusual design for what is presumably an officer's right dress collar emblem B231 is also classified with uncertainty. Unlike B230, there is to date no known service version of it or a matching dress left collar emblem. It is mounted permanently on a square brass buckle stamped "M.E. Sullivan 225 5th Avenue." The permanent mounting prevented an examination of the reverse of this curious emblem. The device may have been struck from a single brass plate or possibly in three pieces: eagle, globe, and anchor, and then reassembled. The quality of the gold plate is better than the thin, weak silver plate on the eagle and globe. Because of its permanent mounting on the buckle, these questions could not be answered.

What is clear is the very unusual design of the eagle, the anchor, and especially the globe, with lines of both latitude and longitude and the extraordinary cartographic rendition of the continents. Special effort was made in the die preparation to depict details such as river systems, including but not limited to the Mississippi and Ohio River system, the Great Lakes, and the Amazon River in South America. These singular features do not appear to be done by hand-engraving but are a part of the die preparation that resulted in a superb die bringing out extraordinary detail. Mass production, where the details of the emblem are almost exclusively a function of die striking, instead of hand craftsmanship, could have been a response to the emblem shortage and increased need for emblems during WWI. This is an additional consideration for tentatively including B231 in chapter 13. Future discoveries of matching emblems in dress and service might help substantiate this interpretation, especially if new information about historical context is forthcoming.

The last example of an officer's dress collar emblem set for this period is the handsome modern reproduction and fantasy creation of a French-made collar emblem of 1918. Joe Weingarten, using investment-casting technology described for B101 in chapter 6, produces these emblems and advertises them as museum quality reproductions. They can be purchased for reasonable prices. The model for the investment castings is B250.

The eagle, globe, anchor, and part of the pin assembly are cast as a single piece, while the original French-made B250 is composed of separate die-struck elements reassembled by soldering. B232 is an excellent casting, but still displays characteristics of investment casting as opposed to die-struck emblems. The silver or white metal alloy is quite soft. Over this white metal, a gold-like plating is used to depict the continents and anchor. A simple drop-in pin assembly with a "C"-shaped catch is the means of attachment. The pin pivot point is not pierced as in most emblems, but is simply wire coiled to form a circle to pivot as well as provide tension on the pin to lock into the catch.

This research has found no known photographs or examples of French-made silver-and-gold collar emblems. It is unlikely that any were ever produced. The emblem shortage was for service emblems, not dress emblems. The service version of B232 is discussed in chapter 14.

CHAPTER XIV

Officer Service Cap Emblems: 1904 through WWI

(B233 to B252)

During the period up through WWI, service collar ornaments, although more numerous than officer dress collar ornaments, actually show less variation than dress collar ornaments. The significant increase in the size of the Marine Corps and the number of Marines serving in field units not only in France, but also throughout the Caribbean and elsewhere, created a great demand for service emblems and a consequent shortage. To fill that pressing need manufacturers resorted increasingly to mass-production that tended to eliminate older handcrafted features. Many service collar emblems seen in this sample are simply die-struck emblems where most, and in some cases all of the details are a function of the die striking a bronze or brass blank. An exception to this efficiency measure is that manufacturers continued to offer a variety of options with variable prices. It is hardly surprising that most sales were not the more expensive options. The manufacturer's various options help to explain the remarkable diversity of both dress and service collar ornaments at this time. The service collar ornaments in this chapter are hopefully a good representative sample of that remarkable variability.

B233

B234

B235

Bailey, Banks & Biddle Service Ornaments

Except for minor differences in the shape of the applied continents, the two BB&B examples are the bronze versions of their BB&B dress collar counterparts described in chapter 13.

The left collar service ornament B233 is an excellent match for the emblem illustrated in the 1907 Bailey, Banks & Biddle Catalog priced at $2.50 a pair.[1] In all probability, it dates back to 1904 (see Figure XIV-1). The distinctive extra fine detail of old style BB&B service emblems likely remained unchanged until 1926. An illustration of B233 also appears in the 1925 changes to the 1922 Uniform Regulations.[2] Significant changes in the old-style BB&B emblems did occur, first in 1926 and then again about 1936. These changes will be discussed in volume 2.

Figure XIV-1
B233 illustrated in 1907 BB&B catalog.

Back-marked "BB&B" and "BRONZE," B233 has a dark brown lacquer finish with struck, not applied, continents. The means of attachment is a pin assembly with a roll-type top loading safety catch. A positive, fine sand pebble pattern for the oceans is a die-strike feature eliminating traditionally hand-engraved effects. Variations in the placement of the back-marks are known, as well as simple drop-in pin assemblies.

With the exception of the shape of the struck continents and anchor, B234 is close enough to B233 to tentatively classify it as a BB&B service collar emblem without back-marks. The differences in the shape of the anchor may simply be a product of using a different trimming tool. The eagle is from the same die as B233, but it is attached differently at the top of the globe. The three elements: eagle, anchor, and globe with continents, are struck in bronze with a dark brown lacquer finish. Continents are not applied, and the struck fine sand pebble depiction of the oceans simplifies the finishing process. The means of attachment for B234 is a simple drop-in pin assembly, but roll-type safety catches are also known. One of only two recent finds of officer's service collar emblems from French battlefields and Marine encampments is the B234 right collar device. It was found at Belleau Wood and reported to Michael O'Shea by Gilles Lagrin.[3] The B234 set has also been identified with a uniform lot including a French-made service collar device (B249) on a campaign cover associated with 2nd Lt. Frederick F. Nagel (see B234, appendix C-1).

Early N.S. Meyer Service Collar Emblems

The following two emblems, even though they are not back-marked, conform very well with their dress collar counterpart B215. The 1918 N.S. Meyer catalog illustration (Figure XIII-1) is consistent with the design of the two service collar ornaments, B235 and B236.

The most obvious features that distinguish the early N.S. Meyer dress and service collar emblems are the long skinny necks and the three huge talons on the feet of the eagles. In addition, the struck continents display a unique shape, especially

Central America. B235 is unusual for having both eagles facing the left and is composed of three separate struck and reassembled elements: eagle, globe, and anchor. The alloy is bronze with a dark brown lacquer finish. "FIRE BRONZE" back-marks are placed in different positions on the reverse of the right and left emblems. The means of attachment is a simple drop-in pin assembly with a "C"-shaped catch.

The differences between B235 and B236 are so minor that B236 is also tentatively classified as an N.S. Meyer variant. The eagle heads are correctly positioned on B236 and are struck from the same die as B235. The globe element of B236 is struck from a different die and can be seen in the shape of the continents. The anchor element of B236 is also struck from a different die and is thicker and less slender than B235. This fat anchor is not simply a feature resulting from a different trimming tool. The angle and uneven spacing of the lines of latitude suggest a handcrafted error when the separate elements were reassembled. Curiously, B236 has the patented Tiffany-type safety catch (Figure XIII-2), instead of the simple drop-in catch of B235. All three elements of B236 are struck in bronze and back-marked "SOLID FIRE BRONZE." Among the options offered in the N.S. Meyer 1918 catalog (Figure XIII-1), "FIRE BRONZE: and "REAL BRONZE" were priced differently. Those marked "REAL BRONZE" were $1.50 each, while those marked "FIRE BRONZE" were only eighty-five cents apiece. Examples of B236 struck in even less expensive brass and finished with a dark brown lacquer finish are also known.

A set of B236 can be found in the USMCHCQV collections on an unidentified officer's service blouse with a Second Division black diamond patch. The Quantico B236 emblem set on that particular blouse was donated in July 2003.

The left and right bronze collar emblems B237came from two separate private collections and are not a matching set, even though the separate elements (eagle, globe, anchor, and continents) are struck from the same dies. B237 right is a pin-back type with a side-loading safety catch; B237 left has a screw post for attachment. Both ornaments have a fine sand pebble stippling effect for the oceans and a distinctive shape to the applied continents. The continents on the right device are superimposed over lines of latitude that are incorrect, a hand-finishing error sometimes encountered. Note also the variation in the angle of the anchors where they are attached by hand to the globes. The left collar emblem has no back-marks while the right collar device is back-marked "SOLID FIRE BRONZE." Without a manufacturer's mark and considering the distinctly shaped applied continents over struck continents, it is uncertain whether this set is a variant of the N.S. Meyer emblems B235 and B236 or a product of an entirely different and unknown manufacturer. Since there is no mention in the

B236

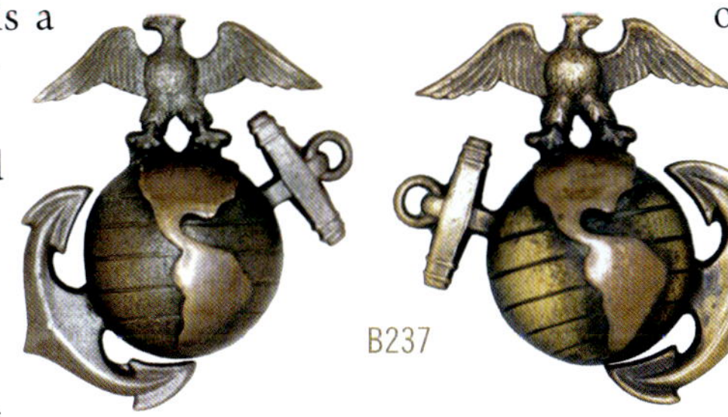

B237

B238

1918 N.S. Meyer catalog of an option to buy service collar emblems with superimposed continents, these may have been made by a manufacturer other than N.S. Meyer.

If the manufacturer of B237 is uncertain, there is excellent information available on the brief period of use for this set. Two minor variants of B237 with the distinctly shaped but struck continents are associated with identified AEF service uniforms worn during WWI by 2nd Lt. Colgate W. Darden, USMC 1918 to 1920, and Capt. Amos Raymond Shinkle, commissioned officer 1917 to 1919. Both officers served in France[4] (see also B237 in appendix C-1). The Shinkle uniform in the USMCHCQV collections has the Second Infantry Division yellow diamond patch for the Second Battalion 6th Marine Regiment and an officer's silk fourragere. Both of these uniform ensembles confirm an unusual and relatively brief period of use by these two officers.

A final example of an officer's service left collar emblem best resembles B235 in having the same eagle and same anchor. Despite a very similar shape, the continents on B238 are separate applied elements, not struck as is B235. These strong similarities between the B235 and B238 emblem suggest that both may be N.S. Meyer products without manufacturer hallmarks. Purchasing an N.S. Meyer bronze set with superimposed or struck continents may have been options, but such an option is not listed in the 1918 price list. B238 is back-marked "FIRE BRONZE," just as the $1.00 pair listed in the 1918 N.S. Meyer catalog. The means of attachment is a side-loading, roll- type catch on a silver or white metal pin assembly. As with B235, the oceans are depicted by a fine sand pebble stippling. A dark brown lacquer finish was applied over the bronze. This research has found no known example of B238 with applied continents in silver and gold for dress collar use.

Officer Service Collar Emblems of the Bent Neck Eagle Group Through WWI

Unlike the dozen variants of dress collar emblems of this group, only three variants could be identified for service use. Although less diverse as a group, they are one of the most commonly encountered emblems for this period. The numbers that have shown up in this research indicate that substantial quantities were manufactured in which handcrafted effects were minimal and mass-production prevailed. As with their dress collar counterparts, a few surely date back to 1904, but the vast majority seem to have been produced in substantial numbers to meet the service collar emblem needs brought on by WWI.

The service version of dress collar B226 in silver and gold is the bronze collar set B239. Like its dress counterpart, it was mass-produced with very few handcrafted finishing features. In their ca.1918 price list, V.H. Blackinton was charging only sixty cents a pair.[5] Further evidence that B239 is an unmarked V.H. Blackinton production can be seen a photo of a V.H. Blackinton salesman's sample board containing various WWI period military insignia. The photo, courtesy of Ray Darida, was found in the W. Stokes Kirk collection (see Figure XIV-2).

B239

Figure XIV-2
B239 on Blackinton salesman's sample board.

It is consistent that Blackinton emblems, mass-produced at low prices, should be the most often encountered WWI period officer's service collar emblem. Two instances can be documented where B239 sets were found in good association with uniform lots identified to specific officers who served during this period. Four other examples of B239 have been associated with the estates of officers, two of whom only served briefly. All of these associations with known WWI period officers have been confirmed by the US Marine Corps muster rolls. All six of these finds are summarized in appendix C-1 (B239).

A seventh example of B239 is one of only two known officer's service collar ornaments recently found in France. This field find of B234 was a single right collar ornament found at Belleau Wood.[6]

Besides lacking time-consuming and expensive finishing features, the entire sample of B239 is single-piece construction, struck from a single plate to produce all details. Consistent with their mass production is the simple white metal drop-in pin assembly as the means of attachment. The examples examined were all finished with a dark brown lacquer and lacked any manufacturer hallmarks.

Several examples of the dress collar ornament B226 (chapter 13) were converted to service use by a black or brown paint or chemical change, to cover or chemically change the color of the original silver and gold elements. These conversions of dress to service emblems further support the contention of a shortage of officer and enlisted service emblems during WWI.

Lacking back-marks, one cannot be certain, but the degree of similarity between the dress set B224 and service right collar emblem B240 is striking. There is a minor difference in the treatment of the oceans. On B240 the oceans are depicted by a struck stippling pattern rather than the struck shark's-tooth pattern of their dress counterpart. The strong similarity in the cartography of the struck North and South American continents would suggest the same manufacturer, despite the fact that the continents are better struck in the service version than on the dress version. The same eagle and anchor elements, as well as the same simple drop-in pin assembly, are consistent on both sets. Over the bronze base metal, a dark brown lacquer finish was applied.

It is known that V.H. Blackinton offered this type in their catalogs and advertisements as early as ca.1918 but probably continued to offer these until 1926, when the size of service collar emblems for officers was reduced 25%.[7] Officers were required to replace the obsolete larger collar emblems on their winter service blouses by July 1, 1927, and January 1, 1928, on their winter service green blouses. This change did not apply to the larger size dress collar silver and gold emblems, which continued to be sold, advertised, and worn through WWII, and in some cases, even later. This official change to a reduced size service collar emblem for officers does not mean, as some mistakenly claim, that all reduced size service collar emblems date to 1926. This issue will be more thoroughly revisited in volume 2.

B240

A set of service collar ornaments that best conforms to the better struck B240 than the weakly struck B239 is a part of a group of emblems from the estate of W.C. Powell USMC1896 to 1927[8] (See also W.C. Powell, appendix C-1, B240).

The last example of the Bent Neck Eagle group is an earlier dress collar gold-and-silver left collar emblem with the pre-1906 back-marking conventions "SILVER" and "GOLD." It was converted to service use by a chemical change to black. Unlike those mass-produced emblems described above, B241 displays other early features such as exceptionally well-struck and reconstructed separate elements of eagle, globe, and continents very similar in shape to earlier dress collar emblems B219, B220, and B225. These handcrafted features also include hand-engraved lines of latitude and a shark's-tooth engraved pattern of oceans. The seldom encountered and distinctive Tiffany-type safety catch and silver pin assembly is the method of attachment.

B241

When the new requirement in 1904 for bronze emblems came into being, it is conceivable that some officers would, by a simple chemical change, convert for service use, a supernumerary set of relatively expensive gold and silver dress collar emblems. Converting more expensive solid silver and gold emblems makes little sense, when the new bronze emblems could be purchased at that time for about sixty cents a pair at the low end, to a maximum of $2.50 for a set of BB&B top-of-the-line bronze emblems.[9] A more likely scenario is that unneeded dress collar sets were converted to service use during the service emblem shortages of WWI. Converting an expensive gold-and-silver set by a chemical change makes great sense when much-needed service sets were simply unavailable for purchase, until manufacturers could meet the requirement, especially through mass production.

Miscellaneous Service Collar Ornaments of the WWI Period

On first glance, the B242 right collar device in bronze appears to be the mirror image of the silver-and-gold dress counterpart B229. On closer examination, especially of the eagle wing feathering patterns and the anchors, the correspondence is not one to one, but B242 is extremely well executed by the use of matching dies displaying marvelous die-cutting skill. In the author's experience, only four examples have been encountered. Two were from private collections and one (B229) is in the USMCHCQV collections. John Driscoll sent the author photos of the obverse and reverse of a forth example in bronze from another private collection (see B242 appendix C-1). B242 belonged to William G. Powell, USMC 1899 to 1927.[10]

It is unusual to be able to confidently identify collar ornaments in old photographs. Figure XIV-3 was discovered in the USMC photo collections in the Washington Navy Yard in 2003 and clearly shows Col. Wendell Neville wearing a set of B242. The photo probably dates closer to 1914 than 1917. This is entirely consistent with the dress version (B229) worn by Capt. Burwell at the same time period.

Figure XIV-3
Col. Wendell Neville wearing B242.

B242

The same fragile, intricate construction is in all respects the same as that described for B229. The anchors of B229 and B242 are very unusual in being two separate elements attached to the globe by means of rectangular tags. The separate eagle is also attached to the globe with this old-fashioned method reminiscent of the work of Karl Breuninger.

The left collar emblem B243 is the service version of B230 in dress. The large and unique eagle head, the shape of the continents, and the anchor stock are distinctive die-struck features, and are exactly the same in both emblems. The almost smooth surface of the oceans is another feature of a weak die strike that contrasts dramatically with hand engraving to depict oceans. Lacking back-marks, these infrequently encountered emblems are problematic to classify with respect to both a manufacturer and a clear period of use. Because of its large size, B243 has to date prior to the changes of 1926 and could be one of those many mass-produced, inexpensive emblems meeting the wartime shortage. All the details of the design are a function of a die strike on the single piece of bronze. The means of attachment is a simple drop-in pin with a "C"-shaped catch. The dark brown finish chips easily, indicating an inexpensive lacquer covering.

B243

In over twenty years of research, this very unusual right service collar emblem is the only one that the author has encountered. John Driscoll's Figure 38, that he dates 1904 to 1914, shows great similarity.[11] The emblem Driscoll illustrates is clearly a variant. B244 is a part of the USMCHCQV collections (Accession #841310 OR). Every element is quite distinctive, especially the remarkable eagle with large, long wings, huge beak, and disproportionately small body and legs. It is consistent with other real bronze constructions and consists of separate elements: eagle, globe, anchor, and applied continents. The weak lines of latitude are uneven, suggesting they were hand-engraved or that the diesinker prepared uneven lines on the die. All of these features, including a complex silver pin assembly with "C"-type catch, are characteristic of emblems dating prior to WWI.

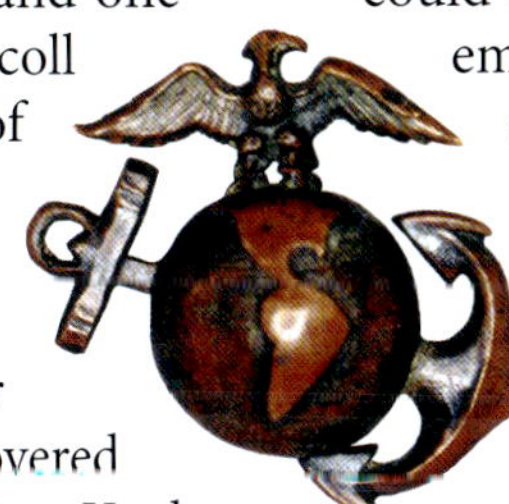

B244

B245

Another example of a one-of-a-kind occurrence in the author's research is B245 from the extensive collection of the late Georg Mennegaux. George was very proud to have acquired this bronze left collar ornament manufactured by the William Link Company and marked by their characteristic trademark (Figure XII-4). When George Mennegaux bought B245, he immediately knew that it was not in his remarkable collection and was an exceptional find.[12] George had an extraordinary ability, somewhat like eidetic imagery, to perceive similarities and differences in emblems. If he already owned it, he could recognize it immediately, thereby avoiding the unpleasantness most of us have experienced of unnecessarily buying expensive emblems already in our collections.

Just about everything on B245 is distinctively designed: the eagle, the anchor, the globe, and the unique shape of the struck continents. One interesting feature is the rare construction of the anchor in two separate elements. An upper element includes the anchor stock and ring, while a separate lower element includes the anchor arms and crown. In this research, this unusual construction feature has only been encountered with B242, which in all other respects is a totally different emblem.

The William Link back-mark appears on the mid-eagle reverse and the lower anchor fluke reverse. A dark brown lacquer finish is evident. When George bought B245, an unknown type of pin attachment had been ground away and in its place, a hole was drilled in the eagle breast to attach the emblem to an officer's swagger stick. There is at this time no known gold-and-silver version of B245.

B246

Another example of a single occurrence in this research is the superbly designed and exquisitely struck B246 left bronze collar ornament by the Tiffany Jewelry Company. Every detail of the design is distinctive. The uniqueness is especially evident in the eagle, its superb pattern of feathers, and the highly realistic cartography of the continents. The device is incised with the back-marks "TIFFANY & COMPANY" on the eagle right wing reverse and "BRONZE" on the eagle left wing reverse. A back-mark that looks like a block letter "E" turned ninety degrees clockwise is also incised on the eagle right wing reverse (see Figure XIV-4). This back-mark is actually a block letter 'M" for John C. Moore, who served as the Tiffany director from 1907 to 1947.[13] All elements: eagle, globe, and anchor are struck from a single piece of very thin solid bronze. The eagle, as well as the upper and lower anchor stock elements, are all one piece and all attached to the globe as a single strike. Instead of a mid-anchor stock, a rectangular bar is hard-soldered between the upper and lower anchor stock to form the base for a silver pivoting pin assembly with the distinctive Tiffany catch (Figure XIII-2). Another unusual construction feature is the attachment of the anchor flukes to the globe. The handsome fire bronze alloy eliminates any need for a brown lacquer finish. The author has not encountered any examples of the dress collar version B246 in silver and gold. Although B246 was authorized for wear up to 1926, it most likely was manufactured earlier than that.

B247

Figure XIV-4
Tiffany director John C. Moore back-mark.

The highly distinctive service collar set B247 is the matching collar emblem set for the service cap emblem B206 (see B247, appendix C-1). With perhaps one exception, there is nothing in the design that matches anything in this inventory. Although many have been examined, none are known with manufacturer marks. The unique design and the tight dating evidence imply a WWI emergency item. The dated photographs of known officers wearing these indicate that they were worn up through the 1930s and probably manufactured stateside. One cannot rule out other possibilities, such as English-made emblems from a manufacturer such as J.R Gaunt. An example of B247 is illustrated in a 1921 publication.[14] Others identified in dated photos (B247, appendix C-1) are worn by officers, all of whom were commissioned in 1918 or 1919. One officer (Thorndike) served only one year before being discharged.

The highly unusual construction has only three elements: 1.) Eagle, globe, and anchor; 2.) applied continents; and 3.) rectangular bar and drop-in pin assembly. The collar version is simply a scaled-down version of the cap emblem (B206). As with the service cap emblem B206, the thick applied continents are placed over struck continents. Variants are known with fine-threaded screw post attachments instead of drop-in pin backs. This simplification of a single die to strike the eagle, the globe, and the anchor elements reflects the manufacturer's trend toward greater efficiency at less cost. The details brought out by the excellent die strike rival the old-fashioned, hand-crafted emblems using several dies and hand-finishing skills.

French-Made Officer Bronze Service Collar Emblems

The splendid group of French-made officer's service collar emblems shares a very strong family resemblance in style, construction techniques, and materials. An attempt was made to include as many variants in this study as possible. Evidently, several dies and craftsmen were involved in their production. It is quite likely that the same unknown French manufacturer that produced the USMC enlisted collar discs described in chapter 15 may have manufactured these superb officer's emblems as well. What is known about this French procurement will be discussed in chapter 15.

The French-made group, in general, has a handsome pattern of weathering. Almost all of those observed have a shiny patina of a dark-brown chocolate-like color. The unique eagle, with long pointed wings and legs shaped like bloused boots, has a vague resemblance to French eagles of the First and Second Empires. All are constructed of three separate die-struck elements then reassembled. Those observed in this research are without manufacturer marks and have bronze pin assemblies with a "C"-shaped safety catch and a distinct coil where the pin pivots. The coil allows the pin to lock in the safety catch. The continents on all varieties are struck, not applied.

B248

The service collar set B248 is the less-often-encountered and diminutive pair with an unusual curved anchor stock. The more common variety is larger and has straight anchor stocks. The B248 set was bought from a man in France who specializes in US Marine WWI sales from battlefield or surplus contexts. The set came from a collector in Belgium, who claims the set was associated with the winter service blouse of 1st Lt. Bert Herried[15] (see B248 appendix C-1). Other features that set B248 apart from the more common straight stock emblems are the small, smooth, featureless anchor arms and crown, a smaller anchor length, and about half the weight of the emblems with the straight stocks. The set is the smallest example of the French-made officer collar emblems.

The set B249 also has a distinctive curved anchor stock, but should not be confused with the smaller, less-often-encountered set B248. Although both sets share the same eagle and globe elements, the anchor element is not only thicker and larger but is struck from an entirely different die. The larger anchor is struck from thicker bronze and accounts for a significant weight difference. In a photo dated 1920, Lt. F.W. Bennett, who served with the AEF, is seen wearing a B249 set (see B249, appendix C-1).

The set B249 comes from two different collections photographed and described fourteen years apart. The left emblem is considerably more worn and was bought on an officer's blouse with French labels.[16] Since B249 occurs in a port and starboard pair, they were obviously meant to serve as collar emblems, but in an emergency would have been worn on headgear. The right collar emblem from another collection is a mirror image of the left emblem, with the exception of showing less wear and maintaining some of the original brown lacquer finish. One curious variant was observed in a collection with the inside of the curve of the anchor stock facing inboard instead of outboard.[17]

B249

B250

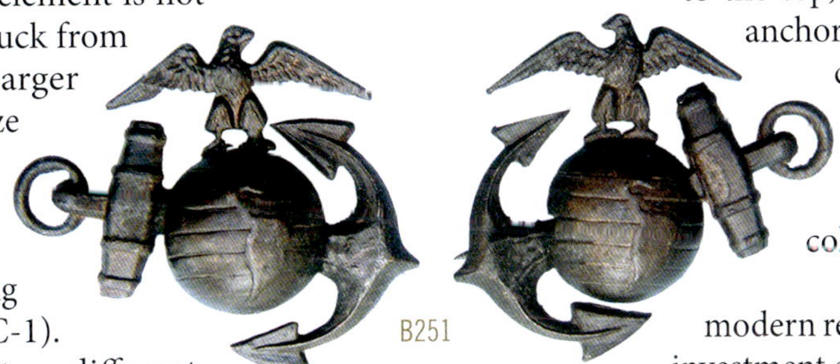
B251

Of the French-made officer's collar ornaments, B250 is the variety most often encountered. Its most distinctive feature is the straight anchor stock, tapered at both ends. It is clearly identifiable in WWI photos.[18] In one photo, a cheeky enlisted Marine is wearing an unauthorized officer's B250 left emblem on his fore and aft cover. A photographic indication that B250 was also used as a cap device is seen in Figure XIV-5.

The right and left emblems of B250 are another example of a good match from separate collections photographed more than a year apart. This set, like all the other French-made collar devices, consists of three separate die-struck elements. The set consists of a globe with an eagle soldered to the top, and a full anchor element from anchor ring to crown attached to grooves cut in the globe element. Note that the craftsman set the globe upside down when the three elements were assembled for the right collar device.

Joe Weingarten produces the modern reproductions B232 and B251 using investment casting techniques as described for making B101 in chapter 6.[19] The most distinguishing feature of B251 is the casting of all three elements: eagle, globe, and anchor, as a single entity. The model for the Weingarten B251 casting was the French-made B250, which consists of separately struck eagle, globe, anchor, and pin assembly elements that were reassembled by soldering after being die struck.

Close examination of B251 reveals subtle investment casting indications, such as flash and a center line seen especially on the upper surface or edge of the eagle wings and anchor arms. This line indicates where the two-piece mold separated. Other subtleties can be seen in tiny pits and protrusions on the casting in places that are smooth as glass on the French-made emblems. By comparison, the French die-struck emblems have a smoother and more uniform surface, perhaps reflecting tumbling in steel shot or burnishing stones.

Nevertheless, B233 and B251 are superb museum quality reproductions. The dark brown, almost black, finish was achieved with a chemical reagent, such as selenium dioxide or other chemicals that result in an even chemical film of a dark-brown color on the surface of the brass. The result is very unlike the thick, uneven covering of dark-brown lacquer commonly seen on service collar emblems of this period. Dark-brown lacquer, as a finish, has a tendency to chip easily.

Figure XIV-5
B250 on fore and aft cover.

The shortage of service collar emblems in the AEF during WWI prompted some officers to purchase French-made embroidered cloth emblems. The well-known photograph previously cited (Brig. Gen. Wendel Neville's staff dated August 11, 1918) clearly shows Lt. W.A. Eddy wearing embroidered collar emblems on his winter service blouse and fore and aft cover[20] (see Figure XIV-6).

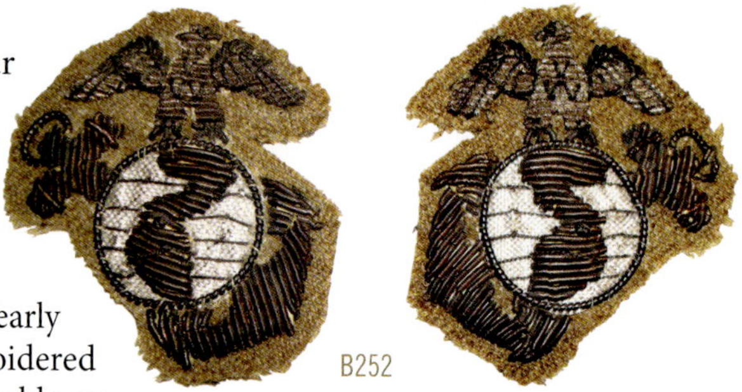

B252

Figure XIV-6
B250 and B252
Lt. Claggett Wilson and Lt. W.A. Eddy.

It is not known who wore the B252 French embroidered set. The set was purportedly sold by the family of the second lieutenant who wore the helmet, trousers, blouse, and boots in the ensemble. The blouse has the second Infantry Division patch, a Sam Browne belt, and fourragère.

The set is highly unusual, in that the embroidered collar emblems are closer to dress collar devices than to service collar emblems. The embroidery is on olive drab wool with a backing of black cotton muslin. The eagle is embroidered in silver bullion thread with black thread highlights. The globe, continents, and anchor are embroidered in gold bullion thread. The means of attachment are twisted gold wires at the anchor ring and border of the globe. The globe is embroidered in a glittery metallic material without tarnish. The lines of latitude are stitched in black thread. Such variation from the norm in officer's emblems had to be driven by the emergency.

A more simplified variant of a French embroidered service collar emblem is also known. Brown thread was used to embroider a port-and-starboard set of eagle, globe, and anchors on squares of olive drab wool.

Chapter XV

Enlisted Dress and Service Cap Emblems: WWI

(B253 to B263)

It is not known with any certainty exactly when the types of enlisted cap ornaments described in this chapter first appeared. Some authorizations for emblems may have gone back to the many important uniform changes that occurred in 1912. Many of these significant changes did not result in actual issues for as much as two years. There was an expectable lag between the authorization, procurement, and the manufacturer's ability to deliver the orders. What is certain is that none of the chapter 15 enlisted cap emblems have been clearly identified in photos or credible and datable uniform ensembles of known Marines prior to late 1916. Despite the huge increase in the number of US Marines from 1917 to 1919, the diversity in emblems is actually less than the period 1904 to 1917. There were five times as many Marines on active duty in 1919 than there were in 1912.[1] Only three distinct types of enlisted cap emblems are known to date ca.1916 to 1919, one of which has never been observed in both dress and service versions.

Type I dress cap emblems are the same as Driscoll figure 53 and can be distinguished from two other main types by the more narrow shape of the eagle's wings and minor differences in the feathering pattern, shape of the eagle's body, the anchor stock, and the cartography of South America. Some of these distinctions are pointed out with tick marks. Attachment is exclusively by means of a screw posts with thirty-two turns per inch.

Manufacturer marks have never been encountered on any of the emblems in this chapter. Like the other types in chapter 15, B253 displays the traditional double lines for the Tropic of Cancer and Tropic of Capricorn as well as a diagonal rhumb line. B253 is struck from a single plate of gilders metal #14 brass.

The manufacturer or seller is questionable but an example of B253 is illustrated on page 53 of an undated catalog by Thomas Parry's Sons Co. (see Figure XV-1). Bruce Bazelon describes the firm of Thomas Parry of Camden, New Jersey, as being in business at that location from 1913 until about 1930.[2] When that firm went out of business, William Horstman dies were found in their inventory. This suggested to Bazelon that the Thomas Parry Company may have been striking insignia for the William Horstman Company.

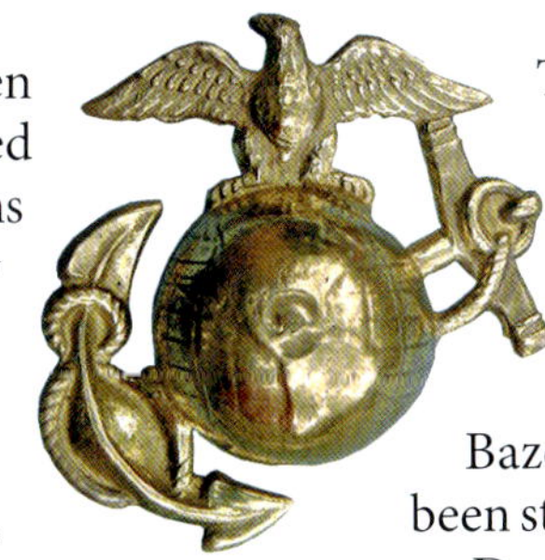

B253

Documents cited in chapter 10 indicate that William Horstman was probably the main source for enlisted cap emblems for the Marine Corps at the turn of the twentieth century. It is conceivable that William Horstman continued to be the primary supplier of enlisted Marine emblems. US Marine Corps Quartermaster procurement records on file with the US Treasury Department Record Group in the National Archives could possibly clarify who sold what to the Marine Corps during WWI.

Of the three types of emblems in this chapter, B253 in dress and B256 in service are the most commonly encountered WWI enlisted emblems.

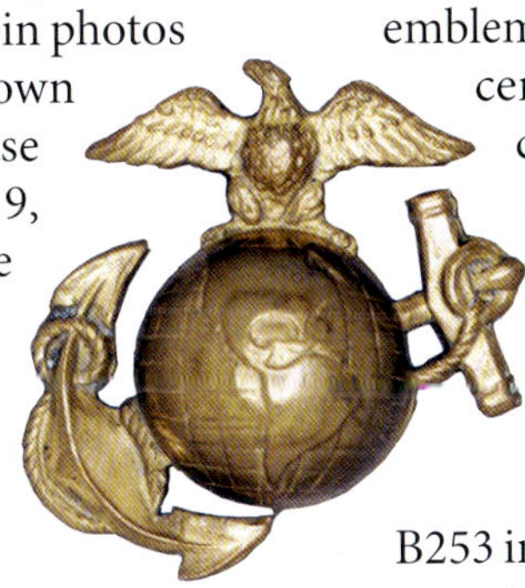

B254

The enlisted gilt dress cap emblem B254 is a minor die variant of B253. Tick marks indicate several differences in the two dies. Both emblems share all other features except that B254 has been salted by cutting away part of the upper anchor stock from the lower part of the eagle's left wing. This cutting is evident by the shortening of the upper anchor stock. Note also that the fouled cable of B254 is not a complete figure eight as is B253.

B255

Type II enlisted dress cap emblems have broader wings and a finer, more distinct pattern of feathering in the eagle's wings. They are less often encountered than the narrow wing emblems. Other differences between B255 and B253 are indicated by tick marks. The photo labeled B255 is the actual emblem illustrated in Driscoll as Figure 53.[3] The best photographic evidence for dating B255 is a superb photo of Medal of Honor winner 1st Sgt. Roswell Winans wearing B255 in a photo that cannot date earlier than September 1916 and no later than April 17, 1917, when he was given a commission. The famous photo probably dates closer to the former Medal of Honor award date rather than the latter commissioning date (see B255 appendix C-1).

The service version of B256 struck in bronze is the most common WWI enlisted Marine emblem. These emblems

Marine Hat or Cap Device

		Per Doz.
No. 1	Bronze or gold plated, with screw, washer and nut on back	$2.40
" 2	Heavy gold plated and burnished	4.50
" 3	Gold and silver plated and burnished	6.00

Figure XV-1
B253 illustrated in Thomas Perry advertisement.

were worn not only on the summer and winter service caps but also on campaign hats and later, during the war, were worn on the US Army fore and aft cover as well as the steel helmets issued in France. There is a photograph of one enlisted Marine wearing, instead of the Army type collar discs, two of these service cap emblems attached to his stand-up collar on the Army-issued olive drab blouse. B256 is in all respects the same as the brass dress cap emblem B253, except that it is usually struck in bronze and given a dark brown lacquer finish.

In the two known varieties, the most obvious difference is the fouled cable. In one variety, the fouled cable is a complete figure eight.

Recent and exciting finds of B256 have been reported by Gilles Lagin and others.[4] These AEF battlefield finds have been further elaborated on with actual provenience information for a large sample of George Bailey's actual finds.[5] These finds from WWI French battlefields cumulatively give us an entirely new and independent perspective on authentic Marine Corps emblems of that time period. Bailey estimates that perhaps as many as 150 US Marine enlisted emblems and a few insignia of Marine officers have been found by individuals using metal detectors and excavations in battlefields, and especially USMC rest areas and encampment sites in France.

This collection of recent field finds shows a fascinating pattern. Between the photos and information provided by Lagin, Bailey and others, this sample of at least thirty-one enlisted service cap ornaments; 28 are B256. The only exceptions are one example of B169, and one of B172, both known to date earlier and probably worn by old salts who enlisted well before WWI.

The single example of B258 in the French field finds is curious and suggests that the Fourth Brigade came to France in 1917 predominantly wearing B256. B258 was likely a later Marine Corps procurement worn mainly by enlisted Marines arriving at the end of the war. This might explain why so few are showing up in France today.

The recent French finds would indicate that B253 (dress) and B256 (service) were procured by the Marine Corps prior to the Fourth Brigade being sent to France. The absence of the other types of service cap emblems described in this chapter strongly suggests that they may have been later Marine Corps procurements or perhaps stateside private purchase items. Emblem shortages that accompanied the explosion in the size of the Marine Corps would be an incentive for the Marine Corps Quartermaster ordering new types from various manufacturers to meet the emergency. The huge increase in enlisted strength would also provide an incentive for manufacturers to produce emblems for private purchase and hopefully government procurement.

Another example of B256 in the USMCHCQV collections is associated with James B. Kimble, who enlisted on October 23, 1916. Kimble served in the Corps from private to gunnery sergeant, and was discharged on November 30, 1920.[6]

B256

B257

B258

B259

The modern investment casting B257 used an original enlisted service cap device (B253 or B256) as the model for the casting. It was sold by Schipper Fabrik of Clearwater, Florida, as an "up-front" modern reproduction. Close comparison with B253 and B256 shows-typical investment casting features such as the muting of sharp details seen in the authentic, superbly struck emblems. Note also the weak depiction of the lines of latitude and longitude and especially the obfuscation of the details seen in the anchor ring and anchor stock of the authentic emblems. A very soft, easily bent copper alloy was used for the casting and is actually lighter in weight than the authentic emblems. The metal is so soft that the globe is out of round. Unlike the authentic models, B257 has a thick, almost black lacquer or paint covering and shows none of the well-developed patina seen on the brass and bronze of authentic emblems. Instead of the traditional thirty-two turns per inch screw post, B257 has a screw post of forty turns per inch.

The broader wings and finer pattern of feathering on the Type II bronze enlisted service cap version of B255 in dress is an excellent strike with fine details. B258 corresponds to John Driscoll's Figure 56. It is finished in a thin dark-brown, lustrous, lacquer. Where the lacquer is worn one can see a healthy, well-developed, handsome and natural long-term patina. The attachment method is the conventional screw post. Type II cap emblems are noted for being well-struck and showing fine, distinct details such as the full figure eight fouled cable.

Only one example of B258 to date has shown up in the recent WWI French field finds.[7] This suggests a later Marine Corps procurement than the B256 enlisted emblem. Surviving photographs support this assertion.

Another modern reproduction of the Type II enlisted cap device using B258 as the model for the investment casting was produced by the Prairie Flower Leather Company. As with the other reproduction (e.g. B257), B259 was honestly sold as a reproduction for a reasonable price and with no intention of purporting authenticity. The casting is in some respects cruder than B257, with many obvious casting flaws, evident even to the naked eye. Note the pits and protrusions caused by trapped air bubbles and the casting flash seen on some edges. The reverse is especially crude with a mat-like finish, where a matting material was used to help separate the two-piece mold. This texture is totally unlike the reverse of authentic original emblems struck under high pressure and giving a smooth surface of condensed, compacted metal. The surface of B259 has instead a gritty texture, like the feel of extra-fine sandpaper. The finish is a spray-dry graphite, lacking any indication of an aged patina.[8]

Molten brass was used to cast this reproduction of a type II broad wing enlisted cap ornament. It is not known by whom or when this casting and its white metal counterpart B261 were made. B260 was part of a collection of cast emblems kindly sent to the author by Carl Carson, who

B260

asked that I examine them and give him an opinion. The collection was purportedly from the estate of a deceased Marine Corps Sgt. Maj. Holiman.

The most obvious casting evidence is the muted detail seen especially in the weak pattern of feathering on the eagle breast as well as the weak pattern of lines of latitude and longitude. The emblem has a black chemical finish that is very uneven and feels grainy and totally unlike the smooth condensed metal of a high-pressure, die-struck emblem. The means of attachment is a cast flat-head wood screw of thirty-two turns per inch and clumsily soldered to the inside of the center of the globe. Another anomalous feature is the incised number sequence ".925" at the anchor crown reverse. These numbers would indicate that the model used for this investment casting (B255) may have for some reason been struck in silver.

B261

With the exception of being cast in a white metal alloy, B261 is exactly the same casting as B260. The weak pattern of feathering, especially at the eagle's breast and on the lines of latitude and longitude, is a function of being cast from the same mold as B260. These weak features are not due to wear. The same chemical black finish of a gritty texture was used to finish the emblem. A cast flat head wood screw of thirty-two turns per inch is used for attachment purposes. The same incised numbers ".925" are seen on the anchor crown reverse.

The final Type III enlisted cap emblem of the WWI period is B262. It is quite distinctive in style suggesting a new manufacturer. The eagle with sharp pointed wings is perhaps the most unique feature. It looks more like a pigeon than an eagle. Oversized anchor flukes are in contrast to Types I and II. All known examples of B262 are finished in a dark chocolate-colored lacquer. The shapes of the anchor stock and continents are also distinctive. Unlike Types I and II the screw post is forty turns per inch. Like Types I and II, it is a superb strike from a single bronze plate.

B262

The absence of an example of B262 in Lagin's French battlefield collection is supported by three examples of B262 associated with known Marines who enlisted later in the war and were discharged after relatively brief service. One example of B262 is associated with numerous photos clearly showing an example of B262 worn by Clayton F. Hawkridge, who enlisted July 1918 and was discharged August 1919.[9] Another example of B262 is associated with a 1924 pattern enlisted winter service barracks cover worn by H.D. Huyck.[10] Huyck enlisted December 15, 1921, and was discharged December 15, 1925.[11] A third example of B262 is associated with the dog tags and collar discs of Albert H. Ross, who enlisted December 26, 1917, and served with the 13th Regiment of the Fifth Brigade in France from October 1918 to August 1919. Richard Forte bought the Ross items from Ross's descendants in Mississippi.[12] This late WWI date for B262 is further supported by seldom seeing the distinctive emblem in photos of WWI Marines serving with the AEF.

B263

The Type III model B262 was used for the modern investment casting B263. It is an excellent casting, lacking many of the more crude features such as obvious air bubbles. It is, nevertheless, not one-to-one with the authentic B262. In particular, details such as sharp lines of latitude and longitude are clearly muted. It also has a grainy feel to the surface and shows obvious edge rounding as an artifact of the casting process. The screw post is forty turns per inch, and like B262, B263 also lacks an anti-twist peg at the reverse of the eagle body. The casting indication in edge rounding contrasts with the sharp edges displayed on the well-struck B261. The high pressure of the die strike effectively forces the metal into every space of the die. The flow of molten metal does not fill that mold as effectively as die striking. A separation line is also discernible where the two-piece mold came together. The reverse is especially crude with filing marks to clean up the casting. All these thick casting features are absent from the thin, well-struck B262. The manufacturer of this reproduction is unknown, but it is distributed as item number RPU008 from Great War Militaria.

Emblems on Steel Helmets

With very few exceptions, the vast majority of AEF photos show Marines wearing the Army-issued steel helmet without the Marine Corps emblem. However, trench helmets with painted AEF patches and emblems like those in this chapter are not rare. Therefore they must have been adopted very late in the war. Service emblems on WWI helmets commonly show up on the market even today. To a large extent this can be explained by provisions that allowed honorably discharged Marines the option to take home their trench helmet and gas mask.[13]

There is a wonderful story told by the late Rick Spooner about the Marine Corps emblem on the trench helmet in 1918.[14] More than one old salt still on active duty during WWII told Spooner the story of how Gen. Pershing, on an inspection tour of the Fourth Marine Brigade, saw a Marine private with a hammer and a heavy nail punching a hole in the front of his helmet for the Marine Corps emblem. Pershing was incensed by this unauthorized damage to government property and expected that those who were participating in this type of activity would be disciplined. According to the oral tradition handed down through Spooner, Gen. Lejeune instead ordered all his Marines to put a service emblem on the front of their helmets. The oral tradition, although it makes a wonderful story of the Marine Corps brotherhood and their admiration for Gen. Lejeune, has yet to be supported by any firm documentation other than oral tradition.

Chapter XVI

Enlisted Collar Emblems: WWI

(B264 to B288)

The enlisted collar discs in chapter 16 are not only some of the most unusual US Marine emblems, but were also remarkably short-lived. From late 1918 through 1919, enlisted Marines serving in the AEF were authorized to wear US Army type collar discs. The discs were discontinued upon the return of the 4th and 5th Marine Brigades to the United States.

The end of the brief period of actual use of collar discs is documented by Warren R. Jackson of the 5th Marine Regiment.[1] Jackson describes the Marines turning in their US Army uniforms for brand-new USMC winter green uniforms without collar emblems just after the Victory parade on August 8, 1919 and just before the August 12 Victory parade in Washington, DC. A photo exists of the entire 5th Regiment at this time on the steps of the US Capitol building in wintergreens without enlisted collar discs. It is also known that Marines were given the option to choose one complete uniform on being discharged.[2] Given the number of US Army olive drab uniforms with collar discs that have survived, it is obvious that many discharged Marines elected to go home in the Army uniforms with collar discs.

Most discs attributed to WWI Marines found on the militaria market today were never worn by Marines. A few of the discs in this chapter were actually authorized and worn by Marines: most discs in this chapter are modern reproductions while a few were probably made by WWI manufacturers for private purchase. Dated photos and surviving uniform lots identified to particular Marines attest to the fact that some WWI period enlisted Marines wore collar discs whether or not they served with the AEF. This is another case of the proverbial 10% who opt to wear something unauthorized. It was also a time when manufacturers knew they could sell what they made, even if the USMC might or might not buy their products.

Written Documentation

The primary source for the US Marine collar disc story is a 1921 *Marine Corps Gazette* article by Maj. Edwin McClellan.[3] Driscoll succinctly reiterates this information in his more readily available publication.[4] On August 5, 1918, McClellan describes an inspection of elements of the 4th Marine Brigade by Assistant Secretary of the Navy Franklin D. Roosevelt. When Brig. Gen. Neville was asked by Mr. Roosevelt to inform him of anything he could do to assist the brigade, Neville told him that, "since there had been considerable difficulty distinguishing between the enlisted men of the Army and those of the Marine Corps, it would be a splendid thing to authorize the Marines to wear the Corps device on their collars in the manner similar to officers, only that the device would be smaller."[5]

Mr. Roosevelt authorized the request, which was expressly for the 4th Brigade of Marines. Since collar discs are seen just as often in photos of 5th Brigade enlisted Marines, it is presumed that the original authorization must have been extended to that later arriving brigade. Interestingly, photos of 4th and 5th Brigade Marines often show that many Marines are not wearing the authorized collar discs, suggesting that the discs may have been in short supply or were not a popular item, or both.

Oral Tradition

In contrast to the skimpy written documentation about the collar discs, there exists a rich oral tradition. During WWII, several versions of the collar disc and "emblems on the helmet" stories were related to Maj. Rick Spooner, USMC (Ret.). These stories were told to Spooner by WWI veterans still on active duty at that time.[6] Chief among those stories were those relayed to Spooner by retired Lt. Col. Robert M. Montague and retired Capt. William Radcliffe. Both were good friends of Spooner and regular patrons at the old Globe and Laurel restaurant in Triangle, Virginia. Both Montague and Radcliffe had served in the 4th Brigade in France.[7]

As this oral tradition goes, Gen. Lejeune ordered a small group of Marines led by Brig. Gen. Wendell Neville to go to Paris to procure the newly authorized enlisted emblems. The group included the Brigade Quartermaster (Brig. Gen. Wendel Neville?), Lt. Col. Frederic Wise, and Gen. Lejeune's driver, an unknown corporal. According to the story, Fritz Wise was favored to go since Gen. Lejeune knew Wise had recently married a young lady now serving as an American nurse in Paris. The corporal driver was purportedly selected by Gen. Lejeune to report any drinking and such on the part of the officers. The only part of this tale with any plausible written substantiation found so far comes from Fritz Wise. In his book, Wise describes his meeting with his nurse wife in Paris after the fighting at Belleau Wood.[8] Unfortunately, Wise made no mention of the emblem mission.

The story, as passed on to Rick Spooner, tells how the Marine officers met with the Parisian insignia manufacturer and explained what they required. The officers were told that filling the order would take four days. To the Marines just off the front lines at Belleau Wood, four days in Paris must have been considered a godsend. The story has it that those four days were indeed well spent.

When the Marines returned to pick up the emblems, they unhappily discovered that the order was not at all what they wanted. McCellan substantiates the oral version; instead of manufacturing the emblems as Lejeune and Neville had wanted, a round US Army-type collar disc with a small eagle, globe, and anchor in relief was delivered. This would really do little to distinguish Marines from other US Army soldiers. Perhaps their limited skill with the French language may have contributed to the misunderstanding. A more likely explanation is that the manufacturer was probably well aware of US Army orders and specifications for collar discs and simply assumed that a disc set with a small port and starboard eagle, globe, and anchor in relief was required.

A mistaken assumption on the part of the French manufacturer is all the more likely since Gen. Pershing had previously ordered that the entire AEF should have a single US Army Quartermaster source of supply. There would not be a separate Marine Corps/ Navy supply line for the Marines in the AEF. The 4th Brigade had been supplied by the US Army Quartermaster since January 1918.[9] It is hard to imagine that the US Army establishment would have concurred with the procurement of US Marine Corps enlisted emblems that did not conform to formal US Army specifications for collar discs.

The oral tradition has it that when the Marines did not get what was intended, they realized that they were going to make Gen. Lejeune very unhappy, not only for bringing back the Army type discs but also for partying four days in Paris with American nurses. The part of the oral version about partying with American nurses is conceivable, given the written account by Wise spending several days in Paris with his American wife. The stories told to Spooner clearly implied that the anger of Gen. Lejeune may have been much worse had his corporal been a teetotaler, which he definitely was not. Evidently the four days in Paris for the anonymous corporal were also very well spent.

Army Discs Worn by Marines

There are at least two documented cases in which enlisted Marines wore discs intended for the US Army. The first is a photograph of the US Marine special escort taken on Bastille Day, July 14, 1918.[10] The photo clearly shows the US Marine escort wearing collar discs. This would have been a good three weeks prior to Mr. Roosevelt's inspection that later resulted in the authorization of the discs. As the chosen escort for this special occasion, perhaps it would have been considered being out of uniform for this special unit of Marines to not wear collar discs on their Army uniforms.

A second example was provided by the late Capt. William Radcliffe USMC (Ret.), who served as a quartermaster sergeant with Headquarters 6th Regiment, 4th Brigade in France.[11] Radcliffe donated his mixed US Army and US Marine Corps collar disc set to Rick Spooner for display in Spooner's wonderful emblem exhibit at the Globe and Laurel Restaurant in Triangle, Virginia. As a quartermaster sergeant, Radcliffe may have had access to a collar disc set not readily available to other enlisted Marines. Radcliffe's set on display at the Globe and Laurel was highly unusual and consisted of the common US Army right collar disc with "US" and the numeral "6" and a left collar Marine Corps disc B269. The Radcliffe set conforms perfectly to 1916 Regular US Army requirements that the disc with the letters "US" be worn on the right collar, while a subordinate unit disc (corps, brigade, regiment, etc.) was worn on the left collar.[12]

Albert Scipio describes the shortage of collar discs with the rapidly expanded US Army.[13] To cope with the impossibility of providing every soldier a set of collar discs that indicated his specific unit, it was decided in June of 1918 to simplify the regulations and place the regimental number under the "U S" on the right collar disc and let the left collar disc indicate the subordinate unit. This provision greatly reduced the variety of collar discs previously required. The Radcliffe set conforms perfectly to this change in Army regulations.[14] When Radcliffe was asked by Rick Spooner why he wore the mixed Army and Marine set instead of the better-known US Marine port and starboard eagle, globe, and anchor disc set, Radcliffe replied, "No one ever said anything to us about it."[15]

Scipio Type I Collar Discs

This classification of authentic Army-type collar discs worn by Marines during WWI relies heavily on the earlier work of Dr. L. Albert Scipio.[16] The classification is further supplemented by Scipio's later work.[17] Dr. Scipio started collecting US Army collar discs as a boy not very long after WWI. That early quest ultimately led to an especially large collection of discs that he acquired over many years. This significant collection and Dr. Scipio's academic training and research skills resulted in the publication of his two superb works on US Army collar discs.

Dr. Scipio's avid collecting and thorough research preceded by many years the earliest known reproductions. Scipio's work therefore gives us a critical pre-reproduction perspective on authentic collar discs. Put another way, if US Marine Corps discs that commonly appear on the market today are not included in Scipio's thorough inventory, then they are probably modern reproductions. With the exception of a very few and rare types described here that Scipio did not have in his collection, his classification is an excellent tool for identifying authentic discs. There is one unfortunate exception in which Dr. Scipio included a modern reproduction in his 1999 work. When the author pointed out this reproduction, Scipio's response was, "that is really discouraging."[18]

By far the most common of the AEF collar discs, B264 conforms to Scipio's Type I #3 Right and #4 Right and #8 Left.[19] The one-inch-diameter disc set is struck from a single bronze or brass planchette with a separate applied screw post and circular base reinforcement with two anti-twist triangular-shaped pegs, (see Figure XVI-1). A dark-brown, almost black lacquer

B264

was used for the finish. Variants of B264 and other Scipio Type I discs are also known to exist, with both metric and English thread sizes on the screw posts. An example of the right collar disc B264 was reported by George Bailey to have been found at the 5th Brigade encampment of Marines at Pontanezen, France.[20]

B265

Unless described separately, all the collar discs in chapter 16 basically conform to the official US Army specifications as described in detail by Scipio.[21] Many variations on this US Army specification are known, especially those made by French and possibly German insignia manufacturers that produced a rounded and a flat metal "C"-type catch for a drop-in pin assembly (see Figure XVI- 2. Variation in the design of the eagle, globe, and anchor, as well as the metal used, will be individually described with respect to the particular "B" number of each disc type.

B266

It is also significant that at least six examples of Scipio Type I discs have been recovered by Gilles Lagin.[22] George Bailey and others have also found Scipio Type I discs from French WWI battlefields and especially Marine rest area and encampment sites.[23] Bailey describes another twenty pristine sets of the Scipio Type I discs that have turned up in France.[24] Consistent with these French finds from the field, B264 is often associated with artifacts identified to AEF enlisted Marines and is the most commonly encountered authentic disc set on the militaria market today. Minor die variants and mixed sets of the Scipio Type I discs were described by Scipio in his earlier work and occur frequently on the militaria market.

B267

B268

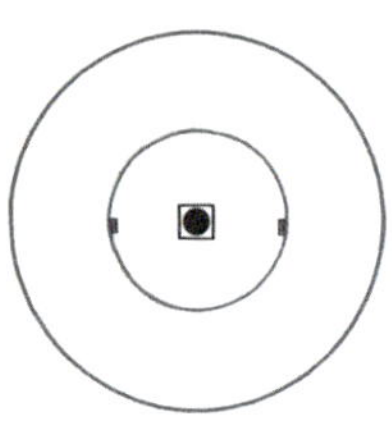

Figure XVI-1
Regulation US Army collar disc with screw post, reverse and side views.

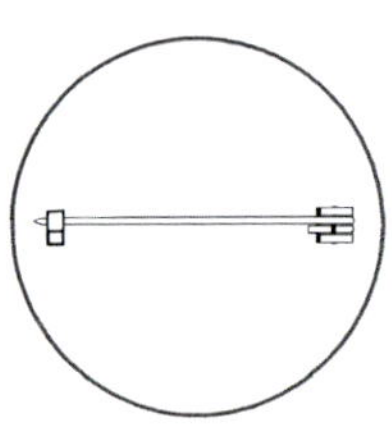

Figure XVI- 2
French and German-made discs with drop-in pin attachments, reverse and side views.

The set B265 was not included in Scipio's two-volume work. It is a die variant of the Scipio Type I collar discs. Besides differences in the shape of the continents, the most obvious differences can be seen in the distinct and strong pattern of feathering on the eagle breast and legs. B265 has the French-type drop-in pin assembly instead of the regulation screw post means of attachment. This kind of variation might simply be a function of the French manufacturer having prepared multiple dies to meet the emblem production requirement and provide a backup for those dies that would eventually wear out or break.

A third die variety of the Scipio type I discs is especially evident in the B266 left disc with an eagle with a squat neck, slender anchor crown, and long, slender anchor arms. The B266 set corresponds to Scipio's Type I #2 left and his #7 right.[25] This set was mixed with others in both the 1981 and 1999 Scipio publications. As with the majority of Scipio Type I discs, the means of attachment is the regulation screw post.

The last known die variety of the Scipio Type I group B267 is a well-matched set that, when compared to the other Type I varieties, has a long-necked eagle, wings of a distinct asymmetrical shape, a thick anchor crown, short anchor arms, and large anchor flukes. This variant set corresponds to Scipio's #5 and #6.[26]

The gilt left collar disc B268 is struck from the same die as the bronze version B264 left. It is Scipio's Type I #2.[27] There is no known requirement for collar discs to have been struck in gilt but some obviously were (see also B272). Scipio also includes in his 1981 inventory an aberrant collar disc with nickel plate. Gilt collar discs occasionally show up in WWI photos of Marines in dress blues. The only two photos that the author is aware of showing gilt discs on dress blues were taken stateside at the war's end.

Despite some instances of Marine replacements arriving in France in newly issued winter service greens, collar discs were authorized for wear on the US Army issue olive drab uniform coat. Mackin describes the contempt displayed by newly arrived Marine replacements in their new winter service Marine greens as they passed grubby Marine combat veterans in their US Army olive drab uniforms. Little did they realize these presumed "Army draftees" were actually combat-hardened fellow Marine volunteers.[28]

With one known and inexplicable exception, the Army-type collar discs should have been worn only by the 4th and 5th Brigades in France. That exception is a yard-long photo of the 10th Separate Battalion taken at Quantico, Virginia, in November 1918. All the enlisted Marines are clearly wearing collar discs.[29] The discs in this photo were probably manufactured in the United States, like B274, by the American Emblem

Company or N.S. Meyer. Other examples of gilt discs worn on dress blues show up occasionally in WWI period photos but all photos seen so far are stateside, probably reflecting manufacturer's selling discs as a private purchase item. Seagoing detachments serving with the European Fleet and wearing dress blues were not designated in the August 1918 authorization. There has never been anything effectively preventing manufacturers from producing and selling non-regulation insignia to any serviceman.

B269

B270

Scipio Type II Collar Discs

The attributes that Scipio probably used to define his Type II collar discs are the distinct shape of the continents and anchors, especially features of the anchor stocks and the inclusion of lines of latitude and longitude on the globes. By comparison, the more common Scipio Type I discs have only lines of longitude. Scipio Type II discs are excellent die strikes, displaying none of the investment casting features of modern reproductions. The well-struck features are especially evident in the sharp and clear details, especially the lozenge shapes in the background. In their construction, the Scipio Type II group conforms to the previously cited US Army collar disc specifications. Those familiar to the author all have a very respectable patina and compare favorably with Scipio Type I discs in all respects of construction and finish, except the design variation.

B271

B272

The set B269 was classified by Scipio as his #11 and #12.[30] It is the most commonly encountered of the Scipio Type II group. In addition to the mixed Marine (B269) left disc and the Army (US 6) right collar disc set worn by Quartermaster Sergeant Radcliffe and described above, a left B269 disc was found in the Argonne Forest near San Mihiel by George Bailey.[31] Compared to the far more numerous Scipio Type I discs found in France, the two Scipio Type II discs known so far would suggest a slightly later date, or perhaps a stateside production. B269 has a close family resemblance to and might be a die variety of B271, known to have been manufactured by the N.S. Meyer Company.

B273

Another set of B269 was included in a large and diverse assemblage of WWI enlisted Marine artifacts that sold on the Internet in June of 1999. This extraordinary group of some 18 artifacts was associated with Arthur Wahl, who served as an enlisted Marine in the 4th Brigade from April 1918 to August 1919.[32] Included in the Wahl group, in addition to the B269 collar disc set, was Wahl's photo in uniform and his emblems B169 and B256.

Scipio classified the B270 set as his #13 Right and #14 left.[33] Driscoll includes the set as his Figure 59.[34] The absence of manufacturer marks or illustrated manufacturer catalogs depicting the set leaves the manufacturer uncertain. Some resemblance to B271 may indicate a die variety by the same manufacturer. The most distinctive features of B270 are the head and wing shapes of the eagle; otherwise, they are quite similar to B271.

Unlike all the other Scipio Type II collar discs with the distinct lines of both latitude and longitude, B271 is clearly illustrated in a 1918 N.S. Meyer catalog (see Figure XVI-3).[35] Ray Darida kindly provided the figure copied from the original 1918 catalog. The distinctive features of B271 are the strange shapes of the continents and the distinctive eagle heads and wings. The set is also weakly struck, as evidenced by the weak lozenge pattern in the background of the disc.

ENLISTED MEN'S COLLAR DISCS

In Right and Left Mated Pairs

		Per Pair
No. 249	Standard Screw Back.	$ .20
PB249	Pin and Catch Back	.25

Figure XVI-3
B271 illustrated In N.S. Meyer catalog, 1918.

Missing from this inventory is the matching right collar disc for the set B272. Scipio illustrates the complete set as his #15 and #16.[36] The set is simply the gilt version of N.S. Meyer B271. Since there is no known record of a requirement for gilt collar discs, these discs may have simply been produced on the initiative of manufacturers. None were known to have been required, but obviously the manufacturers sold some.

Problematic and Miscellaneous Discs

This group is difficult to confidently identify and classify. Two discs (B273 and B274) may have actually been worn by Marines. There is no reason to think that Marines ever wore any of the others in this miscellaneous group.

The port and starboard set B273 came from the collection of the late Joe Lowry. Joe started collecting Marine Corps emblems while serving in the Marine Corps during WWII. By the time the author became friends with Joe in 1997, he had specialized in and put together an extraordinary collection of enlisted Marine Corps emblems. After examining Joe's well-photographed collection, the author found, like George Mennegaux, that Joe also had an eye for distinguishing authentic articles from the plethora of fakes that had begun to flood the market. Photographing and describing large, diverse collections like Joe's that were put together well before the glut of reproductions was a distinct privilege greatly appreciated by the author.

B274

An especially unusual feature of the clearly die-struck B273 set is the "American Emblem Company Utica, NY" back-mark. A very similar reticulate or net-like pattern of the background appears on both the right and left discs. Both discs of the set also share a very similar dark-brown, brittle lacquer finish that chips easily. The right collar disc conforms perfectly to US Army specifications.[37] The left collar disc also conforms as the disc for a subordinate unit.[38] This rare set may have been produced for private purchase instead of an order for the Marine Corps. It seems highly unlikely that the Marine Corps Quartermaster in Philadelphia would have ordered the Army type collar discs for the 4th and 5th Brigades in France.

B275

Another example of B273 left, with the American Emblem Company back-mark and the diminutive but distinct eagle, globe, and anchor design, sold on the Internet in January 2007. A matching right disc with the small distinctive eagle, globe, and anchor design with the American Emblem Company back-mark is unknown, further suggesting that the set may not have been produced in matching eagle, globe, and anchor pairs. To date the American Emblem Company set is known only as a small left eagle, globe, and anchor device meant to be worn with the "US" collar disc on the right collar. This combination is perfectly consistent with US Army collar disc regulations.

Another problematic disc has a small and distinct left eagle, globe, and anchor device separately attached to a conventional right disc with the letters "US." This runs counter to US Army specifications and leaves additional doubt about it ever having been worn by Marines. The disc is an excellent strike, especially the even dot pattern of the background. The strike clearly shows sharp details that tend to be muted in modern reproductions. Another feature of B274 not seen in reproductions is a convincing patina and compound screw post attachment method meeting Army specifications.[39]

The great variation seen in WWI collar discs was probably a function of highly competitive manufacturers taking the initiative to produce whatever they thought might sell, especially during critical shortages of emblems. As private purchase items, manufacturers must have been basically free to interpret needs and specifications for insignia as they saw fit. By contrast, those procured on a purchase order would have had more explicit contract enforcement options to better assure conformity with government specifications.

The right collar disc B275 is another highly questionable anomaly. Although the eagle, globe, and anchor are clearly patterned on the Scipio Type II disc (B269), its construction does not conform to regulations for collar discs. Instead of a single die struck disc, it is composed of a separately struck bronze eagle, globe, and anchor with a screw post that is attached through a square aperture in the center of a plain bronze disc. The disc lacks any of the well-known background designs. A casting flaw can be seen in part of a raised, not incised, segment of a line of longitude. This obvious casting flaw is seen in the southwest quadrant of the globe. Only one other example of a right collar B275 is known to the author. It was seen at a military show in New Orleans in 1998 and was attached as a decorative element to a WWII-era Zippo cigarette lighter.

There is no information that the author is aware of to independently support B276 (see Fig. XVI-4) ever having been worn by US Marines, other than its purported association with Francis G. Miller, based on information from his grandson.[40] Miller served quartermaster duties from July 1918 until at least December 1940 at Headquarters Marine Corps, Washington, DC.[41] There is no record of his service with the AEF in France. Although plausible, it is not known if the letters indicate the United States Marine Corps. In construction and finish, B276 conforms well to the US Army specifications for collar discs. The author drew Figure XVI-4. B276 came from the Michael Manifor collection and is the only example that the author is aware of. It is likely another example of a manufacturer taking the initiative to produce something that could be sold. If it is a stateside private purchase item, then others ought to eventually surface.

Figure XVI-4
B276 obverse top and side views.

B277

Obviously the silver disc B277 is not a US Marine collar disc. It is included in this inventory simply because it is an exceptionally rare and interesting example of a sweetheart pin meant for the mother of an AEF Marine. It is clearly modeled on a 1918-1919 USMC collar disc. The eagle, globe, and anchor, the date 1918-1919, and other sentiments were hand-engraved on a ground-down reverse of a French fifty-centimes silver coin. The means of attachment is a roll-type silver safety-catch and pin assembly soldered to the reverse. The engraver left his name, "O. Roly."

B278

A bronze collar disc with the distinctive design of an eagle, globe, and anchor with a superimposed letter "J" was described in a *Trading Post* article by Kelley.[42] It is the collar disc for Jesuit High School New Orleans (JHSNO). Although it dates later than the WWI period collar discs in this chapter, it is included because it is essentially the same type collar disc. According to Soafer, B278 was worn until 1953.[43] As a collar disc, it is thinner than regulation early US Army bronze discs. For attachment it has a screw post and, at twelve o'clock on the reverse, an anti-twist peg. As with other collar discs, it was finished in a dark-brown lacquer. The manufacturer is unknown, but it has a copyright and was sold by the Taylor and Juden tailor shop in New Orleans.[44] To date, it is only known to the author as a left disc. The same design appears

Figure XVI-5
Ike jacket with B278 worn by JHSNO cadets.

on a cap device as well as large and small buttons for the Ike jacket (see Figure XVI- 5) worn by the JHSNO cadets.[45] Soafer includes photos of five different cap, collar, and button variations of the device.[46]

In 1942, as a JHSNO sophomore, Father Nicholas Schiro recalled the student body receiving olive drab uniforms with B278 collar discs.[47] Two active duty Marine sergeants, probably from the local New Orleans recruiting station, drilled the cadets three times a week. Originally, JHSNO was to have been a Navy ROTC program, but a local congressman and JHSNO alumnus, F. Edward Hebert, insisted that it be Marine. Father Schiro recalls seeing the original document establishing the Marine program before that document was lost in Hurricane Katrina. In the lost document, the word "Naval" in the phrase "Naval ROTC Program" was crossed out and the word "Marine" was written in.[47]

B279

B280

In 1967 JHSNO officially became the first USMC Junior ROTC program in the nation. That program is still in place to this day.

The collar disc B279 does not chronologically belong in this chapter, but it is included because it is also essentially a WWI type disc. Unlike other discs of the US Army type, it is a white metal alloy with a mat black finish and two simple modern clutch type fasteners. B279 is back-marked "KREW G-1."

In February 1986, US Navy Religious Program Specialists (Chaplains Assistants) serving in US Marine units were authorized this device to be worn on the left collars of their winter green service and camouflage utility uniforms.[48] The disc depicts a compass rose, symbolizing the concept of religious direction or guidance. The globe and anchor symbolize religious support provided continuously worldwide for personnel of the sea service. Appropriately, the globe and anchor symbols are also shared with the same two elements on the USMC emblem.

Obvious Modern Reproductions

The last nine entries for chapter 16 are a representative sample of a disturbingly large number of reproductions that have appeared on the militaria market, especially since about 1985. Most have used an authentic emblem as the model for the investment casting; a few are fanciful original creations. A characteristic of investment casting is the ease in which minor variants can be created. The wax product cast in a mold where an authentic or fanciful emblem was used as the model can easily be altered to create a wide variety of discs, each with different numbers, letters, and other minor design variations. In this way the reproductions cover an amazing amount of variation. This would be the bane of the serious collector attempting to find all the different discs, if not for the fact that the vast majority of these reproductions are really quite obvious.

Those who know more about investment casting than the author know that with enough trouble and expense, a modern casting can be virtually indistinguishable from its authentic model. Fortunately, these masterpieces are too expensive to create for anything but the very rarest emblems known. One should be immediately suspicious of considerable numbers of rare emblems suddenly showing up on the market. This is the same dilemma that collectors of rare coins have faced since coins were first minted.

The earliest documented investment casting of a WWI-type USMC collar disc is B280. These discs are thought to have been commissioned on the West Coast by the late Ed Rogers. They were possibly made in Pakistan and are honest reproductions in which Rogers included a raised "R" (see Figure XVI-6) and the raised date 1985. The modern set is quite distinct with unique, sharp, clean details not seen in authentic sets. Especially obvious is the background pattern of small, irregularly sized and shaped squares in a staggered and uneven pattern. This pattern contrasts strongly with the small, neat, regularly shaped lozenges or dots on authentic die-struck discs.

Figure XVI- 6
Rogers back-mark.

Unfortunately, other examples have been sold where the raised "R" and date have been ground away. The presence of a raised back-mark and date is insufficient to identify these reproductions. The dated Rogers casting had a simple one-piece screw post. Figure XVI-7 illustrates the one-piece screw post. Other variants of B280 have a screw post assembly closer to the typical US Army specifications, but are still a one-piece casting. This early Rogers' creation was the only mistaken inclusion of a modern reproduction in Scipio's superb 1999 work. A variety of B280 is also known, with a raised 1992 date.

Figure XVI-7
Side view of B280.

A second commonly encountered modern cast reproduction is the mixed set B281. The left and right discs are cast using different models and have been offered for sale as authentic WWI collar discs. The set is cast in bronze with a dark-brown lacquer finish. Typical investment casting flaws such as pits and small protrusions on the surface of both the obverse and reverse are evident. Other casting traits are flash remnants and edge rounding of the extreme outer edge of the disc. The thickness of the disc in cross section is uneven. The most obvious casting feature is the single-piece casting of the disc, screw post, and combination reinforcement ring and anti-twist points on the reverse. Unlike authentic WWI period discs, there is no indication of being assembled from separate die-struck elements; it is simply cast as a single unit.

B281 left is close to the authentic disc B271 left; compare it with B271 left with B281 left. The authentic B271 has small, evenly patterned diamonds or squares in the background while the investment casting B281 has a larger, uneven pattern of muted and amorphous shapes in the background. B281 right is very similar, but does not bear a one-to-one correspondence with the other investment casting, B280 right. It may have been used as a model for making a new mold for B281 right. This reproduction set has also been seen with an artificial aging effect that looks like an acid bath, giving the discs a flat, crusty, pinkish color and thoroughly corroded effect.

B281

B282

B283

B284

Thanks to Paul Stine, the exact the origin of the B282 set is known.[49] A Scipio Type II disc (B269) was used as the model for this casting in 1991. Only six pair were made by a company in Pennsylvania that cast pewter fantasy figures. The sculptor made these as gifts for Marine friends of his father, like Paul Stine. The six sets were cast in a soft pewter alloy and given a black lacquer finish. The entire screw post assembly was cast along with the disc as a single unit. The usual casting flaws are evident, such as the muted details of the eagle feathering and lozenge shapes of the background. The father of the craftsman could not get his son to cast more than the original six sets. Although a handsome, but obvious, modern investment casting, these six sets are, as a function of numbers cast, rare.

George Peterson and his company, National Capital Historical Sales (NCHS)· commissioned a manufacturer in Thailand to cast the set B283.[50] The set only vaguely resembles B271, suggesting the preparation of a new mold. The set is an excellent casting but still displays typical casting features. These imperfections include minor errors seen especially in the background pattern of the disc. Instead of the tiny, even distinct lozenge-shaped pattern seen in the background of B271, B283 has muted, less-evenly-spaced, and larger dots of indistinct shape. One can also see protrusions and globs of metal, especially on the obverse of the disc. Unlike the clean die-struck B271 set with separate die-struck elements for screw post and reinforcement ring that were reassembled, B283 is another obvious single-piece casting; even the nut for the screw post shows a separation line as an artifact of being cast in a two-piece mold.

The most obvious investment-casting feature is the significantly larger width of the outer rim of the disc. Peterson told the author that he did this on purpose to make it quite obvious that it is a reproduction.[51] The set is openly advertised and sold as a reproduction for a reasonable price by NCHS.

What is immediately striking about the set B284 is the distinct design with clean, deep details of the eagle, especially the feathering in a unique bifurcated pattern in the wings. Details of the continents, lines of latitude and longitude, as well as ironwork on the anchor stock are neat, deep, and clear, therefore lacking the usual muted effects of most castings that use an authentic disc as a model. The casting seems to be an original design, perhaps only vaguely resembling an authentic disc. To date, there is no known authentic disc that clearly served as a model for this particular casting.

The manufacturer of this set is unknown. These discs have been routinely offered for several years on the Internet as WWI French-made discs and in such numbers as to suggest more discs for sale on the Internet than there were Marines in France. Despite a proliferation of this investment casting for sale on the Internet, none have been reported finds on French battlefields or Marine encampments of 1917 and 1918.

B285

Although extremely common on the market, these sets all seem to be in pristine or near-pristine condition, except for a few sets that have apparently been artificially aged, perhaps by a strong acid or caustic reagent giving them a flaky, pinkish, distressed appearance. The usual dark-brown finish appears to be even and thin, suggesting a chemical change rather than the conventional applied coatings of lacquer over bronze. The background consisting of diamond shapes is curiously the opposite of the diamond or lozenge shapes of authentic discs. The diamonds in the background of B284 are not raised but intaglio, with the lines between the diamonds raised rather than the diamond.

B286

There is an amazing variety of this type of disc. Some have what appear to be compound screw posts with anti-twist points and circular retainer elements. Others have drop-in pin assemblies for attachment. Some are cast in brass to mimic fanciful dress collar discs.

B287

Characteristic of investment casting technology is the ease of altering the wax castings to easily create myriad variations. Eagle heads facing inboard can be altered to face outboard instead. Sets without letters and numbers can be altered in the wax model to include a variety of letters and numbers. Included in the variations seen by the author are the numbers "3 and 5" as well as the letters "V and MG." Perhaps the idea of creating all this variation was to appeal to the collector/seller compelled to have one of each of the "rare" types? Were that the case, it might have been a little more clever to exclude numbers of regiments that did not serve in the AEF.

B288

A variant of B284 is the set B285, with eagle heads facing outboard. This set has been honestly advertised as the reproduction RPU006 by Great War Militaria.[52] With the exception of Great War Militaria and a few other venders, notably NCHS, it is the author's experience that many, if not most, of these collar disc reproductions routinely offered on the Internet have not been described as modern castings.

The last three modern cast discs in this chapter are sufficiently similar to indicate the same creator altering the wax castings to make minor variations to lead the unknowing collector/seller into thinking that they were struck for various USMC units in WWI. Despite being excellent castings, seen especially in the sharp detail of the pattern of their background, all three taken together still show a disturbing similarity of color and patina not seen with authentic discs with the accumulated differential patina and wear patterns expected with emblems almost 100 years old.

The extreme similarity of the dark-brown color appears to be an even, thin, chemical change rather than the conventional dark-brown applied lacquer finish of authentic discs. In addition, all three share subtle flaws such as small pits and protrusions as artifacts of molten brass in molds. Note the molten metal flow error on B286 between nine and eleven o'clock on the raised outer rim. These telltale casting errors do not occur with discs struck under tremendous pressure. In contrast, die-struck discs show a compactness of metal, uniformity, and sharpness of details missing in almost all investment castings covered in this study.

The turned brass nut on B286 makes a sloppy fit to the cast screw post, which still shows the two-piece mold separation line running perpendicular to the threads. It is curious that the style of the rifle in B286 is entirely different from the rifle in B287, which is in turn different from the rifle in B288, yet all three have the exact same eagle, globe, and anchor device. It would make little sense for a manufacturer in 1918-1919 to prepare all the dies required to strike discs for each subordinate unit of the Marine 4th and 5th Brigades.

Like the previous investment casting, B287 is the same kind of single-piece casting and not a composite construction of several separate die-struck elements. The same eagle, globe, and anchor device is used, but another style of US Army infantry crossed rifles is seen with another entirely different background pattern of dots and squares.

The last of the group of investment castings, like the two above, is simply a minor variant where it is likely that the wax model was altered to put the same small eagle, anchor, and globe above the crossed rifles and add the letter "B" below the rifles. Figure XVI-8 is an enlargement of the eagle, globe, and anchor used in all three of above castings. Note the obvious casting flaw on the globe.

Finally, there is no good reason to think that the 4th and 5th Marine Brigades would have provided special discs with numbers indicating the individual numbered machine gun battalions and regiments. To ensure that each soldier would be issued a collar disc set, the US Army had been forced in 1916 to greatly simplify the variations in discs.[53] The dramatic increase in the number of soldiers and units created an enormous supply problem. Manufacturers were simply unable to produce the quantity and diversity of the collar discs required under the old system. Under that system over 5,000 variants would have been required. The two Marine Brigades were hard pressed enough to provide each Marine a simple disc set with the small eagle, globe, and anchor device, let alone issue a great variety of distinct battalion level and regimental designations on collar discs. The above reproductions B286, 287, and 288 are the fantasies of wishful-thinking collectors and dishonest or uninformed sellers.

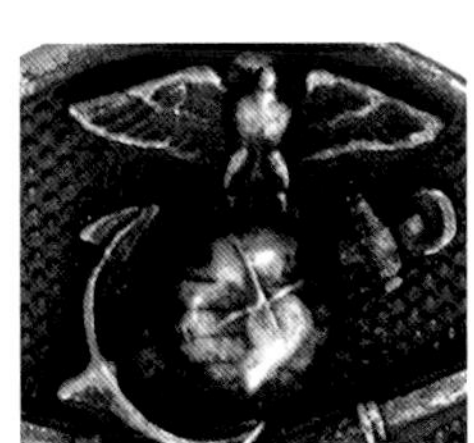

Figure XVI-8
Casting flaw on B288.

APPENDICES

APPENDIX A

To-Scale Line Drawings of Select Emblems

Ten drawings to scale were made using pen, ink, and standard drafting tools. The drawings were in turn scanned, edited, and precisely sized by computer. The selection of emblems was made to graphically depict important distinctions as a tool for identifying and dating purposes. The solid lines depict features of the emblems based on numerical values explicitly described in the Uniform Regulations and summarized in Driscoll 1971. The solid lines are the actual measurements for such features as the length and angle of the anchor, the diameter of the globe, the wingspan and height of the eagle, the width of the anchor stock and anchor shaft and the distance between the anchor flukes and the globe. In other words, the ten drawings offer a graphic summary of important comparative distinctions more readily perceived in the drawings than in the words and numbers in the Uniform Regulations or Driscoll's important summary. The dotted lines are based not on objective measurements from the Uniform Regulations but on the author's more subjective interpretation of distinctions seen in actual emblems in this research. These select distinctions have important chronological and functional significance. Reference to these drawings will be made throughout the chapters in volume 1.

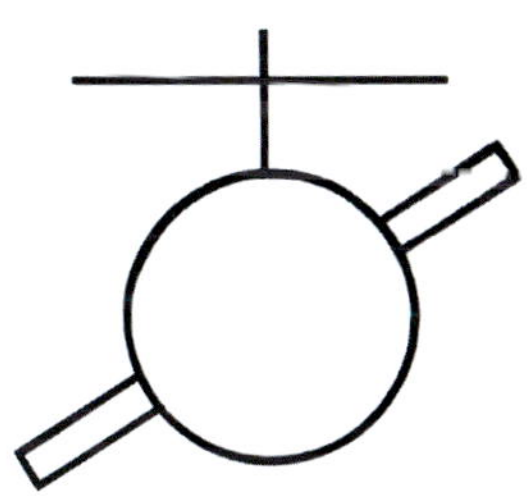

Fig.1
1868 officer and enlisted undress cap (fatigue cap) first eagle, globe and anchor emblem.

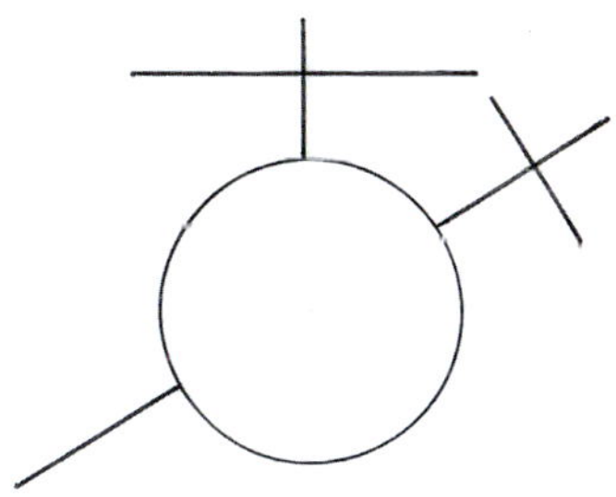

Fig.2
1869 officer's left epaulette ornament.

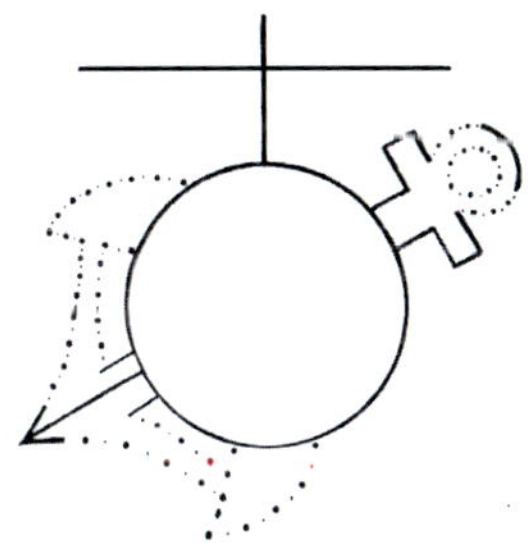

Fig.3
1875 officer and enlisted dress and undress cap and cork helmet ornament, same measurements as 1868 but different die.

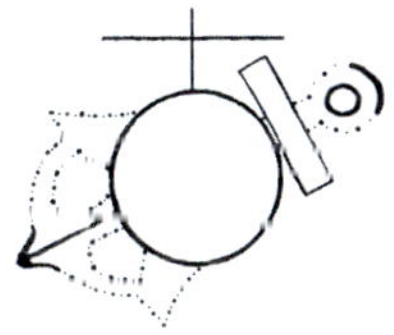

Fig.4
1877 officer's first dress collar emblem with a distinctive shape of anchor flukes.

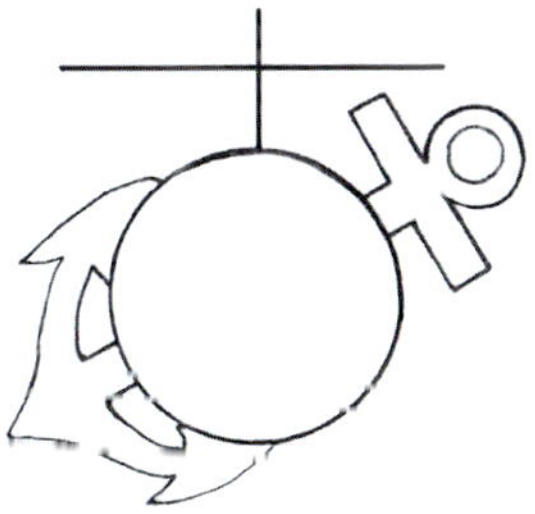

Fig.5
1892 officer's dress and undress cap emblem, same measurements as 1868 and 1875 but struck from another die.

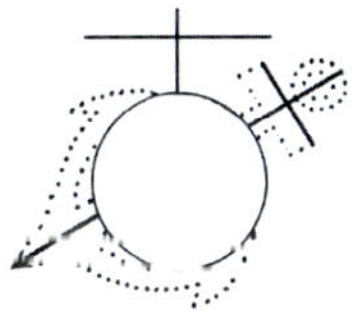

Fig.6
1892 officer's dress coat collar ornament, same measurements as 1877 but distinct pattern of large anchor and flukes still touching the globe, not separated.

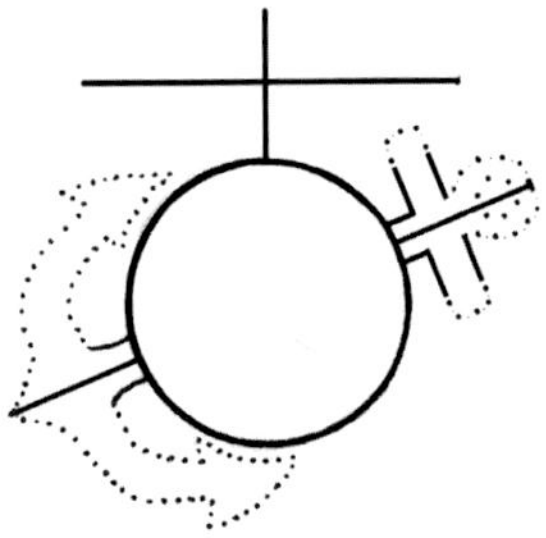

Fig.7
1900 officer's undress cap and campaign hat emblem with distinctive "U" shaped anchor arms instead of the "C" shape characteristic of later emblems.

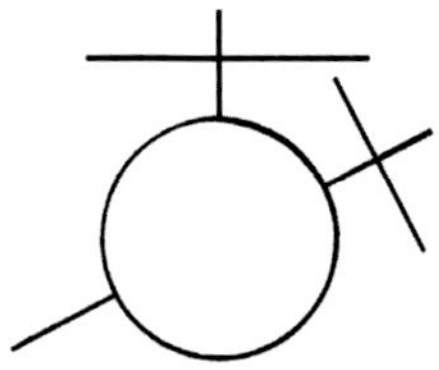

Fig.8
Staff officer's silver and gold shoulder knot ornament 1900 to 1904 only, intermediate in size between the dress collar and dress cap ornaments.

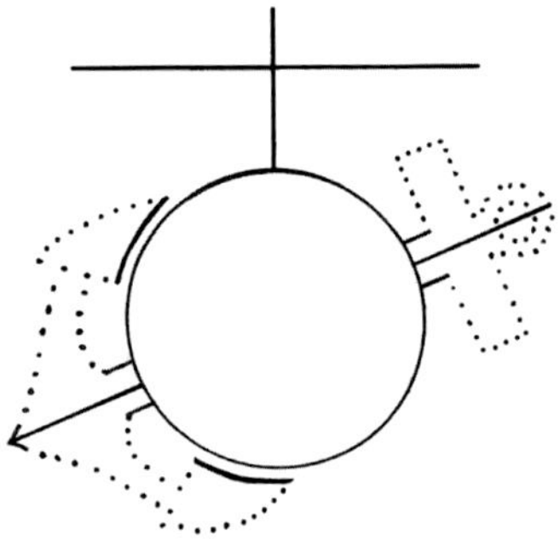

Fig.9
1904 officer's cap emblem that basically established the modern measurements and style for cap ornaments.

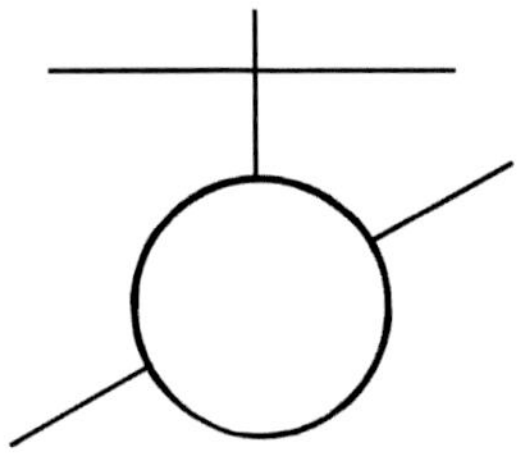

Fig.10
The 1904 officer's collar ornament that established the basic modern measurements and style of officer's collar emblems.

APPENDIX B

Breuninger Emblems: Richard Long Photo

This photograph appeared in Long and Wyckoff and was referred to as "Ornaments made by Mr. Breuninger." On November 28, 2000, after learning that the author would be doing research on Marine Corps emblems at the USMCHCQV, Dick Long kindly shared what could be found of his original research notes. Dick had compiled these notes some thirty years previously at the time of his tasking by Sen. Paul Douglas and the commandant to do an "in depth story" on the first Marine Corps emblem.Long shared with the author his recollection of visiting Mrs. Grigsby, a descendent of Karl Breuninger, to gather information for his research. When Long asked her about emblems, she brought out a small metal candy box (about six inches by six inches) containing the very emblems seen in Dick's photograph. Long and Wyckoff published their article with this photograph but did not mention why these emblems were attributed to the work of Karl Breuninger.

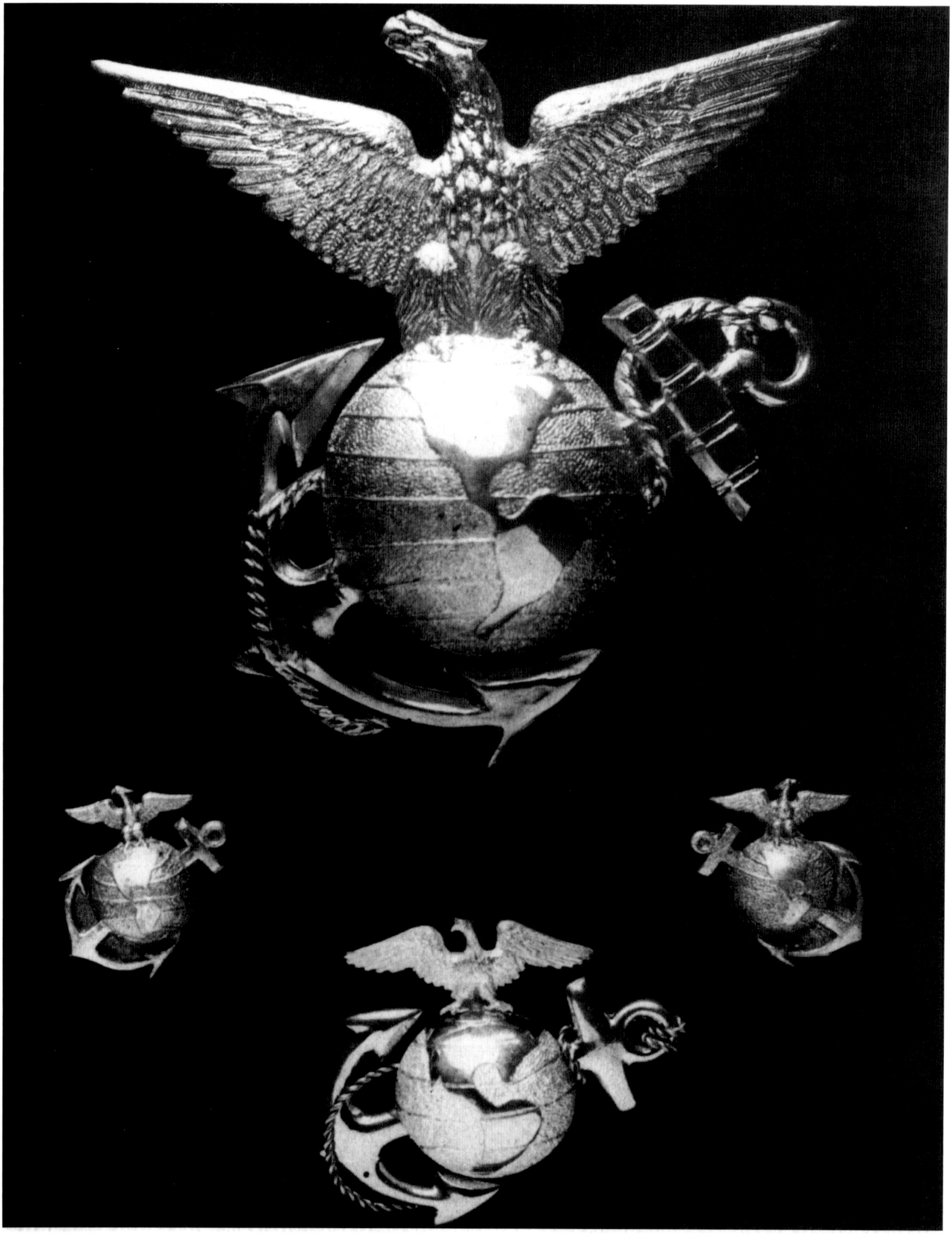

APPENDIX C

Officer Database: Photos and Chronologies Sorted by B Number

Appendix C-1 lists emblems by their B Numbers for which there is independent information for identification and dating. This information comes from a wide variety of sources, including museums, private collections, sales lots, and especially photographic images. In other words, 198 emblems were found in a variety of sources that match one or a small group of the 288 emblems with B Numbers in the volume 1 inventory. Emblems from public museums and private collections with documented context and acquisition records are critical considerations.

Another important basis was to match emblems in this inventory with very select lots of artifact groups, credibly associated with a particular Marine, the larger and more diverse the lot, the better. An example would be lots from Internet auction sales. It is highly unlikely that large, diverse ,artifact lots, clearly associated with a particular Marine, would be regularly cobbled together by dishonest sellers. The few artifact lots in the list that are associated with particular Marines have all been verified in the USMC Muster Rolls, or Annual Registers of Marine Corps officers and warrant officers.

Most of Appendix C-1 is based on original photographs from private and public collections. Relatively few photographs from publications were found to be of sufficient quality to be useful for identifying and dating emblems. The conventional dot matrix print found in most publications usually degrades any clarity that may have once been present in the original photograph. Out of several thousand photographs examined in this research, the following sample was selected for inclusion in the Appendix C-1. This very select sample of useful photographs had adequate focus and clarity to identify with some confidence a particular emblem or at least a group of very similar emblems in the 288 emblems with B numbers in this research. Three photographic collections were extremely valuable: the National Archives photographic collections (NA), the US Marine Corps History Division (HD) and the Library of Congress (LC). The latter two resources present superb collections of high-resolution images that could be enlarged in photo editing software for accurate identification.

Emblems without an asterisk are the most confident identifications. An asterisk in front of the number indicates some qualification. For example, an emblem number with an asterisk could have more than one potential match in this inventory. Also, of the 288 emblems with B numbers in this inventory, none may exactly match the 197 items in appendix C-1. There is extraordinary variation seen in emblems, especially officer's emblems. This inventory of 288 emblems is categorically incomplete. That does not mean, however, that it is all so complicated that meaningful chronological patterns are impossible to discern.

KEY

* Qualified Identification
AEGA: American Embassy Guard Annual
AFM: Annual Fourth Marines 1932-1933
ALGA: American Legation Guard Annual
ANM: Army Navy Magazine 1907
A&SCBLMC: Archives and Special Collections Branch Library of the Marine Corps
Chenoweth and Nihart, 2005
CM: China Marine 1932, 1933
CMMCRDSD: Command Museum Marine Corps Recruit Depot San Diego
CP: Copy of Photo and Name of Contributor
EAL: eBay Auction lot
EAP: eBay Auction Photo
Fleming et al. 1978
Hearn, Chester, 2003
HMCRDSD, 1997: History of Marine Recruit Depot San Diego California
HD: United Sates Marine Corps History Division
LC #: Library of Congress Call Number
LGN: Legation Guard News, 1929
LMCKCMO: Liberty Memorial Collection, National WWI Museum, Kansas City MO
MCBSDCA: Marine Corps Base San Diego California, 1931
MCG: Marine Corps Gazette
MCHCWNY: Marine Corps History Center Washington Navy Yard
NA #: National Archives Photo
OP: Original Photo Owner
P: Provisional
PC: Private Collection
PLGA: Peking Legation Guard News Annual
Quantico Commanders:Fleming, Charles A., et al, 1978
Russell and Moore, no date
T: Temporary
USMCMR: United Sates Marine Corps Muster Rolls 1790 to 1940
USMF: US Militaria Forum
WWM: *Walla Walla* Magazine

B#	NAME	COMMENTS	SOURCES
33	Cash, John C.	* Eagle on cocked anchor device (perhaps 032) worn by Cash as lieutenant; photo dated before 1861, probably 1852	Cureton and Sullivan 2009, p.68
38	Hebb,C.D.	Hebb wears shako plate as 03 in photo dated March 7, 1867	OP Thomas Harris
80	Cochrane, Henry Clay	Dress cap emblem on kepi; photo dated August 20, 1874. First officer's eagle, globe and anchor ornament	EAP #270207224970
80	Wainwright, R.	First officer's eagle, globe and anchor emblem in photo of Wainright as O1; photo dated 1869–1877	NA #517116
87	Hervilly,James D.	Dress cap eagle and globe with embroidered anchor; photo dated 1872 to 1877 before adoption of dress collar ornaments	EAP #290247534334
93	White, Harry Kidder	Small pattern 1875 shield and wreath on white cork hemet in photo of White as O2 dated, c.1889	John Stacey 1999
95	Hall, Newt	* Dress cap with undersized globe worn by Hall as O1; photo dated c.1898	Hearn C., G2003, p.75
95	Harlee, William	* Dress cap with undersized globe; Harlee with group of officers. Photo dated 1900	MCHCWNY no #
97	Butler, Smedley D.	Dress Cap as O1; photo dated 1898	CP Alec Tulkoff
99	Perkins Con, M.	* 1875 pattern white metal officer's device (B099 or B100) on white helmet worn by O2 Perkins; photo dated 1889	CP Alec Tulkoff
99	White, Harry Kidder	Photo dated c.1889 of O2 White with white metal emblem; possibly B099 on white cork hemet	John Stacey 1999
100	Brown, William Rowles	Device worn on 1875 pattern small shield on Brown's white cork helmet, 1881 to 1892	USMCHCQ collections
102	Heywood, Charles	Commandant wears early version of embroidered wreath and dress cap ornament on his cap; photo dated 1894	MCHCWNY #515349
104	Butler, Smedley D.	Dress Collar as O1; photo dated 1898	CP Alec Tulkoff

B#	NAME	COMMENTS	SOURCES
105	Bradman, Frederic L.	Dress collar set	CP Alec Tulkoff
109	Bannon, Philip M.	Dress colar set; photo probably dates to 1897 commissioning	CP Alec Tulkoff
109	Bradman, Frederic L.	B105 * Dress collar set. Several variants known; worn on probable commissioning uniform	CP Alec Tulkoff
110	Bates, John S.	* Spanish–American War period dess collar as O2; photo dated July 1, 1899	NA #520481
116	Stokes, Arthur	Staff Officer's shoulder knot ornament 1900–1904, with 1910 engraved and named rifle expert badge	
118	Long, Charles	Distinctive dress collar set worn by Long as O2 line officer; photo dated November 1897	OP Michael Manifor
118	Murphy, Paul St. Clair	Distinctive left dress collar device associated with Murphy	USMCHCQ collections
119	Smith, Julian, Constable	Right epaulet device associated with Smith and donated by his widow to the US Marine Corps	USMCHCQ Acc. #780048
125	Turrill, Julius S.	Full dress epaulette set associated with Turrill uniform lot	EAL #141053680749
131	Ludlow, Reginald Fairfax 05/08/1907 11/27/1909	Silver epaulet set worn briefly by 1st Lt. Ludlow, c.1910–1913.	OP George Mennegaux
134	Bradman, Frederic L.	* Dress cap emblem, (B099), worn on 1898 pattern dress cap, as O1; possible commissioning photo	CP Alec Tulkoff
147	Santleman, William H.	Officers distinctive helmet plate, photo as Marine bandleader in dress blues dated, NET October 1898, and NLT 1905	OP Frederick L. Briuer
150	Lee Harry	Officers distinctive type II helmet plate; photo as O3, NET 7/1900, and NLT late 1905	OP George Mennegaux
150	Mott, Thomas A.	Officers distinctive type II helmet plate, worn by Mott, 1900 to c.1905	USMCHCQ Acc. #1996.5.1

B#	NAME	COMMENTS	SOURCES
152	Cochrane, Henry Clay	Officer's 1892 dress helmet plate, complete helmet associated with Cochrane; photo dated 1899–1900	NA #522845
155	Pendleton Joseph Henry	Darkened metal helmet plate, as officer's field saddle cloth ornament; photo Col. Pendleton, dated 1913	Chenoweth and Nihart, 2009, p.112
156	LeJeune, John A.	Leather field saddle cloth ornament of mounted O8 LeJeune, and dated after 1918, and NLT 10/11/1929	CP Alec Tulkoff
167	Andrews,John J.	Enlisted service cap, Samar type, as gunner photo dated 1920, with enlisted service prior to 1918	NA #520839
167	Hughes, John Arthur	* Enlisted service cap Samar type, darkened, as O3; photo dated 1909	NA #516897
169	LeJeune, John A.	Enlisted service cap device worn by Lejeune on pre-1912 campaign hat, as O5; photo dated NET 1908, and NLT 1914	LC 2-266-7
169	Rupertus, William H.	* NS Meyer type dress cap, as O4; photo dated 1929, could be post WWI NS Meyer dress cap emblem	LGN, 1929, p.10
173	Butler, Smedley D.	Breuninger type dress cap worn by Butler as O4; photo probably dated 1908 as O4	LC-USZ62-93458
173	Neville, Wendel	Early undersized globe dress cap emblem converted to service use, photo dated c.1914 to 1916	MCHCWNY no #
174	Bigler, Epaminondas, L.	* Breuninger type dress cap (perhaps B175, several close variants) as O2; photo dated 04/13/1913	NA #516548
174	Dewey, Rupert C.	* Breuninger type dress cap (many variants) with very unusual collar set as O3; photo dated 1903 to about 1913	NA #516226
174	McDougal, Douglas C.	Breuninger type dress cap conforms well to B174 or B175, with unique dress collar set as O7; photo dated 1935	NA #307063
174	Pendleton Joseph Henrey	Breuninger type dress cap with unique dress collar set as O6; photo dated 1912	NA photo #514896

B#	NAME	COMMENTS	SOURCES
174	Pendleton Joseph Henry	Breuninger type dress cap; photo dated 1919 as O7	HMCRDSD, 1997, p.23
175	Bannon, Philip M.	Dress cap emblem on pattern 1897 dress cap; photo probably dates to 1897 commissioning	CP Alec Tulkoff
175	Butler, Smedley D.	Breuniger type dress cap with small globe worn by Butler as O4; photo dated 1910	CP Alec Tulkoff
175	Cole, Eli Kelly	* Breuninger Type Dress Cap (variants known) as O8; photo dated Dec. 1925	HD and NA photo #523167
175	Elliott, George F.	* Breuninger type dress cap with undersized globe, variants known, as commandant; photo dated July 1907	ANM 1907
175	Vandergrift, Alexander, A.	* A minor variant of the Breuninger type dress cap emblem, possible commissioning set	HD
177	Cole, Eli Kelly	* BB&B dress cap; photo dated 1924–27	Fleming et al.1978, p.128
177	Fuller Ben H.	Early BB&B type dress cap	AFM 1932-33. p11
177	Lander, F.C. 03/15/1900 03/02/1903 03/13/1908 died on duty	* BB&B type dress cap, conforms best to B177 or B179. Lander is misspelled Landis, as O3; photo dated March 1911	NA #516818
177	Powers, William Channing	BB&B Dress cap device worn by Powers in photo dating NET 1910, and NLT 1914, possible commissioning emblem	LC-B2666-7
177	Shepherd, Lemuel C.	BB&B type dress cap emblem, photo of commandant Shepherd's dress blue cap dating 1952–1956	PC Jerry Goodrich
179	Brown, Philip S.	Dress Cap emblem BB&B type, as O4, photo dated NLT May 15, 1915	CP Alec Tulkoff
179	Hamilton , George W.	Dress cap emblem BB&B type, as O1; photo dated March 25, 1914	NA #516851
179	Russel, John	* B179 dress cap, photo as O7; photo dated 1922	A&SCBLMC

B#	NAME	COMMENTS	SOURCES
179	Taylor, C.B.	Early BB&B type dress cap emblem seen in photo of Taylor as O3; probably dated 1907	EAP #220717793586
180	Schwable, Frank J. 03/21/1900	Distinctive turn of the century dress cap device, possibly Schwable's 1900 commissioning set; from the Schwable estate	PC Bob Gill
181	Cole, Edward B.	Three Big Talons Big Beak type dress cap as O2; photo dated 1912	NA Photo #516544
181	Del Valle ,Pedro A.	Big Talons Big Beak type dress cap, worn by Del Valle; photo dated Sept. 1915	PC Michael Manifor
181	Keyser, Ralph S.	Three Big Talons Big Beak type distinctive dress cap as O7; photo dated 1937	HD
181	Mahoney, James E.	Big Talons Big Beak dress cap worn by Mahoney as O4; photo dated 1904	PC Michael Manifor
181	Myers, John Twiggs	Big Talons Big Beak type dress cap emblem, O7; photo dated 1928	HD
181	Williams, Dion	Big Talons Big Beak type dress cap in photo of Williams as O7; dated 1924–1934	HD
183	Hale, Augustus Boyce	* Asymetrical Wing type dress cap, many variants, as O3; photo probably dated 1920	EAP no #
184	Buchanan, Fitzgerald L.	Variant of the Asymetrical Wing dress cap emblem with applied continents; photo as O2 dated c.1925	PC Michael Manifor
184	Doyen, Charles A.	* Asymetrical Wing type dress cap (several variants), as O7; photo dated c.1917, copy of obituary	EAL #2166447244
185	Burwell, Robert,Oswald, B.	Dress cap associated with Burwell USMC 1915–1920	PC Ed Wages
185	Cukela, Louis	* Asymetrical Wing type dress cap (many variants) as O3 before 1940	EAP #36581352956
185	Thomas, Gerald Carthrae	Asymetrical Wing type dress cap, as O10; photo dated 1956. Thomas may be wearing his commissioning emblems	HD

B#	NAME	COMMENTS	SOURCES
188	Buchanan, Fitzgerald L.	Asymetrical Wing dress cap with distinctive struck continents, as O2; photo dated c.1921	EAP #6635943262
188	Buse, Karl I.	Asymetrical wing dress cap; photo dated November 28, 1917	NA #517476
188	Cukela, Louis	* Asymetrical Wing type dress cap,as O2. Medal of Honor recipient in Haiti; photo dated c.1918–1920	NA #519806
188	Fuller, Edward Canfield	* Asymetrical Wing type dress cap (many variants); photo dated no later than 1918	Fleming et al 1978, p.275
188	Hunter, Tracy G.	* Asymetrical Wing Dress cap as O1; photo no earlier than 4/1911, and no later than 12/1916	NA #516928
188	Skidmore, Robert Louis	Asymetrical wing dress cap emblem with fur cap, and enamel diamond worn by Robert Skidmore 1922–1936	ALGA 1933, 1934
188	Smith, Dwight F.	* Asymetrical Wing type dress cap (many variants), as O2; photo dated July 20, 1914	OP Michael Manifor
188	Wise, Fritz M.	Asymetrical Wing type on dress cap, as O3; photo dated, 1903 to c.1913	NA #516291
189	McGuinness, John Peter	N S Meyer type dress cap, as O1; photo dated 1938	CP Alec Tulkoff
189	Powers, William Channing	Early NS Meyer type dress cap emblem; from the estate of Powers	PC Bob Gilll and USMF
189	Withers, Hartnell, J.	NS Meyer type type dress cap emblem, as O1; photo dates 1926. NSM type bent neck collar (many varieties)	NA #524331
195	Stokes, Arthur	Service cap emblem, possibly Stoke's comissioning emblem; with identified and dated (1910) rifle expert badge	
195	unidentified Officer	* Big Talons big Beak type service cap emblem (B195 or B196) on 1898 pattern campaign hat; photo dated 1909	CP Alec Tulkoff
196	Lee, Harry	Big Beak Big Talons type service cap, as O7; photo dated August 9, 1920	OP Michael Manifor

B#	NAME	COMMENTS	SOURCES
196	Moore, James Tillingham	Big Talons, Big Beak type service cap emblem worn by Moore as O3; photo dated c.1925	OP Michael Manifor
197	Baptist H.	* Asymetrical Wing service cap or B198 as gunner; photo dated 1929	NA #527245
197	Grimm, Charles	Service cap emblem on campaign hat; photo of O3 Grimm dated December 1917	OP George Mennegaux
198	Butler, Smedley D.	Service cap emblem worn by Butler on his fore and aft cover that sold on Ebay for $3,800; photo dated 1918–1919	NA #307655
198	Lay, Harry R.	* Asymetrical Wing type service cap (many varieties); photo dated 1914, as O3	NA #517124
198	Northenscold,Emile, M.	Service cap emblem, distinct applied continents, associated with uniform lot of O2 Nothenscold dated c.1918. EBay auction lot #2285275588, sold 12/03/04	EAL #2285275588
200	LeJeune, John A.	Asymetrical Wing type service cap device, Lejeune as O7; photo dated NET 1916, NLT 7/01/1918	MHCWNY #515720
200	LeJeune, John A.	Asymetrical Wing type service cap emblem, on O7 Lejeune's fore and aft cover, on exibit at Washington Navy Yard in 2003	USMCHCQ collections
200	Neville, Wendel	Asymetrical Wing type service cap emblem on service greens as O8; photo dated 1923	EAP #180263355636
200	Parsons. Miller V.	Most common Asymetrical Wing type service cap emblem with struck continents, as O2; photos dated December 8, 1921	OP Michael Manifor
200	Silverthorn, Merwin H.	Asymetrical Wing type sevice cap emblem, as O9; photo dated 1951–1954	HD
203	Cates, Clifton	NS Meyer type dress cap, as O10; photo dated 1948–1951. Possible commissioning emblem	CMMCRDSD #300000
203	Feland, Logan	NS Meyer type service cap, Feland as O7; photo dated 1928	HD
203	Secor, Theodore	NS Meyer type service cap emblem worn by Secor as O4; photo dated February 1931	

B#	NAME	COMMENTS	SOURCES
203	Smith, Julian, Constable	* NS Meyer type service cap (could be post WWI version), as O4; photo dated 1929	NA #527256
203	Smith, Julian, Constable	NS Meyer type service cap emblem, worn by Julian Smith, and donated by the Smith family	PC Bob Gill
203	Taylor, C.B.	NS Meyer type service cap emblem with straight cable; photo dated 1925–1935	EAP #220717793586
203	unidentified 01/02	NS Meyer type service cap with straight cable in photo of unknown lieutenant	CP Alec Tulkoff
206	Beaumont, John C.	Pete Ellis type service cap emblem worn by Beaumant on winter service uniform as O6	WWM
206	Ellis, Earl H.	Service cap emblem, Ellis as O5; photo dated c.1918	NA #116L-30762, DOD #515720
206	LeJeune. John A.	Service cap emblem (Ellis Type), as O8; photo dated c.1920	LC-USZ62-114896
206	Livingston, Richard	Pete Elllis type service cap, as wounded O3; photo dated 1928, Nicaragua	CP Alec Tulkoff
206	Lloyd,Calvin .A.	Pete Ellis type service cap; photo dated 1931 as C/Gunner	NA #527586
206	Ridderhoff, Stanley E.	Pete Ellis types service cap, as O2; photo dated 02/01/1922. OTC classmate of John Stanton	OP Michael Manifor
206	Thorndike, John T.	Service cap emblem in auction lot including named Good Conduct medal, dog tags, numbered Mexican campaign medal	EAL no #. USMCMR
206	Wiggs, Otho	Pete Ellis type service cap emblem in two photos of Gunner Wiggs dating 1921 and 1928	NA no number
206	Wolever, B.H.	Pete Ellis type service cap emblem; photo dated 1920s	NA #518737
209	Lander, F.C.	* Dress collar set (many variants known B209–214). Photo dated March 1911, as O3	NA #516818

B#	NAME	COMMENTS	SOURCES
209	Myers, John Twiggs	* Big Talons big Beak type dress collar set, (other possibilities B 210 to 216; photo dated probably 1929 as O7	HD
209	Neville, Wendel	* Big Talons Big Beak type service collar set (B209 to B214), as O4; photo dated NET 2/1906, and NLT March 1914	NA #4685-5
209	Powers, William Channing	* BB&B dress collar set (B209 to B214), possible commissioning set; photo dated NET Nov. 1910, and NLT Feb. 1914	LC-B2-2666-7
209	Silard Con D.	* Big Talons Big Beak type dress collar (B209 to B214) O1; 1926	NA no number
209	unidentified O3	Big Talons Big Beak type dress collar set worn by unidentified captain in photo dated 1919	EAP #220892102079
209	Williams, Dion	* Big Talons Big Beak type dress collar set (B209 to B214) in photo of Williams as O7 dated 1924–1925	HD
210	Vandergrift, Alexander, A.	* Big Beak Big Talons type dress collar set (B210 or B212) as O6; photo dated 1934; possible commissioning set	HD
212	Adams, John P.	Big Talons Big Beak left dress collar on Guam Insular Patrol badge; name and September 12, 1917 inscribed	EAP #261070037360
212	Smith, Dwight F.	* Big Talons Big Beak type dress collar set (many varieties) as O2; photo dated July 20, 1914	OP Michael Manifor
212	Smith, Holland M.	Dress collar set worn by Holland Smith and current platoon commanders Marine Corps Silent Drill Team, Washington, DC.	Capt. Aldrich, USMC, 2006
213	Breckeridge, James C.	* Big Beak Big Talons type dress collar set, (many varieties) as O6; photo dated 1934	PLGA 1931, p.8
213	Buchanon, Richard Bell	* Big Beak Big Talons type dress collar set, (many varieties) as O3; photo dated 1927	EAP #2284946372
213	Burstan, Robert M.	Big Talons Big Beak type dress collar set associated with Burstan	PC

B#	NAME	COMMENTS	SOURCES
213	Buttrick, James, Tyler	* BigTalons Big Beak type dress collar worn by Buttrick as O7; photo dated 1935–39	NA #515669
213	Duncan, Donald F.	Dress collar device, dated before 1918, museum holding associated with Duncan; donated by Col. Michael Wiley	LMCKCMO
213	Matthews, Calvin B.	* Big Talons Big Beak type dress collar (B213 or B214,) as O2; photo dated October 17, 1913	NA #516717
213	McClellan, Edwin North	Big Talons Big Beak type dress collar B213 as O5; photo dated NET 1/3/1934, and NLT 6/30/1936	HD
213	McNulty, John Sebastian	Big Talons Big Beak type dress collar, as Chief Gunner; photo dated NET 1932, and NLT 1940	EAP #01/28/2003
213	Osterman, Edward Albert	* Big Talons Big Beak dress collar (B209 to B214) as O7; photo dated c.1939–1943	HD
213	Schwable, Frank J.	Dress collar set, possibly Schwable's 1900 commissioning set; acquired from the Schwable estate	PC Bob Gill
213	Thomas, Gerald Carthrae	Big Talons Big Beak type dress collar, photo dated 1956, Thomas may be wearing his commissioning emblems	HD
214	Long, E.C.	Big Talons Big Beak type dress collar set on dress blues of O4 E.C. Long; estimated date 1916–1923	USMCHCQ Acc. #1988.372.
215	Archer, Percy	Staff officer shoulder knot set worn by Archer as staff officer, c.1904–1912,	PC Bob Gill
216	Butler, Smedley D.	* Dress collar set (variants known) worn by Butler as O4; photo probably dated 1908	LC-USZ62-93375
216	Coffenberg, Bailey	Bent Neck Eagle dress collar set with applied continents, worn by Coffenberg as O2; photo dated 1917	NA #517789
216	Duncan, Donald F.	Pre-1906 dress collar emblem, dating from 1905–1918, associated with Duncan; KIA 1918	LMCKCMO

B#	NAME	COMMENTS	SOURCES
216	Hale, Augustus Boyce	* Bent neck eagle type, applied continents, dress collar set, many variations, as O3; photo probably dated 1920	EAP no #
216	Low, William W.	* Bent Neck Eagle NS Meyer type dress colla set, (many varieties B216 to B228) as O3; photo dated 1916	MCG, Dec.1916, p.397
216	Porter, David D.	* Bent Neck Eagle type dress collar set (many variations B216 to B228) worn by Porter as O4; photo dated 8/2/1915	NA #526119
216	Pugh, Lloyd Randolf	* NS Meyer Bent Neck Eagle type dress colla (many varieties) as O3; photo dated 1934	ALGA, 1934, p.117
216	Vandergrift, Alexander, A.	* NS Meyer or Bent Neck type dress collar (many varieties B216 to B228) as O5; photo dated 1935	AEGA, 1935, p.21
217	Wensinger, Walter W.	Dress collar set associated with Wensiger's dress cap; emblem donated to the Marine Corps by his family	USMCHCQ Acc. #1994.924-5
217	Williams, Ernest, Calvin	* Dress Collar set, (217 or 220) photo of Williams as a lieutenant; dated NET January 1909, and NLT 04/27/1917	HD
218	Burwell, Robert,Oswald, B.	Dressn collar associated with Burwell USMC 1915–1920	PC Ed Wages
221	Metcalf, Clyde	Bent Neck Eagle type dress collar set with distinctive applied continents, as O4: photo dated NET 5/1926, and NLT 8/1936	EAP #400243614056
222	Archer, Percy	Dress collar emblem worn by Archer as staff officer, 1904–1912,	PC Bob Gill
223	Snyder, Harold C.	Dress collar set, pre 1906 back marks, on Snyder's named and 1908 date stamped dress blouse with O3 insignia	
224	McClellan,Edwin North	Bent Neck Eagle type dress collar set, as O4; photo dated 1934–1936	HD
226	Catlin, Albert W.	* NSM Bent Neck Eagle dress collar set worn on pre 1910 patrol jacket, probably as O4; photo dated 1908 to c.1910	CMMCRDSD no #

B#	NAME	COMMENTS	SOURCES
226	Hunter, Tracy G.	* Common Bent Neck Eagle type dress collar set; photo no earlier than 4/1911, and no later than 12/1916	NA #516928
229	Burwell, Robert,Oswald, B.	Dress collar associated with Burwell USMC 1915–1920	PC Ed Wages
233	Feland, Logan	Big Talons Big Beak type service collar left, worn by Feland as O6 with the AEF; c. late 1918	CP Alec Tulkoff
233	Feland, Logan	NSMeyer type service collar set, Feland as O7, photo dates March 1, 1927	HD
233	Smith, Julian, Constable	Service cap, worn by Julian Smith and acquired from the Smith family	PC Bob Gill
234	Nagel, Frederick F.	Big Talons Big Beak type service collar set, struck continents, associated with large WWI uniform lot of O2 Nagel	EAL #6572681128
236	Grimm, Charles	Service collar set on summer service blouse in artifact lot associated with Charles Grimm	USMCHCQ collections
236	Secor, Theodore	Service collar set, applied continents, eagle with skinny neck, small head, photo as O4; dated February 1931	OP
237	Darden, Colgate W.	Service collar set associated with O1 Darden AEF uniform ensemble	EAL #234536546
237	Moore, James Tillingham	Big Talons, Small Beak, Skinny Neck type service collar set with applied continents, as O3; photo dated c.1925	OP Michael Manifor
237	Shinkle, Amos Raymond	Distinct service collar set, struck continents, on O3, Shinkle's WWI winter service blouse with AEF insignia	USMCHCQ Acc. #1995.138.1
238	Neville, Wendel	Service collar set, on winter service greens, as O8; photo dated December 1923	EAP #180263355645
239	Cain, Memory H.	Service collar set on winter service green blouse dated June 1918, worn by Cain 1918–1922; with documents	EAL #6611389525

B#	NAME	COMMENTS	SOURCES
239	Dow, Leon F.	Right collar emblem associated with DOW as officer candidate October 1918 to December 1918 only	EAP #224158367 USMCMR
239	Geiger, Roy	* Service collar set; photo dated May 4, 1923	CP Alec Tulkoff
239	LeJeune, John A.	Service collar set worn by Lejeune as O5; photo dated NET Nov. 1910, and NLT Feb 1914.	CP Alec Tulkoff
239	Powell, William G.	Bent Neck Eagle type service collar set worn by W.G. Powell USMC 1896–1927, from the Powell estate	PC Bob Gill
239	Rowell, Ross	Service collar with small eagle head and skinny neck on fore and aft cover, photo as O4	MCBSDC
239	Russell, John H.	Service collar set worn by Russell as O7; photo dated 2/9/1922	A&SSCBLMC
239	Smith, Harry L.	Pre 1927 Bent Neck Eagle type service collar set, as O4; photo dated c.1923–1927	NA #524316
239	unidentified O2	Service collar set, struck continents; photo of an unknown first lieutenant's WWI uniform with various USMC insignia	PC Alec Tulkoff
239	Vandergrift, Alexander, A.	Service collar set as O2; photo dated c.1914–1915	NA # 517116
239	Wheaton, Ivan P.	Bent Neck Eagle type service collar set on Wheaton's winter service blouse with AEF insignia, as O2 aviator; 1918–1921	USMCHCQ Acc. #87.175 OR
240	Powell, William G.	Service right collar emblem, applied continents, worn by W.G. Powell USMC 1896–1926; from the Powell estate	PC Bob Gill
241	Neville, Wendel	Asymetrical Wing type service cap worn on summer service khaki uniform as O8; photo dated 02/07/1929	EAP #180263355676
242	Neville, Wendel	Highly unusual service collar set; photo dated c. 1914–1918	MCHCWNY no #

B#	NAME	COMMENTS	SOURCES
242	Powell, William G.	Distinctive and seldom seen right service collar emblem, worn by W.G. Powell, from the Powell estate	PC George Mennegaux
247	Doyen, Charles A.	Servicecollar set (Pete Ellis type) as O7; photo dated 1918	CMMCRDSD #1998.948.1
247	Ellis, Earl H.	Service collar set, Ellis as O5; photo dated c. 1918	NA #116L-30762, DOD #515720
247	LeJeune, John A.	Service collar set (Pete Ellis type) worn by Gen. Lejeune as O7; photo dated NET 08/02/1916, and NLT 7/01/1918	MHCWNY #515720
247	LeJeune, John A.	Service collar set (Pete Ellis type) worn by Gen. Lejeune as O8; photo dated c.1920	LC-U5Z62-114896
247	Ridderhoff, Stanley E.	Pete Ellis type service collar set as O2; photo dated 02/01/1922, OTC classmate of John Stanton	OP Michael Manifor
247	Stanton, John T.	Service collar set associated with lot including Stanton's dog tags; OTC classmate of Stanley Ridderhoff, 1918, 1919 only	EAL #190229765370
247	Thorndike, John T.	Service collar set in auction lot including named Good Conduct medal, dog tags and numbered Mexican campaign medal	EAL no #. USMCMR
247	Unidentified Officer	Servtce collar set worn by unidentied officer; photo dated NET 1918, and NLT than 1927; blouse with stand up collar	NA #522854
247	Wiggs, Otho	Pete Ellis type service collar set in two photos of Gunner Wiggs dated 1921, and again 1928	NA no number
247	Wolever, B.H.	Pete Ellis type service collar set; photo dated 1920s	NA #518737
248	Feland, Logan	Small French made service collar set worn by Feland as O6 with the AEF c. late 1918	CP Alec Tulkoff
248	Herreid, Bert O.	French-made service collar set, associated with Herreid	EAL no #, USMCMR

B#	NAME	COMMENTS	SOURCES
249	Bennett, Floyd W.	French-made service collar emblem, as O2 on duty with AEF January 1, 1919; photo dated c.1920	NA #524486
249	LeJeune, John A.	French-made service collar set worn by Lejeune in photo dated after 1918, and NLT 10/11/1929	CP Alec Tulkoff
249	Unidentified officer	Less often encountered French-made service collar emblem worn on officer's fore and aft cover	EAL no #
250	Bogan, Henry S.	French-made service collar set to DSC winner; photo dated 12/1918 to 08/15/1919	EAP no #
250	Claggertt, Wilson	French-made service collar set as O2 in photo dated August 1918	Russel and Moore, p.290
250	Ditto, Holton	French-made B250 service collar set on winter service blouse as O2 with the AEF; photo dated late 1918 to mid 1919.	EAP no #
250	Neville, Wendel	French-made service collar emblem worn on fore and aft cover, as O7, in 1918	Fleming et al 1978, p.290
250	Rea, Leonard E.	French-made service collar with straight anchor stock; photo dated c.1918–1920?	NA #522327
250	Thompson, Claude	Most common French-made left service collar ornament worn by Thompson on campaign hat in photo dated c.1919	NA #519636
252	Eddy, William .A.	Possible B252 or close variant of French-made embroidered service collar devices as O2; photo dated 7/1918	Russel and Moore, p.290
255	Winans.Roswell	Enlisted dress cap device in photo of 1st Sgt. Winans; photo dated NET September 1916, and NLT April 1917	HD
256	Andrews, John J.	Enlisted WWI comon type service cap as gunner; photo dated 1922	NA #526415
257	Doyen, Charles A.	Doyen wears the most common EM service cap emblem as O7; photo dated 1918	Fleming et al, 1978
258	Andrews, John J.	Enlisted WWI common type service cap as gunner; photo dated 1922	NA #526415

APPENDIX C2

Appendix C-2 lists Marines mentioned in appendix C-1 and summarizes, through time, their promotions in grades O1 to O10. This can be an important resource for dating photographs and artifact collections associated with particular Marines. Obviously some Marines are seen in photographs wearing old obsolete emblems. These cases however, should be in the minority. Some dated associations are far better than others. A 1950s photo of a general officer wearing emblems purchased thirty years earlier is not as informative for example as a photo of a new second lieutenant in a photo dating shortly after commissioning and wearing a distinctive and short lived emblem. Another example of a tight window of time are photos or artifact collections worn by Marines who can be documented to have served for very brief periods The overall pattern in this photo sample is what is important. No Marines wore emblems manufactured after the indisputable date of the photograph. Dated photos are more valuable than undated photos but even undated photos can usually be approximately dated by other information in the photo. The evolution of Marine Corps uniforms and insignia usually gives some approximate idea how old the photograph is.

Appendix C shows intuitively time sensitive patterning as well as the objective informational basis for those patterns. The supporting data for appendix C-2 are based mainly on Annual Registers of Marine Corps Officers and Warrant Officers and USMC Muster Rolls 1790 to 1940.

Name	Payclerk	Gunner	2nd LT. 01	1st Lt. 02	Capt. 03	Maj. 04	Lt.Col. 05	Col. 06	Br.Gen. 07	Mj.Gen. 08	Lt.Gen. 09	Gen. 0!0	Ret/Resigned/ KIA etc
Adams, John P.			9/12/1917	11/ /1917	7/26/1923	12/1//1935	9/ /1939						On duty 12/ /1940
Andrews, John J.		3/21/1918											Ret 07/01/1937
Archer, Percy			6/30/1903		3/31/1904				2/11/1923				Ret 1937
Bannon, Philip M.			7/01/1897	6/13/1898	3/3/1899	12/ /1909	10/ /1916	12/ /1917					Ret 3/5/1928
Baptist, H		6/8/1917											Ret 09/01/1934
Bates, John S.				07/01/1899	12/ /1904								Ret 12/1/1904
Beaumont, John C.			2/12/1900					2/24/1926	6/ /1936				Ret 8/ /1940
Bennett, Floyd W.			10/9/1917	11/ /1918	08/ /1931	12/ /1936							On duty 12/1940
Bigler, Epaminondas, L.			1/16/1904	6/27/1910	1/1/1913	11/ /1917							Ret 7/11/1930
Bogan, Henry S.			12/ /1918										Disc 08/15/1919
Bradman, Frederic L.			4/15/1899		7/23/1901		>1919	6/4/1920	5/20/1931				Ret 02/01/1939
Breckenridge, James C.			4[17/1899		7/23/1901			6/4/1920					Ret after 1931
Brown, William Rowles			11/25/1861	8/18/1862	5/18/1871	7/11/1892							Ret 09/05/1892

Brown, Philip.S			06/13/1898	4/ /1899	7/23/1900	5/13/1908							died in line of duty 5/15/1915
Burstan, Rupert M.			6/5/1915		3/26/1917								KIA 09/19/1918
Buchanan, Fitzhugh L.			8/15/1918	6/4/1920									Ret. 06/30/1936
Buchanan, Richard, Bell			8/10/1917		7/1/1918								KIA 05/17 /1927
Burwell, Robert, O, B,			6/5/1915	1916	3/26/1917	7/1/1918							Res 01/31/1920
Buse, Karl I.			10/20/1916	9/ /1917	11/ /1917	10/ /1930	3/ /1935						On duty 12/ //1940
Butler, Smedley D.			5/20/1898	05/08/1899	7/23/1900	5/13/1908	8/23/1916	p 3/9/1919	p 6/4/1920	7/5/1929			Ret. 10/01/1931
Buttrick, James, Tyler			8/2/1900	2/ /1904	7/ /1908	10/ /1916	7/ /1918	12/ /1920	7/ /1935				On duty 12/ /1940
Cain, Memory H.			6/25/1918										Disc 06/24/1922
Cash, John C.			03/16/1845	09/21/1852	06/05/1861	11/20/1862							Died 03/08/1877
Cates,Clifton B.			6/13/1917								<1948 >1951	1948-1951,	Ret 6/30/1954
Catlin, Albertus W.			07/01/1892	9/ /1893		5/13/1908		5/ /1917	8/30/1918				Ret 12/19 /1919
Claggertt, Wilson			10/12/1918	09/ /1919									Gassed and ret 7/ / 1919
Cochrane, Henry Clay			03/10/1863	08/20/1865	03/16/1879			4/24/1899					Ret ca. 11/ /1904

Name	Payclerk	Gunner	2nd LT. 01	1st Lt. 02	Capt. 03	Maj. 04	Lt.Col. 05	Col. 06	Br.Gen. 07	Mj.Gen. 08	Lt.Gen. 09	Gen. O!0	Ret/Resigned/ KIA etc
Coffenberg, Bailey			5/ /1917	9/ /1917	12/ /1917	3/ /1919p							On duty 12/ /1940
Cole, Edward B.			4/2/1904	2/23/1907	6/ /1914	9/ /1917							Died of wounds 6/18/1918
Cole, Eli Kelly			07/ 01 /1890							6/3/1924			Died / /1929
Cukela, Louis			9/26/1918		7/1/1921	6/30/1940							On duty 12/ /1940
Darden, Colgate W.			5/28/1918										Ret 08/02/1919
Del Valle, Pedro A.			6/3/1915		3/26/1917	1/ /1931							On duty 9/ /1934
Dewey, Rupert C.			7/23/1900		6/24/1903	11/ /1916	7/ /1918						Died line of duty 1/13/1920
Ditto, Holton			7/1/1918	3/2/1919									Disc 8/2/1919
Dow, Leon F.			10/ /1918										Disc 12/ /1918
Doyen, Charles A.			7/1/1883				3/11/1905	1/16/1909	3/26/1917				Died 10/06/1918
Duncan, Donald F.			1/6/1909	6/9/1914	8/20/1916								KIA 06/06/1918
Eddy W. A .			6/9/1917	9/ /1918	7/ /1919								Ret 8/30/1919
Elliott, George F.			10/12/1870	03/30/1878	06/15/1892	03/08/1899	09/11/1899		10/3/1903				Ret 11/30/1910

Ellis, Earl H.			12/6/1901	3/3/1903	5/13/2008	8/29/1916	7/1/1918						Died 05/12/1923
Feland, Logan			07/01/1899					3/26/1917	6/2/1920	11/ /1929			Ret 9/1/1933
Fuller Ben H.			7/1/1891	9/ /1893	4/ /1899	12/27/1903	3/ /1911	10/ /1916	2/8/1924P	8/ /1930			RET 3/1/1934
Fuller, Edward Canfield			7/12/1912		3/26/1917								KIA 06/12/1918
Geiger, Roy			2/5/1909						10/1/1941	10/26/1942	06/ /1945?		Died 01/27/1947
Grimm, Charles		7/ /1917	7/ /1917	11/ /1917	11/ /1917								Ret 12/ /1930
Hale, Augustus Boyce			7/ /1917	11/ /1917	6/4/1920 P								Ret ca. 12/ /1930
Hall, Newt			07/01/1897		03/03/1899	01/ /1908	4/ /1917	8/ /1918					Ret 1/2/1929
Hamilton , George W.			08/20 1913	4/ /1917	1/ /1917	t 07/01/1918							Died line of duty 6/20/1922
Harlee, William			2/17/1900	9/ /1905	1/ /1907	9/ /1917	11/ /1918	7/ /1929					Ret 7/1/1945
Hebb,C.D.			3/14/1856	1861	0726/1861	1/12/1970	05/18/1880	08/18/1889					Ret 07/10/1892
Heywood, Charles			4/5/1858	10/ /1861	1/ /1865		1/ /1877 bvt	4/ /1891					Ret 10/3/1903
Herreid, Bert O.			07 /29/1918	7/2/1919									Disc ca. 10/ /1919
Hervilly,James D.			03/05/1872										Res 05/01/1880
Hughes John Arhtur			12/6/1901	3/3/1903	8/ /1908	4/ /1917	8/ /1918						M ret wounds 8/8/1919

Name	Payclerk	Gunner	2nd LT. 01	1st Lt. 02	Capt. 03	Maj. 04	Lt.Col. 05	Col. 06	Br.Gen. 07	Mj.Gen. 08	Lt.Gen. 09	Gen. 0!0	Ret/Resigned/ KIA etc
Hunter, Tracy G.			3/3/1911	12/ /1916	5/ /1917	T3/ /1919							Disc 6/ /1930
Keyser, Ralph S			3/10/1905	1/ /1910	9/ /1916	9/ /1930	11/ /1934						Ret 2/1/1937
Lander, F. C.			3/15/1900	3/2/1903	5/13/1908								Died 6/19/1914
Lay, Harry R.			1/26/1900	08/ /1901	2/28/1905	8/29/1916	8/ /1918	6/ /1925					Died 7/26/1932
Lee, Harry			4/13/1899	5/ /1900	7/23/1900	4/ /1914			6/5/1920	3/1/1934			Died 5/ /1935
LeJeune, John A.			07/01/1890				5/13/1908	3/6/1914	8/29/1916	7/1/1918			Ret 10/11/1929
Livingston, Richard			1/1/1918	3/14/1918	1/27/1926	8/ /1935							Ret.10/ /1937
Lloyd,C.A.		7/19/1918											Om duty 12/ /1940
Long, Charles			07/01/1891	07/01/1891	09/06/1892	03/03/1899		2/ /1911	9/ /1916	8/ /1918			Ret. 12/ /1921
Long, E.C.			8/28/1909		8/29/1916	7/1/1918	2/11/1923	5/1/1928		7/1/1944			Ret 08/ /1946
Low, William W.			07/01/1899		3/3/1904								KIA 10/24/1916
Ludlow, Reginald Fairfax			5/8/1907	11/27/1909									Died 3/11/1913
Mahoney, James E.			07/01/1883	7/ /1890	11/ /1899	10/ /1903	5/1/1905	11/27/1909	t07/18/1918				Ret 2/8/1919
Mathews Calvin B.			12/3/1904	9/ /1907	10/ /1916	11/ /1917	5/3/1929	11/ /1934	8/9/1939				Died 8/20/1939

Metcalf, Clyde Hill					11/11/1912	1/ /1917	4/ /1917	5/ /1926p	8/ /1936				On duty 12/ /1940
Moore, James Tillingham			9/29/1916	10/ /1917	12/ /1917	9/ /1931	7/ /1835						On duty 12/ /1940
Mott, Thomas A.			1/26/1900	7/23/1901	3/1/1908	7/ /1918							Ret, 8/4/1919
Munn, John C.			6/2/1927		6/3/1936					7/1/1954	/ /1957?		Rret 07/ /1964
Murphy, Paul St.Clair			01/01/1890					12/6/1904					Ret 10/10/1910.
Myers, John Twiggs			02/25/1895		7/ /1899	5/1/1905	12/ /1915	6/21/1917	6/ /1929				Ret. 02/01/1935
McClellan,Edwin North			6/18/1907	5/25/1910	8/29/1916	5/22/1917	3/1/1934						Ret 06/30/1936
McDougal, Douglas C.			3/12/1900					10/1/1926	3/1/1934	10/1/1939			On duty 12/ /1940
McGuinness, John P.			4/21/1905	1940	1942	1942	4/27/1905						Ret. 1945
McNulty, John S.	4/4/1905	6/10/1926				05/21/1943							On duty 12/ /1940
Nagel, Frederick			12/4/1918										Disc 1919
Neville, Wendel			06/01/1892		6/4/1904	02/ /1906	3/ /1914	8/29/1916	7/1/1918	12/10/1923			Died 7/8/1930
Northenscold, Emil M.			8/25/1916	8/15/1918	6/ /1919								Ret. 01 after 1932
Osterman, Edward A.			3/20/1907					6/30/1935	02/ /1939	1/1/1943			Ret 01/01/1943
Parsons. Miller V.			5/10/1918	5/16/1919	1/ /1930								On duty 12/ /1940

Name	Payclerk	Gunner	2nd LT. 01	1st Lt. 02	Capt. 03	Maj. 04	Lt.Col. 05	Col. 06	Br.Gen. 07	Mj.Gen. 08	Lt.Gen. 09	Gen. 0!0	Ret/Resigned/ KIA etc
Pendleton, Joseph Henry			07/01/1884	06/28/1891	03/03/1899			5/23/1911	8/29/1916	12/10/1923			Ret 5/12/2024
Perkins Con M.			7/1/1884	1/30/1891	3/3/1899	7/ /1903	6/16/1906						Ret ca. 1906
Porter, David D.			04/26/1898	04/08/1899	10/08/1899	5/14/1908	8/26/1916	7/1/1918	11/ /1935				Ret 3/1/1937
Powell, William G.			07/01/1896	07/01/1899	6/21/1906	5/13/1908	09/ /1917	6/4/1920					Ret 09/ /1927
Powers, William C.			2/5/1906	5/13/1908	12/ /1916	6/4/1920							Ret / /1936
Pugh, Lloy R.			P12/15/1918	6/4/1920	3/ /1931	10/ /1940							On duty 12/ /1940
Rea, Leonard E.			8/15/1918	4/ /1919	10/ /1922	11/ /1934	5/ /1939						On duty 12/ /1940
Ridderhoff, Stanley E.			12/19/1918	4/ /1920	12/ /1934	6/ /1938							On duty 12/ /1940
Rowell, Ross E.			8/3/1906	11/ /1908	9/ /1916	11/ /1917	09/ /1932	8/ /1935	2/ /1940	1/1/1942			Ret / /1946
Rupertus, William H.			11/14/1913	4/ /1917	11/ /1917	9/ /1926							Died 3/25/1945
Russell, John H.			7/1/1894	8/ /1898	3/ /1899	6/ /1906	9/ /1916	12/ /1917	3/ /1922	9/ /1933			Ret 12/01/ 1936
Santleman, William H.						10/ /1898						4/27/1927	Ret 4/27/1927
Schwable, Frank J.			3/21/1900	9/ /1903	10/19/1903	11/ /1916	9/ /1918	7/6/1928					Ret 6/30/1935
Secor, Theodore			2/6/1913	11/ /1916	7/ /1917	9/ /1926							Ret 9/ /1931
Shepherd, Lemuel C.			4/11/1917									1/1/1952	Ret 01/01/1956

Shinkle, Amos R.			07/ /1917	09/ /1913									Disc 9/ /1919
Silard, Con D.			6/3/1926	6/ /1932	10/ /1934								On duty 12/ /1940
Silverthorn, Merwin H.			6/9/1918		7/1/1921						2/22/1951		Ret ca. 7/ /1956
Skidmore, Robert L.			6/3/1922	9/ /1927	3/ /1934								Ret.7/26/1936
Smith, Dwight F.			1/6/1909	8/25/1911	8/29/1916	11/ /1918							Ret ca. 5/ /1920
Smith, Harry L.			8/11/1909			4/4/1923		5/1/1938					On duty 12/ /1940
Smith, Holland M.			2/20/1905	5/13/1908	6/12/1916	6/4/1920		5/29/1934		10/1/1941	2/28/1944	5/15/1946	Ret. 5/15/1946
Smith, Julian, C.			1/22/1909			6/4/1920		7/27/1935					Ret 1 /12/1946
Snyder, Harold C.			07/01/1899	10/ /1900	3/3/1903	12/ /1917	12/ /1918	3/ /1919					Ret. 9/6/1929
Stanton, John T.			12/19/1918	1/2/1919									Disc 3/31/1919
Stokes, Arthur			4/2/1904	12/ /1906	10/2/1914								M ret 8/18/1917
Taylor, C.B.			6/5/1900		/ / 1907		6/4/1920	7/15/1925					Ret 1/26/1935
Thomas, Gerald C.			9/26/1918	T4/ /1919	11/ /1932	8/ /1937			12/7/1943			1/1/1956	Ret 1/1/1956
Thompson, Claude			9 26/1918		?								Disc 09/ /1919

Name	Payclerk	Gunner	2nd LT. 01	1st Lt. 02	Capt. 03	Maj. 04	Lt.Col. 05	Col. 06	Br.Gen. 07	Mj.Gen. 08	Lt.Gen. 09	Gen. 0!0	Ret/Resigned/ KIA etc
Thorndike, John T.			12/16/1918										Disc 7/1/ 1919
Turrill, Julius S.			10/ /1899	1/ /1903	6/ /1903	2/ /1917							Ret. 1943
Vandergrift, Alexander, A.			1/22/1909	1914/1915	08'29/1916	T 7/18/1918					01/ /1944		Ret. 01/31/1947
Wainwright, R.D.			12/04/1869	03/17/1877									Ret 04/17/1893
Wheaton, Ivan P.			06/18/1918 ?	?									Res / /1921
Wensinger, Walter W.			2/16/1918		11/ /1934	7/ /1938		10/15/1942	t7/1/1948	7/1/1948			Ret. 8/1956
White, Harry Kidder			07/01/1883	03/26/1889	02/02/1897	09/11/1899							Ret 11/26/1909
Wiggs, Otho		8/13/1918											On duty 12/ /1940
Williams, Dion			07/01/1893			2/28/1905			6/3/1924				Ret 1/1/1934
Williams, Ernest, Calvin			01/ /1909	10/ /1915	08/ /1917	03/ /1921							Res 03/ 22 /1921
Winans.Roswell			P04/17/1917	never	12/ /1918	6/4/1932	7/27/1935	early 1941	080/7/1946				Ret. 08/07/1946
Wise, Fritz M.			07/01/1899		3/3/1903	after 1913?	3/26/1917	1/1/1922					Ret 01/19/1926
Wolever, Benjamine H.	11/10/1918		.		.		.	.					On duty 12/ /1940

APPENDIX D

Descriptive Data by B Number

The weights were recorded using a digital scale. The measurements were recorded using a set of digital calipers. A total of eight different but standard measurements were originally recorded on a standard form. Only the four most reliable values were included in appendix D. The more difficult and most problematic measurements were excluded in the final appendix. The earliest emblem recordings did not include weights and measurements of metric or English thread sizes for screw posts. Other missing data are do to the problem of not being able to weigh or measure emblems behind glass cases or when the emblems were attached to headgear, uniforms, epaulets etc. Removing emblems in these cases was not possible or advisable. Some missing data are simply the author's inadvertent mistakes. The data in appendix D refer only to that emblem with that particular B number. Any emblem type in this inventory can have a wide range of variations, especially the attachment method and weights. The three measurements A, B, and C are indicated by the illustration below. The measurements for eagle wing span (A) anchor length (B) and thickness of the edge of the globe at four o'clock were less problematic than the more difficult measurements subject to greater measurement error or post production alterations by the manufacturer or the wearer.

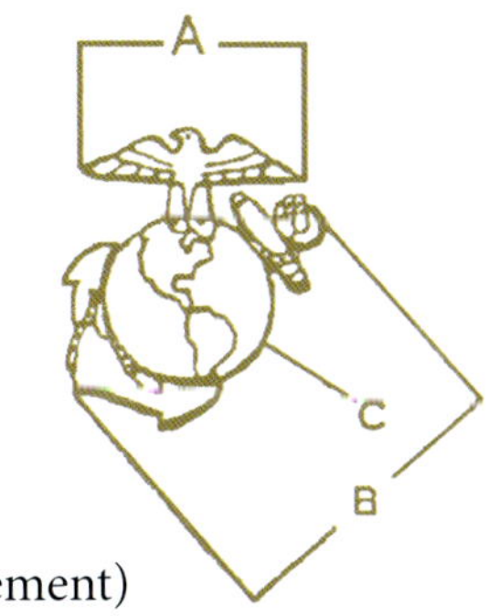

Measurements A, B, and C

* Thickness of the plate
** Original attachment method unknown converted to a white metal oval plate
*** The cavity of the globe is leaded in
BRS: Brass
BRZ: Bronze
HS: Hard soldered
N/A: Not applicable
TPI: Turns per inch (English measurement)
MM: Millimeters (metric system)

B#	METHOD OF ATTACHMENT	WEIGHT GRAMS	A mm	B mm	C mm
1	8 drilled holes in 4 corners for sewing or wiring	26.1	N/A	N/A	0.57*
2	4 drilled holes in 4 corners for sewing or wiring		N/A	N/A	1.49*
3	8 drilled holes in 4 corners for sewing or wiring	36.2	N/A	N/A	0.41*
4	pierced holes in 4 corners for sewing or wiring	10.3	N/A	N/A	0.08*
5	8 drilled holes at 12, 3, 6, and 9 o'clock for sewing or wiring		N/A	N/A	
6	2 flat head rivets at 6 o'clock and a strong metal tongue at 12 o'clock, all BRS	27.2	N/A	N/A	0.86*
7	3 doubled over and inverted iron wires HS at 12, 5, and 7 o'clock REV	37.6	N/A	N/A	

B#	METHOD OF ATTACHMENT	WEIGHT GRAMS	A mm	B mm	C mm
8	2 doubled over BRS inverted wires soldered at eagle mid wings REV	9.3	84.8	N/A	
9	3 single strand BRS wires soldered at mid wings and tail feathers REV	14.4	120.9	N/A	0.45*
10	3 single strand "U" shaped BRS wires soldered at mid wings and shield REV	9.9	78.5	N/A	
11	2 "U" shaped BRS wire loops soldered mid wings REV	10.2	79.6	N/A	0.40*
12	3 single strand BRS wires, at wing tips and tail feathers REV	6.1	77.4	N/A	
13	1 copper wire soldered at base of wings REV, ends free and bent upward	3.9	75.7	N/A	
14	BRS drop in "C" type pin assembly	8.1	76.9	N/A	0.60*
15	2 "O" shaped British single strand BRS cotter pins HS mid wing REV	8.2	74.8	N/A	0.57*
16	2 "U" shaped BRS wire loops soldered mid wings REV		75.8	N/A	0.41*
17	2 "U" shaped BRS wire loops soldered at base of wings REV	9.4	75.8	N/A	0.67*
18	2 single strand wires soldered top of shield REV	2.1	46.3	N/A	0.60*
19	2 single strand BRS wires soldered at base of wings REV		40.7	N/A	
20	2 single strand BRS wires soldered at top corners of shield REV	4.3	40.7	N/A	0.53*
21	2 single strand BRS wires soldered at mid body of eagle REV	5.8	N/A	N/A	0.70*
22	2 single strand BRS wires, soldered at eagle neck and tail feathers REV	1.5	N/A	N/A	0.50*
23	no attachments, device meant to be sewn		N/A	N/A	N/A
24	no attachments, device meant to be sewn		N/A	N/A	N/A
25	no attachments, device meant to be sewn	8.8	N/A	N/A	N/A

B#	METHOD OF ATTACHMENT	WEIGHT GRAMS	A mm	B mm	C mm
26	no attachments, device meant to be sewn	8.8	N/A	N/A	N/A
27	2 "U" shaped BRS wire loops soldered mid wreath REV	8.1	N/A	N/A	
28	2 "U" shaped BRS wire loops HS to wreath at 9 and 3 o'clock REV	12.2	N/A	41.9	.33*
29	no attachments, device meant to be sewn		N/A	36.6	N/A
30	unknown, emblem known only from 1847 illustration				
31	unknown, emblem known only from 1853 illustration				
32	3 doubled over iron wires, mid body, mid anchor stock and mid anchor REV	14.2	96.6	72.8	0.28*
33	original soldered wires missing		92.3	73	0.45*
34	no attachments, untrimmed, unfinished plate	27.8	91.8	70.3	0.46*
35	3 "U" shaped BRS wires soldered to mid body, mid and lower anchor REV	15.8	91.9	70.8	0.50*
36	2 "U" shaped iron wires (magnetic) HS to edges of letters REV	2.3	N/A	N/A	0.60*
37	2 "U" shaped brass wires HS to the periphery of the letters REV	3.1	N/A	N/A	0.40*
38	system of 8 "U" shaped wires HS to rev (loops and eyes and leather triangles)		N/A	N/A	
39	system of 8 "U" shaped wires HS to rev (loops and eyes and leather triangles)	60.2	N/A	N/A	0.55 shield
40	system of 8 "U" shaped wires HS to rev (loops and eyes and leather triangles)		N/A	N/A	0.55 shield
41	system of 8 "U" shaped wires HS to rev (loops and eyes and leather triangles)	60.2	N/A	N/A	0.55 shield
42	6 single strand BRS wires, 2 single strand WM wires soldered to REV	46.4	2.92	40.39	0.55 shield
43	7 "U" shaped wires HS REV: 2 shield, 2 wreath, 2 bugle, 1 letter "M"	29.3	N/A	N/A	

B#	METHOD OF ATTACHMENT	WEIGHT GRAMS	A mm	B mm	C mm
44	7 "U" shaped wires HS REV: 2 shield, 2 wreath, 2 bugle, 1 letter "M"	30.6	N/A	N/A	0.51*
45	2 "U" shaped BRS wires HS to bugle REV, 4 BRS tabs for WM "M" REV	5.1	N/A	N/A	0.51*
46	2 single strand wires HS to bugle REV, 1 "U" shaped BRS wire for letter "M"	5.2	N/A	N/A	0.51*
47	2 single strand wires HS to bugle REV, 1 "U" shaped BRS wire for letter "M"	3.1	N/A	N/A	0.51*
48	device sewn on, 2 holes indicate metal letter "M" were probably wires HS REV	7.9	N/A	N/A	
49	device sewn on, slit indicates metal letter "M" probably had two wires soldered	3.3	N/A	N/A	NA
50	device sewn on, bugle and letter "M" attached by 3 "U" shaped BRS wires	17.8	N/A	N/A	N/A
51	none, untrimmed BRS plate		N/A	N/A	0.36*
52	2 single strand BRS wires soldered at both ends of the bugle REV	4.6	N/A	N/A	0.58*
53	2 single strand BRS wires soldered at both ends of the bugle REV	5.8	N/A	N/A	0.51*
54	2 single strand BRS wires HS to bugle REV	3.9	N/A	N/A	0.44*
55	2 single strand BRS wires soldered to bugle REV, "M" attached by flat tab		N/A	N/A	
56	2 single strand BRS wires, 1 at bell,1 behind chord at small end REV	6.6	N/A	N/A	
57	3 single strand BRS wires, 1 at 12 o'clock, 1 at bell,1 near small end REV	3.6	N/A	N/A	
58	device sewn on, letter "M" has 2 single strand BRS wires		N/A	N/A	N/A
59	device sewn on, letter "M" has 2 single strand BRS wires		N/A	N/A	N/A
60	embroidered device meant to be sewn on	5.1	N/A	N/A	N/A
61	embroidered device meant to be sewn on	2.4	N/A	N/A	N/A

B#	METHOD OF ATTACHMENT	WEIGHT GRAMS	A mm	B mm	C mm
62	device sewn on, letter "M" has 2 single strand brass wires REV		N/A	N/A	N/A
63	device sewn on, letter "M" has 2 single strand brass wires REV		N/A	N/A	N/A
64	sewn on, letter "M" has a single WM wire doubled over and soldered at center	7.8	N/A	N/A	N/A
65	sewn on, letter "M" has 2 single strand WM wires at edge of the letter	7.2		N/A	N/A
66	sewn on, letter "M" has 2 single strand BRS wires at edge of the letter	9.1	N/A	N/A	N/A
67	wires but could not take apart to examine		N/A	N/A	
68	single strand BRS wires soldered to REV	4.1	N/A	N/A	
69	2 rectangular BRS tabs soldered to center of globe REV	9.3	25.1	38.1	1.1*
70	3 "U" shaped inverted BRS wires soldered at eagle head, left wing and legs REV		90.3	22.5	0.24
71	4 "U" shaped BRS wire loops, 2 shield, 2 anchor stock and crown REV		25.8	37.3	0.43
72	2 "U" shaped BRS wire loops on anchor stock and crown REV	3.1	25.3	36.4	0.43
73	4 "U" shaped BRS wires soldered at 12, 3, 6, and 9 o'clock REV		N/A	N/A	
74	2 "U" shaped BRS wire loops soldered at 3 and 9 o'clock REV		25.6	36.9	0.47
75	2 "U" shaped BRS wires soldered at anchor stock and crown REV	3.5	25.7	37.2	0.39
76	4 BRS wire loops, 2 at anchor stock and crown, 2 shields at 3 and 9 o'clock REV	19.4	25.9	36.2	0.44
77	2 BRS wire loops soldered at anchor stock and crown REV	3.4	25.9	36.2	0.44
78	4 BRS wire loops at 12, 3, 6, and 9 o'clock, 1 anchor stock and 1 crown REV		N/A	N/A	

B#	METHOD OF ATTACHMENT	WEIGHT GRAMS	A mm	B mm	C mm
79	4 BRS wire loops 12, 3, 6, and 9 o'clock, 2 at anchor stock and crown REV	20.9	29.3	41.4	0.36
80	single long WM flat rectangular tab soldered to inside of globe REV		24.5	41.5	
81	2 silver wires HS to circular silver disc in turn soldered to globe REV	11.7	23.9	50.5	
82	2 BRS wires with pointed ends soldered to inside of globe REV	8.2	25.9	51.4	0.83
83	2 "U" shaped BRS wire loops soldered at eagle body and bottom of globe REV	5.2	29.9	N/A	0.51
84	2 long WM rectangular tabs soldered to inside of globe REV	8.8	29.1	N/A	0.93
85	2 "U" shaped BRS wires soldered at eagle body and bottom of globe REV	5.5	29.8	N/A	0.56
86	2 single strand BRS wires soldered at eagle body and bottom of globe REV	6.1	28.8	N/A	0.55
87	flat rectangular silver tab doubled over and silver soldered to center of globe REV	4.6	25.6	N/A	1.13
88	sewn to kepi, has aperture for attaching metal eagle and globe	1.9	N/A	47.1	0.56
89	sewn to kepi, has holes for attaching metal eagle and globe		N/A	N/A	N/A
90	sewn, device has long pointed BRS tab doubled over and soldered to globe REV	11.2	29.9	57.4	1.43
91	2 "U" shaped BRS wire loops soldered at anchor stock and crown REV	3.2	25.3	36.9	0.57
92	2 heavy BRZ "O" shaped cotter pin eyes, soldered at 3 and 9 o'clock REV		N/A	N/A	
93	3 single strand BRS wires soldered at 12, 3, and 9 o'clock, shield edge REV	15.5	N/A	N/A	
94	2 single strand BRS wires, soldered to eagle body and anchor crown REV	2.8	25.4	no stock & ring	0.54
95	BRS screw post 40 TPI, HS to mid anchor shaft REV	10.5	25.8	47.5	0.71

B#	METHOD OF ATTACHMENT	WEIGHT GRAMS	A mm	B mm	C mm
96	pin back, "C" type drop in catch	9.6	24.5	43.8	
97	BRZ jeweler's pivoting pin back, "C" type drop in catch		25.6	45.5	
98	converted to pinback on an oval plate, original attachment method unknown	12.2**	26.3	46.3	
99	3 heavy BRZ wires, soldered at eagle body, anchor stock, and fluke REV	8.2	28.7	38.6	0.62
100	2 WM wires, soldered to mid anchor stock and anchor crown REV	4.7	28.5	40.9	0.52
101	2 "U" shaped silver wires. All elements of a single investment casting	10.7	27.5	40.9	1.16
102	missing from this inventory, known only from photographs				
103	sewn to collar, could not remove, original attachments unknown		R 17.0 L 16.5	R 25.9 L25.4	
104	compound hinged jeweler's pin back with "C" type drop in catch	R 3.6 L 3.2	R 17.3 L 17.0	R 25.1 L 24.9	R 0.68 L 0.62
105	pin back "C" type catch, single piece investment casting	L 4.0	L 15.9	L 23.8	L 0.74
106	jeweler's compound pivoting pin back with "C" type catch	R 2.8 L 2.5	R 14.2 L 14.3	R 22.9 L 22.9	R 0.89 L 0.88
107	jeweler's pivoting pin back, drop in "C" type catch		15.1	24.1	
108	jeweler's pivoting pin back, drop in "C" type catch		15.1	28.2	
109	BRS screw post, 40 TPI, HS globe center REV	R 3.8 L 3.8	R 16.1 L 16.1	R 26.7 L 26.3	R 0.63 L 0.60
110	single rectangular, pointed brass tab, doubled over soldered to globe center REV	R 5.3 L 5.5	R 16.7 L 15.7	R 26.4 L 26.1	N/A
111	BRS screw post HS at globe center REV		R 16.5 L 17.2	R 26.8 L 26.5	R 0.90 L 0.80
112	doubled over flat rectangular WM tabs set in REV of solid silver emblem	R 5.9 L 6.4	R 14.9 L 15.9	R 24.4 L 26.1	solid silver

B#	METHOD OF ATTACHMENT	WEIGHT GRAMS	A mm	B mm	C mm
113	2 single strand BRS wires soldered to middle of eagle wings REV		38.5	N/A	
114	2 single strand BRS wires soldered to mid wings REV	5.1	38.6	N/A	0.83
115	jeweler's pin back, pivoting pin, drop in "C" type catch HS anchor shaft REV	7.1	24.5	41.2	0.41
116	jeweler's pin back, top loading rolling type catch HS anchor shaft REV	6.3	24.4	34.6	0.75
117	complex jeweler's pin back, drop in "C" type catch HS anchor shaft REV	4.9	21.5	35.4	0.44
118	complex jeweler's pin back assembly	5.9	19.9	25.7	0.83
119	4 single strand BRS wires, soldered to ends of anchor stock and flukes REV	8.8	25.4	54.1	1.01
120	4 single strand BRS wires soldered to anchor flukes and ends of stock REV		26.4	52.9	
121	5 "U" shaped BRS wires HS at mid anchor shaft, ends of stock and flukes REV	4.6	25.6	52.8	0.13
122	3 long silver pins, 1 at anchor stock and 2 at flukes REV	9.8	24.9	47.9	0.67
123	3 single strand BRS wires soldered to eagle body, mid stock and crown REV	7.2	24.9	45.5	0.77
124	brass screw post 36 TPI, HS to ancher mid shaft REV	11.1	24.8	46.6	0.61
125	3 silver plated pins HS at anchor stock and flukes for easy attachment to epaulette	8.7	27.3	47.6	0.93
126	3 single strand wires, HS to upper anchor stock and flukes REV	6.2	24.8	44.1	0.88
127	4 double strand inverted WM wires HS at anchor stock, crown and flukes REV	R 6.5 L 6.5	R 27.2 L 27.4	R 47.2 L 47.3	R0.15 L 0..21
128	BRS wires probably 3 or 4, could not disassemble the epaulette to examine				
129	3 single strand BRS wires soldered at anchor ring and flukes REV	R 8.2 L 8.7	R 24.3 L 23.9	R 48.4 L 49.0	R 0.60

B#	METHOD OF ATTACHMENT	WEIGHT GRAMS	A mm	B mm	C mm
130	1 flat rectangular, pointed BRS tab doubled over, HS to inside of globe REV	10.3	27.6	46.1	L 0.28
131	3 single strand silver wires, HS at anchor stock and flukes REV		R 31.9 L 30.4	R 41.4 L 41.0	R 0.87 L 1.30
132	jeweler's complex silver pin back, drop in "C" type clasp HS 6 to 12 o'clock REV	R 9.1 L 8.8	R 29.2 L 29.2	R 41.2 L 41.2	R 0.71 L 0.73
133	2 double strand silver wires HS at REV	8.4	29.4	42.5	0.71
134	2 rectangular single flat BRS tabs soldered at mid anchor stock and crown REV	R 10.1. L 9.6	R 29.2 L 29.2	R 40.7 L 40.4	R 0.79 L 0.74
135	2 single strand BRS wires soldered at mid anchor stock and mid crown REV	4.1	29.2	40.9	0.5
136	2 single strand BRS wires soldered at mid anchor stock and anchor crown REV	7.8	29.1	41.9	0.91
137	2 "U" shaped iron wire loops soldered to mid anchor stock and anchor crown REV	4.3	29.3	40.9	0.31
138	BRS screw post, HS at globe center REV		28.5	39.7	
139	doubled over BRS wires soldered at mid anchor stock and anchor crown REV	5.7	29.2	41.5	0.61
140	2 "U" shaped WM wire loops soldered to mid anchor stock and crown REV	7.5	28.7	41.6	0.55
141	Original double wires missing and converted to a brass screw post 32 tpi HS	10.3	28.9	42.1	0.45
142	pivoting pin back "C" type catch soldered to anchor stock and crown REV	8.1	28.9	41.7	0.56
143	2 single strand WM wires soldered to anchor stock and anchor crown REV	3.6	29.2	40.4	0.36
144	BRS screw post, 32 TPI, HS globe center, anti-twist pins at wing tips REV	26.8	84.1	80.2	0.61
145	BRS screw post, 32 TPI, HS center of globe REV, no anti-twist pins at wing tips	44.9	86.8	802	1.01
146	BRS screw post, 32 TPI, HS at globe center, anti-twist pins at wing tips REV		86.5	80.4	0.55

B#	METHOD OF ATTACHMENT	WEIGHT GRAMS	A mm	B mm	C mm
147	3 flat, pointed BRS tabs soldered at eagle back, mid anchor stock and crown REV		86.3	81.7	0.46
148	unknown, was behind a glass frame and could not be examined		84.1	80.2	
149	3 BRS screw posts, 40 TPI, HS at eagle neck, anchor stock and crown REV	41.8	86.1	80.7	0.93
150	BRS screw post, soldered to center of globe REV		78.4	81.4	
151	3 BRS wires,eagle back, stock, crown, "U" shoped loop at globe center REV	49.1***	85.4	79.3	0.82
152	screw post and two flat brass tabs soldered at anchor crown and stock REV		80.2	80.2	
153	4 single strand long silver wires HS to wing tips, anchor stock and crown REV	51.9	100.3	99.7	1.21
154	no data, known only from a period photo				
155	4 probable BRZ single strand wires HS at wings,anchor mid stock and crown REV		86.3	81.7	0.51
156	brown leather ornament sewn to officer's field saddle cloth		R 84.5 L 84.7	R 82.5 L 83.0	
157	scarlet leather ornament sewn to officer's dress saddle cloth		R 82.2 L 88.0	R 81.0 L 82-1	
158	BRS screw post 32 TPI, HS at globe center REV, anti-twist pin at eagles neck	15.4	28.3	40.9	0.99
159	BRS screw post 32 TPI, HS at globe center REV, anti-twist pin at eagles neck	14.2	29.2	41.5	1.14
160	BRS screw post, 32 TPI, HS at globe center, anti-twist pin at eagle neck REV		27.4	42.6	1.56
161	BRS screw post, 32 TPI, HS at globe center, anti-twist pin at eagle neck REV	13.5	28.7	41.2	0.9
162	BRS screw post, HS at globe center, anti-twist pin at eagle's neck REV		29.1	44.1	0.98
163	BRZ screw post, 32 TPI, HS to center of globe REV	14.5	30.2	41.9	1.51

B#	METHOD OF ATTACHMENT	WEIGHT GRAMS	A mm	B mm	C mm
164	BRS screw post, 40 TPI, HS to globe center REV, anti-twist pin at eagle's back	15.5	30.1	42.6	1.77
165	BRS screw post, 32 TPI, HS to globe center rev, anti-twist peg at eagle's back	12.8	29.6	41.5	1.12
166	jeweler's pivoting pin back assembly with side loading roll type catch, cast emblem	13.6	27.7	41.7	1.87
167	BRZ screw post, 32 TPI, HS to globe center REV, anti-twist peg eagle's back	15.1	28.8	40.9	0.48
168	BRZ screw post, 40 TPI, HS to globe center REV	8.7	29.2	40.9	0.77
169	BRZ screw post, 32 TPI, HS to globe center REV	15.3	30.1	41.9	1.49
170	short wing die variety in BRZ, missing from inventory				
171	BRZ screw post, 32 TPI, HS to globe center REV, anti-twist peg eagle's back	14.5	25.1	41.6	1.47
172	BRZ screw post, 32 TPI, HS to globe center REV, anti-twist peg eagle's back	15.9	28.7	40.9	1.27
173	silver pin back, pivoting pin, with "C" type drop in catch HS to anchor shaft REV	10.7	26.4	45.8	0.47
174	silver screw post attached to silver and gold rectangular bar HS globe edges REV	9.1	27.2	40.9	0.33
175	silver screw post, HS to mid anchor shaft REV	9.2	24.9	45.1	0.52
176	silver pin back with "C" type drop in catch, HS to mid anchor shaft REV	10.3	26.4	44.5	0.71
177	silver screw post, 32 TPI, HS to mid anchor shaft REV	13.9	29.9	44.3	0.41
178	screw post converted to WM pin back with roll type catch HS anchor shaft REV	13.9	29.2	43.9	1.26
179	silver screw post 50 mm HS to anchor shaft REV, anti-twist peg at eagle back	12.9	30.2	43.9	0.89
180	screw post, HS to silver and gold clad rectangular bar at edges of globe REV	10.4	25.3	42.5	0.64

B#	METHOD OF ATTACHMENT	WEIGHT GRAMS	A mm	B mm	C mm
181	screw post HS to mid anchor shaft REV, anti-twist peg at eagle's back	11.5	28.7	44.5	0.59
182	missing from inventory, known only from photos and uniform regulations				
183	silver screw post 36 TPI, HS at mid anchor shaft REV no anti-twist peg		25.9	42.9	0.93
184	screw post, 32 TPI, HS at mid anchor stock REV, no anti-twist peg	13.9	31.2	43.9	0.55
185	silver screw post, 32 TPI HS to mid anchor shaft REV, anti-twist peg eagle's back	11.3	31.2	43.4	0.56
186	silver screw post, 32 TPI, HS to mid anchor shaft REV, anti-twist peg eagle's back	13.4	31.9	44.1	0.73
187	silver screw post HS to mid anchor shaft REV, anti-twist peg broken off	12.9	28.1	43.6	0.39
188	screw post, 32 TPI, HS to mid anchor shaft REV, no anti-twist peg	11.1	31.3	43.5	0.63
189	screw post, HS mid anchor shaft REV, anti-twist peg at eagle's neck REV	11.2	28.8	44.3	0.71
190	3 BRS wires HS at mid anchor stock and both flukes REV	R 9.5 L 9.3	R 29.9 L 29,5	R 44.1 L 43.9	R 0.59 L 0.74
191	3 silver wires HS to eagle body, mid anchor stock and mid anchor crown REV		R 30.8 L 30.8	R 45.3 L 45.8	
192	silver screw post 32 TPI, HS to mid anchor shaft REV, anti-twist peg eagle's neck	11.7	31.1	43.5	0.48
193	3 silver wires HS eagle's back, mid anchor stock and mid crown REV	R 11.8	R 31.4	R 43.7	R.0.55
194	BRZ screw post HS to mid anchor shaft REV, anti-twist peg at eagle's back	10.9	26.9	43.6	0.88
195	WM pin back, pivoting pin , drop in "C" type catch HS anchor mid shaft REV	10.1	28.5	43.8	0.56
196	BRZ screw post 36 TPI, HS to mid anchor shaft rev, anti-twist peg at eagle's back	11.1	28.4	43.7	0.61
197	BRZ screw post, 32 TPI HS to mid anchor shaft REV, anti-twist peg eagle's back	11.3	31.2	43.6	0.53

B#	METHOD OF ATTACHMENT	WEIGHT GRAMS	A mm	B mm	C mm
198	BRZ screw post, 32 TPI HS to mid anchor shaft REV, anti-twist peg eagle's back	12.1	29.4	43.4	0.66
199	BRZ screw post, 32 TPI HS to mid anchor shaft REV, anti-twist peg eagle's back	11.3	31.3	43.6	1.12
200	BRZ screw post, 32 TPI, HS to mid anchor shaft REV, anti-twist peg eagle's back	11.1	31.6	43.7	0.68
201	BRZ screw post, 32 TPI, HS to mid anchor shaft REV, anti-twist peg eagle's back	10.4	29.9	43.7	0.68
202	silver screw post HS to mid anchor shaft REV, metric data not recorded				
203	BRZ screw post HS to mid anchor shaft REV. anti-twist peg eagle's back	14.4	29.8	44.1	0.68
204	BRZ four point star nut, screw post, 60 mm thread size, HS to anchor shaft REV	17.2	27.1	52	0.44
205	BRZ screw post, >60 mm thread size, single piece casting except nit	heavier than B204	26.7	45.6	>2.00
206	BRZ screw post 32 TPI, HS to a rectangular bar across globe REV	17.9	34.2	45.9	1.06
207	BRZ jeweler's pivoting pin, rolling type catch HS to anchor shaft REV		30.4	43.9	0.8
208	BRZ screw post HS to mid anchor shaft REV	14.9	32.4	43.2	1.19
209	WM screw post HS to anchor shaft REV, anti-twist peg at eagle's back	R 8.9 L 8.8	R 25.3 L 24.8	R 34.6 L 34.3	R 0.99 L 0.74
210	silver jeweler's compound pin back, Tiffany type catch, HS to anchor shaft REV	R 7.7 L 7.7	R 24.1 L 24.3	R 34.9 L 34.7	R 0.63 L 0.60
211	silver pivoting pin back, side loading roll type catch HS anchor shaft REV	R 7.7 L 7.7	R 26.0. L 26.4	R 35.0. L 35.0	R 0.85 L 0.82
212	WM jeweler's pin back HS to anchor shaft REV	R 9.2 L 9.2	R 25.6 L 26.0	R 34.9 L 34.9	R.0.63 L.0.61
213	silver pivoting pin back, drop in "C" type catch, HS to anchor shaft REV	R 7.3 L 7.2	L25.9	L 34.2	L 0.81
214	silver pivoting pin back, "C" type catch, HS to anchor shaft REV	R 9.2	R 26.6	R 34.0	R 0.45

B#	METHOD OF ATTACHMENT	WEIGHT GRAMS	A mm	B mm	C mm
215	silver pivoting pin, side loading roll type catch, HS to anchor shaft REV	R 7.8 L 7.5	R 26.6 L 27.6	R 34.7 L 34.8	R 0.90 L 0.80
216	WM pin back, "C" type drop in catch, HS to anchor shaft REV	R 7.8 L 7.9	L 26.1	L 33.8	L 0.91
217	silver pin back, pivoting pin, Tiffany type catch, HS to anchor shaft REV	R 7.5 L 7.2	R 24.8 L 25.1	R 34.1 L 34.1	R 0.80 L 0.68
218	silver pin back, pivoting pin, top loading roll type catch, HS to anchor shaft REV		R 26.3 L 25.2	R 33.9 L 33.8	R 0.77 L.0.78
219	silver pin back, pivoting pin, top loading roll type catch, HS to anchor shaft REV	L7.9	L 24.6	L 33.7	L 0.81
220	screw post, 32 TPI, unusual rounded disc shape nut, HS to anchor shaft REV	R 5.8 L 6.7	R 26.1 L 26.5	R 33.6 L 33.9	R 0.50 L 0.58
221	pin back, coiled pivoting pin, side loading roll type catch, HS anchor shaft REV	R 7.3 L 7.2	R 26.0 L 26.0	R 33.8 L 34.1	R 0.52 L 0.68
222	WM pin back, pivoting pin, top loading catch, HS to anchor shaft REV	R 5.6	R 26.5	R 34.0	R 0.49
223	WM pin back, pivoting pin, top loading catch, HS to anchor shaft REV	L 5.8	R 26.6	R 33.8	R 0.64
224	WM pin back, drop in "C" type catch, HS to anchor stock and crown REV	R 5.4 L 6.0	R 25.0 L 25.2	R 34.1 L 34.0	R 0.57 L 0.52
225	2 screw posts, fine threads, small toothed nut, HS mid anchor stock and crown	R 7.6 L 7.6	R 26.4 L 25.9	R 33.8 L 33.8	R 0.51 L 0.50
226	WM pin back, pivoting pin, "C" type drop in catch, HS to anchor shaft REV	R 5.1 L 5.6	R 26.5 L 26.2	R 34.0 L 34.2	R 0.60 L 0.70
227	WM pin back, side loading roll type catch, with pin sleeve, HS anchor shaft REV	R 7,0 L 7.2	R 25.9 L 25.8	R 34.0 L 34.1	R 0.81 L 0.88
228	silver drop in "C" type catch, single piece casting except pivoting pin.	R 6.9 L 5.9	R 24.6 L 24.3	R 33.0 L 33.0	R 0.63 L 0.87
229	unusual WM 5 element drop in pin assembly, HS to globe periphery REV	L 4.4	L 19.4	L 32.7	L 0.67
230	WM "C" type drop in catch, HS to anchor shaft REV	L 5.5	L 25.2	L 34.8	L 0.69
231	2 single brass wires at 6 and 12 o'clock peamed to holes in square plate REV	48.2 plate and device	R 25.8	R 32.8	N/A*

B#	METHOD OF ATTACHMENT	WEIGHT GRAMS	A mm	B mm	C mm
232	silver single piece casting except WM pivoting pin	R 10.3 L 9.8	R 28.1 L 27.3	R 43.3 L 43.2	R 0.47 L 0.51
233	BRZ pivoting pinback, top loading roll type catch, HS to anchor shaft REV	L 8.6	L 25.2	L 34.9	L 0.89
234	BRZ "C" type drop in pinback HS to anchor shaft REV	R 7.4 L 7.0	R 26.5 L 26.6	R 34.2 L 34.4	R 0.63 L 0.53
235	BRZ "C" type drop in catch, HS to anchor shaft REV	R 8.2 L 7.8	R 27.1 L 26.9	R 34.6 L 34.7	R 0.60 L 0.58
236	BRZ Tiffany type catch pinback HS to anchor shaft REV	R 8.0 L 7.5	R 27.3 L 26.8	R 34.4 L 34.6	R 0.48 L 0.52
237	L screw post, R side loading catch pinback, all HS to anchor shaft REV	L 8.0	L 27.0	L 33.7	R 0.48 L 0.53
238	BRZ pin back side loading roll type catch HS to anchor shaft REV	L 9.3	L 27.0	L 34.1	L 0.87
239	BRZ pinback drop in "C" type catch HS to anchor shaft REV	R 5.1	R 25.8 L 25.8	R 34.0 L 34.0	R 0.91 L 0.90
240	BRZ pinback drop in "C" type catch HS to anchor shaft REV	R 5.4	R 26.2	R 34.9	R 0.56
241	silver pivoting pin, Tiffany catch HS to anchor shaft REV	R 7.3	R 26.2	R 33.8	R 0.68
242	BRZ pinback, same complex six element pin assembly as B229	R 4.5	R 20.7	R 32.5	R 0.49
243	BRZ pinback drop in "C" type catch HS to anchor shaft REV	L 5.5	L 25.3	L 35.1	L 0.58
244	BRZ pivoting pin, drop in "C" type catch, HS anchor shaft REV	R 5.7	R 25.6	R 34.6	R 0.88
245	BRZ pinback converted by grinding off pin and drilling 2 holes to attach	L 5.8	L 23.5	L 31.6	L 0.62
246	BRZ pinback, Tiffany catch, HS to anchor shaft REV	L 6.0	L 25.2	L 32.8	L 0.74
247	BRZ pinback, "C" type catch HS to rectangular bar at edges of globe REV	R 10.0 L 9.5	R 25.1 L 25.2	R 34.8 L 35.0	R 1.24 L 0.88
248	BRZ drop in "C" type catch, spring loaded pin HS to anchor shaft REV	R 6.7 L 6.7	R 27.4 L 27.7	R 37.0 L 36.7	R 0.53 L 0.51

B#	METHOD OF ATTACHMENT	WEIGHT GRAMS	A mm	B mm	C mm
249	BRZ drop in "C" type catch, spring loaded pin HS to anchor shaft REV	R 10.1.	R 27.6 L 26.6	R 42.3 L 42.0	R 0.53 L 0.65
250	BRZ drop in "C" type catch, spring loaded pin HS to anchor shaft REV	R 13.6 L 10.2	R 27.9 L 27.5	R 43.4 L 43.3	R 0.62 L 0.76
251	darkened silver single piece casting except pivoting pin, same mold as B232	R 10.4 L 9.9	R 28.1 L 27.3	R 43.3 L 43.2	R 0.47 L 0.51
252	sewn embroidered emblem	R 1.8 L 1.8	R 25.2 L 26.9	R 35.5 L 36.5	R 0.28 L 0.29
253	BRS screw post 32 TPI, HS to globe center REV, anti-twist peg at eagles neck	9.1	30.5	41.1	0.78
254	BRS screw post 32 TPI, HS to globe center REV, anti-twist peg at eagles back		29.9	41.2	1.12
255	BRS screw post 32 TPI, HS to globe center REV, anti-twist peg at eagles neck	13.3	30.3	41.2	1.18
256	BRS screw post 32 TPI, HS to globe center REV, no anti-twist peg	13.1	30.4	40.9	1.29
257	BRS screw post 40 TPI, soldered to globe center REV, cast emblem	10.2	27.5	38.8	1.51
258	BRZ screw post 32 TPI, HS to globe center REV anti-twist peg at eagle neck	13.3	29.9	41.2	1.29
259	cast screw post 32 TPI, cast anti-twist peg and emblem	20.7	29.7	41.5	4.09
260	BRS cast emblem, 75 mm, BRS flat head screw soldered at globe center REV	12.1	29.6	40.9	1.33
261	silver casting except 75 mm flat head screw soldered to globe center REV	13.7	29.4	40.9	1.19
262	BRZ screw post 40 TPI, HS to globe center REV no anti twist peg eagle's back	12.8	30.4	41.3	1.1
263	BRS single piece casting of emblem, 40 TPI screw post and anti-twist peg	13.6	30.1	41.1	1.67
264	BRZ screw post 36 TPI, 2 anti-twist points on circular base HS to disc REV	R 8.0 L 8.2	R 16.3 L 16.4	R 20.9 L 20.8	1.56
265	Iron spring loaded pin, BRZ "C" type catch, 4 piece pin back assembly	L 8.3	L 16.5	L 20.9	1.55

B#	METHOD OF ATTACHMENT	WEIGHT GRAMS	A mm	B mm	C mm
266	BRZ screw post 36 TPI, 2 triangular anti-twist points on HS circular base REV	R 8.4 L 8.0	R 16.6 L 16.2	R 17.3 L 20.7	R 8.4 L 0.80
267	BRZ screw post		R 17.2 L 16.8	R 21.3 L 21.5	R 1.41 L 1.30
268	iron screw post, 40 TPI, HS to circular base with 2 anti-twist points brass REV	L 8.1	L 16.2 L 21.0 L 1.95	L 21.0	L 1.95
269	BRZ 75 mm screw post, 2 anti-twist points HS to BRZ circular base REV	R 7.9 L 8.3	R 17.5 L 18.1	R 22.0 L 22.0	R 1.56 L 1.58
270	BRZ screw post HS to circular base with 2 anti-twist points HS to the disc REV	L 8.1	L 16.6	L 22.0	L 1.66
271	BRZ screw post 36 TPI, 2 anti-twist points HS to circulat base at disc REV	R 7.8 L 7.0	R 17.0 L 16.9	R 22.5 L 22.5	R 1.17 L 1.63
272	BRS screw post, HS to circular base with 2 anti-twist points, all HS to disc REV	L 7.8	L 16.5	L 22.1 L 1.30	
273	L, WM screw post with round base, R BRZ screw post with square base		R N/A L 17.6	R N/A L 17.2	R 1.20 L 1.75
274	BRZ screw post, 40 TPI, HS to BRZ circular base, 2 anti-twist points HS disc REV	L 8.6	L 9.4	L 13.0	L 1.72
275	BRZ screw post HS to globe REV, screw post passes through hole in the disc		R 18.1	R 22.2	R 1.10
276	BRZ screw post, 2 anti-twist points on circular base HS to disc REV				
277	WM pivoting pin and top loading rolling type catch HS at 6 and 9 o'clock REV		L 2.0.6	L 29.8	
278	BRZ screw post HS center of disc REV, no anti-twist points or circular base	L 2.0	L 14.2	L 17.6	L 0.34
279	WM, 2 modern clutch type fasteners at 9 and 3 o'clock REV	6.2	N/A	20.7	1.59
280	BRZ ? screw post 40 TPI, HS to directly to disc REV no anti-twist triangles	R 7.3 L7.2	R 16.7 L 17.5	R 22.4 L 22.6	R 1.40 L 1.30
281	BRZ ? screw post, 40 TPI, 2 anti-twist points on a single piece investment casting	R 7.1 L 7.5	L 16.2	L 22.3	R 1.57 L 1.27

B#	METHOD OF ATTACHMENT	WEIGHT GRAMS	A mm	B mm	C mm
282	single piece pewter casting including cast screw post and anti-twist points		R 18.3 L 25.1	R 22.3 L 31.5	
283	BRZ screw post 40 TPI, single piece casting including post and anti-twist points	R 9.2 L 9.3	R 16.3 L 16.5	R 21.5 L 22.5	R 1.65 L 1.69
284	BRZ ? screw post 40 TPI, 2 anti-twist points all part of a single casting	R 7.8 L 8.0	R 18.3 L 18.4	R 22.0 L 22.5	R 1.51 L 1.59
285	BRZ ? screw post 40 TPI 2 anti-twist points all part of a single casting	R 7.3 L 7.2	R 18.3 L 18.5	R 22.2 L 22.2	R 1.44 L 1.80
286	BRS screw post sloppy 36 TPI, 2 anti-twist points, all part of a single casting	7.6	11.1	12.8	1.35
287	BRS screw post sloppy 36-40 TPI, 2 anti-twist points, all part of a single casting	7.5	11.1	12.8	1.49
288	BRS screw post 40 TPI, 2 anti-twist points, all part of a single casting	8.2	11.1	12.9	1.96

ENDNOTES

Introduction

1. Personal communication, John A. Driscoll, 2006.
2. John A. Driscoll, *Eagle Globe and Anchor* (Washington, DC, History and Museums Division, Headquarters, USMC, 1971).
3. Albert L. Scipio II, *EM Collar Discs 1907–1926* (Silver Spring, MD, Roman Publications, 1981).
4. Albert L. Scipio II, *The Collar Disc Story, 1907–1999* (Silver Spring MD, self published, 1998).
5. Richard Long and Don R. Wykoff, "The Marine Corps Emblem: The First Hundred Years" (United States Naval Institute *Proceedings*, 95, no.11, 1969), pp.49-55.

Chapter 1

1. Edwin N. McClellan, "Uniforms of American Marines, 1775–1829" (unpublished mimeographed manuscript, 1932a, vol.1, chapter IV), p.23.
2. McClellan, "Uniforms of American Marines, 1775–1829," pp.1-39.
3. Edwin N. McClellan, *Uniforms of American Marines, 1775–1829* (Marine Corps History and Museums Division, USMC Washington, DC, 1974), pp.1-99.
4. McClellan, *Uniforms of American Marines 1775–1829*, 1974, p.26.
5. McClellan, *Uniforms of American Marines 1775–1829*, 1974, p.35.
6. McClellan, *Uniforms of American Marines 1775–1829*, 1974, p.44.
7. USMC Headquarters, Acquisition Record, #1975. 633.
8. Correspondence Don Troiani to Frederick Briuer, July 17, 2012.
9. J. Duncan Campbell and Edgar Howell, *American Military Insignia 1800–1851* (Washington DC, Smithsonian Institution, 1963, figure 28), p.22.
10. Campbell and Howell, *American Military Insignia*, p.22.
11. Campbell and Howell, *American Military Insignia*, figure 28, p.22.
12. Robert H. Rankin, *Uniforms of the Marines* (Putnam Sons, New York, 1970), p.120.
13. J. Duncan Campbell, and Michael J. O' Donnell, *American Military Headgear Insignia, 1799–1861* (O'Donnel Publications, Alexandria VA, 2004).
14. Campbell and Howell, *American Military Insignia*, figure 28, p.22.
15. Correspondence, Kenneth Smith Christmas to Frederick Briuer, July 24, 2012.
16. Personal communication, Richard Spooner, November 1997.
17. Rankin, *Uniforms of the Marines*, p.120.
18. Personal communication, Ray Darida, 2009.
19. Correspondence, George Mennegaux to Frederick Briuer, July 17, 1997.
20. Personal communication, Kenneth Smith, Christmas 1997.
21. Correspondence, Don Troiani to Frederick Briuer, July 17, 2012.
22. McClellan, *Uniforms of Marines 1775–1829*, 1932a, vol.2, (part 1), p.22.
23. Campbell and O'Donnell, *American Military Headgear Insignia*, figure 37, p.35.
24. McClellan, *Uniforms of American Marines 1775–1829*, 1974, pp.12-13.
25. McClellan, *Uniforms of American Marine 1775–1829*, 1974, pp.14-15.
26. Campbell and O'Donnell, *American Military Headgear Insignia*, p.35.
27. Edwin Simmons and J. Robert Moskin, *The Marines* (Marine Corps Heritage Foundation, Quantico, VA, 1999), p.132.
28. Samuel H. Johnston, *Niles Weekly Register*, 1817, List of Officers United States Marine Corps.
29. McClellan, *Uniforms of American Marines 1775–1829*, 1932a, vol.2, p. 160.
30. McClellan, *Uniforms of American Marines 1775–1829*, 1932a, p.168.
31. McClellan, *Uniforms of American Marines 1775–1829*, 1974, p.31.
32. McClellan, *Uniforms of American Marines 1775–1829*, 1974, p.151.
33. Personal communication, Charles H. Cureton, 1997.
34. Michael J. O'Donnell and J. Duncan Campbell, *American Military Belt Plate* (O'Donnell Publications, Alexandria VA, 1996), figure 975, p.579.
35. Campbell and Howell, *American Military Insignia*, 1963, figure 30, p.23.
36. O'Donnell and Campbell, *American Military Belt Plates*, p.585.
37. Charles H. Cureton and David Sullivan, *The Civil War Uniforms of the United States Marine Corps: The Regulations of 1859* (Bender Publications, San Jose, CA, 2009), p.280.
38. Personal communication, Charles H. Cureton, 2002.
39. Campbell and O'Donnell, *American Military Headgear Insignia*.
40. Personal communication, Ray Darida, 1996.
41. Campbell and O'Donnell, *American Military Headgear Insignia*.
42. Personal communication, Charles H. Cureton, 2002.

43. Correspondence, Charles Cureton to Frederick Briuer, May 15, 2002.
44. Correspondence, Charles Cureton to Frederick Briuer, May 15, 2002.
45. Campbell and O'Donnell, *American Military Headgear Insignia*. figure 225, p.104.
46. Edwin N. McClellan, "The Device of the Marine Corps" (*The Recruiters Bulletin*, Battery Press, Nashville TN, 1920a), p.11.
47. McClellan, *Uniforms of American Marines 1775–1829*, 1974, p.67.
48. McClellan, *Uniforms of American Marines 1775–1829*, 1974, p.67.
49. McClellan, *Uniforms of American Marines 1775–1829*, 1974, pp.36 and 37.
50. Campbell and Howell, *American Military Insignia*, p.75.
51. Campbell and O'Donnell, *American Military Headgear Insignia*, figure 203, p.97, and figure 212, p.101.
52. Campbell and O'Donnell, *American Military Headgear Insignia*, figure 212, p.214.
53. Campbell and O'Donnell, *American Military Headgear Insignia*, figure 195, p.95.
54. H. Avery Chenoweth, and Brooke Nihart, *Semper Fi: Illustrated History of the US Marines* (Main Street Publications, New York, 2005), p.60.
55. Campbell and Howell, *American Military Insignia*, figure 37, p.25.
56. Campbell and O'Donnell, *American Military Headgear Insignia*, figure 201, p.97.
57. Jacob Gminder, "Cutting Dies" (unpublished hand traced catalog of stamping dies, 1900), die #4517, p.6.
58. Correspondence, Bruce Bazelon to Frederick Briuer, January 2, 2012.
59. Campbell and O'Donnell, *American Military Headgear Insignia*, p.92.
60. McClellan 1920a, *The Device of the Marine Corps*, p.11.
61. Campbell and O'Donnell, *American Military Headgear Insignia*, figure 229, p.107.
62. Campbell and O'Donnell, *American Military Headgear Insignia*, figure 160, p.86.
63. Campbell and O'Donnell, *American Military Headgear Insignia*, figure 199, p.97.
64. William K. Emerson, *Encyclopedia of United States Army Insignia and Uniforms* (University of Oklahoma Press. 1996, figure 8-19), p.122.
65. Emerson, *Encyclopedia of United States Army Insignia and Uniforms,* figure 8-21.
66. Edgar Howell and Donald E. Kloster, *United States Army Headgear to 1854* (Smithsonian Institution, Washington, DC, 1969, figure 23), p.26.
67. Campbell and Howell, *American Military Insignia*, figure 29, p.27.
68. Campbell and O'Donnell, *American Military Headgear Insignia*, figure 204, p.98.
69. Campbell and Howell, *American Military Headgear Insignia*, figure 39, p.27.
70. Leon W Laframboise, *History of the Artillery, Cavalry and Infantry Branch of Service Insignia* (Watson Publishing Company, 1975, figure 15), p.139.
71. Edwin N. McClellan, "Material and Sources: The History of the US Marine Corps" (unpublished mimeographed manuscript on file at the US Military Academy Library, West Point, NY, 1932b), part 1, p.72.
72. McClellan, *Uniforms of American Marines 1775 to 1829,* vol.I, pp.71, 72.
73. Jacob Gminder, *Cutting Dies* (Baltimore, MD, 1900), Die #4541, p.6.
74. Emerson, *Encyclopedia of United States Army Insignia,* figure 8-12, p.121.
75. McClellan, *Uniforms of American Marines 1775–1829,* 1974, p.47.
76. Campbell and O'Donnell, *American Military Headgear Insignia*, figure 164, p.86.
77. McClellan, *Uniforms of American Marines 1775–1829,* 1974, p.71, 72.
78. Campbell and O'Donnell, *American Military Headgear Insignia*, figure 175, p.88.
79. Campbell and O'Donnell, *American Military Headgear Insignia*, figure 176, 177, p.88.

Chapter 2

1. USMC Orders, Headquarters Marine Corps, Archibald Henderson, 23 January 1840.
2. USMC Orders, Headquarters Marine Corps, Archibald Henderson, 23 January 1840.
3. USMC Orders, Headquarters Marine Corps, Archibald Henderson, 15 September 1845.
4. Joel Thacker, Unpublished Manuscript, 1948, p.2.
5. Emerson, *Encyclopedia of United States Army Insignia,* p.138.
6. Emerson, *Encyclopedia of United States Army Insignia,* p.198.
7. Emerson, *Encyclopedia of United States Army Insignia,* p.600.
8. USMC Orders, Headquarters Marine Corps, January 23, 1840.
9. Charles H. Cureton, *United States Marine Corps, The Illustrated History of the American Soldier, His Uniform and His Equipment* (Greenhill Books, London, 1997), p.17.
10. USMC Orders, Headquarters Marine Corps, March 27, 1850.
11. USMC Orders, Headquarters Marine Corps, July 15, 1851.
12. Huddy and Duval, *United States Military Magazine*, vol.2, 1840–1841, p.30.
13. Personal communication, Ray Darida, 2003.
14. USMC Uniform Regulations, 1852. Last unnumbered page.
15. *Gleasons Pictorial Drawing Room Companion*, 1853, p.47.
16. Cureton and Sullivan, *The Civil War Uniforms of the United States Marine Corps*, p.43.
17. Frederick P. Todd, 1977, p.577.
18. Cureton, *USMC, History of Uniform and Equipment*, pp.18 and 19.

19. Campbell and O'Donnell, *American Military Headgear Insignia*, figure 699, p.304.
20. Personal communication, Ray Darida, 1999.
21. Personal communication, Ray Darida, 1999.
22. Personal communication, Ray Darida, 2002.
23. Personal communication, Ray Darida, 2002.
24. Personal communication, Ray Darida, 2002.
25. Personal communication, Ray Darida, 2002.
26. Personal communication, Ray Darida, 2002.
27. Personal communication, Ray Darida, 2002.
28. Personal communication, John Driscoll, 1994.
29. Cureton and Sullivan, *The Civil War Uniforms of the United States Marine Corps*, p.70.
30. Personal communication, Ray Darida, 1999.

Chapter 3

1. USMC Uniform Regulations, 1859, figure 9.
2. Personal communication, Margerie Bears, July 1995.
3. National Park Service, USS *Cairo* Museum, catalog record.
4. USMC Muster Rolls, 1790 to 1940, http://wwwfold3.com.
5. USMC Uniform Regulations, 1859, p.2.
6. USMC Uniform Regulations, 1859, p.2.
7. Cureton and Sullivan, *The Civil War Uniforms of the United States Marine Corps, USMC Uniform Regulations,* 1859, p.43.
8. Alphaeus H. Albert, *Record of American Uniform and Historical Buttons* (Boyerton Publishing Co., Boyerton, PA, 1976), p.366.
9. Ralph W. Donnelly, *The History of the Confederate States Marine Corps: The Rebel Leathernecks* (White Main, Shippensburg, PA, 1989), p.99.
10. Donnelly, *History of the Confederate States Marine Corps,* p.105.
11. Donnelly, *History of the Confederate States Marine Corps,* p.101.
12. Donnelly, *History of the Confederate States Marine Corps,* p.101.
13. Donnelly, *History of the Confederate States Marine Corps,* p.101
14. Correspondence, Robert F. Hancock to Frederick Briuer, October 21, 2008.
15. Personal communication, Ray Darida, September 30, 1999.
16. USMC Uniform Regulations, 1912, revised May 12, 1917, plate 59.
17. Correspondence, John Magruder to Marine Band Drum Major, July 10, 1962.
18. Personal communication, Jack McCord, 1994.
19. Correspondence, D. Michael Ressler to Frederick Briuer, September 9, 2010.
20. Correspondence, D. Michael Ressler to Frederick Briuer, September 9, 2010.
21. Cureton and Sullivan, *The Civil War Uniforms of the United States Marine Corps.*
22. David Sullivan, *The United States Marine Corps in the Civil War* (White Main, Shippensburg, PA, 1997a, 1997b, 1998–2000).
23. Raymond Darida and Ralph Donnelly, "United States Marine Corps Enlisted Dress Cap Model 1859," *Military Historian and Collector, Journal of the Company of Military Historians,* vol.26, no.4, 1974, pp.10 and 11.
24. Darida and Donnelly, "United States Marine Corps Enlisted Dress Cap Model of 1859," pp.10 and 11.
25. Darida and Donnelly, "United States Marine Corps Enlisted Dress Cap Model of 1859," pp.10 and 11.
26. Personal communication, Ray Darida, 1998.
27. Personal communication, Ray Darida, 1998.
28. USMC Uniform Regulations, 1859, p.7.
29. Jon T. Hoffman (editor), *USMC: A Complete History* (Marine Corps Association, Quantico, VA, 2002), p.137.
30. Emerson, *Encyclopedia of United States Army Insignia,* figure 5-32, p.42.
31. Emerson, *Encyclopedia of United States Army Insignia,* figure 5-32, p.42.
32. Emerson, *Encyclopedia of United States Army Insignia,* figure 5-32, p.42.
33. Personal communication, Edward Sies, S&S Firearms owner, 1994.
34. Correspondence, Enrico Saccone to the USMCHCQV, October 16, 1976.
35. USMC Uniform Regulations, 1859, p.6.
36. USMC Uniform Regulations, 1859, figure 17, p.12.
37. Personal communication, Ray Darida, 2001.
38 Campbell and O'Donnell, *American Military Headgear Insignia*, figure 350, p.151.
39. Personal communication, Ray Darida, 2006.
40. Campbell and O'Donnell, *American Military Headgear Insignia*, figure 355, p.152.
41. Cureton and Sullivan, *The Civil War Uniforms of the United States Marine Corps*, p.238.
42. Campbell and O'Donnell, *American Military Headgear Insignia*, figure 352, p.152.
43. Chenoweth and Nihart, *Semper Fi: Illustrated History of the US Marines*, p.76.
44. Personal communication, Rick Spooner, 1998.
45. Personal communication, Ed Wages, 1997.
46. Cureton and Sullivan, *The Civil War Uniforms of the United States Marine Corps*, p.233.
47. Personal communication, Ray Darida, 1997.
48. USMC Uniform Regulations, 1859, p.6
49. USMC Uniform Regulations, 1859, p.6.
50. Personal communication, Ray Darida, September 30, 1999

Chapter 4

1. Personal communication, Richard Long, September 21, 2001.
2. Driscoll, *Eagle Globe and Anchor.*
3. Long and Wyckoff, *The Marine Corps Emblem: The First Hundred Years.*
4. John H. Magruder III, "The Eagle Globe and Anchor," *Marine Corps Gazette,* 52, no.11, November 1968.
5. Long and Wyckoff, *The Marine Corps Emblem: The First Hundred Years*, p.52.

6. USMC Quartermaster Correspondence, March 8, 1869.
7. USMC Quartermaster Correspondence, July 10, 1869.
8. Long and Wyckoff, *Marine Corps Emblem: The First Hundred Years*, p.55.
9. Long and Wyckoff, *Marine Corps Emblem: The First Hundred Years*, p.52.
10. USMC Quartermaster Correspondence, September 25, 1869.
11. Sullivan, *The United States Marine Corps in the Civil War, The Second Year*, p.267.
12. Long and Wyckoff, *The Marine Corps Emblem: The First Hundred Years*, p.51.
13. USMC Quartermaster Correspondence, April 2, 1869.
14. USMC Quartermaster Correspondence, April 2, 1869.
15. Personal communication, John Stacey, 1999.
16. Personal communication, Ed Wages, 1998.
17. USMC Uniform Regulations, 1875, p.6 and plate 10.
18. USMC Uniform Regulations, 1875, p.6 and plate 10.
19. USMC Uniform Regulations, 1875, pp.1 and 5, and plate 10.
20. USMC Uniform Regulations, 1892, p.7.
21. Personal communication, Ray Darida, September 1999.
22. Personal communication, Ray Darida, September 1999.
23. USMC Uniform Regulations, 1975, pp.1 and 5, and plate 10.
24. USMC Uniform Regulations, 1975, p.5 and plate 10.
25. USMC Uniform Regulations, 1859, p.2.

Chapter 5

1. Personal communication, John Driscoll, August 18, 2002.
2. Personal communication, Kenneth L. Smith, Christmas 2000.
3. Personal communication, Kenneth L. Smith, Christmas 2000.
4. Magruder, "The Eagle Globe and Anchor," *Marine Corps Gazette,* p.39.
5. USMC Order, November 20, 1869.
6. Cureton and Sullivan, *The Civil War Uniforms of the United States Marine Corps,* p.242.
7. Long and Wyckoff, *The Marine Corps Emblem: The First Hundred Years*, p.51.
8. Long and Wyckoff, *The Marine Corps Emblem: The First Hundred Years*, p.51.
9. Personal communication, Carl Carson, April 2002.
10. Personal communication, Ray Darida, September 29, 1999.
11. Chenoweth and Nihart, *Semper Fi: Illustrated History of the US Marines*, p.82.
12. Correspondence, Rick Spooner to Frederick Briuer, February 3, 2006.
13. Personal communication, Ray Darida, September 30, 1999.
14. USMC Uniform Regulations, 1875, p.5.

Chapter 6

1. USMC Uniform Regulations, 1875, p.54.
2. USMC General Order #4, 1877.
3. M. Almy, Aldrich, *History of the United States Marine Corps* (Boston, Henry L. Shepard and Company, 1875), pp.257.
4. Personal communication, Ray Darida, September 30, 1999.
5. Emerson, *United States Army Insignia,* p.600.
6. Chester G. Hearn, *The Illustrated History of the United States Marine Corps* (London, Salamander Books, 2003), p.75.
7. USMC Muster Rolls 1798 to 1940.
8. Edward W. Callahan, (editor), *List of Officers of the Navy of the US and of the Marine Corps from 1775–1900*, 1969, p.682.
9. USMC Uniform Regulations, 1892, p.5.
10. USMC Uniform Regulations, 1904, p.29.
11. Alec S. Tulkoff, *Equipping The Corps 1892–1937* (Bender Publishing, 2010), p.209.
12. USMC General Order, no.4, 1877.
13. USMC Uniform Regulations, 1892.
14. Driscoll, *Eagle Globe and Anchor,* p.12.
15. USMC Uniform Regulations, 1904, p.35.
16. USMC Uniform Regulations, 1904, p.36.
17. USMC Uniform Regulations, 1904, p.36.
18. Gminder, *Cutting Dies*, dies #4024, #4025.
19. Personal communication, John Driscoll, May 31, 1996.
20. Personal communications, Ray Darida, September 30, 1999.
21. USMC Uniform Regulations, 1892, p.25.
22. USMC Uniform Regulations, 1904, p.31.
23. US Navy Department, General Order No.4, 1900, p.2.
24. Campbell and O'Donnell, *American Military Headgear Insignia*, p.104.
25. Emerson, *United States Army Insignia,* p.123.
26. USMC Uniform Regulations, 1875, plate VI.
27. USMC Uniform Regulations, 1892, p.5.
28. USMC Muster Rolls, 1798 to 1940.
29. Campbell and O'Donnell, *American Military Headgear Insignia,* p.104.
30. Emerson, *United States Army Insignia,* p.12

Chapter 7

1. USMC Uniform Regulations, 1900, p.14.
2. USMC Uniform Regulations, 1900, p.14.
3. US Navy Department, *List and Station of the Commissioned and Warrant Officers of the United States Navy and the Marine Corps* (Washington, DC, July 1, 1906).
4. USMC Uniform Regulations, 1904, p.10.
5. USMC Uniform Regulations, 1904, p.35.
6. USMC Uniform Regulations, 1904, pp.35-36.
7. USMC 1869, Order, Adjutant and Inspector's Office.
8. USMC Uniform Regulations, 1875, p.10.
9. USMC Uniform Regulations, 1900, p.7.
10. Magruder, *The Eagle Globe and Anchor,* p.39.
11. Magruder, *The Eagle Globe and Anchor*, p.39.
12. USMC Muster Rolls, 1798 to 1940.
13. USMC Uniform Regulations, 1904, pp.31 and 37.
14. USMC Uniform Regulations, 1904, p.35.
15. USMC Uniform Regulations, 1900, p.10.
16. US Navy Department, *Register of the Commissioned and Warrant Officers* (Washington, DC, 1912).

17. USMC Muster Rolls, 1798–1940.
18. USMC Muster Rolls, 1798–1940.

Chapter 8

1. USMC Uniform Regulations, 1892, p.19.
2. USMC Uniform Regulations, 1892, p.19.
3. USMC Uniform Regulations, 1892, p.19.
4. Driscoll, *Eagle Globe and Anchor*, p.12.
5. USMC Uniform Regulations, 1892, p.23.
6. Driscoll, *Eagle Globe and Anchor*, p.107.
7. USMC Muster Rolls, 1798 to 1940.
8. Personal communication, Ken Smith, Christmas 2011.
9. John Stacey, "The USMC Campaign Hat," *Military Images Magazine*, II, no.3 (1980), p.11.
10. Personal communication, Ray Darida, 2002.
11. USMC Uniform Regulations, 1904, p.50.
12. USMC Uniform Regulations, 1900, p.20.
13. Personal communications, Paul Stine, February 2, 2001.
14. US Navy Department, Secretary of the Navy Annual Report, 1900, p.2.
15. S&S Firearms, catalog, 2006, p.119.
16. Personal communication, Ray Darida, 2001.
17. Cureton, Charles, *USMC: History of Uniform and Equipment*, p.26.
18. USMC Uniform Regulations, 1892, p.29.
19. Personal communication, Emile Stefanacci, May 29, 2003.
20. USMC History Division, Annual End Strengths.
21. USMC Quartermaster Receiving Reports 1897–1901.
22. USMC Quartermaster Receiving Reports 1897–1901.
23. USMC Uniform Regulations, 1900, p.20.
24. USMC Uniform Regulations, 1892, p.11.
25. USMC Uniform Regulations, 1912, plate 59.

Chapter 9

1. USMC Uniform Regulations, 1892, p.7.
2. USMC Uniform Regulations, 1892, pp.10 and 20.
3. USMC Uniform Regulations, 1892, p.10.
4. USMC Uniform Regulations, 1904, p.40.
5. USMC Uniform Regulations, 1912, p.61.
6. USMC Uniform Regulations, 1912, revised 1917, p.62.
7. USMC Uniform Regulations, 1922, p.84.
8. USMC Uniform Regulations, 1929, p.102.
9. USMC Uniform Regulations, 1937, p.7.
10. William H. Horstmann, Correspondence with Assistant Quartermaster, May 26, 1898.
11. War Department, Annual Report of the Quartermaster General, 1895, p.5.
12. Alec Tulkoff, *Equipping the Corps*, p.226.
13. William H Horstmann, Correspondence with Assistant Quartermaster, May 26, 1898.
14. Personal communication, Richard Long, 2000.
15. Long and Wyckoff, *The Marine Corps Emblem: The First Hundred Years*, p.53.
16. Correspondence, John Brunner to Frederick Briuer, August 2005.
17. Personal communication, Alec Tulkoff, 2010.
18. Gminder, *Cutting Dies*, p.2.

Chapter 10

1. Tulkoff, *Equipping the Corps*, pp.210-231.
2. USMC Uniform Regulations, 1900, p.20.
3. Tulkkoff, *Equipping the Corps*, pp.225, 226.
4. USMC, Quartermaster Receiving Reports, 1898.
5. USMC History Division, Annual End Strengths.
6. USMC Muster Rolls, 1798 to 1940.
7. US Navy Departmant, Secretary of the Navy Annual Report, 1900, p.119.
8. US Navy Department, General Order #437, 1894, p.2.
9. Personal communication, Paul Stine, February 17, 2002.
10. Driscoll, John, 1971, figure 17, p.16.
11. US Navy Department: Secretary of the Navy Annual Reports, 1898–1901.
12. Tulkoff, Equipping the Corps, p.235.
13. US Navy Department, General Order #4, 1900, p.2.
14. US Navy Department, General Order #166, 1904, p.3.
15. USMC Quartermaster Correspondence, April 29, 1898.
16. USMC Quartermaster Correspondence, April 29, 1898.
17. USMC Quartermaster Correspondence, May 12, 1898.
18. USMC Muster Rolls, 1798–1940.
19. USMC Index to Quartermaster Files, August 5, 1907.
20. Tulkoff, *Equipping the Corps*, pp.226 to 264.
21. USMC Uniform Regulations, 1912, pp.71-74.
22. Correspondence, Lemuel C. Shepherd to Mrs. S.D. Butler, January 15, 1953.
23. Kathleen Golden, Outgoing Report to USMCHCQV, October 27, 2006.
24. USMC Uniform Regulations, 1904, p.50.
25. US Navy, General Order #437, 1894, p.1.
26. USMC Order, Headquarters, No.47, 1917.
27. Correspondence, Giles to O'Shea, February 11, 2010: O'Shea to Briuer, December 21, 2011.
28. Correspondence, Giles to O'Shea, February 11, 2010: O'Shea to Briuer, December 21, 2011.

Chapter 11

1. Marine Corps Order P1020.34B, April 1966.
2. N.S. Meyer Company, catalog, 1918, p.6.
3. USMC Uniform Regulations, 1904, pp.36 and 37.
4. *Military and Naval Insignia and Novelties*, Bailey, Banks, and Biddle Company, catalog, 1907, emblem no.29372.
5. *Military and Naval Insignia and Novelties*, Bailey, Banks, and Biddle Company, catalog, 1907, emblem no.29372.
6. USMC Uniform Regulations, 1904, p.26.
7. USMC Uniform Regulations, 1912 revised 1913. Figure 1, plate 23,
8. USMC Uniform Regulations, United States Marine Corps Muster Rolls, 1798 to 1940.
9. USMC Uniform Regulations, 1900, p.19.
10. USMC Uniform Regulations, 1904, p.24.
11. USMC Uniform Regulations, 1917 revisions, p.44.
12. Driscoll, *The Eagle Globe and Anchor*, figure 44, p.41.
13. USMC Uniform Regulations, 1912, plate 16.
14. USMC Muster Rolls, 1798 to 1940.
15. J.W. Bunkley, *Military and Naval Recognition Book*, 1917, p.119.

16. USMC Muster Rolls, 1798 to 1940.
17. USMC Muster Rolls, 1798 to 1940.
18. Correspondence, Michael Manifor to Frederick Briuer, 2009.
19. V.H. Blackinton, advertisement, Attleboro, MA, p.8.
20. V.H. Blackinton, advertisement, *American Rifleman* (National Rifle Association, March 1943), p.6.
21. N.S. Meyer Company, catalog, p.6.
22. J.R. Gaunt, *Insignia, Equipment, Trimmings, Pricelist*, 1940, p.19.
23. USMC Uniform Regulations, 1904, p.30.
24. USMC Uniform Regulations, 1912, plate 17.
25. USMC Uniform Regulations, 1929, p.59.
26. J.R. Gaunt, *Insignia, Equipment, Trimmings, Pricelist,* p.19.
27. J.R. Gaunt, *Insignia, Equipment, Trimmings, Pricelist,* p.19.
28. USMC Uniform Regulations, 1912, plate 23.
29. USMC Uniform Regulations, 1929, #52, plate 34.

Chapter 12

1. Bailey Banks and Biddle, catalog, 1907, p.14.
2. USMC Uniform Regulations, 1912, revised 1913, plate 23.
3. Personal communication, Michael O'Shea, 2002.
4. USMC Muster Rolls, 1798 to 1940.
5. Pinkerton, *US Marines,* cover illustration, 1912.
6. Department of Defense, photo #525801.
7. USMC Muster Rolls, 1798 to 1940.
8. Correspondence, Gilles Lagin to Michael O'Shea, August 2004: O'Shea to Frederick Briuer, December 12, 2011.
9. Marc Cerasini, *Heroes, US Marine Corps Medal of Honor Winners* (Berkely Press, New York, 2002), p.93.
10. Personal communication, Neil Abelsma, 2010: Bazelon, and McGuinn, 1999, p.188.
11. Bruce Bazelon and William F. McGuinn, *A Directory of American Military Goods Dealers and Makers, 1785–1915* (self published, 1998), p.188.
12. N.S. Meyer Company, catalog, 1918, p.6.
13. Personal communication, Bob Gill, 2009.
14. Personal communication, George Mennegaux, 1999.
15. Correspondence, Gilles Lagin to Michael O'Shea, August 2004.
16. USMC Muster Rolls, 1798 to 1940.
17. D.A. Ballendorf and Merrill Lewis Bartlett, *Peter Ellis: An Amphibious Warfare Prophet 1880–1923* (Naval Institute Press, Annapolis, MD, 1997), cover photo.
18. Robert E. Wylie, *Orders, Decorations and Insignia Military and Civil,* 1921 (Putnam's Sons, New York and London), plate opposite p.256.
19. Bazelon and McGuinn, 1998, p.165.
20. Bazelon and McGuinn, 1998, p.165.
21. Scipio, *The Collar Disc Story. 1907–1999,* pp.132, 133.

Chapter 13

1. USMC Uniform Regulations, 1912, plate 23, no.2.
2. Bailey, Banks, and Biddle, catalog, 1907, p.14.
3. USMC Uniform Regulations, 1912, plate 23, no.2.
4. Bailey, Banks and Biddle, catalog, 1907, p.14.
5. USMC Uniform Regulations, 1904, p.35.
6. Bailey, Banks, and Biddle, 1907, p.31.
7. Bailey, Banks and Biddle, catalog, 1919, p.3.
8. Bailey, Banks and Biddle, catalog, 1919, p.3.
9. Giles Kyser, Letter to all Silent Drill Platoon Commanders, 1990.
10. Giles Kyser, Letter to all Silent Drill Platoon Commanders, 1990.
11. Personal communication, R. Kyle Aldrich, 2006.
12. Personal communication, anonymous collector, 2002.
13. USMC Muster Rolls 1798 to 1940.
14. Personal communication, Michael O'Shea, 2006.
15. USMC Register of Officers, 1918.
16. N.S. Meyer Company, catalog, 1918, p.6.
17. USMC Uniform Regulations, 1904, p.32.
18. Personal communication, anonymous collector, 2010.
19. Francis Bannerman, catalog, 1907, p.182.
20. USMC Muster Rolls 1798–1940.
21. Personal communication, Bob Gill, 2008.
22. Personal communication, Ed Wages, 2001.
23. V.H. Blackinton, price list, c.1918, plate #4.
24. Personal communication, Michael O'Shea, 1998.
25. USMC Register of Officers, 1912 and 1913.
26. Personal communication, Alec Tulkoff, 2010.
27. V.H. Blackinton, catalog of Marine Corps insignia, c.1930, p.8.
28. V.H. Blackinton, price list, 1918.
29. *American Rifleman,* 1943, p.6.
30. USMC Uniform Regulations, 1904, p.28
31. Personal communication, Ed Wages, 1999.
32. USMC Muster Rolls 1798 to 1940.

Chapter 14

1. Bailey, Banks, and Biddle Co., catalog, 1907, #3812-13, p.27.
2. USMC Uniform Regulations 1922, Changes of 1925, no.53, plate 35.
3. Correspondence, Lagin, Giles to Michael O'Shea, February 11, 2010: O'Shea to Frederick Briuer, December 21, 2011.
4. USMC, Muster Rolls 1798 to 1940.
5. V.H. Blackinton Company, Inc., c.1918, price list, plate 4.
6. Correspondence, Lagin to O'Shea, February 11, 2010: O'Shea to Briuer, December 21, 2011.
7. USMC Circular Letter, #46, December 6, 1926.
8. Personal communication, anonymous collector, 2009.
9. Bailey, Banks, and Biddle, catalog, 1907, #3812-13, p.27.
10. Personal communication, George Mennegaux, 1999.
11. Driscoll, *Eagle Globe and Anchor*, p.34.
12. Personal communication, George Mennegaux, 1998.
13. Personal communication, Joseph Weingarten, 2011.
14. Wylie, plate 28, p.261.
15. Personal communication, Michael O'Shea, 2003.
16. Personal communication, Richard King, 1994.
17. Personal communication, Frank Heins, March 18, 2000.
18. James C. Russell and William E. Moore, *US Official Pictures of the World War* (Army and Navy Union, USA), p.290, vol.III, 1928.
19. Personal communication, Joseph Weingarten, 2011.
20. Russell and Moore, vol.III, p.290.

Chapter 15

1. USMC Fiscal Year End Strengths 1798–1995, n.d, http://www.usmc.mil/wwwmain/end.htm
2. Bazelon and McGuinn, p.205.
3. Driscoll, *Eagle Globe and Anchor*, p.45.
4. Correspondence, Lagin to O'Shea, February 11, 2010: O'Shea to Briuer, December 21, 2011.
5. Correspondence, George Bailey to Michael O'Shea, January 22, 2010: O'Shea to Frederick Briuer, December 21, 2011.
6. USMC Muster Rolls, 1798 to 1940.
7. Correspondence, Lagin to O'Shea, February 11, 2010: O'Shea to Briuer, December 21, 2011.
8. Correspondence, Flower Leather Company to Frederick Briuer, May 22, 2004.
9. USMC Muster Rolls, 1798–1940.
10. Personal communication, anonymous collector.
11. USMC Muster Rolls, 1798–1940.
12. Personal communication, Richard Forte, 1994.
13. USMC, Orders, #46, Revised December 3, 1917, p.143.
14. Personal communication, Rick Spooner, 1996.

Chapter 16

1. George B. Clark, (editor), *His Time in Hell, A Texas Marine in France* (Presidio Press Inc., 2001), p.248.
2. USMC Orders, No.47 (Series 1917), p.143.
3. Edwin N. McClellan, "The Marbache Sector," *Marine Corps Gazette,* 1920b, No.3, Vol.6. pp.257, 258.
4. Driscoll, *Eagle Globe and Anchor,* p.39.
5. Driscoll, *Eagle Globe and Anchor,* p.258.
6. Personal communications, Rick Spooner, March 1996, November 1997, and December 2000.
7. USMC, Muster Rolls 1798 to 1940.
8. Frederic M. Wise and Meigs O. Frost, *A Marine Tells It To You* (J.H. Sears Company, New York, 1929), p.244.
9. Doyen, Charles A. Doyen, Brigadier General Memorandum, January 3, 1918.
10. Russell and Moore, p.281, vol.III.
11. USMC, Muster Rolls 1798 to 1940.
12. Scipio, *EM Collar Insignia (1907–1926),* p.181.
13. Scipio, *EM Collar Insignia (1907–1926),* p.21.
14. Scipio, *EM Collar Insignia (1907–1926),* p.21.
15. Personal communication, Rick Spooner, December 2000.
16. Scipio, *EM Collar Insignia (1907–1926),* plate 36, p.171.
17. Scipio, *The Collar Disc Story,* plate 35, p.207.
18. Personal communication, Albert L. Scipio, 2005.
19. Scipio, *EM Collar Insignia (1907–1926),* plate 36, p.171.
20. Correspondence, George Bailey to Michael O'Shea, January 22, 2010: O'Shea to Frederick Briuer, December 21, 2011.
21. Scipio, *EM Collar Insignia (1907–1926),* pp.27 and 28.
22. Correspondence, Lagin to O'Shea, February 11, 2010: O'Shea to Briuer, December 21, 2011.
23. Correspondence, George Bailey to Michael O'Shea, January 22, 2010: O'Shea to Frederick Briuer, December 21, 2011.
24. Correspondence, George Bailey to Michael O'Shea, January 22, 2010: O'Shea to Frederick Briuer, December 21, 2011.
25. Scipio, *EM Collar Insignia (1907–1926),* plate 36, p.171.
26. Scipio, *EM Collar Insignia (1907–1926),* plate 36, p.171.
27. Scipio, *EM Collar Insignia (1907–1926),* plate 36, p.171.
28. Elton E. Mackin, *Suddenly We Didn't Want to Die, Memoirs of A World War One Marine* (Presidio Press, San Francisco, CA, 1993), p.139.
29. Kenneth, L, Smith-Christmas, "Acquisitions," *Fortitudine, Newsletter of the Marine Corps Historical Program,* 1980, vol.X, No.1, p.10.
30. Scipio, *EM Collar Insignia (1907–1926),* plate 36, p.171.
31. Correspondence, George Bailey to Michael O'Shea, January 22, 2010: O'Shea to Frederick Briuer, December 21, 2011.
32. USMC Muster Rolls 1798 to 1940.
33. Scipio, *EM Collar Insignia (1907–1926),* plate 36, p.171.
34. Driscoll, *Eagle, Globe and Anchor,* p.47.
35. N.S. Meyer Catalog, 1918, p.6.
36. Scipio, *EM Collar Insignia (1907–1926),* plate 36, p.171.
37. Scipio, *EM Collar Insignia (1907–1926),* 1981, p.181.
38. Scipio, *EM Collar Insignia (1907–1926),* 1981, p.181.
39. Scipio, *EM Collar Insignia (1907–1926),* 1981, p.181.
40. Personal communication, Michael Manifore, October 2008.
41. USMC Muster Rolls, 1798 to 1940.
42. Clement V. Kelley, "Insignia Worn by the First Marine Corps High School Unit," *Trading Post, Journal of the American Society of Insignia Collectors*, 1989, Vol.XLVIII, No.3, pp.70 and 71.
43. Raymond Soafer, "J in the EGA," *Trading Post,* 1998, April /June Issue, pp.22-24.
44. Soafer, "J in the EGA," pp.22-24.
45. Correspondence, Fr. Nicholas Schiro, January 18, 2012.
46. Soafer, "J in the EGA," p.24.
47. Correspondence, Fr. Nicholas Schiro, January 18, 2012.
48. Correspondence, Fr. Nicholas Schiro, January 18, 2012.
49. USMC Uniform Regulations, 1989, p.88.
50. Personal communication, Paul Stine, February 20, 2001.
51. Personal communication, George Peterson, July 16, 2003.
52. Personal communication, George Peterson, July 16, 2003.
53. Great War Militaria, http://www.greatwar.com.

PHOTOGRAPH CREDITS BY B NUMBER

Anonymous, 6
Anonymous, 20
Anonymous, 21
Anonymous, 23
Anonymous, 27
Anonymous, 28
Anonymous, 39
Anonymous, 40
Anonymous, 41
Anonymous, 45
Anonymous, 55
Anonymous, 57
Anonymous, 59
Anonymous, 62
Anonymous, 63
Anonymous, 70
Anonymous, 75
Anonymous, 81
Anonymous, 91
Anonymous, 95
Anonymous, 98
Anonymous, 106
Anonymous, 116
Anonymous, 117
Anonymous, 122
Anonymous, 129
Anonymous, 132
Anonymous, 133
Anonymous, 136
Anonymous, 144
Anonymous, 147
Anonymous, 149
Anonymous, 155
Anonymous, 156
Anonymous, 161
Anonymous, 166
Anonymous, 168
Anonymous, 171
Anonymous, 172
Anonymous, 173
Anonymous, 174
Anonymous, 178
Anonymous, 180
Anonymous, 181
Anonymous, 183
Anonymous, 184
Anonymous, 185
Anonymous, 186
Anonymous, 187
Anonymous, 188
Anonymous, 191
Anonymous, 192
Anonymous, 193
Anonymous, 194
Anonymous, 195
Anonymous, 196
Anonymous, 197
Anonymous, 203
Anonymous, 207
Anonymous, 209
Anonymous, 210
Anonymous, 211
Anonymous, 213
Anonymous, 214
Anonymous, 215
Anonymous, 218
Anonymous, 219
Anonymous, 220
Anonymous, 221
Anonymous, 224
Anonymous, 225
Anonymous, 226
Anonymous, 227
Anonymous, 230
Anonymous, 233
Anonymous, 234
Anonymous, 237
Anonymous, 238
Anonymous, 240
Anonymous, 247
Anonymous, 248
Anonymous, 253
Anonymous, 256
Anonymous, 258
Anonymous, 264
Anonymous, 266
Anonymous, 270
Anonymous, 272
Anonymous, 278
Anonymous, 284
Anonymous, 286
Anonymous, 287
Anonymous, 288
Carl Carson, 84
Carl Carson, 260
Carl Carson, 261

Carl Carson, 281
Col. Frank Heins, USMC (Ret.), 109
Col. Frank Heins, USMC (Ret.), 205
Col. Frank Heins, USMC (Ret.), 208
Col. John A. Driscoll, USMC (Ret.), 110
Col. John A. Driscoll, USMC (Ret.), 111
Col. John A. Driscoll, USMC (Ret.), 157
Col. John A. Driscoll, USMC (Ret.), 162
Col. John A. Driscoll, USMC (Ret.), 167
Col. John A. Driscoll, USMC (Ret.), 255
Col. John A. Driscoll, USMC (Ret.), 267
Col. Michael Kelly USMC (Ret.), 151
Col. Michael Kelly USMC (Ret.), 268
Col. Michael Kelly USMC (Ret.), 274
Dr. Frederick L. Briuer, 3
Dr. Frederick L. Briuer, 4
Dr. Frederick L. Briuer, 11
Dr. Frederick L. Briuer, 14
Dr. Frederick L. Briuer, 15
Dr. Frederick L. Briuer, 17
Dr. Frederick L. Briuer, 22
Dr. Frederick L. Briuer, 25
Dr. Frederick L. Briuer, 26
Dr. Frederick L. Briuer, 34
Dr. Frederick L. Briuer, 35
Dr. Frederick L. Briuer, 37
Dr. Frederick L. Briuer, 42
Dr. Frederick L. Briuer, 46
Dr. Frederick L. Briuer, 52
Dr. Frederick L. Briuer, 53
Dr. Frederick L. Briuer, 54
Dr. Frederick L. Briuer, 64
Dr. Frederick L. Briuer, 65
Dr. Frederick L. Briuer, 66
Dr. Frederick L. Briuer, 76
Dr. Frederick L. Briuer, 77
Dr. Frederick L. Briuer, 79
Dr. Frederick L. Briuer, 85
Dr. Frederick L. Briuer, 90
Dr. Frederick L. Briuer, 93
Dr. Frederick L. Briuer, 101
Dr. Frederick L. Briuer, 105
Dr. Frederick L. Briuer, 114
Dr. Frederick L. Briuer, 137
Dr. Frederick L. Briuer, 142
Dr. Frederick L. Briuer, 143
Dr. Frederick L. Briuer, 163
Dr. Frederick L. Briuer, 228
Dr. Frederick L. Briuer, 232
Dr. Frederick L. Briuer, 257
Dr. Frederick L. Briuer, 259
Dr. Frederick L. Briuer, 262
Dr. Frederick L. Briuer, 263
Dr. Frederick L. Briuer, 269
Dr. Frederick L. Briuer, 279
Dr. Frederick L. Briuer, 280
Dr. Frederick L. Briuer, 285
Emile Steffanaci, 176
George Mennegaux, 71
George Mennegaux, 89
George Mennegaux, 120
George Mennegaux, 126
George Mennegaux, 127
George Mennegaux, 128
George Mennegaux, 131
George Mennegaux, 175
George Mennegaux, 177
George Mennegaux, 189
George Mennegaux, 204
George Mennegaux, 212
George Mennegaux, 242
George Mennegaux, 245
George Mennegaux, 250
Gregory Walseth, 83
Jack Brown, 50
James Phillips, 112
James Phillips, 115
James Phillips, 179
James Phillips, 201
James Phillips, 231
James Phillips, 241
James Phillips, 243
James Phillips, 246
James Phillips, 249
Joseph Lowry, 10
Joseph Lowry, 13
Joseph Lowry, 16
Joseph Lowry, 33
Joseph Lowry, 74
Joseph Lowry, 169
Joseph Lowry, 254
Joseph Lowry, 273
Joseph Lowry, 275
Joseph Musso, 8
Joseph Weingarten, 251
Lt. Col. Michael Manifor, 96
Lt. Col. Michael Manifor, 107
Lt. Col. Michael Manifor, 108
Lt. Col. Michael Manifor, 235
Lt. Col. Michael Manifor, 252
Lt. Col. Michael Manifor, 276
Major Richard Spooner, USMC (Ret.), 24
Major Richard Spooner, USMC (Ret.), 29
Major Richard Spooner, USMC (Ret.), 58
Major Richard Spooner, USMC (Ret.), 86
Major Richard Spooner, USMC (Ret.), 148
Mark Kasal, 150
Mark Kasal, 153
MSgt. Jack McCord, USMC (Ret.), 12
MSgt. Jack McCord, USMC (Ret.), 18
MSgt. Jack McCord, USMC (Ret.), 47
MSgt. Jack McCord, USMC (Ret.), 51
MSgt. Jack McCord, USMC (Ret.), 56
MSgt. Jack McCord, USMC (Ret.), 69

FIGURE CREDITS BY B NUMBER

I-1, Ann S.K. Brown Military Collection, Brown University, Providence, Rhode Island
I-5, Marine Corps Combat Art Collection, National Museum of the Marine Corps, Quantico, Virginia
I-9, Marine Corps Combat Art Collection, National Museum of the Marine Corps, Quantico, Virginia
I-10, Pennsylvania State Library, Harrisburg, Pensylvania
II-1, United States Marine Corps Uniform Regulations, 1839
II-2, United States Marine Corps Uniform Regulations, 1839
II-3, Ann S.K. Brown Military Collection, Brown University, Providence, Rhode Island
II-4, Ann S.K. Brown Military Collection, Brown University, Providence, Rhode Island
II-5, Ann S.K. Brown Military Collection, Brown University, Providence, Rhode Island
II-6, Gleasons Pictorial Drawing Room Companion, January 27, 1858
II-7, Raymond Darida
II-8, Raymond Darida
III-1, Alphaeus H. Albert, 1976
III-2, United States Marine Corps Band, Washington, DC, copy courtesy of MGySgt. D.Michael Ressler
III-3, Marine Corps Order, Commandant John Harris, 23 July 1861
III-4, Raymond Darida
III-5, Alec Tulkoff
III-7, Ann S.K. Brown Military Collection, Brown University, Providence, Rhode Island
III-8, United States Marine Corps Historical Collections, Quantico, Virginia
IV-5, William H. Horstman Photo, 1881
V-1, Col. John A, Driscoll, USMC ret
V-2, Raymond Darida
VI-1, M. Aldrich, 1875, Cover Illustration
VI-3, Alec Tulkoff
VI-4, United States Marine Corps Band, 8th and I Streets, Washington, DC.
VI-6, Marine Corps Combat Art Collection, National Museum of the Marine Corps, Quantico, Virginia
VIII-1, Raymond Darida
VIII-2, Raymond Darida
VIII-3, Brig Gen. Richard Natonski, USMC (Ret.)
VIII-4, Brig Gen. Richard Natonski, USMC (Ret.)
VIII-5, Brig Gen. Richard Natonski, USMC (Ret.)
IX-2, Raymond Darida
IX-5, John Brunner and James Zahkar
IX-6, Alec Tulkoff
XI-1, United States Marine Corps History Division
XI-2, Alec Tulkoff
XI-5, Bailey, Banks and Biddle, 1907 Catalog
XI-6, United States Marine Corps Uniform Regulations, 1913
XI-7, Raymond Darida
XI-8, V.H. Blackinton, 1943, Advertisement in American Rifleman
XI-9, N.S. Meyer, 1918 Catalog, copy courtesy of Ray Darida
XI-10, J.R. Gaunt, 1940 Catalog
XI-11, United States Marine Corps Uniform Regulations, 1912
XII-1, Alec Tulkoff
XII-2, Pinkerton, 1912, Cover Illustration
XII-4, Joseph Weingarten
XII-5, 1918, 1919, Art Metal Works Catalog (Ronson), copy courtesy of Ray Darida
XIII-1, N.S. Meyer, 1918 Catalog, copy courtesy of Ray Darida
XIII-5, V.H. Blackinton, 1918 Catalog, copy courtesy of Ray Darida
XIII-6, V. H. Blackinton, 1943 Catalog
XIII-7, Col. John A, Driscoll, USMC ret
XIV-1, Bailey, Banks and Biddle, 1907 Catalog
XIV 2, Ray Darida
XIV-3, Department of Defense, Marine Corps Photo, Washington Navy Yard.
XIV-4, Joseph Weingarten
XIV-6, Russell and Moore, 1920
XV-1, Thomas Parry's Son's Company Catalog, copy courtesy of Ray Darida
XVI-3, N.S. Meyer, 1918 Catalog, copy courtesy of Ray Darida
XVI-4, Redrawn by the Author, based on a photo by Lt. Col. Michael Manifor
XVI-5, Father Nicolas Schiro, S.J.

MATERIAL CREDITS BY B NUMBER

B Number, Credit For Photos and Figures

B001, New York State Office of Parks, Recreation and Historic Preservation, Waterford, New York

B002, Smitsonian Institution, National Museum, Military Collection, Washington, DC.

B030, Ann S.K. Brown, Military Collection, Brown University, Providence, Rhode Island

B080, Col. John Driscoll, USMC (Ret.)

B096, Lt. Col. Michael Manifor, USMC, Photo, Description, and Recording

B107, Lt. Col. Michael Manifor, USMC, Photo, Description, and Recording

B108, Lt. Col. Michael Manifor, USMC, Photo, Description, and Recording

B138, Paul Stine, private collector, Photo, Descriotion, and Recording

B154, Department of Defence Photo (Marine Corps), Number 515356, Washington Navy Yard.

B182, Col. John Driscoll, USMC (Ret.)

B202, Paul Stine, private collector, Photo, Descriotion, and Recording

B235, Lt. Col. Michael Manifor, USMC, Photo, Description, and Recordding

B252, Lt. Col. Michael Manifor, USMC, Photo, Description, and Recording

B265, Paul Stine, private collector, Photo, Descriotion, and Recording

B276, Lt. Col. Michael Manifor, USMC, Photo, Description, and Recording

B277, Paul Stine, private collector, Photo, Description and Recording

BIBLIOGRAPHY

American Embassy Guard Annual. USMC University Special Collections. (1935): 21.

Annual Fourth Marines, 1932–1933. USMC University Special Collections.

American Legation Guard Annual, USMC University Special Collections. (1934): 117.

Aldrich, M. Almy. *History of the United States Marine Corps.* Boston: Henry L. Shephard and Company, 1875.

Army Navy Magazine, USMC University Special Collections, 1907.

Bailey, Banks and Biddle Company. *Military and Naval Insignia and Novelties.* Philadelphia, PA, 1907.

Ballendorf, D.A. and Merrill Lewis Bartlett. *Peter Ellis An Amphibious Warfare Prophet. 1880–1923.* Annapolis, Maryland: Naval Institute Press, 1997.

Bannerman, Francis. *Catalog of American Military Goods from Government Auctions, For Sale.* Broadway, New York City, 1907.

Bazelon, Bruce S. and William F. McGuinn. *A Directory of American Military Goods Dealers and Makers, 1785–1915.* Combined Edition. Self Published, 1997.

Blackinton, V.H. Company Incorporated. Price List, c.1918.

Blackinton, V.H. Company Incorporated. Catalog, Marine Corps Insignia, c.1930.

Bunkley, J.W., *Military and Naval Recognition Book,* New York: D. Van Nostrand Company, 1917.

Campbell, J. Duncan "An Early Marine Corps Cap Plate," *Military Collector and Historian, Journal of the Company of Military Historians.* 4, no.71, 1955.

Campbell, J. Duncan and Edgar M. Howell. *American Military Insignia 1800–1851.* Washington, DC: Smithsonian Institution, 1963.

Campbell, J. Duncan and Michael J. O'Donnell. *American Military Headgear Insignia 1799–1861.* Alexandria, VA: O'Donnell Publications, 2004.

Cerasini, Marc. *Heroes, US Marine Corps Medal of Honor Winners.* New York: Berkley Books, 2002.

Chenoweth, Avery and Brooke Nihart. *Semper Fi: The Definitive Illustrated History of the US Marines.* New York: Main Street Publications, a Division of Sterling Co., 2004.

China Marine, 1932–1933.

Cureton, Charles H. *United States Marine Corps, The Illustrated History of the American Soldier, His Uniform and His Equipment.* London: Greenhill Books, 1997.

Cureton, Charles H. and David M. Sullivan. *The Civil War Uniforms of the United States Marine Corps: The Regulations of 1859.* San Jose, CA: R. James Bender Publications, c.2009.

Darida, Ray and Ralph Donnelly. "United States Marine Corps Enlisted Dress Cap Model 1859." *Journal of the Company of Military Historians.* 26, no.2, p.10-11, 1974.

Department of Defense, Photo Number 525801, National Archives Record Group (NARG), 127. n.d.

Donelly, Ralph. *The History of the Confederate States Marine Corps: The Rebel Leathernecks.* Shippensburg, PA: White Mane, 1989.

Doyen, Charles A., Brigadier General Memorandum, January 3, 1918.

Driscoll, John A. *The Eagle, Globe and Anchor 1868–1968.* Washington, DC: History and Museums Division, Headquarters, US Marine Corps, 1971.

Emerson, William K. *Encyclopedia of United States Army Insignia and Uniforms.* Norman, OK: University of Oklahoma Press, 1996.

Fleming, Charles A. and Robin L. Austin, *Quantico, Crossroads of the Marine Corps,* USMC University Special Collections, 1978.

Gaunt, J.R. and Sons Inc., *Insignia, Equipment, Trimmings,* Pricelist. New York, 1940.

"Gleason's Pictorial Drawing Room Companion." *Representation of the New Uniform of the United Sates Navy.* (1853): 55-56.

Gminder, Jacob. *Cutting Dies,* Hand-traced catalog of stamping dies. Unpublished catalog of dies, 1900.

Great War Militaria. http://www.greatwar.com., n.d.

Hearn, Chester. *The Illustrated Directory of the United States Marine Corps.* London: Salamander Books, 2003.

Hoffman, Jon T. (editor). *USMC: A Complete History.* Quantico, VA. Marine Corps Association, Beaux Arts Editions, 2002.

Horstmann, Wm. H., Correspondence with Assistant USMC Quartermaster Prince, May 26, 1898, NA. RG 127.

Howell, Edgar M. and Donald E. Kloster. *United States Army Headgear to 1854.* Catalog of US Army Uniforms in the collection of the Smithsonian Institution. I. Washington, DC, 1969.

Huddy and Duval. *1840–41 United States Military Magazine.* II. Philadelphia, PA.

Jackson, Warren R. *His Time in Hell, A Texas Marine in France: The World War I Memoirs of Warren R. Jackson.* Edited by George B. Clark. San Francisco, CA: Presidio Press Inc., 2001.

Kelly, Clement V. "Insignia Worn by the First Marine Corps High School Unit." *Trading Post, Journal of the American Society of Insignia Collectors,* XLVIII, no.3, 1989.

Laframboise, Leon W. *History of the Artillery, Cavalry and Infantry Branch of Service Insignia.* Watson Publishing Company. (1976): 139.

Long, Richard and Don R. Wyckoff. *The Marine Corps Emblem: The First Hundred Years.* Annapolis, MD: United States Naval Institute *Proceedings*, November 1969.

Mackin, Elton E. *Suddenly We Didn't Want to Die, Memoirs of A World War I Marine.* San Francisco CA: Presidio Press, 1993.

Magruder, John. H. III. "The 139. Eagle, Globe and Anchor." *Marine Corps Gazette.* 52, no.11, (November 1968): 38-44.

Marine Corps Gazette, USMC University Special Collections. December 1916.

McClellan, Edwin N. "The Device of the Marine Corps." *Recruiters Bulletin,* Nashville, TN: Battery Press, 1920a.

McClellan, Edwin N. "The Marbache Sector." *Marine Corps Gazette,* No.3, vol.6, pp.257-258, 1920b.

McClellan, Edwin N 1932a *Uniforms of American Marines 1775 to 1829.* Unpublished, mimeographed manuscript, (1932a): 36-37.

McClellan, Edwin N. *The History of the US Marine Corps,* Unpublished mimeographed Manuscript, IV, "Getting Under Way," manuscript on file US Military Academy Library, West Point, NY, 1932b.

McClellan, Edwin N., *Uniforms of the American Marines 1775–1829,* official USMC monograph, reprint of selections from the original 1932 mimeographed version of McClellan's manuscript, 1974.

Meyer, N.S., "Marine Corps Insignia and Buttons." *N.S. Meyer Company Catalogue.* New York: (1918): 6.

Horstmann, Wm. H., Correspondence with Assistant USMC Quartermaster Prince, NA. RG 127, May 26, 1898.

National Park Service. Vicksburg National Military Park, USS *Cairo Museum, Catalog Record,* Vicksburg, MS, n.d.

National Rifle Association. V.H. Blackinton advertisement, *American Rifleman.* (March 1943): 6.

Niles Weekly Register. *List of Officers of the United States Marine Corps,* 1817.

North Carolina Office of State Archaeology. USS *Huron.* n.d., http://www.archaeology.ncdcr.gov/ncarch/underwater/huron.htm

O'Donnell, Michael J. and J. Duncan Campbell. *American Military Belt Plates.* Alexandria, VA: O'Donnell Publications, 1996.

Peking Legation Guard Annual, USMC University Special Collections. (1931): 8.

Pinkerton. *US Marines,* cover illustration, 1912.

Rankin, Robert H. *Uniforms of the Marines.* New York: Putnam's Sons, 1970.

Russell, James C. and William E. Moore. *US Official Pictures of the World War.* Washington, DC: Army and Navy Union. USA, III, 1928.

S and S Firearms. *Catalog of Military Americana.* Glendale, N.Y: 2004.

Scipio, Albert L. II. *E.M. Collar Insignia (1907–1926).* Silver Spring, MD: Roman Publications, 1981.

Scipio, Albert L. II. *The Collar Disc Story (1907–1999).* Silver Spring, MD: Self published, 1999.

Simmons, Edwin Howard (editor in chief) and J. Robert Moskin (editor) *The Marines.* Quantico, VA: Marine Corps Heritage Foundation, Hugh Lauter Levin Association, 1997.

Smith-Christmas, Kenneth. "Acquisitions." *Fortitudine, Newsletter of the Marine Corps Historical Program.* X, no.1, (Summer 1980): 10.

Soafer, Raymond "J in the EGA," *Trading Post,* (April-June issue, 1998): 22 and 24.

Stacey, John. "The USMC Campaign Hat." *Military Images Magazine.* II, no.3, (November-December, 1980): 11.

Sullivan, David M., *The United States Marine Corps in the Civil War, The First Year.* Shippensburg, PA: White Mane, 1997a.

Sullivan, David M. *The United States Marine Corps in the Civil War, The Second Year.* Shippensburg, PA: White Mane, 1997b.

Sullivan, David M.,*The United States Marine Corps in the Civil War, The Third Year.* Shippensburg, PA: White Mane, Shippensburg, PA. 1998.

Sullivan, David M. *The United States Marine Corps in the Civil War, The Final Year.* Shippensburg, PA: White Mane, 2000.

Sullivan, David M. "The 1875 Uniform Regulations of the United States Marine Corps: Original Text, Plates, Changes and Reports." *Military Collector and Historian, Journal of the Company of Military Historians.* Washington, DC: 5, no.4, Winter, 2013,

Thacker, Joel. D., *The Emblem of the US Marine Corps.* Historical Division, Headquarters, US Marine Corps. Unpublished, mimeographed manuscript. Washington, DC: A.G.126B, May 1948.

Todd, Frederick P. "American Military Equipage 1851–1872." *Company of Military Historians.* Westbrook, CT: III, 1976.

Tulkoff, Alec S. *Equipping the Corps, 1892–1937.* San Jose, CA: R. James Bender Publishing, 2010.

US Marine Corps, *Muster Rolls 1798–1958.* The National Archives and Records Administration, http://search.ancestry.com/search.

USMC Circular Letter, Headquarters Marine Corps, no.46, 1926.

USMC Correspondence, Headquarters Marine Corps, Board of Officers to Commandant Zeilen, NA., R G. 127, 13 November 1868.

USMC General Order No.4, Headquarters Marine Corps, NA., RG. 127. 29 October 1877.

USMC History Division, Quantico, VA, *Annual End Strengths.* n.d., http://www.mcu.mil/historydivision.. USMC History Division, Quantico, VA, *Who's Who in Marine Corps History,* (organized by last name). www.mcu.usmc.mil/historydivision/Pages/who's who/whos_who_alpha. aspx

USMC Index to Quartermaster Files, Headquarters Marine Corps, 5 August 1907 to 2 October 1908.

USMC Orders, Adjutant and Inspectors Office, Headquarters Marine Corps, NARG. 127, 20 November 1869.

USMC Orders, Headquarters Marine Corps, Commandant Archibald Henderson, NARG 127, 23 January 1840.
USMC Orders, Headquarters Marine Corps, Commandant Archibald Henderson, NARG. 127, 27 March 1850.
USMC Orders, Headquarters Marine Corps, Commandant Archibald Henderson, NARG. 127, 15 July 1851.
USMC Orders, Headquarters Marine Corps, 20 November 1869.
USMC. Orders, Headquarters Marine Corps, Number 47. NARG127, 1917.
USMC Orders, Headquarters Marine Corps, Number P1020.34B, April 1966.
USMC Quartermaster Correspondence, William Slack to Bent and Bush, NARG 127, 2 April 1869.
USMC Quartermaster Correspondence, William Slack to Jacob Gminder. NA RG.127, 13 April 1869.
USMC Quartermaster Correspondence, William Slack to Bent and Bush. NARG 127, 10 July 1869.
USMC Quartermaster Correspondence, William Slack to Commandant, NARG.127, 25 September 1869.
USMC Quartermaster Correspondence, Assistant Quartermaster Prince to Quartermaster, Washington, DC, NARG.127, 28 April. 1898.
USMC Quartermaster Correspondence, Assistant Quartermaster Prince to Quartermaster, Washington, DC, NARG.127, 12 May 1898.
USMC Quartermaster Receiving Report, Prince to Horstmann, 4 June 1898. NARG. 127, 4 June 1898.
USMC Quartermaster Receiving Report, Prince to Horstmann, NARG.127, 18 June 1898.
USMC *Register of the Commissioned and Warrant Officers of the United States Navy and Marine Corps*, Washington, DC, 1 January 1912.
USMC *Register of the Commissioned and Warrant Officers of the United States Navy and U.S. Naval Reserve Force National Naval Volunteers Marine Corps Medical Reserve Corps and Dental Reserve Corps.* Washington Government Printing Office, 1918.
USMC *Dress of the Officers, Non Commissioned Officers, Musicians and Privates of the Marine Corps of the United States.* Washington, DC, 1 July 1839.
USMC *Regulations for the Uniform & Dress of the Navy and Marine Corps of the United States.* Philadelphia: Lppincott, Grambo, and Co. 1852.
USMC *Regulations for the Uniform & Dress of the Marine Corps of the United States, October 1859. From the Original Text and Drawings in the Quartermaster's Department.* First Edition Philadelphia: Charles Desilver, 1859
USMC *Regulations for the Uniform and Dress of the United States Mariner Corps.* Quartermaster's Department. Washington, Government Printing Office, 1875.
USMC *Regulations for the Uniform and Dress, Equipments, etc., of the United States Marine Corps from the Original Text in the Quartermaster's Office.* Washington Government Printing Office. July 14, 1892 as modified December 5, 1896.
USMC *Regulations Governing the Uniform and Equipments of Officers and Enlisted Men of the United States Marine Corps,* Washington DC, Government Printing Office, 1900.
USMC *Regulations Governing the Uniform and Equipments of the Officers and Enlisted Men of the United States Marine Corps.* Washington, DC, Government Printing Office, 1904.
USMC 1912 Uniform Regulations United States Marine Corps. Headquarters United States Marine Corps.Washington Government Printing Office, printed 1913.
USMC *Uniform Regulations United States Marine Corps. Headquarters United States Marine Corps.* Washington Government Printing Office. 1917 Revisions to the version.
USMC *Uniform Regulations United States Marine Corps. Superseding 1917 Regulations.* Washington, Government Printing Office, 1922.
USMC *1929 Uniform Regulations United States Marine Corps. Superseding 1922 Regulations.* United States Government Printing Office, Washington 1930.
USMC *Uniform Regulations United States Marine Corps. Superseding 1929 Regulations.* United States Government Printing Office, Washington: 1937.
USMC *Marine Corps Uniform Regulations (MCOP.10203AE) 1988,* US Navy Department, p.87. January 4, 1989.
US Militaria Forum, http://www.usmilitariaforum.com/forums/index.php?show
US Navy. List *and Station of the Commissioned and Warrant Officers of the Navy of The United States and the Marine Corps on the Active List & Officers on the retired List Employed on Active Duty.* Government Printing Office, Washington, DC, July 1, 1906.
US Navy. *Register of Commissioned and Warrant Officers of the United States Navy and Marine Corps.* Washington, DC, January 1, 1912,
US Navy . *Register of Commissioned and Warrant Officers of the United States Navy and the U.S. Naval Reserve Force National Naval Volunteers and Marine Corps Medical Corps and Dental Reserve Corps.* Washington, DC, Government Printing Office. January 1, 1918.
US Navy Department: *Secretary of the Navy Annual Report.* Clothing Received, p.883. NARG. 127. 1898.
US Navy Department: *Secretary of the Navy Annual Report.* Clothing Received, p.883, 1898.
US Navy Department: *Secretary of the Navy Annual Report.* General, Order No.437. p.2. December 14, 1894.
US Navy Department: *Secretary of the Navy Annual Report.* General Order. p.3, 1 July 1899.
US Navy Department: *Secretary of the Navy Annual Report (1889),* General Order No.4. p.2, 1 July 1900.
US Navy Department: *Secretary of the Navy Annual Report.* General Order No.166, pp.2-12, 1904.
US Navy Department: *Secretary of the Navy Annual Report.* General Statement of Prices, p.2, 1896.
US Navy Department: *Secretary of the Navy Annual Report.* General Statement of Prices, p.2. 1900.

US Navy Department: *Secretary of the Navy Annual Report*. General Statement of Prices, p.2. 1902.

Vezina, Meredith. R. *The History of the United States Marine Corps Recruit Depot San Diego,* MCRD Museum Historical Society & Heritage Press & Productions, Escondido, CA: (1997): 34.

Walla Walla. US Marine Newsweekly, "Fourth Marines, Shanghai," USMC University Special Collections. July 1933.

War Department. *Annual Report of the Quartermaster General*, (1894): 5.

Wise, Frederic M and Meigs O. Frost. *A Marine Tells It to You*. New York, J.H. Sears Company Inc., 1929.

Wylie, Robert E. *Orders, Decorations and Insignia Military and Civil.* New York and London: G.P. Putnam's Sons, The Knickerbocker Press. 1921.

INDEX